THE GODS OF INDIAN COUNTRY

THE HOUSE OF THE WOLFINGS

The Gods of Indian Country

RELIGION AND THE STRUGGLE FOR THE AMERICAN WEST

Jennifer Graber

OXFORD
UNIVERSITY PRESS

OXFORD

UNIVERSITY PRESS

Oxford University Press is a department of the University of Oxford. It furthers
the University's objective of excellence in research, scholarship, and education
by publishing worldwide. Oxford is a registered trade mark of Oxford University
Press in the UK and certain other countries.

Published in the United States of America by Oxford University Press
198 Madison Avenue, New York, NY 10016, United States of America.

© Oxford University Press 2018

First issued as an Oxford University Paperback, 2022

CIP data is on file at the Library of Congress
ISBN 978-0-19-027961-5 (Hbk.)
ISBN 978-0-19-762544-6 (Pbk.)

9 8 7 6 5 4 3 2 1
Paperback printed by Marquis, Canada

Contents

List of Plates and Figures

PLATES

FIGURES

Acknowledgments

I'M NOT SURE when I decided to write a big book. In order to answer my intellectual questions, I had to work in a new subfield, cover an entire century, and drive to Oklahoma a lot. Writing a book like this requires a great deal of resources and support. In an era with fewer funds devoted to the humanities, I've been lucky to have those things over the past eight years. It's a pleasure to acknowledge the people and institutions that made it possible for me to follow my wandering brain.

Thank you, first, to the University of Texas at Austin (UT). I work with terrific people in the Department of Religious Studies. I'm grateful for the way my department chairs, Martha Newman and Steve Friesen, have supported me. I also thank our department's executive assistant, Aubrey Cunningham. I would be lost without her help. My colleagues and students in the Religion in the Americas concentration deserve special mention, especially Mike Amoruso, who read the finished manuscript and helped me add some important final touches. I've also benefited from interdisciplinary conversations at UT. I'm grateful to my colleagues in the Native American and Indigenous Studies Program, people from whom I've learned so much. I particularly thank Erika Bsumek and Kelly McDonough, who've been wonderful writing group partners and great friends. I'm grateful to UT's Humanities Institute, especially its leader, Polly Strong, for providing a terrific environment in which to improve several chapter drafts. Funds from UT have supported my trips to conferences, libraries, archives, and Kiowa country. I'm grateful for a Humanities Research Award from the College of Liberal Arts. The publication of the images in this book has been especially supported by a subvention grant from the Office of the President at UT-Austin. Clearly, my institution helped this book come to be. That doesn't always happen these days. Let's take note when it does.

I'm grateful, also, to the Louisville Institute, which provided me a Sabbatical Grant for Researchers. The grant funded a year's leave from teaching, allowing me peace, quiet, and time to bring this project to completion. This book would not have come out in 2018 without it.

Thank you to the University of California Press, which granted permission to republish portions of "'If a War It May Be Called': The Peace Policy with American Indians," *Religion and American Culture: A Journal of Interpretation* 24, no. 1 (2014): 36–69.

I must also thank all the librarians and archivists who offered special help. The bibliography includes a long list of places I've either visited or from which I've received documents. Staff at these institutions took special care to make sure I knew the extent of their holdings. Libraries and archives often run on shoestring budgets. The treasures they contain are vital to the work of memory. Let's support them.

A few digital projects have made my research easier. I'm especially grateful to Ross Frank at the Plains Indian Ledger Art project (www.plainsledgerart.org). It's a beautiful website that makes scores of drawings available to those without budgets to visit museums or buy pricey art books. I have also relied on Dickinson College's Carlisle Indian School Digital Resource Center (www.carlisleindian.dickinson.edu.) The site makes thousands of pages of school records and photographs, most of which are kept at the National Archives in Washington, DC, available to all. Both sites are great resources for the classroom. Use them!

I came to this project with a lot to learn. I dedicated several years to the study of Kiowa history, culture, and art in particular, and American Indian history and religion more generally. I could not have done it alone. Specialists in these fields have taught me a great deal and have been generous in their feedback. Michelene Pesantubbee offered comments on a conference paper that were particularly helpful. Thanks to Clyde Ellis and Jenny Tone-Pah-Hote, whose knowledge of Kiowa history and willingness to talk about it helped me a great deal. I offer special thanks to Candace Greene, who read some of my earliest pieces, offered critical feedback, and encouraged me to keep learning and researching. She also shared generously from the documents and materials she has gathered over the years. Finally, I owe a great debt to William Meadows, who read the finished manuscript and offered insights gleaned from his many years working in Kiowa Country. His help with Kiowa names was critical. Thank you, Bill.

My original field of training is the history of religions in the United States. Some of my best friends and most helpful critics have been with me through many years of common work. I single out Jon Ebel, Heather Curtis, and Kip Kosek, who've commented on chapter drafts all along. They're my best readers and dear friends. I've been lucky to have other dear people read pieces over the last several years, including Angela Tarango, Alison Greene, Brendan Pietsch, and Tracy Fessenden. I've benefited greatly from the chance to present work to Judith Weisenfeld and her wonderful cohort of Americanists at Princeton, Pamela Klassen and the religious studies and book studies folks at the University of Toronto, and Sally Promey and her MAVCOR colleagues at Yale. Two other groups of scholars have played a profound role in my life as this project developed. I'm grateful for my cohort in the 2009–2011 Young Scholars in American Religion Program sponsored by IUPUI's Center for the Study of Religion and American Culture. I also benefited from the Religion and US Empire Seminar at Creighton University. I continue to receive unending encouragement from my graduate school cohort at Duke and my doctoral advisor, Grant Wacker. Truly, I feel so lucky to work in this field. Thanks to you all.

I also thank my Oxford University Press editor, Theo Calderara, who did not run away when I asked for fifty images, including some in color, for this book. More than that, Theo understood this project from the very beginning. I'm grateful.

As I get to the end of this list, I also draw closer to my heart. My thanks go out to every person who offered me welcome in Kiowa Country. Thank you to folks at the Kiowa Tribal Museum, Rainy Mountain Kiowa Indian Baptist Church, Hunting Horse United Methodist Church, and the Black Leggings Society for accepting my presence among you and showing me kindness. I was a stranger to you. In time, I found welcome and I can only hope that I have been a decent guest. Although my work draws on historical sources about Kiowas, my time researching and writing has been enriched by getting to know Kiowa people, observing their ongoing work to build community, and learning from the ways they narrate their history.

Finally, to the people who've had everything to do with me enjoying the good days and continuing on through the bad. I have a son with a significant disability. Many mothers of children with disabilities end up leaving their jobs. And many feel crushed by the responsibilities they bear. I, too, would have left my work and been overwhelmed by burden were it not for my family and friends. I've been open, both personally and professionally, about the difficulties with which I live. My friends and family have held me up in those times. I've also tried to communicate the joy my son brings to my life. My family and friends share in this as well. So, thank you, my friends. Thanks for every way you helped me and shared my joy. You did a million things: flew me to Mexico, let me write in your homes, yards, and back porches, visited me, sent me cookies and pizza, and offered me endless encouragement. Every single bit of it mattered.

My final thanks go to my dear family. To my partner, Stacy, who has always believed in my ability and supported my work, even when my own confidence faltered. To Sasha, my little reader, who traveled to archives with me as a tiny child. And to Martin, who has my whole heart in his beautiful and difficult life.

List of Abbreviations

ABBREVIATIONS

ABCFM	American Board of Commissioners for Foreign Missions
ARCIA	Annual Report of the Commissioner of Indian Affairs
BCIM	Bureau of Catholic Indian Missions
BIC	Board of Indian Commissioners
JC	Jerome Commission (also known as the Cherokee Commission)
KCA	Kiowa, Comanche, and Apache Reservation
LIM	Ladies Industrial Mission
LMC	Lake Mohonk Conference of Friends of the Indian and Other Dependent Peoples
MECS	Methodist Episcopal Church-South
NIDA	National Indian Defense Association
NYT	*New York Times*

COLLECTIONS AND RECORD ABBREVIATIONS

AECFIA	Associated Executive Committee of Friends on Indian Affairs
APCR	Anadarko Presbyterian Church Records
ASSNAA	Arthur and Shifra Silberman Native American Art Collection
FWP	Federal Writers' Project
GWFC	George W. Fox Collection of American Indian Ledger Drawings and Photographs
GWHC	G. W. Hicks Collection
IPP	Indian-Pioneer Papers
JMND	James Mooney Notes and Drawings
JSMNAMC	Joseph Samuel Murrow Native American Manuscripts Collection
KAF	Kiowa Agency Files

KDT	Kiowa Drawings and Texts
LR	Letters Received
LTP	Lawrie Tatum Papers
MBC	Mary Burnham Collection
MBP	Mary D. Burnham Papers Related to the Dakota League
OFLC	Oklahoma Federation of Labor Collection
PMP	Parker McKenzie Papers
PYMICR	Philadelphia Yearly Meeting Indian Committee Records
QSC	Quaker and Special Collections
RG	Record Group
RHPP	Richard Henry Pratt Papers
TCBC	Thomas C. Battey Collection
TCBLF	Thomas C. Battey Letters to Family
WBHM	Woman's Board of Home Missions (Presbyterian)
WEC	Woman's Executive Committee (Presbyterian)
WHC	Western History Collections
WPA	Works Progress Administration
YCWA	Yale Collection of Western Americana

ARCHIVE ABBREVIATIONS

ASBS	Archives of the Sisters of the Blessed Sacrament, Bensalem, Pennsylvania
ASGA	Archives of St. Gregory's Abbey, Shawnee, Oklahoma
ASSF	Archives of the Sisters of Saint Francis of Philadelphia, Aston, Pennsylvania
AAOC	Archives of the Archdiocese of Oklahoma City, Oklahoma City, Oklahoma
AEC	Archives of the Episcopal Church, Austin, Texas
BL	Beinecke Rare Book and Manuscript Library, Yale University, New Haven, Connecticut
DRC	Dickinson Research Center, National Cowboy and Western Heritage Museum, Oklahoma City, Oklahoma
GM	Gilcrease Museum, Tulsa, Oklahoma
HRBML	Hargrett Rare Book and Manuscript Library, University of Georgia, Athens, Georgia
HC	Haverford College, Haverford, Pennsylvania
MHM	Missouri History Museum, St. Louis, Missouri
NAA	National Anthropological Archives, Smithsonian Institution, Suitland, Maryland
NA	National Archives and Records Administration, Washington DC
NAMA	Nelson-Atkins Museum of Art, Kansas City, Missouri
OHS	Oklahoma Historical Society Research Center, Oklahoma City, Oklahoma

OSU   Oklahoma State University, Special Collections and University Archives, Stillwater, Oklahoma

PHS   Presbyterian Historical Society, Philadelphia, Pennsylvania

PPM   Panhandle-Plains Historical Museum, Canyon, Texas

RCHS   Rice County Historical Society, Faribault, Minnesota

SHSI   State Historical Society of Iowa, Research Center, Iowa City, Iowa

SI   Smithsonian Institution, Washington DC

UO   University of Oklahoma, Norman, Oklahoma

A Note on Terms

INDIANS—WRITTEN SOURCES BY Americans commonly employed the term "Indians" to refer to Native Americans or American Indians. I use all three designations in the book. I also employ the term "Native." For the sake of avoiding repetition, I sometimes use the word "indigenous," which is a category that stretches outside North America.

INDIAN LEADERS—Many English sources from the period use the word "chief" to denote Indian leaders. I typically use the words "headmen" or "leading men," along with some Kiowa terms for different types of leaders.

DEROGATORY TERMS—American sources I used include several derogatory terms, including "redskin," "squaw," and "half-breed." I use these terms only in direct quotation and, even then, sparingly. Americans also frequently referred to American Indians as "savages," "barbarians," and "heathens." These terms came from a long history of colonial encounters between Europeans and people across the globe. They also played a key role in the developing academic study of religion. I use them when discussing how Americans understood Native cultures and ritual practices in light of their assumptions about how civilizations progressed over time.

AMERICANS—I use this term to denote citizens of the United States in the nineteenth century. When discussing assumptions that Americans had about culture and ethnicity, I employ specific designations such as Euro-American and Anglo-American. To discuss episodes when Americans considered Native people within emerging systems of racial classification, I use terms such as "white," "black," "negro," "yellow," "red," and "Mexican." These were commonly used descriptors in nineteenth-century discourse about race.

CIVILIZATION—Many Americans assumed the superiority of Anglo-American cultural practices for home, family life, eating, dress, and work. These practices signaled their position at the highest level of civilization. They considered other populations, including Native Americans, to be lower on the scale of civilized societies and therefore recommended their cultural transformation. Americans often discussed civilization in tandem with Christianity, or in some cases, considered it to be integral to civilized living.

FRIENDS OF THE INDIAN—This phrase identifies a range of Protestants and Catholics active in Indian affairs who considered themselves to have Native people's best interests at heart. Two points about them are important. First, they sometimes used this characterization informally. For instance, in debates about Indian policy, they often referred to themselves as "the Indian's friend" in order to construct and affirm benevolent identity. I chart this informal usage, especially in the early nineteenth century. Second, in the 1880s, a group of Protestant reformers and civic leaders formed an organization called the Lake Mohonk Conference of Friends of the Indian and Other Dependent Peoples (LMC). I chronicle this group in the book's later chapters and capitalize "Friend" in order to designate that my reference is to this formal organization.

PROTESTANTS—This term encompasses non-Catholic Christians in the nineteenth-century United States. In this study, that umbrella term specifically includes Episcopalians, Methodists (members of the Methodist-Episcopal Church, both north and south), Presbyterians, and Unitarians, as well as a variety of Baptist and Quaker groups. Some of the people leading and participating in these movements might also properly be termed "evangelical," but certainly not all of them. The variety of Protestants participating in this study can be best understood as having shared interests in social reform or benevolent activity, some of which was inspired by revivalist energies in the first half of the century.

QUAKERS—People associated with the Society of Friends are referred to in several ways in the sources, including Quakers, members of the Society, and Friends. During this period, Quakers experienced some schisms, leading to the emergence of Hicksite, Orthodox, and Gurneyite groups. Those splits, while important within the internal life of the Society, are not a crucial part of my story about interactions with Native people and I do not dwell on them. Further, I typically include Quakers in my larger discussions of Protestants in this period. There are many ways, namely theology and worship, that such a connection is problematic. But my account focuses on Quaker action in the public sphere, in which at least some Friends participated in broader Protestant coalitions.

THE CHURCH OF JESUS CHRIST OF LATTER-DAY SAINTS (LDS)— Popularly know as the Mormons or the Saints, the LDS played only a small role in Indian Territory. However, their experiences of discrimination and legal coercion make them a crucial group for understanding pressures to "Americanize" in this period.

CATHOLICS—The Catholics in this book considered themselves in full communion with Rome. When discussing anti-Catholic attitudes held by Protestants in this period, I sometimes reference terms they used, such as "papists" and "Romanists."

INDIAN OFFICE—What is now known as the Bureau of Indian Affairs, the federal department tasked with interacting with American Indians, has had several names and has been attached to different parts of the federal government throughout its history.

I use the generic term "Indian office" for what has alternately been known as the Indian Department, Indian Bureau, and Office of Indian Affairs.

PEACE POLICY—In 1869, President Ulysses S. Grant put in place a new policy regarding the administration of Indian reservations. He turned over the appointments of reservation officials to Christian denominations. He also established a Board of Indian Commissioners staffed with Christian leaders and tasked with advising the Indian office. The policy was popularly known by a variety of names, including the Grant Policy, Quaker Policy, and Peace Policy. The last two terms highlight the policy's direction insofar as the military typically could not enter or interact with Native people on reservations. They had full authority, however, to engage Indians outside reservation boundaries.

RESERVATION—By the 1850s, many Americans supported a policy of placing Indian nations on bounded areas of land called reservations. Reservations were managed by agents, and the offices where agents worked were referred to as agencies. Indians typically had to travel to agencies in order to collect rations guaranteed to them by treaties. Some reservations, such as the Kiowa, Comanche, and Apache (KCA) Reservation, were adjacent to a military post so that agents could be in close communication with military officials.

RELIGION—Many Protestant Americans in this period used the word "religion" or the phrase "true religion" to refer to their particular experience of Protestant faith and practice. As I discuss in the Introduction, some Americans also employed the term "religion" to denote what was considered a universal category of human experience, an idea developed by scholars in this era. Kiowas had no word that translates neatly as "religion." I do not use the term in my discussions of their ritual practice or understanding of sacred power. Kiowas did not employ the term until the early twentieth century, when they played a role in a pan-Indian movement to seek protections under the First Amendment for ritual practice involving peyote. Americans working on the KCA Reservation, on the other hand, employed language about Kiowa "religion" much earlier. I note when Protestants labeled particular Kiowa actions and sentiments using words such as "reverential," "sacred," "solemn," "priest," "medicine," "medicine men," "ritual," and so on. These labels had both positive and negative meanings, depending on the context and speaker. Protestants drew many of these descriptors about religion from anti-Catholic discourse in the period, as well as language about the "religions of the world" developed in colonial settings.

GREAT SPIRIT—From the colonial era, documents in English aiming to translate and transcribe Indian speeches often employed the phrase "Great Spirit" to refer to some sort of high god worshiped by Native people. The use of the phrase betrays a Euro-American penchant for establishing the possibility of monotheism among Indians. I use it only when quoting American sources. To be sure, American Indians who spoke English also employed this term, especially during treaty negotiations. But Kiowas in this period of study almost always used translators in their discussions with Americans and attributing the phrase "Great Spirit" to them, as opposed to their translators, would be misleading.

RECTIFICATION MOVEMENTS—I borrow this term from a scholar of religion to interpret specific Native responses to colonialism. It refers to movements in which people seek supernatural intervention to address suffering and rectify their situation. Scholars have also described these movements as "prophetic," "millenarian," or "seeking revitalization." I avoid these terms for a few reasons. First, Americans used the term "prophet" derisively to describe Native leaders of these movements. Second, an emphasis on millennial visions has led some interpreters to classify these movements as doomed to failure. Finally, analysis of revitalization does not necessarily account for imbalances of power that participants seek to address.

GHOST DANCE—Americans used this term to refer to a pan-Indian rectification movement that spread across the plains in the 1890s. The movement began with Wovoka's activities on the Paiute reservation. Native nations across the West adapted it to their particular contexts and needs. I use the term "Ghost Dance" when referring to Americans' discussion of the movement. When discussing the Kiowa practice, I use the term "Feather Dance," an English translation of one of their names for the dance, as well as the phrase Kiowas use to refer to the practice today.

THE GODS OF INDIAN COUNTRY

Introduction

THE MAN PAINTED his body white. He stretched out his arms and stared directly into the sun. He asked the sun to pity him and give him *dwdw*, or sacred power. He needed it to aid him in hunting and war. He also implored the sun, one of the many natural phenomenon imbued with *dwdw*, to bless his family that they might live long and be healthy. The man danced for hours and did not eat or drink for four days. He stood near the banks of the *You'-guoo-o-poh'*, or Sweetwater Creek, which flowed east through the southern portion of the North American Great Plains. The land surrounding the creek lay flat and waved with tall grasses. Clumps of mesquite and juniper trees stood nearby. In winter, strong winds raced across the waters. In summer, the sun bore down, with few options for shade. On this day in the season of picking plums, or the month of June, the man painted white stood by the creek seeking *dwdw* to aid his people.[1]

His people were Kiowa Indians, who migrated from the north and had lived near Sweetwater Creek for just under a century when they gathered in 1873 for the Kiowas' version of the Plains Indian Sun Dance.[2] In their ritual encampment of a few thousand people, they told stories about their ancestors who had once lived farther north in the mountains near the Yellowstone River's mouth in what is now western Montana.[3] These ancestors had migrated eastward onto the northern plains and close to the Black Hills, where neighboring Indians taught them skills in horsemanship.[4] They learned to hunt buffalo, not only with bows and arrows, but also with guns made available by Spaniards and brought northward through vast networks of Indian trade. Eventually, Kiowas moved to the southern plains, where they capitalized on their hunting skills to make a place for themselves near Sweetwater Creek and a massive rock formation, *Xoqaudauha*, or the Medicine Bluff.[5] Chálkǫ́gái (Black Goose) noted these and other special sites in maps he made of his homeland (Figure I.1).[6]

I

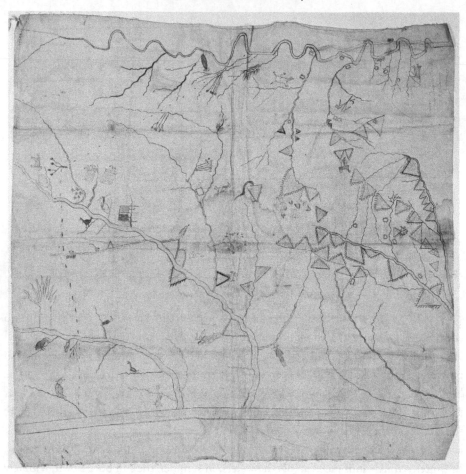

FIGURE I.I.   Chálkógái's (Black Goose) map of Kiowa lands and sites of significance. Two Sun Dance lodges, commemorating celebrations in 1869 and 1870, are featured by the side of a tributary in the left center of the map. Sweetwater Creek, the site of the 1873 Sun Dance, is the tributary further south on the same river.

Credit: Department of Anthropology, American Museum of Natural History, catalog no. E233091, photo by Donald E. Hurlbert

When Kiowas migrated south, they brought with them rituals they had learned from their neighbors on the northern plains. Crow Indians had befriended them and shared their Sun Dance ritual, an annual celebration that acknowledged the sun's power and showed gratitude for the abundance of buffalo.[7] In their new southern homeland, Kiowa bands that were scattered across the region for most of the year came together for the summer ceremony. Over the course of several days, they made offerings, fulfilled vows, and socialized with relatives and friends. They prayed for the people's welfare.

The Sun Dance required a specialist to gather the scattered community, handle special objects, and direct ritual action. In 1873, Jòhéjè (Without Moccasins) served in this role. Kiowas called him the *Táimé* keeper for his care of the *Táimé,* the people's most sacred

FIGURE I.2. Replica of the *Táimé*, the sacred object at the center of Kiowa Sun Dance practices and considered a mediator between the sun and the people.
Credit: National Anthropological Archives, Smithsonian Institution, GN 01458

object. The *Táimé*, a replica of which is pictured in Figure I.2, came as a gift from the Crows. It epitomized the sun's power and mediated between the sun and the people.[8] Jòhéjè avoided dangerous conditions that threatened its power. He kept the *Táimé* safe during winter while he considered a site for the next summer's Sun Dance encampment. Once decided, Jòhéjè sent a messenger to Kiowa camps, telling the people where and when to gather. Kiowa artists created many visual accounts of their Sun Dance activities, including the image in Plate 1 of people receiving news about the upcoming celebration.[9]

As Kiowas moved toward the Sun Dance site, Jòhéjè prepared them for their ritual undertaking. He rode out to the camp's periphery. Carrying the *Táimé* in a bag around his neck, Jòhéjè circled the people and called them to come together. He brought the people into a posture of respectful devotion to the buffalo, animals that received *dwdw* from the sun. They began with a buffalo hunt designed to respect taboos against bloodshed during the Sun Dance. Rather than use more recently available technologies such as rifles, Kiowas chased, killed, and processed the animal using older methods. Hunters used bows and arrows and directed them at the bull's heart, but not the lungs, as depicted

FIGURE 1.3. Gùhâudè's (Stripping Off of a Rib Cage) image of Kiowa men hunting a buffalo with bows and arrows. The hide then hangs on the Sun Dance lodge's central pole.
Credit: Missouri History Museum, St. Louis, image no. 1882-018-005

in Figure I.3. They aimed carefully lest any blood come out of the animal's mouth and bring misfortune.[10]

Once they killed the animal, the hunters processed its body and implored the sun to look on them with pity. One Kiowa informant recalled the hunters' words as they transported the hide to the Sun Dance site: "Look at me, Sun! Let our women and children live good, and buffalo cover the earth. Let sickness be put away."[11] Once brought into the encampment, the section of hide was subjected to a purifying sweat. Kiowas then presented offerings to it, including cloth, beads, and feathers.[12]

With the buffalo hide procured and purified, it was time to establish the central ritual space, the Medicine Lodge, which housed the encampment's primary activities. The process began with a battle performance in which men fought over a tree that would serve as the lodge's central pole. After making offerings to the tree and cutting down the pole, the people took up the pipe. Ceremonial smoking, practiced widely across Native North America, marked the people's efforts to engage sacred power. Kiowas then brought the tree pole to the encampment's center. Informants recall that the *Táimé* keeper shook rattles, blew whistles, and sang songs during the transport. American observers of later celebrations noted the community cooperation and pleasant mood. Good times continued through the lodge's construction, which was accompanied by

FIGURE I.4. Zǫ́tâm's (Driftwood) rendition of Kiowa women and men building the central Sun Dance lodge. Note the forked pole, made from a cottonwood tree, at the center.
Credit: Richard Henry Pratt Papers, Yale Collection of Western Americana, Beinecke Rare Book and Manuscript Library, Yale University

singing and dancing.[13] As shown in Figure I.4, Kiowas worked to clear a space, install the central pole and other branches, and hoist the section of buffalo hide with its attached offerings to the top.

Jòhéjè then called for the buffalo to enter the lodge, but he did not anticipate the arrival of actual animals.[14] Instead, he gathered people. Kiowas of all ages dressed in buffalo hides and acted the part of their favored prey, as depicted in section (b) of Figure I.5. Two men worked to lure the "buffalo" into the lodge, encouraging them to dance around the central pole. Their effort, which also involved no weapons, recalled older forms of buffalo hunting in which Kiowas trapped buffalo in closed areas. In the process of bringing the people into the lodge, Jòhéjè and the hunters mimicked an ideal hunt.

With the central pole planted, the buffalo hide in place, and the lodge finished, Jòhéjè put other special objects into place. He removed the *Tʼáimé* from its protective wrappings and carried it inside, as depicted in Figure I.6. Jòhéjè placed it in a screened area, to which other important objects would be added. Over the years, Kiowas supplemented the *Tʼáimé* with other figures, creating a *Tʼáimé* complex.[15]

Jòhéjè then invited bearers of *Tʼáimé* shields to hang them on a cedar screen behind the central pole.[16] The shields displayed powerful symbols and colors in designs received in visions. Along with other decorated shields, Kiowas considered the *Tʼáimé*

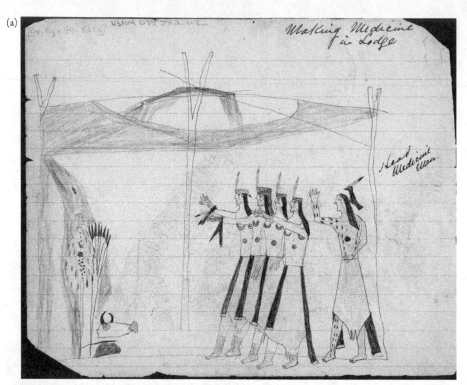

FIGURE 1.5. Unidentified artist's drawing of the "calling of the buffalo." The lower drawing shows Kiowas dressed in buffalo hides as they processed toward the central lodge. The drawing above depicts the lodge, ritual specialist, and several sacred objects.

Credit: National Anthropological Archives, Smithsonian Institution, manuscript 392725

FIGURE I.6. Hǻugú's (Silver Horn) image of the primary ritual specialist bringing the *Tǻimé* to the Sun Dance lodge.

Credit: Silverhorn (Haungooah) (1860–1940), Kiowa, Oklahoma. *To-hane-daugh and Party Carrying "Medicine" to Medicine Lodge, as captioned by D. P. Brown, 1883.* One of the 75 drawings contained within a bound book; graphite and colored pencil on paper, 11¾ × 14¾ inches (29.8 × 37.5 cm). The Nelson-Atkins Museum of Art, Kansas City, Missouri, Gift of Mr. and Mrs. Dudley C. Brown, 64-9/14

shields to be powerful objects. The men who owned them were considered to have *doi*, or medicine.[17] As such, they had access to sacred power for healing, discernment, and success in war. They held prominence in Kiowa society. With the shields in place, Jòhéjè's assistants brought the last of the necessary items, including earthen censors for cedar smoke, ceremonial fans, rattles, and animal skulls into the lodge.[18] At this point, the lodge was ready and the central rites of the Sun Dance could begin.

Jòhéjè and other men who had taken vows began a four-day process of dancing and praying without the benefit of food or water. The *Tǻimé* keeper asked the sun to bestow its protective power through the *Tǻimé*, depicted in the lower right corner of Plate 2. Other men raised their arms, prayed, sang, and stared into the sun. Hungry and humbled, they asked the sun, the buffalo, and the *Tǻimé* to pity them and protect their families. Unlike some other Plains Indian nations, Kiowas did not practice any form of cutting or bleeding. But they modified their bodies in other ways, usually by painting themselves. The *Tǻimé* keeper painted his body yellow, with images of the sun on his chest and back. The men who joined him were painted white. Dancing continued most of the day, demanding perseverance. Female relatives looked on and encouraged the dancers.[19]

The 1873 ceremony along Sweetwater Creek also included the introduction of medicine bundles, sometimes referred to by outsiders as the "grandmothers."[20] The bundles
predated Kiowa Sun Dance practices. Some Kiowas affirmed that the bundles "grew
up with Kiowa" and went back to the people's time of origin.[21] Keepers, or custodians,
passed on these sacred items to their descendants. Bundle keepers talked to them and
approached them with prayers for the people. They consulted the bundles when asked
to settle disputes. Men going out to raids or battles made vows before them. Informants
recall that bundle keepers brought them to the central lodge in order to smoke with them
in the *Táimé*'s presence. During the Sun Dance, bundles were placed on a platform of sage
and subjected to a sweat. Fanning the steaming rocks, the *Táimé* keeper and his assistants
prayed for those who had brought the bundles, asking for good life, success in war, and
healing from sickness.[22] *not asking for anything materialistic*

As the Sun Dance progressed, Jòhéjè received people as they made more offerings
to the *Táimé*.[23] When the men who made vows finished their four days of dancing and
fasting, Jòhéjè brought the *Táimé* down from its central position and wrapped it carefully. He called for women to bring food to those who had fasted. He took water, made
it powerful by adding elements from the bundles, and distributed it to the people as they
departed.[24] In this way, every person ingested a substance empowered by contact with the
lodge and its sacred contents.

During the Sun Dance, Kiowas declared who they were as a people and engaged the
dwdw, or sacred power, present in their homeland.[25] Unlike centuries before, when they
lived in the northern Rocky Mountains, or even more recently when they lived on the
northern plains near the Black Hills, they were now a southern plains people. They were
connected to Sweetwater Creek, Medicine Bluff, and the surrounding landscape. Living
there meant adapting to the place and relating to the sun, buffalo, mountains, rivers, and
plants. Kiowas also acknowledged the special people among them who engaged *dwdw* on
their behalf. These included Jòhéjè, the *Táimé* keeper, as well as other leading men who
healed, sought visions, and beseeched a number of animals and natural elements capable
of bestowing protection and providing guidance. While these special people certainly
harnessed these powers for their benefit, Kiowas did not monopolize them. Just as Crow
Indians shared the Sun Dance with them generations before, Kiowas in 1873 celebrated
with Comanches, Apaches, Cheyenne, and Arapahos, their Indian allies and friends.[26]

That summer, a new friend joined Kiowas as they celebrated the Sun Dance.
A Quaker schoolteacher named Thomas Battey sat on the banks of Sweetwater Creek
and watched the Sun Dance unfold.[27] Battey had been assigned to teach school on the
Kiowa, Comanche, and Apache (KCA) reservation in what the United States designated as Indian Territory (Figure I.7). He had arrived in the autumn of 1872 and started
teaching a few months before the Sun Dance. For a variety of reasons, Kiowa parents
were reluctant to send their children to the already established school at the nearby military post. As a result, Battey volunteered to live in a Kiowa camp and presented lessons
in his tipi. Embedded in camp life, he encountered Kiowas' starkly different cultural

FIGURE I.7. Charles Roeser's 1879 map of Indian Territory. The Kiowa, Comanche, and Apache (KCA) Reservation is in the territory's southwest section.

Credit: American Geographical Society Library, University of Wisconsin-Milwaukee Libraries

all about culture

practices: nomadic movement; hunting game and drying meat; using skins and blankets for clothing; no discernable structures for educating the young. Battey hoped to trigger the transformation of Kiowa ways by modeling Anglo-American alternatives. In time, he convinced a few parents to send their children to his lessons. But most in the camp expressed suspicion about schooling and kept their children away. Frustrated, Battey concluded that Kiowa "heathenism," or non-Christian religion, explained the people's resistance to education.[28]

Nothing symbolized that "heathenism" like the 1873 Sun Dance that Battey witnessed. Over many days, the Quaker teacher encountered painted bodies dancing, special objects he perceived to be "idols," and leaders who used their power to change the weather. He had never seen anything like it. He later wrote that what he "saw and heard of this pagan rite" was "enough to cause my heart to swell with deep and conflicting emotions in beholding the depth of heathen superstition into which this people have fallen."[29] Battey, convinced of all people's need for the Christian God, as well as the joy and consolation this communion provided, worried about Kiowas' lack of "true religion."[30]

The Quaker teacher's considerable concern did not overwhelm the confidence he had in his mission. Referring to the Christian God as the "Great Disposer of all things and events," Battey affirmed that "[God] saw fit to cast my lot on earth in a land where the blessed light of the gospel of truth shines."[31] Battey counted himself part of a nation

destined to bestow true religion upon Kiowas and other heathens. He shared this attitude not only with other Quakers concerned about Native Americans, but with a range of
Protestant ministers, missionaries, and reformers who deemed themselves "friends of the
Indian."[32] As such, Battey and his contemporaries claimed a superior knowledge about
Native life. They deemed their approach to the "Indian problem" less self-interested and
more effective than solutions proffered by most government officials and nearly all mili-
tary leaders.[33] As "friends of the Indian," they planned to civilize, and thereby Christianize,
Native people.

In several respects, the civilizing project advocated by "friends of the Indian" overlapped
with missions targeted at other groups living in the United States and around the globe.[34]
These Christian workers promoted an internal process of religious conversion signaled
by external markers of newly adopted Anglo-American cultural practices. But engagement with the nation's Native peoples involved an additional feature. Indians occupied
lands that the United States did not yet fully control, and some Indian nations had successfully resisted US rule for decades. When Americans spoke of the "Indian problem,"
they referenced not only Native people and their uncivilized practices, but also the lands
they inhabited, which Americans desired.

Over the course of the nineteenth century, American officials used diplomacy and
military power to exert authority over lands stretching from the Appalachian Mountains
to the Pacific Ocean. Securing these lands seemed crucial as Americans migrated west in
search of new places to settle. But when Thomas Battey entered a Kiowa camp in 1873,
tens of thousands of American Indians still lived to some degree outside of American authority. Kiowas and Comanches in Indian Territory, Apaches in the Southwest, Sioux on
the northern plains, and a number of Indian nations in the Pacific Northwest thwarted
US efforts to reduce their lands and make way for American overland migrants. "Friends
of the Indian" sought to change this situation. As Battey noted after the Sun Dance,
I "hope that the day might not be far distant when the darkness enshrouding this portion
of our country may be dispelled by the everlasting Sun of Righteousness."[35]

To support their civilizing work, "friends of the Indian" relied on church resources.
They also partnered with the federal government to direct the pace and nature of
American expansion.[36] Battey, again, provides a useful example. Prominent Quakers
serving on the Society of Friends' Indian committee nominated him to teach. But the
federal government provided financial support for his efforts, and Battey reported to the
Indian office in Washington, D.C.[37] Through this partnership, Battey and other "friends
of the Indian" hoped to convince federal officials and the American public that theirs was
the only ethical and practical way to transform Indian people and claim the vast lands
that Native nations controlled.

But in the hot summer of 1873, things were not going as planned. As noted earlier,
only a few Kiowa parents sent their children to Battey's tipi-school. Little could be
shown after more than four years of Quaker effort to promote civilization. Kiowas still
lived in tipis and moved them frequently in order to follow the game herds. The Indians

showed little interest in farming and their fields languished despite the Friends' encouragement to plow and plant seeds. To Battey and other Quakers' chagrin, Kiowas had not changed their ways. Most unnerving, they continued to raid for horses, mules, and human captives deep into Texas and Mexico. Settlers in these frontier regions sought to defend their families and resources against Indian plunder. Some retaliated, and still others initiated counter raids by attacking Native people's camps and stealing from their horse herds. Encounters between settlers and Indians in the region often erupted in spectacular violence.

Indeed, violence between Americans and Kiowas had prompted Battey's visit to the 1873 Sun Dance.[38] He came to deliver a message about Kiowa leaders incarcerated at the nearby military post. The two men had led an 1871 attack and had killed seven Americans. They served two years in a Texas prison and had been returned to Indian Territory. Kiowas expected their imminent release. But Battey had bad news. Modoc Indians in Oregon had recently attacked and killed Americans at a meeting to negotiate peace. The incident fueled a surge in anti-Indian sentiment across the country. American officials felt they could not release the Kiowa leaders given the national mood. Kiowas expressed outrage. They could hardly see why Indian actions in Oregon affected them. Several demanded an immediate response, calling for Indians across the southern plains to rise up against the Americans. As Kiowas debated their options, Battey counseled peace. By the time the Sun Dance ended, Kiowas and their allies decided not to engage in armed resistance, at least for the moment.[39]

While Battey came away from the Sun Dance relieved that war had been avoided, the experience unnerved him. He watched as Kiowas and their allies gathered in an enormous encampment to express their attachment to each other and their homeland, as well as the sacred power that circulated among them. He looked on as Kiowas considered violent resistance to the Americans. From Battey's perspective, much work remained to be done before Kiowas could be freed from their savagery, heathenism, and violence. "Friends of the Indian," with the government's support, had a monumental task before them in transforming Kiowas into civilized, Christian, and peaceful citizens of the American republic. The Quaker teacher, ever an optimist, was sure it could be done.

THE GODS OF INDIAN COUNTRY

Thomas Battey's visit to the 1873 Sun Dance was one of many meetings between Kiowas and Americans. This book traces these encounters between 1803 and 1903 in order to make two arguments. First, in light of American expansion into Indian lands and encounters with Native peoples, Christian ministers, missionaries, and reformers cast themselves as "friends of the Indian" who could acquire land and achieve Native people's cultural transformation through peaceful means.[40] They presented their methods as an alternative to the argument made by some politicians, army officers, and settlers that expansion necessitated force, and perhaps the extermination of Native people. By contrasting their approach to the violence of Cherokee removal, the Indian wars, and settlers' assaults, "friends of the Indian" rendered benign acts of physical and cultural dispossession they both supported and perpetuated. These acts ranged from cutting children's hair and suppressing Native languages to calling on the military to threaten, arrest, and incarcerate Indian people. In bringing the Christian God to Indian Country, these Protestants obscured their role in violent and coercive expansion and constructed an image of themselves as benevolent believers who imparted life-saving gifts to Indian people.

Second, Kiowas relied on their practices of making kin, giving gifts, engaging in diplomacy, as well as their rites for engaging sacred power, to respond to American efforts to reduce their lands, change their way of living, and break their tribal bonds.[41] They continued and adapted practices, including the Sun Dance, which had sustained them throughout their long history of migration. They also engaged new sources of power and experimented with new rites, such as ritual peyote ingestion, Ghost Dancing, and affiliation with Christian churches.[42] They evaluated these new options in light of their capacity to protect their families, fulfill communal obligations, and secure blessings and protection. In terms developed by one scholar of religion, Kiowas invoked "gods" insofar as they had "relationships" with "special, suprahuman beings" imbued with power.[43] For Kiowas, the "gods" both old and new were central to their struggle to survive and flourish as Americans invaded Indian Country.

Americans often referred to "religion" as they sought to transform Kiowa culture and secure Kiowa lands. They considered the ethical implications of their own Christianity on westward expansion, as well as the meaning of the non-Christian ritual practices they observed among Kiowas. As theorists of religion have demonstrated, myriad intercultural encounters during the modern era shaped the creation of "religion" as a category.[44] As English speakers, the Americans chronicled in this book inherited ideas about religion from their Christian European forebears, who had developed it as a way to understand and categorize a variety of peoples. These included Jews and Muslims, as well as so-called pagans, primitives, Orientals, and idolaters.[45]

Like their European ancestors, these Americans developed their identities as Protestant Christians in the midst of encounters with not only American Indians, but also Africans and African Americans, Catholic immigrants from Europe and Mexico, immigrant workers from Asia, practitioners of new religions like Mormonism, and a variety of other peoples outside their ken.[46] "Religion" served to mark one of many differences Protestant Christians perceived between themselves and others. It played a central role in American debates about Native peoples' place in the nation's future.[47] Kiowas and other indigenous societies, on the other hand, had no word that translated as "religion." Instead, they had ways of interacting with a variety of powerful beings and forces, as well as a multitude of words that described or dictated the forms of these interactions. Even so, Kiowas eventually classified some aspects of their ritual power-seeking as "religious" in order to secure protection for these activities.[48]

This book, then, tracks the ways that "religion" was central to Americans' acquisition of Indian lands, as well as Kiowa efforts to defend their sovereignty and secure their community's survival in the face of American territorial expansion.[49] For Protestant "friends of the Indian," "religion" made an ethical demand on methods the nation used to acquire Indian lands and civilize Indian communities, as well as validated their campaigns to bring "true religion" to Native people.[50] But Protestants were not the only Christians interested in the nation's Indian peoples. America's period of westward expansion coincided with a surge in its Catholic population. Leaders in the emerging American Catholic Church leaned on their European co-religionists to assist in the work of civilizing and evangelizing American Indians. Catholic missions to Native people in the United States reflected broader developments in the global church, as well as American Catholics' efforts to gain a foothold in a nation dominated by Protestants and teeming with anti-Catholic sentiment. Within this context, Catholics developed a distinctive sense of themselves as the Indians' "friend." They emphasized the long history of Catholic missions in North America, work that both predated the United States as a political project and contributed to a centuries-long effort to create a universal church. In missions started in the decades after the nation's founding, Catholics aimed to civilize Native people, but often lacked the Protestants' assumption that this process overlapped precisely with Americanization.

Over time, however, Catholics reframed their efforts on Indians' behalf. As Americans debated the role of religious schools in American democracy, Catholics demanded religious freedom for Catholic Indians who experienced discrimination at the hands of government officials and Protestant reformers. They argued that support for Catholic schools on reservations signaled the nation's commitment to religious freedom for all. Catholic leaders considered their efforts to start religious schools on reservations as central to their labors as the Indian's "friend." By century's end, they also claimed that these schools achieved the goal of transforming Indians into proper American citizens.

Kiowas, of course, had their own ways to determine who their friends were. For centuries, they had migrated among and lived near other Indian nations. Upon their arrival in the southern plains, they participated in a borderlands economy that included Spanish officials, French traders, New Mexican leaders, as well as numerous Native peoples. In this context, Kiowas participated in a gift-based trading economy that relied on kinship ties. They made alliances and economic partnerships sealed with gifts and strengthened by shared rituals for seeking sacred power. Kiowas' reception of the Sun Dance from Crow Indian allies is only one example of this dynamic. When the Americans arrived on the plains, Kiowas came to the encounter with these expectations about how nations interacted, how they worked to benefit each other, and how rituals like the Sun Dance could solidify such relationships. In sum, both Kiowas and Americans made "religion" central to their determination of who their friends were, how friends acted, and how relationships with other people affected their territorial claims.

METHODS AND SIGNIFICANCE

Indian people and Indian lands have been mostly absent from narratives about nineteenth-century US religious history. To be sure, scholars have produced outstanding studies focused on particular Native nations and their interactions with sacred powers.[51] But these rich and detailed stories have yet to be integrated into broader interpretations of the period. Indeed, our histories mirror nineteenth-century policy goals in which white Americans occupy the center and Native people dwell on the periphery. In contrast, the scholarship on colonial-era engagements offers excellent accounts of the ways encounter transformed both Native and British settler communities.[52] Work on the early republic, however, quickly loses track of Indians and mentions them primarily as the subjects of a fiercely debated removal policy.[53] Scholarship on the middle part of the century rarely references Native people, reflecting the policy of separation that drove reservation building in this era. At best, Indians appear throughout the rest of the century only as practitioners of a new religious movement, the Ghost Dance, and victims of horrific colonial violence, namely the 1890 massacre at Wounded Knee.[54] Readers are left with histories that are, at best, partial in terms of Native people. More worrisome, this absence betrays scholars' unwillingness to grapple with American acquisition of Indian lands and the actions that US citizens took to effect that dispossession.[55]

Placing Indian lands and nations at the story's center seems obvious when we consider that these lands made up most of the nation's massive expansion.[56] Growth during the nineteenth century was staggering. The 1803 Louisiana Purchase was by far the most significant acquisition, but expansion also included Spain's cessation of Florida, the annexation of Texas, treaties establishing the Oregon Territory, and forced land cessations from Mexico. The United States also invaded Hawaii, acquired Alaska from Russia, American Samoa from Germany, and the Philippines, Puerto Rico, and Guam from Spain. These new possessions prompted questions about how to govern the hundreds of thousands of Indians, Mexicans, Chinese immigrants, and others who occupied newly acquired regions. Complicating these debates were shifting ideas about racial and religious difference.[57] Taking Indian land and governing Native people, then, prompted serious debate about integrating these particular lands and peoples into the United States.[58] It also connected to similar issues raised by the acquisition of other places.

The study of settler colonialism and imperial history offers particularly helpful tools for understanding the ways that managing lands and peoples, as well as indigenous peoples' responses to those efforts, shaped American religion in this period. Historians of settler colonialism explore intercultural contacts that came *after* colonizers' early efforts to explore new places and extract resources from them.[59] These scholars investigate how colonists settled permanently in new lands and established dominance over indigenous populations through policies of segregation and exclusion. They also analyze the ways indigenous societies unwilling to cede their claims to land and autonomy responded to settler colonial policies. Scholars engaged in the critical study of empire also offer models for exploring Indian-American encounters.[60] They analyze the ways colonizing societies established social hierarchies, regulated space, and theorized differences in terms of race and culture. They consider how imperial outposts connected to and impacted colonial centers. I use tools from both subfields to understand how "friends of the Indian" participated in US expansion into Indian lands and how Kiowas reacted to the Americans' colonial strategies.

As noted earlier, the situation in Indian Country reflected other issues in American life. Questions raised by taking Indian lands and the effort to manage Native populations connected to debates about Mexicans who became American citizens and the status of Hawaiians and Filipinos after the United States acquired and colonized them. More broadly speaking, Americans' efforts to transform Kiowa cultural practices, including those understood as religious, reflected white Americans' campaigns to change the ways of life of numerous peoples, including formerly enslaved African Americans, Chinese workers, Mormons, and immigrants from southern and eastern Europe, especially if they were Catholic or Jewish. Kiowa responses also connect to broader themes in this period. Numerous people dealt with white Americans' efforts to transform them. The realm called the "religious" was one place in which these responses could be formulated.

SOURCES

The sources for this book include local and national stories that come from both Kiowa and American perspectives. While no one group can represent the diverse Indian communities across the American West, I focus on the Kiowa for a number of reasons. Their migration onto the southern plains and their shifting cultural practices show that Indian worlds were already changing prior to contact with Europeans and Euro-Americans.[61] As a thriving plains culture by the turn of the nineteenth century, Kiowas make for an interesting comparison with other groups living as far south as Texas and as far north as southern Canada. Further, Kiowas' alliance with one of the most powerful Indian nations at the time, the Comanches, made them central to American debates about westward expansion and the "problem" of ongoing Indian political autonomy.[62]

Kiowas also created materials that allow us to study their perspectives. In the last quarter of the nineteenth century, some Kiowas learned to speak, read, and write in English. We have some letters and diaries written in their hand. Even so, most Kiowas hardly had access to print publications or fluency in the English language. While Kiowas may not have written their history, they had alternative forms for recording their past. Like indigenous cultures across the Americas, the Kiowas developed ways of carving, painting, and drawing about their communal and personal histories.[63]

I employ these sources, particularly *sai-cut* (calendars), ledger drawings, tipis, and shields. Like many Plains Indian nations, Kiowas created rock art that depicted supernatural encounters as well as personal and tribal histories.[64] They also developed modes of painting on bison hides. Again, this production recorded events from the past and signaled personal and communal accomplishments. Older Kiowa men made calendars, on hide and later on paper, which included symbols meant to recall memorable events from each year. Through the work of early ethnologists, we have access to several Kiowa calendars, some of which include entries dating back to the 1820s and 1830s (see Figure I.8). More recent anthropologists have offered contextual details and interpretive tools for understanding these sources.[65]

I also use Kiowa drawings on paper made in ledger notebooks, such as the ones featured in my earlier description of the 1873 Sun Dance. Scholars have collected and studied Kiowa ledgers, which they view as an extension of an earlier tipi and hide painting tradition. These ledger notebooks include depictions of Kiowa life both before and during their containment on a reservation. Anthropologists have carefully documented the way that these forms of material culture track changes in Kiowa life.[66] Art historians have deciphered many of the colors, objects, and symbols depicted in the ledgers and have considered how ledgers and other drawings can be used as sources in historical inquiry.[67]

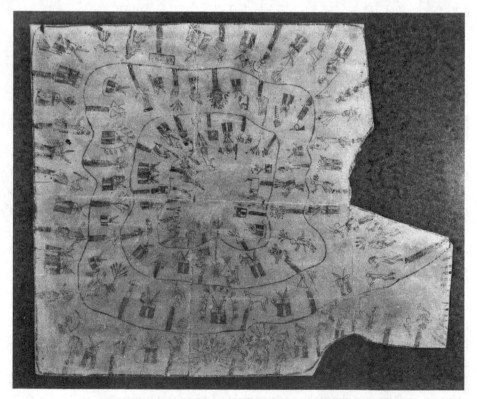

FIGURE 1.8. Jòhâusàn's (Little Bluff) *sai-cut*, or calendar, with entries about memorable events dating back to the 1830s. Winter events are marked by a black rectangle and summer events with the lodge built for Sun Dance rites. An infrared camera was used to make the entries more legible.

Credit: Phoebe A. Hearst Museum of Anthropology and the Regents of the University of California, catalog no. 2-4933

The calendars and ledgers, as well as oral histories and historical work documenting Kiowa engagements with the Spanish, Comanches, and Americans, serve as sources for considering Kiowa perspectives on the changes they experienced in this period.

Americans interested in this land, whether they visited it or not, left behind reams of reflection. They wrote endless reports issued for governmental and denominational authorities. They penned newspaper and magazine articles in national, local, denominational, and religious outlets. They published memoirs. The archive they left behind features the full array of players in Christian endeavors to civilize Indians, including Catholics and a variety of Protestants, men and women, and workers from throughout the country and beyond its boundaries. Americans such as Thomas Battey, who visited and worked among the Kiowas, left documents of a more personal nature, including diaries and letters that spoke to their aspirations, difficulties, and unresolved questions. These written sources are crucial to my historical labor to capture the variety of American viewpoints on Indian lands and "religion" as they developed over the course of the nineteenth century.

ORGANIZATION

Part I, "Open Lands," covers the period in which Kiowas maintained political autonomy within their homeland. It begins in 1803 when the Louisiana Purchase made the southern plains a part of the United States. It ends with the 1867 Treaty of Medicine Lodge, which created the Kiowa, Comanche, and Apache (KCA) Reservation. It traces American ideas about acquiring the vast Louisiana Territory, including arguments for its potential as a site for separating Indians from Americans and the debates surrounding Indian removal. It also traces Kiowa alliances within the Southwest borderlands and the prosperity they experienced in the decades before Americans arrived in the region. It continues with American settler migration across the Mississippi River and corresponding ideas about maintaining Indian separation despite this movement. It focuses on proposals to achieve separation through the creation of reservations. It also follows Kiowa responses to Americans heading west, exiled Indian nations settled on nearby lands, and federal proposals about a reservation. During this period, Protestant activists fashioned themselves as "friends of the Indian" and Catholics slowly established a series of western missions. Meanwhile, Kiowas maintained their ritual work as Americans came increasingly close to their lands.

Part II, "Closed Lands," examines life on the KCA Reservation from 1868 to 1881, spanning the reservation's early years to the eventual calls for its dissolution. It details President Ulysses S. Grant's so-called "Peace Policy," by which he turned reservation administration over to Christian denominations. It also chronicles Kiowa responses to Quakers' civilizing mission. The section considers the resulting conflict, the 1874–1875 Red River War, in which Kiowas and their allies mounted a campaign to push the Americans out of Native homelands. The military crushed the endeavor and sent some fighters to a military prison. Part II also follows the war's aftermath, in which Kiowas experienced separation from kin and increasing pressure to change their way of life. Throughout the period, American Protestants and Catholics debated what it meant to be the Indians' friend, especially during times of violent conflict. Kiowas, under mounting pressure and newly introduced to Christian missionaries, struggled to maintain their ritual obligations, even as they adjusted them in the midst of changing circumstances.

Part III, "Divided Lands," spans 1882 to 1903 and follows the efforts of "friends of the Indian" to dissolve reservations and break down tribal bonds, as well as the myriad Kiowa responses to that process. It focuses on American arguments for individual landholding, economic activity, and citizenship as keys to Indians' cultural transformation. Because breaking apart reservations threatened their livelihoods and tribal connections, Kiowas mounted a campaign to block it. The section follows the Americans' success in securing this dissolution, along with the "surplus" lands left over. It ends with Kiowas' last-ditch effort to defend their lands before the Supreme Court. Throughout this period, "friends of the Indian" promoted multiple forms of dispossession as benevolent gifts to Indians. Kiowas, facing the Americans' campaign of cultural genocide, experimented with a variety of new powers and rituals in order to secure their lands and community.

ECHOES FROM INDIAN COUNTRY

The story that unfolded in 1873 on the banks of Sweetwater Creek reveals that Kiowas and Americans made their gods central in the contest over Indian Country. But the significance of that story is hardly limited to that distant time or place. Stories of contact and transformation intersected with territorial claims starting in 1607 when British settlers set foot on North American soil and engaged with indigenous people. It continued as Americans claimed their freedom and expanded their country's boundaries throughout the entire nineteenth century. The story, then, stretches over centuries and spans the continent. It continues as Americans expand their global influence. In the end, we might consider how the peoples and gods who came together in Indian Country remain with us even today.

PART ONE

Open Lands

1

1803 to 1837

IN 1803, THOMAS Jefferson's administration negotiated with French officials to purchase the vast Louisiana Territory. The purchase more than doubled the size of the young United States. Jefferson had not necessarily sought out this major acquisition. The frontier regions of Ohio, Indiana, and Tennessee still provided ample space for American settlers. But the surprising opportunity presented the possibility of securing American economic interests at the mouth of the Mississippi River. It also made incursions from European enemies far less likely. The purchase also offered another potential benefit: land for removing Indians from the East and settling them at a distance from American citizens.[1]

Reducing Indian landholdings had been an important feature of US Indian policy since George Washington's presidential tenure. While some Americans argued that Indians had forfeited their lands by siding with the British during the Revolution, Washington disagreed. He affirmed Native peoples' right to occupy their homelands and established an Indian Department to carry out diplomacy with indigenous leaders. He supported his colleague Henry Knox's effort to make treaties with Indian nations. In what some scholars have called a "limited notion" of the "doctrine of discovery," Washington's administration considered themselves the rightful first purchasers of Indian lands and offered compensation to Native people who chose to sell.[2]

Washington's vision for Indians' future also assumed their "progress" toward "civilization." He shared with many Americans a sense that Native people were both capable of and should practice Anglo-American cultural habits. These included a settled life built around agriculture, use of tools and the practice of skilled trades, monogamous families with patriarchal leadership, written language and literacy, and women's duties focused on the home. Washington and others promoted this way of life based on an

Enlightenment-era confidence that humanity progressed from savagery to barbarism to civilization, of which Anglo-American cultural practices were the pinnacle.[3]

According to many Americans, "civilization" also involved the affirmation of Protestant Christianity.[4] Drawing on missionary efforts that predated the revolution, American Protestants quickly organized efforts to evangelize Native Americans. In 1787, New Englanders founded the Society for the Propagation of the Gospel Among the Indians and Others in North America and opened schools to which Indian children could travel for an American-style education. New Yorkers started three different mission societies dedicated to sending missionaries to Native people both upstate and in the American Southeast. The Society of Friends also took an interest. In 1795, Quakers inaugurated their mission to New York's Seneca nation. Friends opened schools and encouraged a transition from hunting to farming. They held meetings for Christian worship and advocated the transition from the Senecas' traditional longhouse dwellings to log cabins. Quaker women encouraged Seneca wives to take up the domestic arts, which included sewing American-style clothes. Several Protestant denominations and mission organizations received federal funds to support their "civilization" programs.[5]

The Friends saw themselves not only as part of the nation's plan to civilize Indians, but also as the right people to ensure Native nations' fair treatment at the hands of government officials. This approach did not mean that Quakers disagreed with US Indian policy. Like most Americans, Society members affirmed that Indians ought to become civilized and give up some of their lands. Once Native people became subsistence farmers, they would not need as much land and could sell the excess to the government for distribution to settlers. But Quakers worried that federal officials, local leaders, or greedy traders might take advantage of Indians as they progressed toward civilization. The Friends hoped that their public influence would ensure the nation's "expansion with honor."[6]

Thomas Jefferson shared Washington's Indian strategy of promoting civilization and making treaties. From the moment of his election, Jefferson argued that Indians needed to live on less land, making room for yeoman farmers. During his presidency, Congress passed the Indian Trade and Intercourse Act, which set the terms for acquiring Indian lands. His administration promoted several treaties to acquire land, some of which also initiated Indian westward movement. With the Louisiana Purchase, Jefferson saw even greater prospects for removal, especially for Indians who were not ready to move toward civilization. For these Native peoples, Jefferson recommended an exchange of their lands in the East for permanent lands across the Mississippi River. Once there, Indians could continue, at least for a time, their own cultural traditions.[7]

Removing Indians westward not only opened up land, but also established a physical barrier between Indians and settlers. Jefferson was not the first to recommend this kind of separation. In 1795, General Anthony Wayne proposed a neutral zone between Indians and Americans, affirming the need for a "kind of consecrated ground" between them. Jefferson agreed. Physical separation kept conflicts to a minimum and eliminated the possibility of frontier citizens, with their less than upstanding behaviors, corrupting Indians. The Louisiana Territory buoyed the president's confidence that such a barrier was possible.⁸

Jefferson's desire for Indian separation did not imply a lack of confidence in Indians' capacity for civilization. Like Washington, Jefferson affirmed that they could gradually be civilized and assimilated into American society. In this way, Jefferson's view of Native Americans diverged sharply from his highly negative views of people of African descent. For Jefferson, as with many Americans, the question of the Indians' future rested on their behavior and cultural practices, which he affirmed could change. He saw evidence for this potential in the lives of some Indians, such as the Cherokee, who were viewed as already being on a path toward assimilation. But American settlers needed more land, and Native people unwilling to relinquish their old ways might best maintain them in America's vast new western territory.⁹

LIFE IN THE OPEN LAND

On the southern plains of this territory, Kiowas also made agreements with other nations. They had struggled against their powerful Comanche neighbors for several years.¹⁰ But in the 1790s, they moved toward peace. In 1806, Kiowas met Comanches at the home of a Spanish trading partner in New Mexico.¹¹ A Kiowa leader named Cûiqáuje (Wolf Lying Down) initiated contact and signaled his peaceful intentions. Surprised at the gesture, the Comanches signaled their willingness to negotiate, and the two nations celebrated the new alliance with gifts and feasting. They solidified their bonds through a series of marriages. While the Kiowas were still a relatively small nation, their alliance with the powerful Comanches firmly established their presence in the area. Their trading relationships now extended beyond the southern plains to include Spaniards, French traders, and numerous Indian nations. Partnership with the Comanches allowed Kiowas to benefit from a booming regional trading market.¹²

Allying with the Comanche also had implications for Kiowa ritual life. While Comanches often came together in summer for hunting and raiding parties, they had no ceremony like the Kiowas' Sun Dance. After 1806, Kiowas opened up their summer ritual encampment to them.¹³ In this way, Kiowas shared their methods for accessing sacred power. The benefits of such sharing were clear: Sun Dance practices invoked blessing, health, and protection. Kiowas could only be as strong as their closest allies. Empowering their Comanche friends made sense.

The Kiowa-Comanche alliance also encouraged joint hunting expeditions and raids for horses and mules. Kiowas joined Comanches on long-distance, dangerous raids into the Spanish frontier. These men had great need of protection.¹⁴ Kiowas considered shields essential to raids and other dangerous activities. Men received shield designs through dreams or vision quests. In the case of the latter, men traveled to special places, fasted for several days, and asked beings of great power to help them. Some men received designs and later painted them on buckskin. The colorful shields, typically adorned with other items, indicated men's relationship to protective powers. As long as they carried them, men obeyed required proscriptions and performed rituals associated with their shield's possession.[15]

Stories about Páuthòcáui (White-Faced Bison Bull) receiving his shield offer a helpful example of this process (Plate 3). According to descendants, an invisible spirit spoke to Páuthòcáui around the time the Kiowas made peace with the Comanches. The spirit promised to give him a "shield to help [him] through life." A flock of birds then appeared before Páuthòcáui and then transformed into beautifully adorned warriors on horseback. The shield's design, a combination of yellow and green, came to him from one of the vision's riders. By the time Páuthòcáui wielded it in battle, he had added a horsetail, cowtails, a cowbell, eagle feathers, and hooves from a young antelope. Páuthòcáui's shield was one of many that Kiowa men carried to protect themselves while doing the dangerous and cooperative work of securing prosperity on the plains.[16]

In the first decade of the nineteenth century, Americans claimed sovereignty over lands that Kiowas occupied, but they were more concerned with Indian nations living east of the Mississippi River. These Indians needed to relinquish at least some of their lands. Their way of life required change, a total transformation to take on Anglo-American cultural habits. Among these was affirmation of "true religion," a Christianity freely chosen and non-specifically Protestant. Government officials worked toward these ends by making treaties that established reservations, reduced landholdings, and by encouraging some removals. They also partnered with a variety of Protestant clergy, missionaries, and reformers to civilize American Indians. And while these religious representatives cooperated eagerly, they also developed the notion of their particular duty to ensure that Indians were treated fairly. They conceived of themselves as "friends of the Indian" and guarantors of an ethical American expansion.[17]

Kiowas, on the other hand, had never encountered the Americans who now claimed authority over their lands. Their world centered on the southern plains and their people's flourishing within it. Kiowas organized themselves around shared obligations to each other and social duties based on status and place in life. They also related to outsiders, whether Comanche, French, or Spanish, in ways to benefit their people. These interactions included rites for invoking sacred power, such as the Sun Dance, and material objects, including powerful shields. During this period, Kiowa alliance making and ritual power seeking accompanied a period of strength and prosperity. Along with the Comanches, Kiowas owned some of the largest horse herds of any Indian nation in the West.[18] They had made a good place on the southern plains, and the Americans were not there yet.

During the early nineteenth century, Kiowas and their Comanche allies played an integral part in a complex southern plains economy. This enormous trading network included Spaniards from New Mexico to Mexico City, French traders who traveled the Mississippi, and numerous Indian nations. The trade centered on horses and mules, but also included trade goods, guns, powder, and human captives.[19] Communities connected to these markets made alliances for peace and trade, but their agreements were hardly permanent. Indeed, Kiowas and their allies sometimes overlooked old pacts. As New Spain lurched toward civil war after 1810, Kiowas and Comanches took advantage of the northern frontier's poorly guarded horse and mule herds.[20] They used the spoils not only to enrich their own status as horse-owning men, but also as valuable trade commodities to make connections and gain desired items from trading partners throughout the region. For Kiowas in this place and at this moment, life was good.

EAST OF THE RIVER

The southern plains and its internationally connected market were mostly unknown to the Americans who now claimed dominion over them. As a result, Thomas Jefferson initiated several expeditions to survey the vast territory. While Lewis and Clark, the most famous of these explorers, took a route running north of Kiowa lands, other government-sponsored expeditions ventured into the southern plains. Zebulon Pike passed through during his 1806–1807 journey, meeting some Native peoples, although not Kiowas. He later reported that the region had some commercial prospects, but little agricultural value. Several years later, an American military officer had a brief encounter with some Indian nations in the region. But a decade after the 1803 Louisiana Purchase, Americans still had little information about Native people living on the southern plains. Maps from the period represented the region as largely unknown. They featured unclear boundaries and highlighted the presence of multiple Indian nations with whom Americans had no formal relations.[21]

Matters east of the Mississippi, on the other hand, appeared clear and pressing. Despite winning the Revolution, Americans had not ejected their British enemies from the continent. Conflict brewed as Britain tried to reassert itself. Some Indian nations sided with their old colonial ally in what would become the War of 1812. Native people, including Tecumseh and other Shawnees, used the conflict as an opportunity to press their own concerns. They organized a pan-Indian alliance aimed at pushing out the Americans. As the War of 1812 ended, Britain relinquished its claim to lands east of the Mississippi. Their exit opened up more land for American settlement. Overland emigrants poured into the trans-Appalachian West by the thousands.[22]

While this postwar American migration pressed Indians for land, Britain's retreat also entailed the loss of a crucial ally. American officials had long considered Indian policy in light of Native peoples' ability to make alliances with other European powers, namely Britain and Spain. Now this option was gone.[23] Further, some Native people's support for the British caused some Americans to question their fitness for citizenship. Increasingly, Americans doubted Indians' willingness and ability to assimilate. These concerns seemed especially acute in settings where Indians lived near American towns and settlements. In response to this skepticism, Protestant reformers and leaders adjusted their approach to Indian affairs. They insisted that Native people could be civilized, but that this goal would be best realized by separating Indians from American communities and sending missionaries to live and work among them.[24]

Missionaries from the American Board of Commissioners for Foreign Missions (ABCFM) were among those eager to send their workers into Native communities. Revival-minded Presbyterians and Congregationalists founded the board in 1810 with the aim to convert all the world's people. In their early work, ABCFM missionaries affirmed that evangelizing and civilizing went hand in hand. They brought their Protestant Christianity, as well as Anglo-American cultural habits, to potential converts in India, Ceylon, the Sandwich Islands, and the Middle East. They wanted "heathens" around the world to accept the Christian gospel, as well as change their gender roles, food subsistence practices, childrearing, and dress. The ABCFM proclaimed a gospel of total transformation.[25]

Despite the word "foreign" in their name, the ABCFM also promoted missions to Native Americans. They opened a mission to the Cherokees in 1817. A year later they started work among the Choctaw. In step with federal policy, they supported American efforts to reduce Indian lands in the East in order to promote a transition away from hunting toward settled forms of agriculture. They also recommended robust payments and annuities for ceded land. Mission officials encouraged Indian nations to use these funds to support mission schools and other civilizing programs.[26] In the face of hardening American attitudes toward Indians, ABCFM workers emphasized that Indians were making the transition. Civilization was possible. They urged government officials to have patience and to act humanely toward Indian nations engaged in the process of cultural change.

But more and more Americans sought land for homesteads and argued for removing all Indians living east of the Mississippi. President Monroe affirmed that removal would benefit Native people, although he insisted that it not be forced. During his 1817–1825 tenure, federal officials promoted treaties, land cessations, and removals. To be sure, Monroe also supported a civilizing mission. During his administration, Congress established the Civilization Fund, which provided $10,000 annually for Indian schools. Monroe applauded Indian efforts to move toward Anglo-American cultural practices. But fewer Americans envisioned the East as a site for long-term Indian settlement. And the Louisiana Territory presented the prospect of an ideal place to relocate Native people. Monroe's Secretary of War soon asked Congress for an appropriation to remove nearly 100,000 Native people.[27]

WEST OF THE RIVER

If Americans knew more about the southern plains, perhaps they might have thought differently about removal as an expedient solution. Massive movement of American settlers, as well as Indians removing west, had triggered a crisis for Native people living just west of the Mississippi, especially the Osage. Pushed out of their homelands and armed with guns procured through the fur trade, Osage warriors ranged west onto the southern plains. The Kiowas and the Comanches felt the threat of their presence. In 1824, they sent out a massive number of fighting men to push the Osage back east. At the same time, Kiowas and Comanches continued large raids into northern Mexico. They needed to refresh their horses and mule herds in order to maintain their strong position as key trading partners in the region. Pressures to raid to the south and play defense in the East stretched Kiowa and Comanche resources thin.[28]

Around the same time, two explorers set out to study the territory that Americans hoped would solve their land and Indian problems. The War Department sponsored explorer and engineer Stephen Long's 1820 expedition. Long trekked westward toward what he called "the Great American Desert" (Figure 1.1). He interacted with several Native nations along the way. He offered gifts and requested safe passage. He encountered some Kiowas and penned one of the earliest American accounts of them, reporting that they "wander" the area and "have always a great number of horses."[29]

Long's report included copious information about Indians whom he encountered. He paid particular attention to religious practices. The explorer recorded his impressions of Omaha "medicine men or magicians." Most, he claimed, were "impostures." They pretended to have prophecies and capitalized on Indian people's "superstitious faith." Long also wrote about a "great medicine dance" he witnessed. He compared the ritual's bodily cutting to the "expiatory tortures of the Hindoos." Tapping into the long tradition of ascribing cannibalism to indigenous people, Long insisted that Pawnees practiced human sacrifice to forestall potential calamities. In his assessments of Native religious life, Long reflected the anti-Catholic discourse of the period, especially the tropes about priests who duped their unschooled congregants. He also engaged in the emerging discourse of comparative religion, in which Europeans and Americans in colonial settings studied and assessed the non-Christian peoples of the globe.[30]

The War Department sponsored a second expedition led by Jedidiah Morse, a geographer and Congregationalist minister. Morse occupied the center of New England clergymen's efforts to reform the nation through evangelization and education. He helped found a seminary, as well as national societies for Bible and tract distribution. He supported global and domestic missions as an ABCFM board member. While the Secretary of War commissioned Morse because of his geographical expertise, Morse also traveled to the West as a Protestant minister committed to the world's conversion. In his report about the expedition, Morse called for an "awakening" to the situation of "neglected and oppressed" Indians just west of the Mississippi. The situation, according to Morse, was dire. American settlers encroached, depleting game herds and taking Indian land. With the exception of Native nations visited by Catholic priests, few western Indians had been introduced to Christianity or the most basic aspects of civilization. Hoping to reverse the trend of hardening attitudes toward Indians, Morse called for a new benevolent society committed to civilizing Native people. He begged Americans to

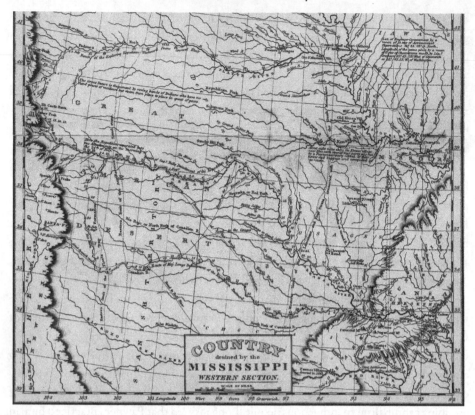

FIGURE 1.1. Detail from Stephen Long's 1823 map of the trans-Mississippi west. He marked the southern plains as the "Great American Desert." In his account of his western travels, Long wrote, "The Great Desert is frequented by roving bands of Indians who have no fixed places of residence but roam from place to place in quest of game."

Credit: Stephen Harriman Long, *Country Drained by the Mississippi* [Philadelphia: Young & Delleker, 1823] map. Retrieved from the Library of Congress, https://www.loc.gov/item/2007630425/. Accessed May 27, 2017.

consider their duty to the continent's first residents. Indians were weak and dependent, he wrote. America was strong and possessed the capacity, with the Christian God's help, to save Native people.[31]

Along with a public commitment to Indians' improvement, Morse recommended western missions modeled on ABCFM Indian stations in the East. He urged the opening of schools and the establishment of model farms. While he envisioned much labor to be done by civilian farmers and teachers, Morse also called for a military presence in the West. Indians needed to know the nation's benevolent purposes, as well as its strength. With an American commitment to Indian improvement, Morse reasoned, Native people would eventually be raised to the rank of "freemen and citizens." And in a tone that anticipated rhetoric by later ABCFM leaders, Morse warned that America's leading position in the world was at stake. If citizens shrugged their responsibilities to Indians, he wrote, "the national charter will suffer."[32]

Like Stephen Long, Morse also used his report to assess Native religious life. He claimed that Indians had ideas about a "Great Spirit" or god similar to the ancient Athenians whom the biblical Paul had confronted. Morse called for modern-day Pauls to serve as teachers, declaring to Indians that their "unknown God" was truly revealed through— and only through—the Christian Bible. Morse acknowledged that the task would be difficult, as Christian teachers would face "medicine men" who were "imposters" and manipulated Indians through their "pretended sorcery." But with Americans' sustained effort, Morse affirmed, victory was possible.[33]

After traveling through the region, both Long and Morse admitted to the southern plains' tough conditions. Long's designation of the region as the "Great American Desert" cast a lasting negative light on the area.[34] Settlers did not seek to make homesteads there until the end of the nineteenth century. But that did not mean that Americans left the southern plains alone. As Long noted, the region had commercial prospects, including the recently opened Santa Fe Trail connecting St. Louis to New Mexico to Mexican Chihuahua. And as both Long and Morse emphasized, huge numbers of uncivilized Indians lived there. They wandered. They hunted. Their "religion" was all pretense and superstition. They needed civilization.

Morse reported to federal officials and then publicized his plans for a new society to encourage Indian civilization. In the *Missionary Herald*, the ABCFM paper with more than 14,000 subscribers, Morse asked readers to support this new effort.[35] The society's agents would learn about Indians' traditions and customs, as well as select spots "for experimental farms." In his description of the society's work, Morse outlined what it meant to be a "friend of the Indian." According to Morse, "friends of the Indian" understood who Native people were, as well as who they should become. They believed they knew Indian cultures and how best to transform them. But according to Morse and his successors, "friends of the Indian" had another crucial role. They partnered with the US government and insisted on Indians' fair treatment at the hands of federal officials. Morse's article about his new benevolent organization listed several government officials as patrons and members, but clergymen and Protestant reformers dominated the group. Their presence ensured sympathy toward Indians and a commitment to ethical expansion.

THE REMOVAL CRISIS

Throughout the 1820s, American officials promoted Indian civilization, made treaties that reduced Indian lands, and encouraged removal. The judiciary enabled these efforts with the 1823 ruling in *Johnson v. McIntosh*, which undermined the strength of Native land claims. The decision declared Indians rightful occupants of their lands, but asserted the nation's primary claim on the land itself.[36] In 1825, John Quincy Adams became president and supported the establishment of the Indian Territory, with exiled Indians settling primarily in its eastern half and "wild" Indians, like the Kiowas, living in the western part. State officials in the eastern United States, especially in Georgia, pressured Adams to accelerate the pace of removal. Adams, however, refused to force the matter. Georgians, who coveted Cherokee lands for both settlement and mining, fumed. They had reason to rejoice with the election of Andrew Jackson.[37]

Jackson's distaste for Indians emerged during his military service in the War of 1812 and his 1813 campaign against Muskogee Creeks. During these conflicts, Jackson confronted pan-Indian coalitions aimed at resisting Americans. Claims to sacred power had enlivened Native fighters. Identifying Americans as physical and spiritual threats, Indian leaders such as Tecumseh and his brother Tenskwatawa called for rejection of colonial products and recommended new ritual forms to empower resistance to American incursion. These Indian coalitions, however, were unsuccessful. Tecumseh died in battle. His brother faced exile. The leaders inspiring a "spirit-based revolt" among Muskogees fared no better. Jackson's soldiers decimated the ranks of Creek fighters and later appropriated lands from even those Creeks who had assisted the Americans.[38]

As a veteran of the Creek War, Jackson recognized Indians' capacity for inter-tribal alliance and resistance. As a statesman, he argued that the federal government ought to forego treaties with Indians and simply legislate in regard to them. Once president, he quickly involved himself in the disputes over Cherokee lands in Georgia, siding with settlers and state officials. In contrast to Washington and Jefferson's affirmation of Indians' potential for "gradual assimilation," Jackson argued that Native people could not survive as free people intermingled with Americans. Settlers would soon overrun the Indians who remained in the East. Jackson claimed he could not guarantee their safety and filled his administration with those who shared his views. War Department officials claimed that removing Native people from their homelands would be a "work of mercy," while Indian resistance would "entail destruction upon their race." Indian Office leaders regularly referred to removal as a "benevolent" and "humane policy." In 1829, Jackson introduced his controversial Indian removal bill to Congress. He pronounced it a humanitarian act.[39]

To be sure, thousands of Indians faced unwelcome removal prior to Jackson's bill, and many Protestant leaders had supported treaties that reduced Indian landholdings and pushed Native people west. These reformers did not object to removal in theory, but rather were opposed to Jackson's bill and its implications for particular Indian nations. They specifically protested the possibility of Cherokee forced removal.[40] From the perspective of clergymen and reformers who considered themselves "friends of the Indian," Cherokees had made great strides toward civilization. They had schools, churches, a newspaper, and an American-style constitution. They also cultivated farms that provided for their subsistence. Removal would force them to start their agricultural efforts all over again. The Cherokees had done everything Americans asked them to do. And now Jackson insisted that even this civilized Indian nation must be removed.

Religious leaders and laypeople responded to Jackson's bill, as well as his insistence that removal could be realized without violence, with incredulity followed by activism.[41] One historian has argued that the campaign against the removal bill "generated the most intense public opposition that the United States has witnessed."

Prominent religious women, including Catherine Beecher, became involved, sending Congress numerous anti-removal petitions anonymously in order to hide their identities as women. Members of the American Anti-Slavery Society also joined the opposition, drawing connections between Indian removal and proposals for African colonization. Protestants against Jackson's bill claimed that forced removal broke an "implicit promise" made to Indians who had complied with American demands and transitioned toward civilization.[42]

ABCFM secretary Jeremiah Evarts played a major role in popularizing arguments against Jackson's removal bill. He claimed that the policy violated Indian rights, did nothing to solve the land problem, and most important, constituted a sin against the Christian God. Evarts, who had visited ABCFM missions to Indians throughout the Southeast, published a widely reprinted set of essays in Washington, D.C.'s *National Intelligencer*. He also penned memorials to Congress. Exploring the history of US treaties with the Cherokees, Evarts affirmed Indians' right to occupancy on at least a portion of their traditional lands. He also claimed that removal provided no real solution. Leaving lands that they had worked so hard to improve would bring misery to thousands. If the government removed them to poor lands in the West, Cherokees could not survive on them. If the lands were good, however, American settlers would eventually try to claim them.[43]

Evarts deemed Jackson's bill a national calamity to which all American Christians should object. The proposed removals, he argued, involved "the character of our government, and of our country." Other nations, including those also dealing with indigenous populations, would take note. Evarts reached to a story in the Hebrew Bible to make his point, comparing Cherokee removal to Ahab and Jezebel's treacherous theft of Naboth's garden. "The sentence of an indignant world will be uttered in thunders, which roll and reverberate for ages," he wrote. Even worse, according to Evarts, was that removal constituted a sin of great consequence. "The Great Arbiter of Nations never fails to take cognizance of national delinquencies," he claimed. If Jackson removed civilized Indians by force, Evarts threatened, God would judge.[44]

Quakers involved in Indian affairs also expressed their displeasure with Jackson's bill. Like Jeremiah Evarts, Friends emphasized Indians' right to stay on their ancestral lands and called removal an offense against the Christian God. In a memorial to Congress, Society members emphasized the connection between permanent lands and Indians' transition to civilization. They complained that Georgia officials had already reduced Cherokee lands to such a degree that the Indians barely had enough to lead a "civilized" (meaning agricultural) life. If the government let the Cherokees remain, Quakers insisted, they would continue on their path to civilization and soon be ready for "amalgamation with the white population." Jackson's proposed removal would stop Cherokee progress in its tracks. Articles in Friends' newspapers reiterated these claims. As one editorialist wrote, uprooting the Cherokees would hinder their progress. The Quakers' connection of permanent land and the possibility of Indian civilization continued for decades.[45]

During the debate over the Indian removal bill, Protestant clergy, reformers, and lay-people galvanized their particular understanding of what it meant to be a "friend of the Indian." "Friends" resisted federal policies that undermined Indian progress toward civilization and relied upon violence for enforcement. They struggled against Jackson and others who argued that removal legislation had humanitarian motivations. To be sure, the president had some Protestant leaders, namely Baptists with strong connections to the South and West, on his side. Baptist missionary to the Cherokee, Isaac McCoy, declared that "benevolent" Americans who understood Indian needs should support Jackson's removal. An article in a Washington, D.C., newspaper called McCoy "one of the most judicious and devoted Friends of Indian reform." But opponents fired back, presenting their alternative understanding of what it meant to be the Indians' friend. One New York congressman argued that Jackson's opponents were the true "Friends of Indian rights." Newspaper editorialists called on "despairing Friends of the Indian" to keep fighting on behalf of Native nations in the Southeast.[46]

A growing number of Protestant clergymen and reformers, especially in the North, rallied in opposition to Jackson's plans for removal. In the course of their effort, they claimed the mantle of the Indians' "friend" and continued to employ this designation for decades. This development coincided with the growth of abolitionist sentiment, which reformers articulated in a similar language of sympathy, benevolence, and friendship. Indeed, one historian has found connections between many removal bill opponents and proponents for both the gradual and immediate end to chattel slavery.[47] Abolitionist newspapers in the 1830s included strong critiques of Jackson's removal plans and embraced their responsibility to ensure Indians' fair treatment and the nation's ethical expansion. Once again, as "friends of the Indian," these reformers claimed to know what Native people needed. They should become civilized and eventually assimilated. Jackson's bill threatened this outcome and, therefore, the nation's reputation.

Protests by Indian nations, Protestant leaders, missionaries, and abolitionists ultimately failed. Congress passed Jackson's bill and authorized funds to carry out removals. Treaty commissioners assigned western lands and arranged for the forced removal of multiple Indian nations in New York, Ohio, Indiana, and Illinois. Over the course of the 1830s, American officials also expelled thousands of Native people in the Southeast. Some Indians found ways to stay on reservations or in eastern settlements. Still others chose to hide until the removal process ended. But many thousands suffered containment, followed by exile to the west. The best-known example of forced removal, the Cherokee Trail of Tears, caused the deaths of one-quarter of the people removed.

FILLING UP THE INDIAN COUNTRY

Removals, whether voluntary or forced, put significant pressures on Indian nations that had long been established in the area designated as Indian Territory. One historian has claimed that by the 1830s the "Indian Country had become a confused and often dangerous jumble of peoples and policy."[48] Kiowas experienced these new dangers. As noted earlier, Indians forcibly removed from the East settled in Osage lands, pushing the Osage further west. Cheyennes and Arapahos to the north came down onto the southern plains to steal Kiowa horses. In order to maintain their relatively strong position, Kiowas joined Comanches on dangerous raids deep into Mexico to replenish their herds. In the 1830s, threats to Kiowa safety and prosperity came from every direction.[49]

Kiowas turned to rituals for seeking sacred power as the region grew more violent. Scattered Kiowa bands and some of their allies continued to gather for Sun Dances. Calendar entries, which recalled memorable events in the past, feature a pipe for the summer of 1828. The pipe image suggests that the people performed ritual adoptions during the ceremony.[50] Kiowas also adopted captives to replace dead relatives and friends. Like Comanches, Kiowas addressed their losses due to epidemic disease and warfare by integrating captives. Through ceremonies of adoption, especially those performed at their primary ritual to reinforce communal identity, Kiowas integrated new people.[51]

Kiowa men also sought out visions. One story tells of a vision received during a raid into Mexico. After taking many cattle and escaping, Cûiqáuje (Wolf Lying Down) stopped to rest. While sleeping, a bull appeared to him and offered him a powerful "medicine." Cûiqáuje later made four shields with elements from his dream. He painted bulls and rainbows on the shields and their covers. To give the shield aural elements, he added metal tinkers and a clanging bell. Cûiqáuje then shared the extra shields with friends and relations, hoping they would bring protection.[52]

Other Kiowa men received dreams for designing tipi covers imbued with protective power. Of course, all Kiowas in this period lived in tipis constructed from bison skins and wooden poles. But prominent men painted their tipi covers. In large Kiowa encampments, as many as one-fifth of the tipis bore such decoration. Some men painted their tipis with images from their life as warriors and hunters, but others integrated designs and referenced powers given to them in dreams. The tipi owned by a leading man named Gúkáulê (Lump On The Rib Cage) is one example (Figure 1.2). As a young man, Gúkáulê shot at a porcupine. To his surprise, the animal caught the arrow in its jaws. Soon after, a porcupine holding an arrow visited Gúkáulê in his sleep and gave him a powerful tipi design. Kiowas affirmed the tipi's power in Gúkáulê's life as he, like the porcupine on the tipi, had a large family. According to Kiowa accounts of the tipi, Gúkáulê's descendants were also protected from illness, especially consumption.[53]

Sometimes the ritual work performed and sacred objects engaged to ensure health and safety were not enough.[54] The summer of 1833 was one of those times. According to one Kiowa source, three bands camped along a river bend. Some young men returned from a hunt and reported finding an Osage arrow in a buffalo they had just killed. The news prompted immediate concern. Two Kiowa leaders called for immediate flight from the area. Another decided to stay until the river waters subsided and his people could cross more easily.[55]

Two groups fled as far as possible. As they made a new camp, young men rode in with news. Osage warriors had "frightfully killed many and left the heads of the killed in traders' brass buckets, for they had beheaded their victims." Because most of the adult men were away on raids or hunts, the women, children, and elderly in the doomed village could make no defense. Many tried to flee. Mothers unsuccessfully tried to hide their small children among the nearby rocks. Once the news came to other Kiowa encampments, men rode out after the Osage warriors but stopped at the site of the attack. The destruction was so "terrifying" that they were detained from their pursuit. The group that stayed behind had been almost entirely destroyed. Decapitated bodies littered the ground. Brass buckets held the heads of women, children, and older people.[56] Kiowa calendars, including Séttàun's (Little Bear) (Figure 1.3), memorialize the carnage with images of severed heads. Others, such as Cûitònqì's (Wolf Tail) (Figure 1.4), depict the Osage knives.

The Osage not only perpetrated one of the most brutal assaults Kiowas had ever experienced, but also captured two children, one of the ten medicine bundles, and the *Tái̧mé*, the people's central sacred object. According to one account of the massacre, the *Tái̧mé* keeper's wife heard warning cries and tried to unfasten it from her tipi pole before fleeing. Osage warriors found and killed her.[57] Without the *Tái̧mé*, Kiowas did not celebrate the

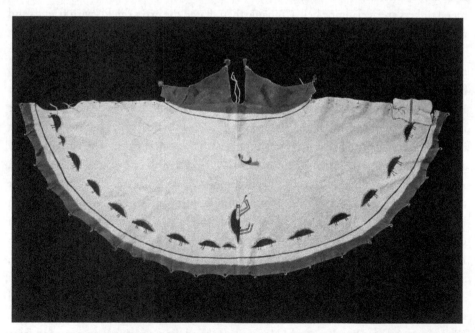

FIGURE 1.2. Gúkáulê's (Lump On The Rib Cage) tipi cover, featuring porcupines that came to him in a vision. Gúkáulê was known to some Americans as Tumor.

Credit: Department of Anthropology, National Museum of Natural History, image no. 229904

FIGURE 1.3. Séttàun's (Little Bear) calendar entry for the summer of 1833, when Osage warriors mounted a devastating attack and killed many Kiowa women and children. In his study of Kiowa calendars, Smithsonian ethnologist James Mooney featured all the entries from Séttàun's calendar, referring to him as Sett'an.
Credit: Mooney, *Calendar History of the Kiowa Indians,* page 258

Sun Dance that summer. The loss was demoralizing. The people had no opportunity to come together, fulfill vows, and offer thanks.

The following winter brought no peace, but instead another unnerving spectacle. In November 1833, a meteor shower dazzled inhabitants across a wide swath of North America. According to later writers, people from Mexico to Missouri interpreted the show of lights as divine displeasure.[58] Indians across the northern and southern plains took note and depicted the event on winter counts and calendars, including the Kiowa image in Figure 1.5.[59] Kiowa adults and children looked to the night sky and wondered what the "awful" sign foretold.[60] Within a year, Kiowas would meet the largest American military force ever sent onto the plains.

PICTURING THE INDIAN COUNTRY

In summer 1834, George Catlin accompanied American troops across the plains. Catlin was neither a soldier nor a Protestant reformer. He was a budding artist with an interest in exploration. But he shared with his reform-minded counterparts a sense that he was the Indians' friend. His fascination began in 1824, when he witnessed an Indian delegation visiting his native Pennsylvania. During his first western journey in 1832, Catlin had sailed up the Missouri River. Along the way, he encountered Crow, Blackfeet, and Mandan Indians. He painted over 180 portraits, as well as myriad landscapes and scenes of Indian life. His most dramatic paintings from the trip were inspired by a Mandan ritual that Catlin called the O-kee-pa ceremony (Plate 4).[61]

At the journey's end, Catlin eagerly presented his work to eastern audiences. He published accounts of his trip in many newspapers and began work on a book. Because

FIGURE I.4. Cûitònqìꞌs (Wolf Tail) calendar entries for the winter of 1831–1832 through the summer of 1833. The drawing on the bottom right memorializes the 1833 Osage attack. Cûitònqìꞌs drawings on cardstock are called the Quitone Kiowa Calendar after another name, Jimmy Quitone, by which the artist was known.

Credit: National Anthropological Archives, Smithsonian Institution, manuscript 2002-27

eyewitness accounts of Indians in the American West were still rare, periodicals often reprinted Catlin's letters. In these early reports, the young artist exhibited a simultaneous ardor and abhorrence of Indian life, an ambiguous feeling of "romance and darkness" that was shared by many Americans. Like other Americans who considered themselves "friends of the Indian," Catlin invoked the nation's "honor" and "humanity" to call for Indians' protection. Even so, he also presented his paintings to a public eager to see images of Native people whose future was uncertain. Viewers in Cincinnati flocked to see them. The exhibition, one newspaper claimed, "perpetuate[d] the remembrance of the vanishing Red Men."[62]

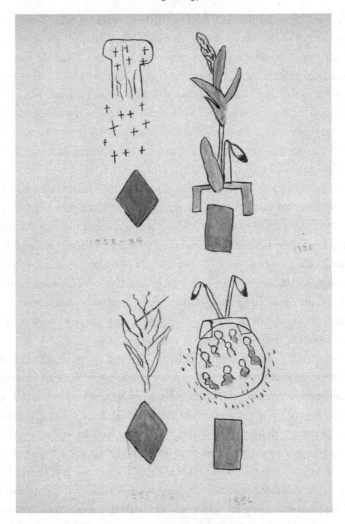

FIGURE 1.5. Cúitònqì's calendar entries for the winter of 1833–1834 through the summer of 1836. The meteor shower that amazed viewers from the central United States to Mexico is featured in the upper left corner.

Credit: Manuscript 2002-27, National Anthropological Archives, Smithsonian Institution

Catlin shared this sense that Indians might soon meet their end, an idea increasingly popular after 1830. Hoping to preserve as much Indian culture as possible, he accepted another chance to go west in 1834. Catlin accompanied Colonel Henry Leavenworth and 400 dragoons, or cavalrymen, on their mission to establish relations with "wild Indians" on the southern plains. Catlin painted and wrote about Indian life along the way. As with his earlier journey, the young artist used dramatic language to describe his experiences. He expressed eagerness to learn more about the "red knights of the lance." Catlin also registered the ways in which American exploration, migration, and settlement disrupted Indian nations in the region. He fretted about federal Indian policies. Officials appeared to punish Indians first and make treaties with them after.[63] Catlin wrote to his family often, telling them, "We are invaders of sacred soil. We are carrying war in our front."[64]

US officials purposefully outfitted Leavenworth with a huge number of soldiers. They wanted to impress Kiowas, Comanches, and other western Indians with a display of American strength.[65] But the expedition did not go as planned. Struck by malaria, Leavenworth and his troops staggered across the plains. Dozens became ill each day. The expedition encountered Pawnees and Comanches, who showed peaceful intentions and extended care to the sick men. Leavenworth was injured and sent his second-in-command, Colonel Henry Dodge, onward. Despite the expedition's struggles, Dodge made it to a Wichita village. There, he met more Comanches and some Kiowas.[66]

Catlin took notes on Kiowas at the meeting. As with his other Indian encounters, Catlin described them using the racial and religious taxonomies that circulated in this period. Comparing them to the Comanches and Pawnees, he remarked that Kiowas were a "much finer looking race of men." He mentioned their long hair, appreciated the outline of their heads, and noted their "easy and graceful gait." These assessments fit with the categories Catlin associated with Indians uncorrupted by contact with Americans. Unlike Indians who had suffered by way of exposure to settlers, Kiowas were handsome. Rather than "crooked," they were "straight."[67]

Catlin's assessment of "uncorrupted" Indians reflected a common sentiment that contact with Americans had mostly negative consequences for Indians. His response also reflected romantic attitudes about "wild" Indians' danger, as well as allure. Catlin mused about the meeting with Kiowas and other Indians: "I cannot name a scene more interesting and entertaining than it was: where, for several days in succession, free vent was given to the feelings of men *civilized, half-civilized*, and *wild*; where the three stages of man were fearlessly asserting their rights, their happiness, and friendship for each other."[68] The artist acknowledged that Indians understood their rights and articulated notions of "happiness" or the good life. He also noted that Indians valued relationships, including potential friendship with American newcomers. While offering some praise, Catlin considered the Kiowas to be "wild," a status that implied their need to progress toward the state of "half-civilized" and eventually "civilized." In this way, Catlin and other "friends of the Indian" participated in widespread imperial discourse that characterized foreign peoples as needing rescue and foreign spaces as ripe for "improvement."[69]

Catlin's fascination, mingled with disdain, was also evident in his reflections on indigenous concepts of sacred power. As noted earlier, Catlin claimed to have observed Mandan ceremonies on his 1832 journey. He had also visited sites sacred to Dakota Indians. His behavior during these episodes prompted Indian anger. Catlin expressed his disbelief when Mandans refused to give him sacred objects.[70] Undaunted, he decided his pencil was all the "medicine" he needed to preserve Mandan culture for American viewing. Catlin also failed to heed Dakota warnings about visiting the source for sacred red pipestone. The artist emphasized that his "curiosity" simply required him to go. He later reported on the incident with details about the sacred site. He painted images of it to share with interested Americans.[71]

As Catlin later reflected on Mandan ritual life, he used tropes about indigenous religions established in imperial settings around the globe. Scholars working on the history of comparative religion have found that colonial officials in South Africa initially claimed that Native peoples had no religion, but later "identified" indigenous religions as they increasingly exerted control over Native populations.[72] Colonial officials used comparisons with Judaism and Catholicism to document their process of "discovering" religion among Native peoples in South Africa. Although a world away from the South African setting, Catlin employed similar comparisons. In order to detail the Mandan's "great religious ceremony," he borrowed language about sacrifice and secrecy, as well as an anti-clerical tone from anti-Catholic polemics of the day. Catlin also focused on portions of the ceremony he considered highly sexualized, including what he called Mandan women's "lascivious" dancing. He wrote pages about a naked villager painted as an owl spirit and sporting a wooden phallus. Catlin called him a "modern Priapus," the Greek god of fertility best known for sporting a permanent erection.[73]

A variety of religious newspapers published Catlin's descriptions of Indian ritual life. Methodist, Quaker, and Baptist newspapers included the story of Catlin's effort to visit the Dakota sacred pipestone site. The stories included breathless descriptions of the landscape's beauty, an account of the Indians' belief that they were created from the red stone, as well as the distress caused by Catlin's unwelcome visit. A Catholic paper published another of Catlin's accounts of the sacred pipestone site. He described Dakota men, women, and children who cried out and groaned as he made his way to the area. Catlin understood his offense. "[The Dakotas'] sacred rights had been trampled upon— their religion was invaded and their *Wakons* [or powerful spirits] insulted, by the ruthless feet of white men!" Catlin, however, did not take the offense too seriously. While he registered the Dakotas' horror, he also proceeded with full confidence that their taboos about footsteps on a rocky landscape were nothing he needed to honor.[74]

Catlin observed and wrote about many events during his travels, including the 1834 meeting between Dodge and the Kiowas. As noted earlier, the artist was fascinated by the coming together of "civilized" and "wild" people. While Catlin mused, the Americans and Indians initiated a variety of political exchanges. The military expedition included thirty Indian scouts, some of them Osage. Kiowas bristled at the sight of them. These enemies had brutally attacked them just the year before. Seeing the upset Kiowas, Osage scouts used the meeting to initiate a peace process. They returned one of the children taken captive during the attack. Kiowas celebrated her return. While Dodge was certainly encouraged by signs of better relations between Indian nations, his objective was to initiate treaty negotiations. After conversation and invitations, some Indian men accompanied the American expedition back to Fort Gibson for talks. A few Kiowas agreed to attend.[75]

Federal Indian officials had much to report after the "expedition to the far west" and "regions almost unknown." In correspondence with the Secretary of War, they claimed that Colonel Dodge's contact with the "wild Indians" had been productive. He had asked Kiowas and Comanches to cease their attacks on eastern Indians now living in the region. The "wild" Indians, it seemed, had agreed. But the situation remained delicate. Kiowas and Comanches sometimes camped and often hunted beyond US boundaries in Texas and New Mexico. Officials referred to them as "borderers" and even "foreign tribes." Despite this ambiguous status, officials emphasized the importance of defending the region's American traders and removed Indians from possible Kiowa and Comanche attack.[76]

When officials considered their relations to "wild" Indians they also contemplated the future of the broader American West. In a proposal to Congress, Indian office administrators recommended the creation of a permanent Indian Country to serve as a homeland for multiple Native nations at various stages in the "progression from savagery to civilization." Congress would apportion parts of the land to various tribes, within which they could live as they wished. According to this plan, government officials in St. Louis would administer the region while scattered militia posts ensured security. To be sure, the United States retained title to these lands, but would apportion them to Indians nations and guarantee it to them forever. This pact, officials argued, would be sealed by the "faith of the nation." Unlike earlier broken agreements, they claimed, this one would be "sacred."[77]

While the Indian Department confirmed the government's commitment to Native peoples' future west of the Mississippi, their plans presumed continuing cultural transformation within Indian nations.[78] Some Indians who had been forcibly removed, particularly the Cherokee, already exhibited the virtues of American dress, housing, female domestic arts, schooling, and churches. This progress would continue in the new Indian Country. The land offered great opportunities for stock raising and agriculture. But official reports also revealed the limits to Indian political and cultural autonomy. Native people could practice self-government if it was "somewhat analogous to the international laws among civilized nations." They could continue their cultural practices for now, but it would be best if "their heathenish superstitions and customs [were] wholly abandoned." According to officials, Indian Country would be the last stop on Native people's long journey toward their "ultimate participation in the advantages of civilization and free Government."[79]

With this view of the blessings and opportunities of Indian Country, federal officials de-emphasized the realities of bureaucratic monitoring and military occupation. Further, they amplified their arguments about removal's humanitarian purposes. Since the western lands offered Indians the prospect of civilized living, the process of getting them to that land seemed therefore justified. Officials ended one report to the War Department with a bold assessment: removals had proved to be "the greatest blessing that has ever been conferred upon the red men of the wilderness, by any nation since the discovery of

America." Indeed, "divine wisdom" had ordained them and used America as an "instrument" to lead Indians to a new land and to true civilization. Creating the Indian Country was part of God's providential plan.[80]

While many Protestant "friends of the Indian" still objected to the workings of Cherokee removal, they shared government officials' vision for political and religious arrangements in Indian Country. If Jackson's removal bill had made them adversaries, managing Indian affairs in the West made them allies again.[81] In time, government officials praised missionaries for bringing the "pure doctrines of [C]hristianity" to Indians who lived in the East prior to their forced removal. They considered Protestant workers crucial to moving Native people from the "cold and barren confines of savage life" to the "sunny and fertile regions of civilization and religion."[82] Like the new land beneath their feet, removed Indians would live in the light. They would soon produce good fruit.

BRINGING GOD TO INDIAN COUNTRY

But for Protestant clergy and reformers, the fertile soil of Indian Country and the greater American West was not quite enough. More was needed, as the new lands filled not only with forcibly removed Indians, but also with settlers who brought rowdiness and revivals with them. In 1835, prominent reformer and minister Lyman Beecher launched a speaking tour focused on the future of the American West. According to Beecher, the nation's destiny would be decided west of the Mississippi. The United States had the unique potential to extend "civil and religious liberty," allowing for the flowering of "universal Christianity." Those on the Mississippi's eastern side needed to work toward the West's proper development. They must lay the foundation of educational and moral institutions. Given the "vastness" of the West, Beecher urged his audience to act right away.[83]

While Beecher started his lectures with generalizations, he quickly became specific about the obstacles to political and religious liberty in the American West. The problem, he argued, was Roman Catholicism. European immigrants from Catholic countries flooded the United States. Priests claimed an improper dominion over parishioners' minds and hearts. According to Beecher, Catholic clergymen also controlled the laity's political activity, implying that Catholic immigrants voting in the United States were beholden to European clerical and political powers. Only robust Protestant institutions could withstand the surging Catholic population. In a West replete with common schools, Protestant churches, and moral societies, Beecher concluded, Catholics would realize the nature of "Protestant independence." The experience would "awaken" their "desire of equal privilege." Catholics would then appreciate ministers' proper role and the correct relationship between church and state. As a group, they would function as "another religious denomination," accommodating to the American political and religious landscape.[84]

Beecher's speeches are perhaps best known for accusations that they provoked anti-Catholic violence, including the burning of an Ursaline convent. But Beecher also mentioned Indian affairs. He worried about potential Native converts to Catholicism. According to Beecher, Bishop Fenwick of Cincinnati supported Indian schools and missions not to bring civilization to heathens, but to secure a larger Catholic population as part of a larger plan to dominate American life.[85] The race to settle the West involved shaping not only newly arriving settlers, but also Indians already living there.

Beecher was right. To his dismay, immigration from regions of Europe with large Catholic populations had picked up after 1815, just as many Americans were moving into the trans-Appalachian West. Catholic leaders in the United States, at the helm of a territory considered a mission rather than a national church, struggled to supply priests and institutional structure. Following the settlers, Vatican officials established the nation's second diocese at Bardstown, Kentucky, in 1808. They also began to organize missions and churches in the Louisiana Territory. But the United States produced nowhere near enough priests to serve the population, especially as more immigrants from Ireland and Germany arrived. Increasingly, priests from France, Belgium, Germany, and Italy served Catholics who migrated to the American West.[86]

While they focused on American settlers and recent European immigrants, some priests also established Indian missions. The desire to serve Native people, as well as the possibility of being martyred like colonial-era Jesuit Jean de Brebeuf, fueled the imaginations of many French priests who traveled to the United States. But few worked in missions with regular contact with Native people. Some Jesuits initiated a mission to the Osage in 1822. But a report published the same year described a "dilapidated Indian mission system" in American states and territories. Catholic leaders faced the difficult position of having numerous potential audiences—underserved and lapsed Catholics, heretical Protestants, enslaved people, and Indians—and far too few priests to serve them all.[87]

Catholics in Europe offered support for US Indian missions. The Vatican's Sacred Congregation for the Propagation of the Faith provided direction and resources for Catholic missions around the globe, including in North America. In 1823, Pope Pius VII offered both plenary and partial indulgences to those who raised funds for these missions. Support came specifically from French Catholics, who sent a number of missionary priests to the United States. In 1822, they founded their own institution, the *Oeuvre de la propagation de la foi*, to support evangelism. The *Oeuvre* supported one American bishop's efforts to send missionaries to Indians in the Northwest Territory and publicized the results to lay readers and potential missionary priests in France.[88]

The *Oeuvre* also supported Bishop Fenwick, whom Beecher accused of using missions to cultivate an indomitable Catholic population in the United States. Fenwick had traveled to France to request more missionary priests. He hoped to appoint some of them to Indian missions. He later brought Native children to Cincinnati to study in the seminary and convent. In 1831, he traveled to the Michigan Territory to visit

Catholic missions to Native people. While there, he met a federal Indian Department official who promised that the missionary's school was eligible for monetary support from the government's Civilization Fund.[89] The money likely drew Beecher's ire. While Protestant reformers and missionaries received thousands of dollars every year to support their schools and civilization programs for Indians, Beecher could not countenance Catholic participation in a federally funded civilizing project. Catholic immigrants from Europe needed Protestant institutions just as much as Indians did. They, too, needed lessons in American democracy and true religion. And now, federal dollars supported the enrollment of Indian children in Catholic schools. It was more than Beecher could bear.

THE GODS ALREADY THERE

As Beecher fretted over Indians choosing Catholicism over Protestantism, Kiowas had yet to encounter Americans concerned about their Christian conversion or acquisition of cultural practices associated with civilization. After meeting with Colonel Dodge and initiating peace with the Osage, Kiowas had one primary ritual concern: getting back their *Tấimé*. According to one story, the Kiowas' recently named leader, Jòhâusàn (Little Bluff), set about the task. He traveled to an Osage camp and offered several ponies for the object's return. As a gesture of friendship, the Osage returned the *Tấimé* in exchange for only one pony.[90] By the summer of 1835, Kiowas could again gather for a Sun Dance. Àunsójèqàptàu (Old Man Foot), the recently named *Tấimé* keeper, called the people together.[91]

Despite the shortness of his tenure, the new ritual leader emerged as a person of significant power. According to one of his granddaughters, Àunsójèqàptàu once confronted an oncoming cyclone. He placed the *Tấimé* around his neck to protect it from the wind, held out his arms, and spoke words to keep the storm at bay. The same relative recalled how Àunsójèqàptàu's power drew Kiowa people to him. He often led ceremonies to name and bless babies. He took medicine from the *Tấimé*, chewed it in his mouth, and placed it in babies' mouths, transferring to them the *Tấimé's* blessing and protection.[92] Under Àunsójèqàptàu's leadership, Kiowas reinvigorated their ritual work. They sought sacred power to ensure their safety in the increasingly dangerous southern plains.

A new sacred object also entered the people's life around the same time. Kiowa oral histories maintain that the young girl taken captive by the Osage was returned to her people not through an American-brokered truce, but because she implored a medicine bundle to help her. During her journey home, she received new powers from a buffalo.[93] Seeing the girl's suffering, the buffalo offered to guide her travel and provide a new "medicine" for her people. Once home, the girl transferred the power to men who became known as the buffalo doctors.[94] In time, they emerged as important healers of war-related wounds. They also wielded powerful buffalo shields believed to stop bullets.

Jòhâusàn and the warriors who followed him needed this sort of power as they raided into Texas and Mexico, which during these years were engaged in civil war.⁹⁵ On an expedition near El Paso, Kiowas found themselves trapped in a cave and surrounded by Mexican soldiers. Jòhâusàn led a daring escape.⁹⁶ Accounts of the raid's aftermath include the story of a wounded warrior left behind. The man despaired when he considered that his death would cause his relatives grief. At this vulnerable movement, a wolf appeared and cared for him. Then the man heard a *Táimé* whistle, along with a voice that said, "I pity you and will care for you." The wounded man claimed that the *Táimé* sent rain to wash his wounds and directed some traveling Comanches to find him and care for him. On the trip home, the man saw what he called a "*Táimé* stone" in the ground and reached for it. Feeling certain it had appeared to him in his earlier vision, he took it home and added it to the sacred items assembled for the Sun Dance.⁹⁷

This story captures something about the Kiowas' strength, as well as their adaptability, in the early years of Jòhâusàn and Àunsójèqàptàu's leadership. Kiowas performed successful raids deep into the south. They had strong allies in the Comanches. They welcomed captives and other outsiders into their community. They acknowledged the *Táimé*'s power and its ability to ensure protection. With the wounded man's new "*Táimé* stone," Kiowas continued to add to the array of techniques and objects designed to offer thanks and secure blessing. As one ethnohistorian has argued, embracing and initiating change allowed for survival, if not flourishing, on the southern plains in this period.⁹⁸ In politics, trade, and ritual life, Kiowas move in new directions. When Indians, French, Spaniards, and Mexicans found ways to make joint work of shared goals, such as material prosperity and physical safety, alliances in the region flourished.⁹⁹

MAKING PROMISES IN INDIAN COUNTRY

But the Americans were coming closer, and they had different goals. When Kiowas finally sat down for treaty talks in 1836, they brought with them their long-held expectations about making agreements with other nations. For them, treaties involved a "powerful mix of ceremony, negotiation, and legally-binding promises."¹⁰⁰ Kiowas considered the Americans' demands, including ending attacks on traders traveling the Santa Fe Trail, as well as on Indians forcibly removed from the East. Officials also sought an end to raiding for horses, mules, and captives in Texas. Kiowas deliberated carefully. Leaving traders alone was certainly possible, although difficult to ensure as the route traveled through the lands of multiple Indian nations. Kiowas agreed to stop their assaults on Indians crowding into the eastern side of Indian Territory, although they worried that the growing population there would result in declining game herds. They also promised to refrain from raiding in Texas, although Kiowas were baffled that US officials attempted to control their relations with independent Texas.¹⁰¹ While these demands were significant, Kiowas realized the Americans had no immediate plans to settle in the region, nor had they made attempts to reduce their landholdings. Jòhâusàn and other leading Kiowa men signed the treaty, considering it a "sacred promise."

By agreeing to end raids into Texas, Kiowa leaders jeopardized their strong position on the southern plains. Many Kiowa and Comanche men were unwilling to give up the lucrative herds to the south. Before long, Kiowas broke the agreement.[102] Americans fumed. Their efforts to establish relations with western Indians had failed. As one official wrote, the United States needed compliance from these "predatory Indians" and the treaty had not accomplished it. Federal officials countenanced the possibility that resistant Indians might need to be "subdued and even destroyed." Given the US record of dispatching Indian nations in the East, officials assumed they could do the same in the West. But government leaders were not eager for conflict. As one treaty official put it, such destruction would be "revolting to humanity," as well as "expensive."[103]

When federal representatives considered the "humanity" of possible solutions, they had self-designated "friends of the Indian" in mind. While not exclusively aligned with Protestant denominations and reforming organizations, self-described "friends of the Indian" disapproved of the government's use of force to pursue Indian policies. At the same time, they heralded the prospect of Indian "civilization." They had objected to Cherokee removal not only because they assumed it would require force, which it did, but also because the Cherokees had attained a level of civilization that satisfied them. Facing west, "friends of the Indian" encountered a different situation. They needed to acquire knowledge about a new set of Indian nations in order to preserve their self-ascribed expertise on Indian cultures. They also needed to determine what ethical expansion beyond the Mississippi looked like.

Debates about Indian civilization and Native lands paralleled arguments about slavery and the status of African Americans, as well as conversations about missions around the globe. Most "friends of the Indian," who were also typically antislavery and supporters of global missions, assumed the superiority of Anglo-American cultural practices and the exclusive truth of Christianity in its Protestant forms. In their position of self-claimed privilege, these Americans struggled to articulate a "humane" relationship with marginalized peoples, while at the same time enforcing the boundaries and hierarchies that inscribed difference. By emphasizing their sympathy for Indians and the benefits of Anglo-American habits, "friends of the Indian" also managed to characterize land dispossession and removal as a gift to Indians. To be sure, they could not countenance removals carried out at the point of a gun. But in naming Jacksonian removal to be the primary moral problem, "friends of the Indian" avoided the possibility that other dispossessions harmed Native people. And once removal was over, they partnered once again with government officials to provide "civilizing" programs. As one missionary boasted to Baptist readers, now was the time for "friends of the Indian" to initiate their "grand scheme of deliverance."[104]

When Jefferson purchased the Louisiana Territory, he assumed the new lands would establish a barrier between Native peoples and American settlers. Jefferson not only envisioned a place for Indians in the West, but also for men and women freed by slavery's abolition. The president was one of many Americans who saw the positive potential of physical barriers. Andrew Jackson also argued for a barrier. With his forced removals, Jackson established the Mississippi as the dividing line between Indians and Americans. But by 1837, Americans' trust in the barrier's feasibility started to fade. Inter-Indian conflicts complicated matters on the western side of the river, and there was no reason to believe that American settlers would stay on the eastern side. The West might have contained the "Great American Desert," but it also had grassy plains and rugged mountains. It had fertile valleys and powerful rivers. Its mineral wealth was as yet unknown. American settlers would not leave these resources untouched. "Friends of the Indian" hoped that the Christian God might temper the settlers' behavior and bring salvation to Indians living there.

Kiowas registered the Americans' reach into the region. The new nation's policies and future actions were as yet unknown to them. For now, they maintained their alliances and practices for seeking sacred power and protection. They stayed near to their gods. At least for the moment, they still lived freely in Indian Country.

2

1838 to 1867

EVENTS IN 1848 confirmed the impracticality of Andrew Jackson's plan to make the Mississippi River a physical barrier between settlers and Indians. In January of that year, prospectors discovered gold in California, prompting a rush of migrants from around the globe. Americans east of the Mississippi crossed through Indian Country on their way to the gold fields. In February, American and Mexican officials signed the Treaty of Guadalupe Hidalgo, in which Mexicans ceded not only their claims to Texas, but also lands stretching from New Mexico to California.[1] Americans secured not only regions east and north of Kiowas, but also lands to the west and south. The nation's Indian policy of physical separation, enacted with forced removal after 1830, needed to be reconfigured in an era of expansion and increased migration into the West.[2] Self-described "friends of the Indian," many of them representing Protestant denominations, played a prominent role in debating and shaping the new policy of separation that emerged in 1850s and 1860s. With Jackson's removal bill and its accompanying violence as their foil, "friends of the Indian" called for containing and civilizing Native people on reservations. They cast these policies as nonviolent, benevolent, and the necessary prerequisites for Indian freedom.

The failure of the Mississippi to serve as a barrier did not immediately impact Kiowas negatively. Indeed, in the years after signing their 1837 treaty with the Americans, Kiowas experienced a period of relative strength. They prospered from raids for horses and mules deep into Mexico. They made peace with the Cheyenne and Arapahos, which allowed them greater freedom of movement and access to trade opportunities. But they also faced difficulties. Diseases circulated through the plains. Smallpox, measles, and cholera devastated Kiowas and other Indian nations. And though Kiowas had made peace with some of their neighbors, Indian Territory was crowded with Native people pressured by American westward movement. To adjust to changing circumstances, Kiowas continued to revise their rituals for engaging sacred power. They tried old and new ways to seek protection from enemies and disease. They shared their power-seeking practices with old and new allies. They employed these activities to empower their defense against Americans who, after 1860, pushed hard into their country.

DANGER IN THE OPEN LANDS

In June 1838, Kiowas camped with their Comanche allies. It would soon be time for the Sun Dance. But before the ceremony could begin, Cheyenne and Arapaho warriors attacked them by surprise, as depicted in Séttàun's calendar entry (Figure 2.1). As the attack unfolded, Cheyenne fighters ambushed and killed a group of Kiowa men hunting beyond the encampment. Women out digging for edible roots were also taken by surprise and killed. As the Cheyenne and Arapahos rode into the main Kiowa camp, a devastating, hours-long battle commenced. Even though nearby Comanches came to their aid, Kiowas could not expel their enemies. The battle, which cost many lives on all sides, ended in a stalemate. With more than forty men killed, as well as some women and children, Kiowas entered a time of mourning. They held no Sun Dance that summer. The attack also affected Kiowa interactions with special objects, namely warriors' shields imbued with protective power. Cûiqáuje (Wolf Lying Down), who had received his shield design in a dream and gifted it to four other men, died in the Cheyenne attack. Three of the men who shared the design discarded theirs because it had failed to protect its bearer.[3]

FIGURE 2.1. Séttàun's calendar entry denoting an 1838 attack by the Cheyenne and Arapaho.
Credit: Mooney, *Calendar History of the Kiowas*, page 273

The 1838 attack and stalemate serve as just one example of the inter-Indian disputes that resulted as Indian Territory became increasingly crowded. In 1840, Kiowa leader Jòhâusàn (Little Bluff) responded to this dangerous situation by signaling his willingness to make peace with the Cheyenne and Arapahos. Later that summer, Kiowas camped with their Comanche allies on a site in which their potential allies could join them. The parties negotiated what has come to be called "the Great Peace of 1840." With it, these Native nations ensured greater physical safety and expanded their trading networks. As with their earlier alliance with the Comanches, Kiowas solidified their new relationship in several ways, including intermarriage.⁴ In coming years, Kiowas also invited their new allies to join their Sun Dance.

Because Kiowas no longer worried about Cheyenne and Arapaho attacks from the north, more men could dedicate themselves to raiding south into Texas and Mexico. While expeditions brought prosperity, they were also dangerous. Kiowa calendars include references to numerous men who died. The risks involved with raiding impacted ritual power seeking. In 1842, for instance, the Kiowas held an extended Sun Dance. Some scholars speculate that two men must have received instruction in their dreams to sponsor dances. That is one possibility. But Kiowas also sponsored Sun Dances for other reasons. Men in dangerous situations sometimes made vows to the *Táimé* with the hope of securing protection. In a time when so many men perished on raids, it would be no surprise for multiple Kiowa warriors to vow a Sun Dance to secure protection on these expeditions. The revised "double Sun Dance" provided Kiowas an extended opportunity to come together as a people and invoke the blessing of sacred powers.⁵

Extensive raiding also afforded more chances for protective powers to fail. In the winter of 1844–1845, a Kiowa warrior named Àthàuhâuiqì (Warbonnet Man) joined a 200-man raid deep into the Mexican state of Tamaulipas. He carried with him a powerful shield and wore a shirt with corresponding symbols. A drawing made by a descendant shows the crescent moon and morning stars (Figure 2.2). Despite these items, the design of which had been given in dreams, Àthàuhâuiqì was killed. His power had failed to protect him.⁶

Even more often, death came from disease. The Kiowas had already suffered from smallpox on several occasions. In late 1839, the disease struck the Kiowas once again. Because smallpox spreads through contact, many Kiowas simply scattered and fled to the plains. Many tried to avoid large groups. Despite the disease, Kiowas risked gathering for a Sun Dance the next summer, which calendars commemorate with figures bearing smallpox scars (Figure 2.3). They continued to assemble for the ritual, even as new diseases such as measles struck them in 1846.⁷

As with raiding, disease presented the prospect that protective powers could fail. Besides shields and war paraphernalia, Kiowas also signaled their connection to supernatural powers through symbols painted on tipi covers. As noted in the previous chapter, some men attested to receiving powerful tipi designs in dreams. Sétbáujè (Bear Bringing It) was given his tipi design some time before a cholera outbreak. The decorated cover included images of a bear and several bear paws against a bold red background. (Plate 5).

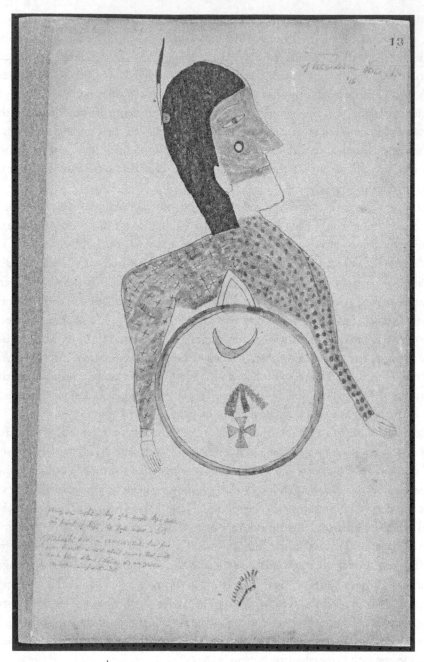

FIGURE 2.2. Drawing of Àthàuhâuiqì's (Warbonnet Man) shield, featuring a crescent moon, morning star, and war paint.

Credit: Manuscript 2538, National Anthropological Archives, Smithsonian Institution

FIGURE 2.3. Séttàun's calendar entry featuring a man with smallpox during an 1839–1840 outbreak. Credit: Mooney, *Calendar History of the Kiowas*, page 274

The design signaled the promise of protective power he had received. But cholera was stronger, and Sétbáujè was one of hundreds of the outbreak's Kiowa victims.[8]

In the 1840s, then, Kiowas struggled against things close at hand. They battled Indian enemies. They suffered from disease. They accepted the risks of raiding as a way to prosper within the borderlands economy. The Americans still figured only minimally in their calculations. To be sure, soldiers, settlers, and traders crossed Kiowa lands via the Santa Fe Trail. But they hardly lingered. The Americans' transient presence in western Indian Territory belied the nation's growing administrative and military apparatus for dealing with both removed Indians from the East and the "wild" Indians on the plains. As Americans moved deeper into Indian-controlled lands west of the Mississippi, the nation engaged in yet another round of debating the ethics of expansion. These debates grew particularly heated as the United States fought Mexico and then annexed territory that not only bordered Kiowa lands, but also raised the question of slavery's expansion.

EXPANSION INTO INDIAN COUNTRY

Americans began to pay attention to Mexican *Tejas* in the lead-up to Anglo-Texans' 1835 claim of independence. While complex reasons lay behind the settlers' dispute with

Mexico, the region's Indians played a central role in their arguments for revolution. In what one historian has called the "Texas creation myth," Anglo settlers claimed that prior to their arrival in the 1820s, Texas had been a desolate land of "wandering savages." Mexican officials had been unable to neutralize the threat posed by Comanches, Kiowas, and other Native peoples. But Anglo-Texans arrived and subdued the land. They "made the desert smile." Because Mexicans had squandered their opportunity to settle this "neglected Eden," Texans were justified in claiming it. And if Mexicans did not agree, Texans declared they would take it by force.[9]

The "Texas creation myth" was one of many ways that Americans encountered Kiowas and Comanches, the "wild tribes" at the center of an emerging discourse about Indians of the southern plains. Government officials reinforced these claims in their reporting on efforts to maintain treaty terms with both Indian nations. They repeatedly claimed that Kiowas and Comanches violated terms by hunting on lands designated for Native people forcibly moved to eastern Indian Territory, attacking traders and other Indian nations, and holding both Mexican and American captives. The latter practice proved especially inflammatory. In 1844, a federal official reported that Kiowas and Comanches were rumored to hold between one hundred and two hundred white female captives, which was patently untrue. A government representative further west shared his dismay about the borderlands captive trade. He called for the ransom of America women, who were in the most "terrible position into which civilized women [can be] placed."[10]

Government officials pledged to deal with these threats and treaty violations by placing more troops in Indian Territory. US military presence in the region was admittedly thin. Administrators regularly referred to the need for a "sufficient military force on the frontier." But the nation had far too few troops or funds to sustain a presence across such an immense region. Local Indian agents protested the lack of dedicated resources. Securing the Indians' cooperation was difficult, one complained, as they had "no idea of [America's] physical power."[11]

Because neither forced cooperation nor allusions to military strength were options, officials emphasized treaty making, gift giving, and the benefits of civilization already realized by some Indian nations in the region. Administrators often repeated their hopes that the Cherokees' example of settled living and agricultural labor would inspire Native people further west. While the diminishing bison herds encouraged administrators that such a change was inevitable, they also focused on education's crucial role in the process. Every year, officials praised ongoing education projects in eastern Indian Territory, especially manual labor schools teaching Native people about agricultural and industrial skills.[12]

In this way, administrators based their plans for dealing with "wild tribes" such as the Kiowas on their experiences with Indians who had once lived east of the Mississippi. Officials assumed that initial encounters involving gifts and treaties would be followed with policies to promote settled living, agriculture, education, evangelization, and a reduction in hunting. Their approach reflects how little they knew about Kiowas and other nomadic Native people. They had not adjusted their expectations to the vast territory in which Plains Indians lived. Indeed, federal agents sometimes could not find them and failed to meet with them for years at a time. Kiowa movement across international borders further complicated the situation. As one official complained, he simply could not keep an eye on them. "They have neither belonged hitherto to the one government [Mexico] nor the other [the U.S.]."[13]

Americans wanted information about these "wild Indians" moving between Mexico, independent Texas, and the United States. How had they evaded Mexican control? Had the Texans successfully subdued them? If so, how? Would Kiowas and Comanches willingly relinquish their nomadic living and hunting life? Would they give up their captives, many of whom had been integrated into family networks? How could they be brought into the American fold now that the nation's interest encompassed not only Indian Territory, but also Texas and the greater Southwest? Americans wanted to know, and self-styled "friends of the Indian" were happy to oblige. Newspapers reprinted almost any information they could provide.[14] This growing stream of reportage included work by the artist and explorer George Catlin.

Catlin published his first book on the western Indians in 1842. It included drawings of Native people whom the artist had observed during his travels. It also featured his notes about the journey. The book was well received. As one reviewer noted, Americans greeted it as a "desideratum" offering valuable information on Indian life where none had been previously available. Curious readers, the reviewer insisted, wanted stories about these "fierce, warlike, and barbaric tribes." Catlin delivered. In his extensive sections on the Mandans, Catlin described scenes that startled his readers: underdeveloped agriculture, polygamy, women engaged in domestic drudgery, and children learning to wield weapons and dance with scalps. Reviewers agreed with Catlin's assessment. Western Indians had much progress to make before they could be considered "Christian and civilized."[15]

Catlin specifically addressed the religious difference of the "wild tribes." His book included a chapter-long discussion of a four-day Mandan ritual he claimed to have witnessed.[16] Catlin described "medicine men" acting with "Satanic Majesty." He told of entering the "medicine house" with the reverence of a churchgoer, only to find a "temple turned into a slaughter-house." According to Catlin, Mandans fasted, mutilated their bodies, and suspended themselves in painful positions to appease good and evil spirits. The artist found the spectacle horrifying, although he watched long enough to inspire several drawings and paintings. Concluding his remarks on the ritual, Catlin acknowledged that the event was "abominable and ignorant." But he cautioned his readers to pity the Indians. The practice was founded, he assured them, in "superstitions and mysteries" of unknown origin.[17]

Catlin's concern about false authority, misdirected ritual, and improper use of the body reflected popular discourse about non-Protestant religious forms. According to this logic, Mandans and other Native people engaged in one of the world's many false religious systems. Catlin and his readers interpreted the Mandan ceremony in comparative terms that reached back into ancient history and stretched outward around the globe. As noted in the previous chapter, Catlin compared Mandan rituals to ancient Greek religion. Readers of his book also considered resemblances. One reviewer claimed that the Dakotas' sacred pipestone quarry, which Catlin described in detail, served as "another Delphic temple of Diana." Relishing the book's detailed description of Kiowas, Comanches, and Pawnees, of whom little was known, the reviewer referred to them as the "Arabs of the Southwest."[18]

Protestant "friends of the Indian" employed similar comparisons. Baptist missionary Isaac McCoy claimed that western Indians' nomadism kept them from developing religious systems, which distinguished them somewhat from the "Hindoos," who in their settled communities had developed mythologies of great "absurdity." Missionaries did not always look beyond the Christian communion to deride Native religious practices. In his discussions of Kenekuk, who led a revitalization movement among the Kickapoo, McCoy described his use of material objects and penitential discipline as an "absurdity" similar to Catholicism. An ABCFM missionary also relied on long-circulated anti-Catholic rhetoric to describe Native peoples' tendency to "stand on the ground of their own works for salvation."[19]

Despite the dramatic religious difference they asserted, Protestant "friends of the Indian" also drew on their experiences among some Native peoples to insist that religious transformation was indeed possible. As the ABCFM missionary continued in his mission update, he had preached to hundreds of Indian people. A few candidates had requested baptism. "Scarcely a pagan can be found, at the present time, who will deny that the gospel is 'good.' "[20] According to these "friends of the Indian," Native people could be civilized. The nation's ethical expansion demanded material support for this project.

"Friends of the Indian" and their defense of civilizing and Christianizing efforts took on greater importance as some Americans voiced their skepticism. Increasingly, citizens saw African Americans, Mexicans, and Indians as incapable of participation in free institutions. As one writer argued in a Freethought newspaper, Indian missions were nothing but an "expensive hoax." The writer's doubts reflected not only a public dubious about the possibility of Indian civilization, but also qualms about the increasing size of the government's Indian affairs budget.[21]

Quakers, in turn, were among the "friends of the Indian" who defended the cause against such attacks. Friends focused on unregulated settler migration that resulted in frontier violence, traders acting as bad influences on Native communities, and squatters who impinged on Indian lands. They held up their own relations with Indians as the ideal. Their pacifism, they claimed, kept them from perpetrating violence against Indians. Benevolence prompted their work to promote civilization through schools and farms. Quakers relished the possibility that their efforts would someday result in Indians' true freedom: a day when their "improved condition" included education, agriculture, and Christian worship. Baptist missionaries to Native people joined in this defense. In a widely reprinted pamphlet, one called on American Christians to acknowledge their responsibility to Indians and join the "grand scheme of deliverance" that benevolent citizens had devised to save them.[22]

But Protestant "friends of the Indian" were not the only ones promoting civilizing and evangelizing projects among Native peoples. After the 1833 Second Baltimore Council, American Catholics partnered with their European co-religionists to establish more missions for settlers moving west, as well as for Indian nations. American Catholics welcomed priests from several European missionary orders, especially the newly restored Society of Jesus.[23] In the 1830s, Jesuits established missions among Kickapoo and Potawatomie Indians just west of the Mississippi River and with Flatheads in the Pacific Northwest. The Belgian Jesuit, Pierre De Smet, played an influential role in scouting and establishing missions in the plains, northern Rockies, and Pacific Northwest. If Protestants cultivated their special role in civilizing and evangelizing Native people, American Catholics framed their work somewhat differently. They hoped to increase Catholicism around the globe and battle anti-Catholicism in the United States.[24]

Jesuits working in the American West relied on long traditions of Catholic mission work in the Americas. De Smet and others drew inspiration from the *reductions* of the seventeenth century, especially the Paraguay missions. After arriving in 1841 among Salish Indians in the Pacific Northwest, De Smet and his fellow Jesuits erected a village with cross, chapel, cabins, and Native dwellings modeled on the Paraguayan example. They supplemented the older design with signs of a new spirituality flourishing in nineteenth-century global Catholicism: devotion to the Virgin Mary. As seen in a Jesuit's drawing of the St. Mary's Mission, the Virgin Mary looks down upon the tipi encampment (Figure 2.4).[25]

Jesuits also used pedagogical strategies from their long history of missions in the Americas. Based in the Pacific Northwest, François Norbert Blanchet crafted catechetical tools based on Native forms of recording history and organizing knowledge. In 1839, he developed the Sahale stick, meaning "stick from above," with hashmarks and images depicting biblical history. Blanchet used the visual form to organize his telling of salvation history from earth's creation to the life of Jesus to the church in the present age. Sensing the tool's success, Blanchet transferred the components to cloth and paper. Handmade copies, eventually called "Catholic ladders," circulated to other missions (Figure 2.5).[26]

The ladders soon came to symbolize the budding competition between Catholics and Protestants working in Indian missions. Catholics added to their ladders, depicting Protestants deviating from the true church. This view, of course, replicated animosities from the 1500s. But it also reflected what one historian has called the nineteenth-century move toward an "ultramontane" Catholicism. Missionaries in the United States understood their Indian work as a way to build up the global Catholic communion, with its ever-growing emphasis on papal authority and experiential piety. De Smet and Blanchet also hoped to save Indians from aligning themselves with Protestants heretics. One Methodist missionary to Indians in Oregon Territory took umbrage at Blanchet's

FIGURE 2.4. Detail from Jesuit missionary Nicolas Point's *Notre Dame de la Prière* (Our Lady of Prayer) featuring the Virgin Mary appearing to a Native person attending mass.
Credit: The Archive of the Jesuits of Canada

creation and created a rival "Protestant ladder" (Figure 2.6). It featured the pope descending to hell. Another Protestant missionary threatened to throw blood on Blanchet's ladder as a symbol of martyrs from the Reformation era. They worried that Catholic ladders and the missionaries who used them would guide Indians out of one religious system at odds with enlightenment and freedom and into another.[27]

Catholics and Protestants approached Indian missions with centuries-old enmity, including their exclusive claims to absolute truth, as well as their newly realized competition with each other in the American West. For all their animosity, however, there were similarities in their Indian work. Both Catholic missionaries and Protestant "friends of the Indian" considered Native people to be part of the larger human family, hindered in their cultural progress not by innate inability or racial difference, but by lack of proximity to civilizing influences. Both were committed to Indians' potential for civilization, which included settled living, agriculture, productive labor, and conversion to Christianity. Both identified the dangers posed by westward-moving settlers when they came in proximity to Indian communities. In response, Catholics and Protestants sought ways to create new kinds of barriers between Indians and Americans.

Further, both sides were willing to partner with the US government, using federal funds to establish civilizing missions. Protestant "friends of the Indian" had accepted monies from the Civilization Fund for decades. They used the support at their mission

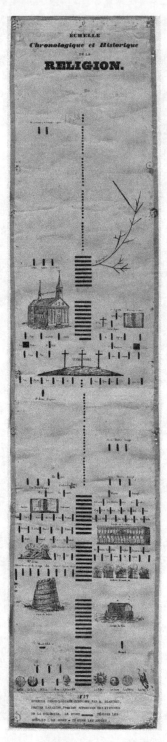

FIGURE 2.5. Catholic missionary François Blanchet's *Echelle Chronologique et Historique de la Religion* (Chronological and Historical Ladder of Religion), which he designed as a catechetical tool for Native Americans. It begins with the earth's creation and proceeds through the history of the Israelites, the life and death of Jesus, the early church, and the conflicts resulting in the Protestant Reformation. The ladder ends with Catholic missions to Native people.

Credit: Department of Special Collections and University Archives, Marquette University Libraries

FIGURE 2.6. Henry and Eliza Spaulding's catechetical ladder, which begins with Adam and Eve and proceeds through other events in the Hebrew Bible and New Testament. The track on the left depicts the Catholic Church, ending with the martyrdom of Protestant leaders and the pope falling into hellfire. The smaller track on the right includes events from biblical history, including the apostle Paul and proceeds directly to Martin Luther and into the contemporary age.

Credit: Oregon Historical Society, Image OrHi 87847

stations to found schools, supply teachers and farmers, and provide agricultural equipment. Catholics had some participation in the early years, but hoped to increase this activity. For Catholic missionaries writing to officials in Europe, the arrangement could be a difficult sell. European church leaders were nervous about the United States. The country featured religious disestablishment and sometimes violent anti-Catholicism. But missionaries such as De Smet tried to calm their fears.[28] The Jesuit reported on his pleasant conversations with federal Indian agents and emphasized the US government's power to assist in the "worthy" work of Indian missions.[29] Federal officials were only too happy to rely on religious workers, both Protestant and Catholic, to administer and staff the "civilizing" programs.

Government leaders extolled Christian workers involved in civilizing Indians. As the commissioner of Indian Affairs noted in 1847, the "labor of the Christian denominations" made the "most efficient way" to civilize Indians.[30] This approach seemed to win the day in 1849, when Congress transferred Indian affairs out of the War Department and into the newly created Interior Department. Civilian officials, rather than military representatives, would direct the course of the nation's Indian policy and would work with religious organizations to implement it.[31]

But this administrative change hardly silenced those who doubted Indians' capacity for civilization and advocated, instead, for a military solution to the nation's "Indian problem." These counterarguments were amplified as the Texas creation myth—about Texan settlers' ability to neutralize threats caused by the "wild tribes"—circulated in the lead-up to the US-Mexico War. As Kiowas and Comanches continued raiding deep into Mexico, some US officials considered an aggressive approach that they associated with the Texas Rangers.[32] One western Indian agent reported that Comanches and Kiowas were "formidable tribes of savages" and knew nothing but war and plunder. He called on federal officials to send forces. He argued that a show of strength would subdue the "wild tribes," saving the bloodshed and money to be spent in a prolonged conflict with Indians. Ultimately, the agent argued, an overwhelming show of force would be "the most philanthropic."[33]

Events in Oregon also contributed to arguments that Indian submission could be gained only by force. In late 1847, Cayuse Indians attacked a Protestant missionary compound, killing fourteen and taking dozens hostage. Political and religious leaders responded to the brutal assault by calling for quick American expansion into and settlement of the region. Although the conflict between Cayuse Indians and Protestant missionaries grew out of long-standing cultural misunderstandings and occurred when Indians believed that missionaries deliberately spread measles, supporters of expansion capitalized on the tragedy to promote rapid expansion, aided by the use of force. In short order, appeals to "manifest destiny," a phrase coined during the conflict with Mexico and repeated in the struggle over Oregon, assumed a willingness to use force against Native people in the way.[34]

Officials in Washington concerned about the southern plains concurred. As the Secretary of War wrote, there was no way to teach Comanches and Kiowas "proper respect" for the United States but by military force sent to "chastise them."[35] Developing relations with the Republic of Texas added yet another reason to pacify the region quickly. After the republic's 1845 annexation, Americans had a greater interest in stopping Indian raiding in Texas. With the Treaty of Guadalupe Hidalgo a few years later, the nation accepted an even greater responsibility. Not only did federal officials gain massive new tracts of land, stretching from New Mexico to California, to administer, but they also made a promise to Mexico. In the treaty, the United States agreed to stop "wild" Indians living north of the Rio Grande from raiding south of the new international border. Northern Mexicans, who had been devastated by these raids for more than a decade, were relieved. The Americans, who figured their success in removing most Native nations from the East, as well as Texans' ability to deal with the "roving tribes," assumed they would have no trouble using military force to bring Indians to heel.[36]

HOLDING ON TO THE OPEN LANDS

Kiowas knew little of the Americans' new treaty obligations to Mexico. Nor did they know of officials' desire to send troops to subdue them and missionaries to civilize them. Soon after Americans and Mexicans met to sign their 1848 treaty, Kiowas gathered for their Sun Dance. It was a time of relative strength for the people. Raiding had made their horse herds large. Peace with other Indian nations made the southern plains safer than any time in recent memory. At this moment of relative prosperity, Àunsójèqàptàu (Old Man Foot), the Táimé keeper, called Kiowas together for the days-long ritual.

Along with the usual buffalo hunt, medicine lodge construction, and dancing before the Táimé, the 1848 Sun Dance featured the initiation of prominent men into the Qóichégàu (Dog Society), the Kiowas' elite warrior society.[37] Some adorned themselves with red or black sashes, in addition to personal body paint, weapons, and shields. Qóichégàu (Dog Society) members vowed particular acts of courage when faced with enemies. They pledged to die in battle rather than surrender. Kiowas came together for the Sun Dance ceremonials and celebrated the strength and power of their most esteemed warriors.[38]

But the security that Kiowas felt in the summer of 1848 faded quickly.[39] A period of drought had recently begun. Dry conditions weakened the already dwindling bison herds. By winter, southern plains Indians were hungry. The next year, conditions became staggeringly worse when cholera swept the plains. The disease devastated Kiowas. Descendants tell of the 1849 Sun Dance in which a man rode through the encampment, calling out that a disaster was about to befall them. Having hardly finished his statement, he doubled over with terrible cramps, fell off his horse, and died. Calendar entries from that summer show figures bent over in pain. The disease struck with ferocious speed. Descendants claim that it reduced their nation's numbers by half.[40]

Just as the dangers of raiding prompted ritual revisions, so too did changing environmental conditions and the devastations of disease. In the winter of 1848, Kiowa men endowed with "antelope medicine" addressed the people's hunger.[41] The process involved building a tipi and singing songs. The men led the people out onto the plains, singing and praying before hunters set out to procure food in a time of scarcity. While Kiowas reacted to conditions with infrequent practices such as the antelope drive, they also brought their concerns to their regular Sun Dance ceremonials. Descendants report that the cholera epidemic provoked new offerings to the *Táimé*. The people had long made gifts of fabric, feathers, and other natural items. In 1849, however, a man seeking protection from the disease tied a horse to the medicine lodge. He offered his animal to the *Táimé*. His family did not become ill.[42] But many others succumbed to the disease, decimating the population.

Kiowas and their allies replenished their ranks by taking captives on raids into Mexico and Texas. Rather than sell them through the borderlands trade network, they were more likely to keep them. Kiowas used captives to perform much needed labor, such as minding herds and preparing hides. They incorporated some of them into family life. Kiowas also revised their Sun Dance practice in order to integrate them. A variety of sources attest to adopted captives cutting down the cottonwood tree used as the central pole for the medicine lodge.[43] The task was considered a dangerous one. One informant claimed that Kiowas did not want to imperil their own women, so they instead chose a captive for the job. But the same speaker also noted that the task was a great honor and that the captive woman designated for the duty was required to dress beautifully. It is unclear if Kiowas were engaged in extensive captive taking and trading when they received the Sun Dance from the Crow further north. Coming to the plains and becoming a part of the borderlands economy prompted them to adapt their ritual practice in ways that both capitalized on the liminal character of captives and the integrative function of Sun Dance ceremonies.

Kiowa ritual activity, including its innovations, allowed the people a way to respond to hunger, disease, and the difficulties associated with losing loved ones and repopulating their community. But sometimes events and conditions overwhelmed their most basic efforts at ritual regularity. Kiowa calendar entries for the summer of 1852 attest to this struggle and its many possible causes. Drawings allude to a terrible defeat that prevented Kiowas from gathering for the Sun Dance. The entries diverge, however, when identifying the enemy. Elders interviewed about Séttàun's (Little Bear) calendar reported that Kiowas lost a battle against the Pawnee.[44] When the same anthropologist asked another calendar artist about that summer, he was told that Kiowas had lost a battle to Mexicans.[45] Two other calendars feature entries with details related to the American army, including an American flag and distinctive soldier caps.[46] To be sure, comparing calendars often reveals differences, and the form itself obliged keepers to record memorable events, rather than designate a single occurrence of greatest importance. Kiowas might have been involved in multiple conflicts that summer. In 1852, they still considered Pawnees to be enemies, continued their raids into Mexico, and might have encountered an American army captain leading an expedition through the region. Despite the multiple possibilities behind the diverse entries, the calendars agree on one thing: violent conflict sometimes contributed to Kiowas' inability to gather for their most important ritual.

As Kiowas faced these challenges, they also resisted American efforts to meet for new treaty talks. When officials invited them to a massive council at Fort Laramie in what is now Wyoming, Kiowas and some of their allies refused. Even so, in 1851 government officials met there for negotiations with several northern plains Indian nations, including the Sioux, Cheyenne, and Arapahos.[47] Observers estimated that more than 10,000 people attended the talks. The Americans voiced a desire to increase their presence on the plains. They presented a treaty that established boundaries for Indian nations' land claims, mandated the construction of more forts and roads, and required safe passage for Americans traveling through the region. In return, Americans promised to keep settlers out of Indian lands and pledged annuities for fifty years.

The treaty talks showed not only what American officials wanted, but also their willingness to partner with religious representatives to achieve those ends. Government leaders attributed at least some of the council's success to the presence of Jesuit Pierre De Smet. The priest had long-established relations with many of the Indian nations involved in the treaty. Federal representatives invited him with the hope that he would be a pacifying presence during what could be potentially tense negotiations. De Smet reported that the talks were a major success. In letters to his European superiors, he recounted peaceful interactions between Indian nations often at war with one another. He claimed that federal officials and military representatives, who sometimes disagreed on policy, held opinions in common. The Indians' promise to stop attacking overland emigrants meant the inevitable American expansion into the Pacific Northwest could proceed without delay. "It will be a commencement of a new era for the Indians—an era of peace," the Jesuit proclaimed.[48]

According to De Smet, the treaty also provided opportunities for Catholics to establish missions among Native peoples with reduced lands. To be sure, the treaty set apart huge tracts of land to be occupied by Native people. But as one ethnohistorian has observed, the treaty also established the government's ability to determine the extent of Indian landholding. Further, it reserved smaller tracts of land to support agricultural practice among communities of "half-breeds." De Smet saw these "new colonies" as a boon to evangelization. He called on Europeans to send more priests before those hostile to the faith, namely Protestants, could establish a foothold among them. According to De Smet, the treaty's initiation of a "new era of peace" offered an opportunity to send an influx of priests to Indian nations living on bounded lands delineated by the US government.[49]

OCCUPYING THE INDIAN COUNTRY

The Fort Laramie treaty talks included an unprecedented number of Plains Indians, but not all of the nations that prompted government concern. Kiowas and Comanches had refused to attend. They continued to live without firm territorial boundaries and periodically attacked traders, settlers, and northern Mexicans. As noted earlier, some government officials prescribed military force as the only way to gain their compliance. But these promoters also anticipated the ethical questions that such an approach would raise.

On the other side of the debate, officials who objected to a military solution had lost their patience with Kiowa and Comanches' slow pace of change. If the two sides disputed the military's role in achieving policy goals, they could agree on one thing. They increasingly argued that reduced Indian landholdings would prompt the cultural changes that Americans desired. Reservations would establish the physical boundaries necessary to keep whites and Indians from harming one another. As one official put it, once Indians are "colonized," they "learn to appreciate how the white man lives." Confining them to smaller lands, along with a decrease in game herds, he argued, will "compel" them to farm. He also assured his readers that the plan to colonize Indians on reservations was "agreeable to every Christian and philanthropist."[50]

The official was right. Protestant "friends of the Indian" embraced the idea. The Quakers' Indian committee echoed the official's assessment and proposed solution. "The annexation of Texas, and the acquisition of California and New Mexico, have given increased importance to our Indian relations," a Friend noted in a popular periodical. The situation on the southern plains proved especially problematic. The Indians there are a "source of constant terror," roving in "small predatory bands" that destroyed crops and kidnapped settlers. Friends drew on their interactions with the once mighty Iroquois to champion their "milder mode of restraining."[51] The Seneca nation, they argued, had once roamed over huge tracts of land and engaged in warfare with colonial powers and other Indian nations. But all that had changed after the Society's arrival on the Seneca's recently restricted landholdings. In a short time, Senecas had farms and schools. They had access to bibles. Settlers, who might bring bad influences with them, were restricted from the reservation. In just fifty years, Senecas had transitioned from wandering heathenism into the fullness of civilized living.[52]

ABCFM leadership also boasted about the successful transformation of Indian nations contained on reduced lands. Commissioner Selah Treat insisted that the Choctaws had been degraded heathens prior to the ABCFM's arrival. After years of missionary effort in both Mississippi and Indian Territory, the fruits of their labor were now evident. Treat argued that many Choctaws not only attended worship, but also met the high bar demanded for church membership. The Choctaws had also waged a successful campaign against intemperance. They farmed. They sent their children to school. They had a constitutionally based tribal government. "There is hope for the red man," argued Treat. That hope, he insisted, had been realized on the Choctaws' greatly reduced lands.[53]

The growing clamor for reservations is evidenced in the differences between the government's terms for the 1851 Fort Laramie treaty and what they presented to Kiowas and their allies at Fort Atkinson in 1853. Both treaties required Native people to remain at peace among themselves and stop attacking overland emigrants and settlers.[54] Both also established the Americans' right to build forts and roads in lands occupied by Indian nations. Finally, both promised annuities as compensation. But government negotiators at Fort Atkinson added a further stipulation: the Americans claimed the right to establish reservations for Kiowas in the future.[55]

Jòhâusàn (Little Bluff) and other Kiowa leaders accepted the Americans' call for peace between Native nations and a stop on attacks on overland emigrants who respected Indian land claims. But they objected to the Americans' demand that they stop raiding into Texas and Mexico. From the Kiowas' perspective, Mexico and Texas were not part of the United States. The Americans had no authority over actions there. Government officials grumbled that Kiowas seemed not to understand that the United States now included Texas and that treaties with Mexico obliged Americans to take action against raiding.

This was not the only demand that Jòhâusàn rebuffed. During the talks, he also rejected American demands to build forts and railroad lines across the southern plains. He claimed that military posts depleted timber reserves, drove off game herds, and brought bad white people into the area. Military posts led to an atmosphere of hostility. Most important, Jòhâusàn rebuffed the Americans' call for future reservations.[56] Despite his objections, the American negotiator stuck to his position, emphasizing that none of the proposed changes was immediately forthcoming. He also highlighted the offer of annuities, which would make Kiowa life easier in a time of hunger.

Despite his concern about some of the terms, Jòhâusàn signed the agreement.[57] As one historian has observed, Kiowas seem to have come away from the process convinced that they had at least established peace and secured their material needs with the promise of substantial annuities. These needs were real given the recent cholera epidemic and ongoing drought. The concessions to which they agreed seemed far off in the future. But while Kiowas' consent to the treaty involved significant compromise, Americans wanted still more. When the commissioners took the treaty to Congress for ratification, senators demanded that the terms be amended so that annuity money would be used for farming implements and supplies, rather than given as cash for Native people to use at their discretion. The frustrated commissioner returned to Indian Territory with hopes of getting Kiowa signatures for the amended treaty. Jòhâusàn joked that the government would need to send not only farmers and agricultural tools, but also different land if they wanted productive farms in western Indian Territory. The joke, it seems, was about more than the land's limited agricultural potential. Kiowas had yet to see a substantial number of Americans. Where were these farmers who would make their lands into an agricultural paradise? Where were the soldiers who would stop their raiding? For the time being, hardly any Americans ventured into Kiowa lands. The Americans, it seemed, were still the least of the Kiowas' problems.[58]

Kiowa challenges close at hand continued through the 1850s. Small groups of American soldiers sometimes came after Kiowas who raided in Texas and Mexico. Men from other Indian nations sometimes stole horses and crucial supplies. Prominent warriors, including Thẹ̀nébáudài (Bird Appearing), died in violent encounters with other Native people. Calendar entries show that Kiowas held no Sun Dance the summer Thẹ̀nébáudài was killed.[59]

As with this esteemed warrior's death, environmental pressures and epidemic disease also led to adjustments in Sun Dance practice. During the scorching summer of 1855, for instance, Kiowas simply did not hold one.[60] Informants reported that the summer was so hot that the people stopped often to rest themselves and their weakened horses. Such conditions would have made travel to the Sun Dance encampment difficult. A smallpox outbreak in 1861–1862 also affected ceremonial practice. As with the earlier cholera epidemic, a Kiowa man tied his horse to the medicine lodge with hope that his sacrifice might stave off the disease. Several calendar entries show Kiowas with smallpox scarring.[61]

If Kiowas had so far been able to avoid settling on a reservation, many Indian nations in the West had not. Ritual life in these communities changed as a result. These adjustments and innovations fell within a pattern of activity similar to Indian nations east of the Mississippi.[62] In the Pacific Northwest, a Wanapum man named Smohalla traveled to a beloved mountain, fasted, and sought a vision. He said he received a message from the "land of the dead." In what one scholar has identified as a movement to "rectify" a world gone wrong, Smohalla directed the Wanapum to return to the old ways that had once sustained them.[63] He told them to avoid materials made available by trading with colonizers. He attracted followers, many of whom became central to the Wanapum resistance to a reservation. Smohalla later gave them songs and dances to ritualize their participation in the movement.[64]

Even if federal officials had not yet pushed for a reservation for Kiowas, the people felt increasing American pressure. Robert Miller, the new federal agent in the region, expressed particular frustration with his charges. His reports to Washington frequently complained about treaty violations. In 1857, he grumbled that Kiowas continued to attack travelers on the Santa Fe Trail. He asked federal officials to punish the Indians by withholding their promised annuities. He threatened Jòhâusàn with the possibility. To Miller's chagrin, Kiowas said they doubted that the Americans could make good on the threat. When Miller met Kiowas to distribute annuities the next year, he again warned them that continued raiding would result in suspended annuities and the arrival of US troops.[65]

Even Indian agents more sympathetic to the Kiowas expressed frustration with them. William Bent, an American with strong ties to the Cheyenne nation due to his trading post and marriage to a Cheyenne woman, also worked for a short time as a federal Indian agent.[66] Writing to officials, Bent noted that food shortages and white encroachment gave Indians "the exasperating sense of decay and impending extinction with which they are surrounded." Bent warned that "a desperate war of starvation and extinction is therefore imminent and inevitable" unless the government acted to ameliorate the Indians' situation. But Bent's solution to the Kiowas' distress reflected increasingly popular views about colonization. He argued that Plains Indians required settlement on smaller, restricted lands that would require them to farm. While he noted that these should be decent lands with good resources, the message was the same: reservations on reduced landholdings. He shared an approach endorsed by many Protestant "friends of the Indian."[67]

Quakers were among the loudest voices calling for reservations. Throughout the 1850s, they argued that smaller, bounded lands provided not only the permanent base necessary for Indians' civilization, but also the solution to Americans' insatiable greed for land and resources. Contact between Indians and Americans, they argued, usually led to violence. Reservations would allow separation and would provide Indians with adequate space in which they could transform their cultures and rebuild their lives. The need was pressing, the writers claimed. Society periodicals in the 1850s frequently featured articles on the issue, many of which framed the question in the dire language of Indian extinction. Pointing again to their experience with the New York Senecas, Quakers argued that it was possible for Indians who were once "nearly as savage in their manners as any of those scattered over the wilds of North America" to make the transition to settlement and peaceful farming.[68]

According to Quakers and other Protestant "friends of the Indian," abandoning Native people to the whims of settlers or the military would be a national disgrace exceeded only by chattel slavery. As with earlier overlaps between opponents of Cherokee removal and advocates of slavery's abolition, some Protestant "friends of the Indian" again linked the degraded political status of Native people and African Americans.[69] Even that diminished status was increasingly threatened. In 1850, Congress passed the Fugitive Slave Act, mandating that Northerners return any enslaved person who escaped captivity to his or her enslavers. The year 1857 brought another blow. The Supreme Court decided *Dred Scott v. Sandford*, excluding black people from constitutional rights. Both actions jeopardized even the most basic freedoms of African Americans. Escape to the North provided no guarantees.[70] Courts were no recourse for protesting the infringement of black rights.

Antislavery supporters, with Quaker leaders among them, objected to these developments.[71] They understood them both as the entrenchment of Southern political power, as well as the inevitable spread of slavery into the West. In light of these developments, antislavery advocates saw little possibility for a political resolution ending chattel slavery and ensuring even the most basic freedoms for black Americans. Specifically, these activists worried that the continuation of chattel slavery allowed African Americans little chance to access the benefits of civilization and Christianity.

While the potential westward spread of slavery prompted dismay for these reformers, they also worried about another population living in the heart of the West. In 1849, Mormons had petitioned to enter the Union as the state of Deseret. They were granted, instead, status as the Utah Territory. A few years later, Mormon leaders announced "the Principle," claiming the practice of plural marriage as given to them in divine revelation. Protestant reformers expressed outrage and labeled polygamy a "relic of barbarism." As with their concerns about slavery and uncivilized Native people, these activists looked to the government to address the problem. Federal officials responded in 1862 by passing the Morrill Anti-Bigamy Act, outlawing bigamy in federal territories.[72]

During the 1850s, Protestant "friends of the Indian" identified several groups in need of federal protection: enslaved people, Mormon wives, and Indians. Concerning the latter, they argued that treaties had failed to provide sufficient civilizing programs and offered no guarantees against future removals. They accused the government of failing to protect Native people from settler squatting, theft, and violence.[73] Federal officials, they claimed, provided no workable plan for Indians transitioning to civilized living. Critically, proposed military approaches could wipe out Indian nations entirely. In this situation, Native people were hardly free to enjoy the blessings of civilization and Christianization.

In the run-up to South Carolina's secession, Quakers and other "friends of the Indian" continued to press their points about chattel slavery, Mormons, Indian policy, and a proper ethic of expansion.[74] Members of the Society of Friends' Committee on Indian Affairs warned that "a fearful reckoning" over Indian lands was imminent. Calling on Friends to advocate for Indian justice, writers offered up the prospect of divine retribution for the nation's sins against Indians. The Society must desire justice, one wrote, "in order to avert the reaction of suffering to ourselves and our posterity." On the eve of the Civil War, the writer argued that the Christian God's judgment "must certainly follow upon the continued violation of the laws of justice and humanity."[75]

VIOLENCE IN THE OPEN LAND

Plains Indians knew that Americans were on the brink of a bloody conflict over chattel slavery. For a little while, they were able to use this knowledge to their benefit. At an 1858 meeting, the government's agent to the Kiowas threatened that the president would send troops to stop Indian raiding. The agent's warning was hardly the first Jòhâusàn (Little Bluff) had received. In response, the Kiowa leader insisted that raiding was the only thing keeping Kiowas from going hungry. Then he pointed to a valley full of Kiowa and Comanche lodges. The "white chief" did not have enough troops to contend with so many Indian fighters, he claimed. "I have looked for [the troops] a long time, but they have not come." Pushing further, Jòhâusàn declared, the president is "a coward; his heart is a woman's." For the moment, at least, he was right about military resources. Washington was not willing to send the number of troops necessary to subdue Plains Indians. With conflict brewing between North and South, no federal authorities tried to force them onto a bounded piece of land, at least not yet. Kiowas, it seemed, had a little more time.[76]

But debates about expansion and Native people never went away entirely, even as Union and Confederate troops fought the most deadly conflict in US history. As historians have observed, the Civil War was also about the future of the American West.[77] It would decide the future of chattel slavery there, as well as in the South. Further, some Native people fought in the war, including many men from forcibly removed Indian nations who enslaved people of African descent. Some Choctaws, among others, joined the Confederates with the hope of maintaining this unequal system of economic exploitation. Confederate officials sought support throughout Indian Territory. Kiowas and Comanches, while not formally fighting for either side, accepted Confederate arms and agreed to turn their raiding practices north toward Union-aligned Kansas and away from Confederate Texas.[78]

The Civil War's western theater also affected Native people across the Mississippi. As a result of early Union victories, campaigns in Louisiana, Mississippi, and western Tennessee were practically over by 1862. Many military units involved in these battles had been formed from men living in states and territories west of the Mississippi. They returned home, and their commanders refocused their efforts on suppressing Indian resistance.[79] As a result, the plains became increasingly militarized. Concerned to stay in the Union's graces and avoid military attack, Kiowas and other southern plains Indians embarked on an 1863 delegation to Washington, D.C. They met President Lincoln, who counseled them to emulate the civilizational practices of white people, make peace with the government, and keep their treaty obligations. He urged them to give up the warring tendencies so common to Indian peoples. Jòhâusàn and his fellow leaders saw the irony in Lincoln's recommendation. They knew the president was embroiled in a war that had ground on beyond anyone's expectation. The Kiowa leaders returned home with the sense that the Americans were busy killing each other. Perhaps they would soon leave Indian Country to the Indians.[80]

But they did not. Throughout the West, state and territorial militias went after Native people. In 1863, troops from California entered Utah and attacked Shoshoni and Bannock people camped along the Bear River. They killed over 300 people and took more than 100 women and children as prisoners. That same year, Colonel Christopher "Kit" Carson led troops in New Mexico on a campaign against Mescalero Apaches, eventually confining them to a militarized reservation called Bosque Redondo. In 1864, Carson turned east toward Kiowa lands.

Unaware of Carson's approach, Kiowas and their allies camped near Adobe Walls in the Texas Panhandle. More than 300 American troops and five dozen Indian scouts moved toward them for a surprise attack. Carson's men struck an encampment of 176 tipis first, depicted in the calendar entry shown in Figure 2.7. Taken by surprise, Kiowa men tried to fight back, but eventually abandoned the village. Reinforcements finally arrived from encampments downstream, and the allied Indians initiated a counterattack. Carson could not overwhelm the combined forces and decided to withdraw, but not before burning the Kiowa village along with a large share of the winter food supplies it held.[81] As Sherman burned through Georgia, Carson moved across the West.

As they engaged this new enemy, Kiowas took objects imbued with protective power into battle. Oral traditions about Carson's attack focus not so much on the Americans' methods or devastating results, but rather on Kiowa men's ingenuity and the sacred power that energized their struggle. Stories tell of Sétthâidé (White Bear), who used a stolen bugle to mimic cavalry calls and confuse American soldiers. Others tell of Sétèmqià (Bear That Runs Over Them), who put on his feathered warbonnet, with a magpie attached to its base, before racing into the battle. Fighting at close range, American bullets tore the feathers off the headdress, but the magpie's body stayed in place. Onlookers said that as Sétèmqià continued to fight "the wings of that magpie [were] flapping like it was alive or something." Kiowas affirmed not only their warriors' willingness to defend their free life on the land, but the sacred power that enlivened their struggle.[82]

FIGURE 2.7. Calendar entry by an unknown artist depicting Kit Carson's 1864 attack on Kiowas, in which the American military leader relied on scouts from other Indian nations.
Credit: Kiowa Tribal Museum, photograph by Jennifer Graber

While Carson's troops and their Indian allies did not totally overwhelm the Kiowa, the Battle of Adobe Walls had significant costs.[83] Estimates of casualties were low. But the fire set by Carson's men destroyed all the tipis and winter provisions stored in the first Kiowa village. This included several hundred dressed buffalo skins ready for use within Kiowa circles or for trade in the borderlands market. The attack, Kiowas' first major battle with the Americans, resulted in significant difficulties for people already struggling against disease and reduced game herds.[84]

Carson's attack did not receive extensive media coverage, but another military assault on Indians, just a few days later, did. On November 29, 1864, a Colorado militia unit led by Colonel John Chivington attacked a camp of Southern Cheyenne and Arapahos who were understood by other government officials to be at peace with the United States. Chivington's men killed about 200 people in the encampment, including women, children, and elderly people.[85] While Chivington and his supporters recounted the engagement as a fierce battle, others quickly provided alternative accounts. Some eyewitnesses described it as a massacre of innocents. Eastern newspapers decried Chivington. Congressmen called for an investigation. The committee on the conduct in war, established to adjudicate Civil War military operations, was employed to investigate events at Sand Creek.

The attack, which came to be known as the Sand Creek massacre, shocked Americans, at least those living east of the Mississippi. Even if some citizens doubted civilizing missions and groused at the federal Indian office's costs, Chivington's assault failed to meet their standards of "ethical expansion."[86] Federal Indian agents also expressed outrage. The Kiowas' new agent wrote to federal officials that Chivington's attack on "friendly Indians" "destroyed the last vestige of confidence between the red and white man."[87] He worried that Sand Creek would not suppress Indian resistance, but would lead instead to conflagration on the plains.

Protestant "friends of the Indian" shared this view and pointed to Chivington's attack as evidence for the superiority of a non-military approach to Indian relations. The controversy surrounding the massacre became an important episode in the ongoing debate about the military's role in settling the West and assimilating Indians. Concerned about Sand Creek's aftermath, federal officials renewed efforts to make peace with Plains Indians. Officials dispatched a commission to go west, make new treaties with Indians, and define the extent of Indian lands. They also hoped to convince Indian nations to move onto reservations.

A few months after Adobe Walls and Sand Creek, Kiowas came together for their 1865 Sun Dance.[88] Àunsójèqàptàu (Old Man Foot) still served as the *Táimé* keeper. He was aging, but hardly flagging. "He was an old, old man, and just by looking at him you knew that every year he had more wisdom," one Kiowa informant recalled. She recounted Àunsójèqàptàu's kindness to children and willingness to share food with others. She also spoke of his power. Standing outside his tipi, Àunsójèqàptàu "looked wise and kind and good; but he looked strong, too, as if all the power that was inside him had been gathered together in his heart and showed through his face." He lifted his arms, painted yellow and green, and prayed before a large crowd. "More and more power seemed to come into his face."[89]

The woman who recalled Àunsójèqàptàu in such vivid detail also focused on two objects that Àunsójèqàptàu held. Neither was the central *Táimé* figure. Rather, the informant remembered Àunsójèqàptàu tying two small rawhide forms to the buffalo hide hanging from the medicine lodge's central pole. The first, she said, was a buffalo figure that "stood for all the earth spirits." The second was "like a man" and was painted red.[90] Accounts from Sun Dances in the middle decades of the nineteenth century attest to a variety of objects that accompanied the powerful *Táimé*. Some stories refer to a set of male and female figures that became integral to Sun Dance practice.[91] As noted in the Introduction, Kiowas welcomed new objects into their ceremonial practice, creating a *Táimé* complex. Their ritual revisions continued as the people faced ongoing difficulty.

Kiowas remembered the 1865 Sun Dance as a joyous occasion. But the same year also featured incredible stresses as Americans ended their internal conflict over slavery and turned to colonizing Plains Indians and suppressing any resistance. That fall, General John Sanborn represented the government in meetings with Kiowas and their allies. He took a stern approach. He argued that Kiowas hardly deserved the president's mercy or a chance to make another treaty. From the federal government's perspective, Kiowas had violated the 1853 treaty by raiding in Mexico and attacking Americans on the Santa Fe Tail. Sanborn claimed that Kiowas' "interest" required them to cede all their land south of the Canadian River. In return, Americans would pay Kiowas and "give" them a reservation. Sanborn also addressed Kiowas' standing in relation to the government. The United States was large and powerful, the general claimed. A small tribe's resistance was as a "mosquito troubles a horse."[92]

Jòhâusàn offered a different perspective. He argued that leaders in Washington, not the Kiowas, had failed to keep their sacred promises.[93] To substantiate his claim, the elderly chief inquired about annuities the Americans had failed to deliver. Jòhâusàn also identified Americans, not Kiowas, as Indian Country's true aggressor. Attacks at Adobe Walls and Sand Creek lent credence to his claim. Finally, Jòhâusàn addressed Sanborn's land proposal. The Kiowa leader was clear. He did not want to cede his land. He had no interest in the "freedom" to pursue civilization on bounded territory. "I want a big land for my people to roam over," he said. I "don't want to stay long in one place, but want to move about from place to place." Jòhâusàn promised to end attacks on Americans traveling on the Santa Fe Trail, but paired it with a demand that the Americans leave other parts of Kiowa land undisturbed. "The rest of the country I want let alone," Jòhâusàn said. "I want to tell you again and again to throw away the soldiers, and I will get all badness out of my heart, so that we can all travel kindly together."[94]

Sanborn continued his effort to secure Kiowa land concessions and was ultimately successful. As one historian has observed about treaty making in this period, there was no "sharp distinction" between voluntary and involuntary agreement to terms.[95] It is possible that Kiowas signed the treaty because it offered good annuities and promised American soldiers' exit. It is unclear, however, how much they understood about the government's claim to Kiowa lands. We also do not know if Kiowas ever learned that the Senate failed to ratify the treaty. Without ratification, promised annuities never arrived and Kiowas were left to wonder why Washington failed to keep its promises.

MAKING PROMISES IN INDIAN COUNTRY

Just a few months after the treaty talks, Jòhâusàn died. Kiowas lost their longest serving leader. Men holding different views about how to deal with the Americans emerged as possible replacements. Sétthạidé (White Bear) was among them. He articulated a deep frustration with the Americans, especially their calls for land concessions and failure to deliver annuities. He urged resistance. Some Kiowas agreed. American officials maintained their stern approach. By the time their irritated agent investigated the extent of Kiowa treaty violations, he lost the sympathy he had expressed a few years earlier. He threatened Kiowas in no uncertain terms. Stop raiding, he declared, or be wiped from the face of the earth. An official with the agent expanded on the warning. He told Kiowas, you will get the "muzzle of a gun if you do not conduct yourselves properly."[96]

In the face of American demands, O-tank (White Bird), an older Kiowa man endowed with power, stood up to speak. He questioned the Americans' claim to such overwhelming authority. Addressing the question of who had final authority over Kiowa lands, O-tank said it was not the Great Father in Washington. It was the "Great Father, the Sun." Unlike any American president, the Sun gave Kiowas the land and animals. According to his bewildered observers, O-tank then stopped speaking and laid two circles of paper on the ground. He "went through a form of prayer." Addressing the crowd again, O-tank spoke in Kiowa, which was translated into Comanche and then into English. He said he knew Americans were coming. They would kill the buffalo. The Kiowa might not escape. But, he insisted, the buffalo and the Kiowa belonged to their Great Father, the Sun. They relied on the Sun to sustain them.[97]

Kiowas had revised several rituals during their decades on the southern plains. They revered new objects, rejected others that failed, made new kinds of offering, and integrated outsiders into their ritual performance. But O-tank's words detail the epistemology behind the people's ritual work and revision. The Sun was their father. The sun had *dwdw*, or sacred power. The sun provided their sustenance. Americans might conquer the Kiowa, but they had no power over the Sun.

O-tank's speech was recorded as part of negotiations prior to the 1867 Treaty of Medicine Lodge. When Americans and Kiowas finally signed it, many eastern newspapers celebrated. Their pages featured lengthy accounts of Séttháidé's speech before the American commissioners. Protestant "friends of the Indian" praised the Kiowa leader's eloquence.[98] Reporters heralded Séttháidé as the "Webster of the Plains." One reporter observed, "Never have I seen and known true eloquence before this day." He then compared Séttháidé's speech to the "voice of nature and of God."[99]

But what did Séttháidé actually say? Of course, he spoke in Kiowa, so we know only what a transcriber recorded of a translator's words. But that translation and transcription had an impact. According to newspaper accounts of the speech, Séttháidé said Kiowas intended to make and keep the peace. Committed to his end of the treaty, Séttháidé waited only for the Americans to keep or break their word, a critique that "friends of the Indian" must have relished. He also looked back on an earlier and easier time: "In the far distant past there was no suspicion among us. The world seemed large enough for both the red and the white man." Séttháidé's speech, then, seemed in line with many Protestant "friends of the Indian." The government had erred in sending troops instead of assistance. Séttháidé continued, "The old days of peace and friendship [are] to come again." For readers eager to settle the Indian question without violence, newspaper words confirmed that Kiowas would enjoy safety and freedom on reduced lands conducive to their civilization.[100]

Newspaper accounts, however, failed to include some of Séttháidé's statements as they were recorded in the proceeding's minutes. The Kiowa leader made his wishes clear. He wanted peace, but he also wanted his people to keep all their lands south of the Arkansas River. He wanted to hunt and be left alone. He did not desire schools or churches. He wanted the freedom to live among his people as he wished. Because Kiowas were divided on the matter of signing treaties and abiding by American demands, Sétth̜áidé requested two agents to work separately with the divided segments of the Kiowa community. To the commissioners' demand that Kiowas remove to a reservation, Sétthạidé was straightforward. "I don't want to settle there. I love to roam over the wide prairie, and when I do it, I feel free and happy, but when we settle down we grow pale and die."[101]

American commissioners were not deterred. They pushed for reservations to address "the Indian problem" and settlers' needs. The 1862 Homestead Act demanded federal action to open up as much land possible for white settlement. The American negotiators worked with this need in mind. The resulting treaty stated that Kiowas and Americans were finally at peace. It established a reservation of 3.5 million acres in the Indian Territory's southwest corner (Figure 2.8). By treaty, Kiowas were now contained. They could go off-reservation to hunt south of the Arkansas River only with the agent's permission. In return for these concessions, the treaty promised annuities for thirty years, as well as funding for schools, churches, and a physician on the reservation.[102]

Quaker periodicals' coverage of the treaty negotiations cast the reservation's creation as an act of benevolence. The columnist, who also wrote a biography of William Penn, praised the Americans commissioners for supporting Indian civilization, as opposed to a military approached that would lead to "slaughtering [Indians]." Rescued from a nomadic life that relied on hunting, Native people were now free to learn agriculture and animal husbandry, reading and writing, American forms of government and individual

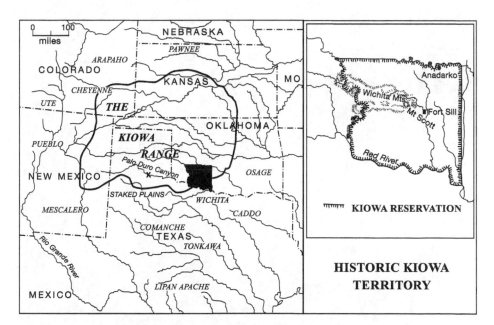

FIGURE 2.8. Kiowa lands before and after the 1867 Treaty of Medicine Lodge, which created the Kiowa, Comanche, and Apache (KCA) Reservation.

Credit: Department of Anthropology, Smithsonian Institution

property holding. The writer also referenced the Society's labors among Indians since colonial times and their willingness to do it again. The reservation, he insisted, was America's gift to Native people.[103]

Kiowas, however, did not see it that way. Unable to secure their demands during negotiations, Sétthái̩dé and his fellow leaders signed a treaty that ended their free occupation of Indian Country. On the last day of the proceedings, Sétthái̩dé made what would become his famous speech about making and keeping the peace. But he had made other speeches in the previous days. "I don't want any of these medicine homes [churches] built in this country. I want the papooses brought up just exactly as I am."[104] Again, Sétthái̩dé could not make the Americans concede. By 1867, the Society of Friends and other Protestant "friends of the Indian" mounted a successful campaign to direct Indians' civilization on newly formed reservations. Within a few years, Kiowas not only had churches and schools among them, but Quakers ran their reservation.

PART TWO

Closed Lands

3

1868 to 1872

THOMAS BATTEY, A Quaker schoolteacher, wondered why Kiowas would not grow corn. It had been more than two full growing seasons since the reservation's establishment. Still, the people would not farm. They lived in tipis rather than wooden houses. They wore blankets instead of American clothes. They were dubious about school and showed no interest in Christian worship. Battey had heard that Kiowas' "superstitious" beliefs convinced them that eating corn would make them sick and die. In fact, one Kiowa man announced he would not grow it because the "Great Spirit" had never told him to do so. Kiowas' false religion, Battey concluded, lay behind their resistance to reservation life, civilization, and assimilation into the American populace. His assessment reflected widespread ideas about Native cultures as primitive, irrational, and on the brink of extinction.[1]

Quakers such as Battey worked among southern plains Indians not as missionaries, but as employees of the federal government. The 1867 establishment of the Kiowa, Comanche, and Apache (KCA) Reservation was quickly followed by Ulysses S. Grant's election and the transformation of the nation's Indian policies. Protestant "friends of the Indian" played a central role in formulating and implementing what came to be known as the "Peace Policy," which put representatives from Christian denominations in charge of more than seventy reservations across the American West.[2] According to Grant's policy, religious workers had authority within reservation boundaries, while the military stayed strictly outside them. They encouraged "civilizing missions" through new forms of land use, foodways, family organization, dress, and religious practice. Protestant representatives also served as formal advisors to the federal Indian office.

"Friends of the Indian" in this period contrasted the Peace Policy with those who advocated military campaigns to subdue Native nations. Quakers, especially, played an important role in this debate that pitted the Interior Department's civilizing policy against the War Department's more aggressive tactics. By asserting a stark difference between these approaches, Christian workers viewed themselves as the Indians' "friends" despite engaging in a variety of coercive practices, such as restricting food rations, cutting hair, forcing forms of dress, silencing Indian languages, and cooperating with military efforts to monitor and arrest Indian people both on reservations and off. They also constructed a notion of "friendly" Indians who participated in their civilizing efforts, most notably by living on bounded pieces of land. Consequently, they also identified "hostile" Indians, including many Kiowas who refused to grow corn, settle down, or go to school, based on their lingering "superstition."

After their reservation's establishment, Kiowas faced increasing pressure to live within bounded lands and transition toward Anglo-American cultural practices. Throughout the Peace Policy's early years, Kiowas often resisted American demands. They hunted and raided, lived nomadically, maintained their forms of political organization, and continued their ritual practices. But the reservation's pressures prompted revisions. New ritual leaders emerged with ideas about resisting American efforts to control their land. In following these leaders, Kiowas found themselves labeled as "hostile" and placed in even more restrictive conditions.

While the post–Civil War era is most often discussed as the period of Reconstruction, one historian suggests thinking about it as an "Era of Citizenship."[3] Political leaders, cultural elites, and marginalized populations battled over the future of African Americans' rights and status. They also debated the potential citizenship of populations in the West, including Native Americans, Chinese immigrants, and Mormon homesteaders.[4] In all of these contexts, Americans deliberated the nature of citizenship, including the racial and religious qualities associated with it. They also considered the ways that force and coercion could be used in the work of defending rights, as well as in motivating more civilized living.

Debates about Indian civilization and citizenship paralleled broader discussions about other marginalized populations. As with considerations of Reconstruction and Chinese exclusion, questions about race and its meanings mattered greatly. Like disputes about Mormons and Chinese workers, concerns about "foreign" religion also came to the fore. But more than any other group struggling for rights in this period, Native people faced American objections to their use of land. As historians have noted, the period "tested the reach and authority of the national government over its own territory."[5] In order to take control while simultaneously obscuring the violence of this takeover, federal officials and "friends of the Indian" promoted visions of proper land use that rendered dispossession as a gift to Indian people.

THE RESERVATION AS BLESSING

The 1867 Treaty of Medicine Lodge designated a reservation of three million acres for Kiowas, Comanches, and Apaches. It provided for an administrative agent in charge of distributing rations of food and clothing. The agent hired staff, including teachers, farmhands, and a doctor. The treaty also promised cash annuities in exchange for land, as well as monetary support for schools and churches. For Americans seeking a more peaceful approach to the "Indian problem," recent treaties seemed to be successful.[6] Indians across the northern and southern plains moved to designated reservations, out of the way of American emigration and settlement. The treaties also anticipated the future. They authorized the eventual construction of railroads, if not roads and forts, throughout the region. Americans hoped the process would lead to Native people's settlement and ownership of individual land plots.[7]

Supporters of a more "peaceful" approach argued that using treaties and gifts not only reflected a spirit of sympathy and charity, but also saved money. Maintaining a standing army to suppress Native resistance across the West would cripple the federal budget and provoke avoidable conflicts. Indeed, critics of a military-driven policy toward Indians offered eye-popping estimates. In 1868, the commissioner for Indian Affairs used financial records related to the earlier suppression of Seminole, Sioux, and Cheyenne Indians to estimate the cost of subduing the nation's 300,000 remaining "wild" Indians. It would take 25,000 years and cost $300 billion.[8] In light of the absurd costs, officials recommended civilian leadership, focused on establishing peaceful relations with Native peoples.[9]

Protestant "friends of the Indian" praised the treaties and the growing support for a "peaceful" Indian policy. They saw a heartening convergence between their plans for Indian assimilation and programs designed to assist the formerly enslaved. These Protestant activists also started a number of new organizations to promote their views. In 1867, Quakers sent a memorial to Congress declaring their "double sorrow" for Indians suffering under bad policies, as well as for federal officials who "fail to afford [Indians] better protection." The next year, they founded a committee dedicated to Indian affairs. Members visited the capital to speak with federal officials and published in Quaker periodicals to promote sympathy toward Indians. Well-known abolitionist Lydia Maria Child also employed the language of sympathy to engage the public. In 1868, she published a popular pamphlet, "An Appeal for the Indians." In it, she criticized military approaches and claimed that a program of gradual civilization could bring Native people into the national family. Child's writings, along with other voices drawing attention to Indian affairs, prompted wealthy industrialists and Protestant reformers in New York to found the US Indian Commission. Through it, prominent ministers such as Henry Ward Beecher called for the "protection and elevation" of Indian people.[10]

The election of Ulysses S. Grant in November 1868 offered "friends of the Indian" an opportunity to advance their agenda. Contemporary readers might find this development surprising given Grant's reputation for political conservatism and lack of sympathy for some ethnic and religious groups.[11] But Grant had served in the American West after the Civil War and knew well the extent of violent conflict between Indian nations and American soldiers. While in the West, Grant befriended James Henry Carleton, a general who orchestrated efforts to civilize captive Navahos at Bosque Redondo. Carleton convinced Grant that a new effort at civilizing work was not only required, but also ripe for success.[12]

"Friends of the Indian" got to work even before Grant's March 1869 inauguration. Quakers met with him in January and asked him to support civilizing programs. They encouraged him to commit to a "humane" policy relying less on military force.[13] In the first month of his term, Grant called for a new Indian policy. He also solicited the Quakers for names of men among them willing to serve as agents on a few western reservations. Other interested reformers followed suit. William Welsh, an Episcopal reformer from Philadelphia, met with Grant and his Interior Secretary to advocate for a policy shift.[14]

Their efforts paid off in spring 1869 when Congress authorized $2million to support programs designed to make peace with Indian nations. They also established a civilian-led Board of Indian Commissioners (BIC) to administer the funds in concert with the Interior Department.[15] By June, Grant appointed not only Welsh, but also a number of prominent Protestant industrialists and reformers, to the board. Along with business interests in steel, banking, railroads, mining, and shipping, these men had extensive denominational and social reform credentials. Members represented the Episcopalians, Presbyterians, Methodists, Baptists, and Quakers.[16] A few had experience in the evangelical revivals of the 1850s and had worked with evangelist Dwight L. Moody. They participated in and supported a variety of missionary and reforming efforts, including global missions, the US Christian Commission, the Sunday School movement, Freedman's Aid Society, Freedman's Bureau, US Sanitary Commission, American Bible Society, public schools, and the abolition of slavery. They took up their new work with a reformer's zeal for "improving" marginal populations and a businessman's interest in opening the West.

Around the same time, the Quaker Indian committee provided Grant with names of men to serve as reservation agents. In May 1869, the president began assigning reservations to Quakers. Grant intended to start small with his experiment in civilian leadership. Even so, his administrators emphasized what the shift to Quaker participation symbolized. The Secretary of the Interior, for instance, wrote that the government appointed Friends because "their selection would of itself be understood by the country to indicate the policy adopted, namely, the sincere cultivation of peaceful relations with the tribes."[17] To be sure, some citizens criticized not only the new "peaceful" approach, but also the reliance on an often-misunderstood religious minority group to do it. But the war-weary and budget-conscious postwar population mostly welcomed the new policy with Quakers as its symbolic heart.[18] The pace of the policy change accelerated in the spring of 1870 when Congress passed a law forbidding military officers from serving as Indian agents.[19] With this change, the small experiment on a few reservations grew to encompass scores across the West. Needing more agents, officials in the Grant administration looked to Protestant "friends of the Indian."

What would come to be known alternately as the Grant Policy, the Quaker Policy, and the Peace Policy was born. With it, American officials and "friends of the Indian"

claimed that violence in the American West was caused not primarily by Indian savagery, but rather by American misdeeds against Native people. They argued that
Indians, for their own protection and good, needed permanent reservations where they
could avoid contact with frontier settlers and concentrate on progressing toward civilization. Under the tutelage of agents and staff from religious denominations, Indians
would be ushered into a life of settled agriculture, education, Christian practice, and
eventually individual landholding. They would someday assimilate into the wider
American populace.[20]

Religious groups eagerly responded to these opportunities. The struggle over allocating
assignments, however, revealed deep divisions within American Christianity. Given their
long-standing presence among numerous Indian nations, Roman Catholics disputed the
small number of reservations they were assigned.[21] They also resented their exclusion from
a place on the BIC. Catholics' experience of the Peace Policy sparked new levels of public
activism. They claimed their place on the American religious scene and their position
as "friends of the Indian." Protestants, also, squabbled over the Peace Policy's workings.
Some resented the Quakers' symbolic importance and overrepresentation in reservation
assignments. Others argued about the inclusion of those whom many Protestants found
suspicious, including not only Catholics, but also Mormons. The Peace Policy, while
signaling Protestants' extensive political influence and power, also revealed the fissures
within a community fretting about American religious diversity.

LANDS NOT YET CLOSED

While the 1867 Medicine Lodge treaty established numerous constraints on Kiowa
freedom, the people did not feel them immediately. On the one hand, it is not clear
if Indian leaders fully realized the extent of the treaty's restrictions. On the other, it
allowed for Kiowas to be outside reservation boundaries, with permission, for the purpose of hunting. For several years after the treaty's ratification, some Kiowas hunted and
camped outside the reservation and traveled to the agency headquarters only to receive
biweekly rations. The reservation had yet to feature schools or churches for the purpose
of promoting assimilation. In many respects, Kiowas could maintain their patterns of
living, including hunting, raiding, nomadic living, and ritual practices.

Kiowa calendars attest to this continuity. Several entries for the winter of 1867–1868
refer to the Medicine Lodge treaty with images of men talking alongside American goods,
such as hats, cloth, buckets, and pitchers (Figure 3.1).[22] But others allude to initiation rites
for men joining the Qóichégàu (Dog Society), Kiowas' elite warrior society.[23] As noted
in the previous chapter, Qóichégàu men evidenced their bravery in battle. They wore
red body paint to signal their status. One calendar entry indicates both events. In these
reservoirs of cultural memory, calendar keepers noted the treaty's significance, while at
the same time recognizing the people's ongoing effort to flourish in a mobile southern
plains economy.

FIGURE 3.1. Háugú's (Silver Horn) calendar entries for (a) the summer of 1867 and (b) the winter of 1867–1868, featuring (on the left) men's initiation into the Qóichégàu (Dog Society), the Kiowas' elite warrior society, and (on the right) negotiations and gift-giving at talks prior to the Treaty of Medicine Lodge. The Qóichégàu are referred to in many sources as the Koitsenko.

Credit: National Anthropological Archives, Smithsonian Institution, manuscript 2531

Maintaining a strong cohort of fighters was still necessary. In July 1868, a Kiowa man who lost a close relative in battle invited others to join him on a raid against the Utes. Sétjáuáuidè (Many Bears) joined him and sought to acquire protective power by asking the *Tàimé* keeper if he could take two related sacred objects on the journey. Kiowas kept a central *Tàimé* given to them long ago by the Crows. They later added other figures, creating what might be called a *Tàimé* complex. While the keeper could not allow the main *Tàimé* to leave camp, he gave two smaller figures to Sétjáuáuidè, who shared one of them with another fighter, Páugùhéjè (Hornless Bison Bull). Possessing these objects offered the promise of great protective power. Sétjáuáuidè also painted crescent moons and a sun on his chest and forehead. He tied the sacred objects around his neck and joined the raid.[24]

Carrying them also entailed significant responsibility, especially observing taboos associated with the objects. From participation in Sun Dances in which *Tàimé* figures were central, Sétjáuáuidè knew to avoid skunks, mirrors, and bears. Kiowa accounts of the raiding party, however, claimed that he failed to observe these protocols. During their pursuit of the Utes, a skunk crossed the warriors' path. Some Kiowas wanted to turn around, but Sétjáuáuidè refused. While camping one evening, Kiowas discovered that a Comanche man in the raiding party had a small mirror among his belongings. Again, some Kiowas counseled the raid's cancellation. Sétjáuáuidè pressed on. Finally, a black bear appeared before the riders, stood on its hind legs, and "held up its forepaws to warn them." At this point, even Sétjáuáuidè worried. He left the group, painted himself white, and asked the *Táimé* to ensure their safety. Confident once more, he returned and the party continued.

The raiders came upon a small group of Utes, which they should have easily defeated. But the Utes overpowered them, as depicted in Plate 6. They killed both Sétjáuáuidè and Páugừhéjè and captured the *Táimé* figures.[25] Kiowas considered the defeat by the Utes, including the ritual objects' loss, to be a disaster second only to the 1833 Osage massacre detailed in Chapter 1. Kiowa calendars include name glyphs for the men who died at the Utes' hands.[26] And while the sacred objects' capture certainly impacted subsequent Sun Dance practice, the defeat also affected warriors and their power seeking. Men who carried *Táimé* figures and painted their bodies had died. While some blamed Sétjáuáuidè for his failure to observe taboos, others did not. One calendar notes that a Kiowa warrior involved in the battle "killed his shield" upon return.[27]

While Kiowas continued to face traditional enemies such as the Utes, they also felt the US military's growing presence on the southern plains. As noted in the previous chapter, this process began already in the second half of the Civil War. Kit Carson had attacked Kiowas camped at Adobe Walls in 1864. Once the war ended, some of the nation's most famous generals, including Philip Sheridan and William Tecumseh Sherman, made their way west to subdue Indian nations.[28] And while federal Indian officials established a policy grounded in civilian leadership, military leaders still advocated their priority to identify and chastise Indians who broke treaty provisions. They used the term "hostile" to designate them.[29] And when "hostiles" left their reservations, they faced soldiers who patrolled the boundaries with vigor. Some historians borrow a term from Civil War scholarship to describe US military strategy against Indians in this period. They call it "total war."[30]

Kiowas witnessed this strategy in action as military units assaulted their Indian allies, including Cheyenne and Arapaho neighbors who abided by treaty provisions. In an unprecedented move, General Sheridan called for a campaign to push Native people back onto reservation lands and show the army's willingness to attack even in winter, a time when Indian food stores became low and horses lacked grass to strengthen them.[31] Leading the Seventh Cavalry, George Armstrong Custer attacked a Cheyenne village camped along the Washita River. The Cheyenne leader, Black Kettle, had barely survived the 1864 Sand Creek massacre and was among those considered "friendly" by the federal Indian office. Custer and his men tore into the unsuspecting village at dawn, killing Black Kettle.

Some Kiowas, camped further down the Washita, came to the Cheyennes' aid. When the shots woke him from sleep, Éàunhâfàui (Trailing The Enemy) ran barefoot to join Cheyenne men defending the village with bow and arrows. He saw women and children running for their lives. While Kiowas successfully protected a group of about twenty

Cheyenne, they also witnessed the magnitude of Custer's destruction. Soldiers killed more than one hundred people, including many women and children. They took dozens of captives, burned the village to the ground, including its winter food stores, and killed approximately 650 horses and mules.[32] Kiowas recognized the vulnerability of their winter camps. Several calendar keepers marked the winter of 1868–1869 with images evoking the attack on Black Kettle's band.[33]

SACRED POWER IN THE CLOSING LANDS

As American officials mandated the reduction of Indian lands through treaties and as army leaders struck Native bands, several Indian nations underwent rectification movements.[34] In late 1868 and into 1869, a Paiute named Wodziwub issued proclamations and ritual instructions to his community living on Nevada's Walker River Reservation. Wodziwub had a dream telling him of a train's imminent arrival from the East. The train brought American settlers into their country. Wodziwub called on his kin to paint their faces, participate in the nation's long-practiced Round Dance, and bathe after dancing. He also told them their fathers and mothers would soon return. At the dance's end, Wodziwub entered a "trance-state" and visited with the dead. He claimed that those who had recently died would come back to earth. With his message, Wodziwub drew on older dance forms and healing rites to envision the earth renewed and beloved relatives restored. His message involved a direct response to colonial expansion, namely train cars of American emigrants moving westward.[35]

Wodziwub's movement, which has come to be known as the Ghost Dance of 1870, did not last long on the Paiute Reservation, but it quickly spread to others. Native people in Utah, Oregon, and California considered the new message and what it had to offer. Shoshones living on Idaho's Fort Hall Reservation heard about Wodziwub's dream and incorporated his message into their Round Dance tradition. Some Shoshones embraced the Paiute's claim that deceased relatives would soon return. They also supplemented his message with calls for resistance to American cultural practices.[36]

In the same period and under similar colonial stresses, Kiowas experienced a movement to rectify their unwelcome situation. The man responsible, Cą́umâmâjè (Goose Flying Overhead), had a history of accessing sacred power. He claimed a "medicine dream" in which he received a tipi design. It featured a buffalo bull along with a Spanish long-horn, each animal exhaling its powerful breath. Birds with lines denoting power rested on the larger animals' backs. One anthropologist argues that this combination of images signaled a "medicine complex" into which Cą́umâmâjè was likely initiated. Cą́umâmâjè also possessed a shield painted with images of a bear and a bullet on the outside cover. The inside, adorned with eagle feathers, featured images of an owl and pipe.[37]

While Cą́umâmâjè (also known as Mamanti) had connections to the animals featured on his tipi and shield, he was known particularly for his ability to communicate with owls. According to some, Cą́umâmâjè offered a pipe to owls at night and in return received messages about impending events. He was also known for his work among the Kiowa buffalo doctors, a group of men expert at treating war wounds. Cáumâmâjè also claimed to have visited the "village of the dead," the Kiowa afterworld, where he said things were "good." He told others that he received "dead men's medicine" during this encounter.[38]

Cáumâmâjè's works of power took on new dimensions in 1869 when federal officials planted the first corn and melon crops on the reservation. While somewhat familiar with corn made available through trade markets, Kiowas had no history of eating melons. They picked and ate them while still unripe. Many became sick. Some feared that government officials were poisoning them. Cáumâmâjè became ill, falling into a four-day sleep in which relatives thought him dead. Upon waking, Cáumâmâjè claimed that owls had given him a message. He told listeners that he could heal gunshot wounds and kill enemies with darts hidden inside his body. Such claims were hardly new among Kiowas. Around 1810, a Kiowa man claimed a vision in which birds not only gave him a shield design, but also powers allowing him to "throw off bullets," hide lethal objects in his stomach, and produce them from his mouth when needed. At least some Kiowas respected Cáumâmâjè's newfound abilities. He eventually claimed an ability to see the future and predict a war party's success, which would make him a pivotal figure in Kiowa responses to reservation life in coming years.[39]

Kiowas continued many of their cultural practices, including hunting, raiding, nomadic living, and Sun Dancing, during the early reservation years. But they also enacted changes in response to the reservation's establishment and administration. Government agents grew new kinds of food and sought to contain at least some of their movement. Soldiers policed the region, ready to suppress Native people they perceived to be hostile. Even so, a national movement for a more peaceful approach to Indians also took hold. With it, Protestant "friends of the Indian" assumed an important role in federal Indian policy. And despite characterizations of Grant's policy as peaceful, some of these "friends" engaged with army officers and considered the usefulness of coercive practices deployed to civilize Native people.

STRUGGLING OVER THE RESERVATION

In May 1869, an Iowa Quaker named Lawrie Tatum opened his diary and wrote about the surprising assignment he had just received. The farmer and Sabbath School leader had been asked to serve as reservation agent among Kiowas and Comanches, the "most hostile Indians in the U.S." Tatum worried about leaving his family, traveling to an unknown region, and working among such "notorious" people. But his grounding in Quaker practice reassured him. "Believing that the Lord had called me into the service," he wrote, "it was for me to obey, trusting that he would overrool [*sic*] all things for the best."[40]

Tatum arrived in Indian Territory after a grueling overland trip. He was among several Friends appointed to serve as agents on the southern plains.[41] He was also one of Grant's first appointees from the Christian denominations to begin service. Once on the reservation, Tatum began his many administrative tasks, including distribution of biweekly rations. As agent he had authority over more than 5,000 Indians.

Tatum started his service convinced of the Peace Policy's potential, but figured that its implementation would be difficult. A few weeks into his term, he wrote to the commissioner of Indian Affairs of his firm belief that most of the Indians wanted to travel the "white man's road." He worried, however, that the government's low-quality and meager rations did little to support this impulse. In his letter to Washington, Tatum quoted the golden rule and asked, "for humanity's sake," that the rations be increased. He was convinced that Indians with rewarding work and enough to eat would stop raiding in Texas, would stay on the reservation, and would move toward Anglo-American cultural habits. In this way, Tatum's rhetoric reflected Quakers' confidence that Native people would choose civilization when offered the proper inducements.[42]

During his early service, Tatum followed in the Society's long history of calling the United States to be a truly Christian nation. The agent employed the language of benevolent paternalism to convey his message. "May God grant wisdom [to federal officials,]" he wrote in one letter, "that they may act as becomes a Great and Christian Nation to perform towards its long neglected wards."[43] Tatum's colleague, Enoch Hoag, represented the Society as superintendent over several reservations and shared Tatum's views about Indians' need and America's duty. In his first report to federal officials, Hoag recommended more money to support Indians' transition to farming. He urged the government to keep American settlers off reservation lands, calling on officials to protect vulnerable Indians or accept "the penalty of a righteous retribution."[44]

Federal officials worked with the recently appointed Quakers to implement Grant's new policy. They also insisted on the necessity of a military presence throughout the southern plains. They had particular concerns about reigning in Kiowas and Comanches who continued to raid into Mexico and Texas. In December 1868, the army established Fort Sill to monitor Kiowas and their allies. When Tatum arrived the next spring, he not only moved into agency headquarters located on the grounds of Fort Sill, he also met the commanding officer, with whom he was required to coordinate some of his activities.[45]

Tatum often reported on his interactions with Fort Sill's commander. Within a few months of his arrival, he commented that the major general lent him a hand when he needed it. By autumn, Tatum reported that the fort's military leadership "enter[s] heartily into President Grant's plan of civilizing the Indians." Quaker leadership in Indian Country agreed and pointed to the relationship between Tatum and the fort's commander as a model for the future. "The success of our labor," Superintendent Hoag wrote, demanded "the Military command there be of that character that will harmonize with [Quaker] agents."[46]

This early concord did not reflect national opinion, which ranged from strong critique of the military to growing criticism of Grant's Peace Policy. On the one hand, citizens expressed outrage at periodic army attacks on Indians they considered "friendly," including a January 1870 assault on Piegans in which soldiers killed 200 women, children, and old people. Even supporters of some military presence worried that forts full of single, male soldiers posed a danger to Indian communities. On the other hand, some Americans criticized Grant's policy as hopelessly naïve. Within weeks of the policy's start, a Washington, D.C., newspaper reported that congressional representatives from western states asked the president that they not be "inflicted with the Quakers." Western editorialists concurred. A Colorado paper referenced ongoing "frightful murders and mutilations" to argue that Indians must be "caught and tamed before the Quaker plans can be applied."[47]

The national conversation contrasting Quaker service with military surveillance obscured Native people's experiences. From their perspective, the two groups worked together to contain Indians on reservations and radically transform their way of life. Tatum's diary notes that Kiowas often saw little distinction between Quakers and other federal representatives. When members of the Friends Indian committee visited the reservation, one Kiowa leader considered him a conduit to Washington and gave a long speech about not taking the white man's road.[48] In a report to federal officials, Tatum reported that the Indians came to him and claimed the government had no right to "pen them up on this small tract of land."[49] Kiowas considered Tatum a representative of the federal government and its armed forces.

Resistant to containment and cultural transformation, Kiowas cited their right by treaty to hunt beyond reservation boundaries. They also broke treaty provisions as small groups of men continued to raid into Texas and Mexico. Given recent army attacks on Native people, including those considered to be in good relationship with the government, Kiowas experienced significant anxiety about these actions. Decades later, an anthropologist heard many recall this period as a "winter of chronic alarm."[50] Kiowa calendars memorialized this anxiety. Several include drawings of a bugle.[51] The entries recall a young man outside a Kiowa winter camp who blew a horn in jest. Alarmed residents worried that Americans were about to attack. Some began to flee before the origin of the sound was finally known.

Kiowas continued to seek out sacred power in this period of increasing military presence. Men carried shields, as well as other objects imbued with protective power. One example of the use of objects comes from reservation officials curious about ongoing Kiowa raiding despite its dangers. They were told about Cûifâgàui's (Lone Wolf the Elder) "bit of stone." According to Cûifâgàui, he could not be killed while he carried the stone. The object's power was strong enough to overcome grievous injuries, including a lightning strike. Confident that he would be protected, Cûifâgàui was among many Kiowa men who frequently moved beyond reservation boundaries to hunt, raid, and participate in war parties against other Indian nations.[52]

Younger Kiowa men involved in these activities also sought sacred power. In this period, one traveled to a swamp to seek instruction from water spirits. A turtle gave him power, as well as a new name, Tónàuqàut, meaning "rough tailed" or "snapping turtle."

Tónàuqàut received the power to heal battle wounds. He shared this power with sixteen followers who made up a small sodality of healers to accompany war and raiding parties.[53]

Older men supported war and raiding efforts by hosting feasts in which they prayed for direction. Sétthái̯dé (White Bear) offered one such prayer. "You see us sitting here. We are small, poor men, and we can do nothing unless you help us." He acknowledged the threats. "The new people . . . they cut open the earth and put strange seeds in it. They build boxes to live in . . . They say they own the land." Sétthái̯dé and his guest, Sétái̯gài (Sitting Bear), acknowledged that the Americans had the upper hand. They asked for guidance as they faced an unequal situation. "We will fight if we are driven to fighting. Perhaps we can save our children and our women without battles. Teach us," they prayed.[54]

Kiowas also continued their Sun Dance rites. In May 1870, they gathered with allies to construct their ceremonial encampment. At the time, the people did not realize the importance of the event. It was Àunsói̯jèqàptàu's (Old Man Foot) last Sun Dance. He had served as *Tái̯mé* keeper for nearly thirty years. He died that winter and Kiowas did not replace him. That same Sun Dance also hosted an important debate about how to respond to Quakers' and army officers' insistence that Kiowas stop raiding. Some leaders argued for making peace with the Americans, while others insisted on the need to hunt and raid, especially given the low quality and unpredictable delivery of rations. Young men, in particular, went further and argued for a war to push the Americans out of their lands altogether.[55]

Tatum sensed the tensions and told his employees they could leave if they felt unsafe. Committed to staying, the Quaker agent continued his effort to persuade Kiowas to stay on the reservation and convince government officials that better and timelier rations would assist in the cause of peace. Tatum's wife, Mary Ann, expressed her concern for his health and safety. She also considered how the Christian God remained present during difficulty. God tested them, she wrote, in "this land of heathen darkness." She keenly felt her lonely position on the plains. "Vain is the help of man situated so far from the Christian world and surrounded by wild men of the woods." Tatum sent her back to Iowa in early July.[56]

Tensions increased between Tatum, Kiowa leaders, and army officials. In mid-June, Fort Sill's commander ordered all Kiowas and Comanches onto the reservation under threat that troops would apprehend any who failed to arrive.[57] Many Indians were so angered that they came to the fort and promptly stole a herd of horses and mules adjacent to it. The commander sent troops in pursuit, but had no luck finding the Indians.[58] Neither could Tatum persuade Kiowas to follow his direction. Under orders to bring two Kiowa leaders to Washington, D.C., for talks, Tatum admitted that he could not because he had no way of finding them.[59]

The situation deteriorated, at least from the Americans' perspective, in subsequent months. Kiowas continued raiding and stealing cattle to supplement their diminished diets. They also refused Tatum's and military officers' requests for meetings. In time, the Quaker agent distributed rations only to Indians who had returned any and all goods stolen from Texans and other American settlers. Just three months into his tenure as agent, Tatum admitted that many Kiowas did not want to travel the "white man's road." They wanted to continue their own way of life. In mid-July, he met with Kiowas who requested that their reservation be enlarged. Tatum flatly refused. Demanding to know who had been raiding and that all stolen property be returned, Tatum told them the Americans "had given them no cause" for their terrible behavior.[60]

Tatum's opinion of the Kiowa continued to diminish. In early August, he reported that the Indians held their weapons in view during discussions about stolen animals. The agent continued to withhold rations unless Kiowas brought in goods or captives. To be sure, Tatum at times acknowledged Kiowa struggles and dissatisfactions. In a report to federal officials, he noted that the Indians had suffered significantly from malaria in the last year, as well as from eating unripe crops. Annuities were small and rations came late. He recognized that Kiowas resented that the reservation "limited their ability to roam." But none of these things, in Tatum's mind, justified raiding, stealing, and killing. The Quaker had no experience of the long economic history of raiding and captive taking that constituted economic and political strength on the southern plains. To him, these acts proved Indians' propensity for violence and the urgent need for their civilization.[61]

In September, Tatum's tone sharpened once again. Angry about Kiowa raiding, he removed sugar, a prized resource, from rations. In a letter to his Quaker supervisor, Tatum explained that "I did it to punish them and . . . I believe it had a very salutary effect upon them. They have not appeared to be nearer conquered since I have been here than they did on that day."[62] He also wrote in his diary that he lost his temper during interactions with individual Indians. Of an encounter with a man who would not leave the ration storage building, Tatum wrote, "I got tired of waiting on him . . . took holt [*sic*] of his arm and put him out and closed the door all with more energy than prudence."[63]

In his frustration, Tatum called on Fort Sill's commander for help. He requested troops to assist him during ration distribution.[64] Tatum later reported "the presence of the troops I believe had a good effect." In a letter to Superintendent Hoag, he recounted his request for troops and his experiment with withholding sugar as punishment for raiding. Tatum said he believed "it will be the best." He also acknowledged that his fellow Quakers might not approve. He would continue, however, "unless I am ordered by superior Officers to not punish [the Indians] in this way."[65]

Tatum was right about his co-religionists' hesitation. Earlier in the summer, Hoag had expressed concern about the ration policy. In November, the superintendent arrived at the reservation with members of the Society's Indian committee. Tatum wrote in his diary that the committee "had heard reports . . . which had caused them uneasiness." But the agent reassured his colleagues. Hoag and the other Quaker leaders then tried to assuage fellow members of the Society. They penned editorials in praise of Grant's Indian policy. They extolled its design to "rescue" Native people and "elevate them so as to be fit for citizenship and a place in the Christian community." They acknowledged that Quaker agents sometimes found themselves in trying situations, but assured readers that they stayed true to the Society's "doctrines and testimonies." They also addressed the policy's inability to prompt quick transformation. "While this path doesn't always bring success," one wrote, "it does always prevail." But in the midst of this effort to maintain Quaker support, Hoag also admitted his concerns. In the last line of his otherwise cheering editorial, he wrote that Kiowas and Comanches were the only Indians who still worried him.[66]

Society members concerned about the ethics of reservation administration were not the only problem Quakers faced.[67] Skeptics criticized the central role that Friends played in President Grant's policy. Some of these critiques came from other Protestant "friends of the Indian." Writers for a Congregationalist paper wondered why the president had overlooked the American Board of Commissioners for Foreign Missions (ABCFM) and other Protestant bodies with long histories of Indian mission work. They asked why the Society of Friends, a group "few in number, and whose distinctive principles are an offence [sic] to [other Christians]," should play such a predominant role.[68]

Protestants found a way to address their concern about a Quaker monopoly on Indian work when, in December 1870, President Grant announced the Peace Policy's expansion. His officials assigned a range of denominational representatives to scores of reservations across the West. When the Protestants serving on the BIC met soon after, they reported that Baptist, Congregationalist, and Presbyterian leaders were searching for men to nominate to these positions. With the prospect that religious representatives would be running most reservations, missionaries also envisioned an expansion of their work. In 1870, Southern Baptists who had been active in eastern Indian Territory for decades began plans to send preachers to the "wild tribes" further west. That same year, Episcopalians named a missionary bishop to the newly created jurisdiction of Arkansas and Indian Territory. Protestants saw the chance to expand their influence in government and their civilizing work among Native peoples.[69]

Catholics also positioned themselves to take advantage of the policy's expansion. They argued that their long mission history on dozens of reservations proved they should receive priority. Oregon's archbishop, François Blanchet, wrote to President Grant with an offer of cooperation. He also requested three reservations with a history of Catholic activity to administer through the expanded policy. The bishop encouraged the president to act quickly, as a Methodist missionary was already trying to establish himself.[70]

If Blanchet's communications were a bit bossy, his colleague Pierre De Smet took a more irenic approach.[71] The Jesuit wrote congenial letters about Indian nations with a history of Catholic missions among them. He politely urged federal officials to name Catholics to these posts. His interactions with Protestant leaders on the BIC, however, were much more antagonistic.[72] As a guest at their first meeting after Grant announced the policy expansion, De Smet raised concerns about Protestant agents being assigned to reservations with substantial numbers of Catholic Indians. He noted reports that some agents, inspired simply by anti-Catholic animus, barred priests from entering and distributing sacraments. He worried that the situation would deteriorate if the Peace

Policy expanded without Catholic representation. Would Catholic Indians be at liberty to practice their religion, De Smet asked?[73]

What started as a rift over reservation assignments soon developed into a national conflict over federal support for Catholic schools and missions for Indians.[74] Grant's Peace Policy, intended to draw on religious organizations to provide a "humane" answer to the "Indian problem," also prompted significant conflicts within and between Christian groups. Despite this growing controversy, most Americans trained their eyes on Native people's responses to Grant's policy. How would the Indians, especially "wild tribes" like the Kiowa, react to civilizing programs on newly formed reservations?

OUTSIDE THE BOUNDS

Kiowas continued to invoke sacred power in response to American occupation of the southern plains. As Agent Tatum and his staff attempted to plant crops, Kiowas tried to discourage them. According to Tatum, one man said the "Great Spirit" had never told him to grow corn. Even so, the man had tried the year before. Kiowas became ill and died after eating the crop. The man concluded that the tragedy resulted because "he had done what the Great Spirit did not want him to do." Other Kiowas sought guidance at Sun Dances, hoping to receive wisdom about navigating the reservation's perils. Tatum noted that a Kiowa leader named Cújòkǫ́gai (Black Eagle) attended the "medicine dance" and went out to raid shortly after. He was inspired to take the risk because living on the reservation left them starving. Cújòkǫ́gai also felt emboldened to confront Tatum. He demanded that Americans lift their limits on trade goods, including ammunition, and stop limiting Native peoples' ability to move freely.[75]

But free movement, especially when it involved raiding, involved many dangers. In response, Kiowas adjusted their ritual practice. In the winter of 1870–1871, two young men were killed while outside reservation boundaries. In their grief, the young men's fathers, Sétągài (Sitting Bear) and Cûifągàui (Lone Wolf the Elder), departed from standard practices regarding men killed on raids. Instead of allowing his son to be buried at the battle site, Cûifągàui insisted on bringing his son's body back. As Kiowas faced increasing limitations on their movement and forced enclosure on the reservation, Cûifągàui decided a burial far away was not acceptable. Sétągài offered to wrap up the young men's bones in a new blanket and bring them home. After gathering them, he talked to them and cried over them. Sétągài brought them back, declared a feast, and distributed gifts on behalf of his dead son. In a surprising move, he gave away a treasured possession, a medicine bundle that had been in his family for at least four generations. In more ordinary times, he would not have passed it on until his own death neared. But Sétągài presented the bundle to his living son, hoping that in this new and dangerous time, it would ensure his long life.[76]

Sétągài, along with other Kiowa leaders, struggled against an increasingly difficult situation. They resented the reservation, the soldiers, and the settlers. At every turn, it seemed, the situation deteriorated both locally and nationally. In early 1871, Congress voted to suspend all treaty making with Indian nations. The government no longer interacted with Native peoples as sovereign nations. Instead, they structured relations along the lines of guardians and wards, or parents and wayward children. This shift certainly undermined Native sovereignty and did not result in more sympathetic treatment of the nation's new "wards." Army patrols across the West continued to attack Native people. In late spring 1871, US forces coordinated an assault on Apaches who had surrendered and were being held in Arizona's Camp Grant. Eastern newspapers called it a massacre. From the Kiowas' perspective, Grant's "Peace Policy" had not improved their situation. It undermined their autonomy and failed to secure them from attack.[77]

In mourning over his lost son, Sétą̀gài joined young Kiowa men interested in continued raiding and fighting. In his interactions with military officials, he emphasized his desire to live in a Kiowa way and listed the problems caused by American farmers and settlers. "Land doesn't want to be worked," he claimed. "Land gives you what you need if you're smart enough to take it. This is good land. This is our land. We know how to take what it gives us. It takes care of us." Sétą̀gài was right about the threat. Some Americans advocated opening Indian Territory to settlement and farming. Big-game hunters were moving south from the northern plains where they had already devastated the herds. Of the settlers and buffalo hunters moving in, Sétą̀gài claimed, "When they work the land they kill it and drive the buffalo away . . .. We have to protect ourselves. We have to save our country. We have to kill off those men who are killing our land and driving the buffalo away." In May 1871, he did just that.[78]

VIOLENCE IN THE INDIAN COUNTRY

According to its primary leaders, the attack was essentially a revenge raid.[79] Following cultural codes of warfare, friends of Sétą̀gài and Cùifàgàui organized an expedition in retaliation for their sons' deaths. Led by Sétthą̀idé (White Bear), several men rode south into Texas and attacked a wagon train and its occupants. They burned everything in the wagons. They killed seven men, including the grisly murder of one man they tied to a wagon wheel and set on fire. Some Kiowas reported that Cą̀umâmą̀jè (Goose Flying Overhead), the man who earlier claimed the power to forecast the success of raids and war parties, suggested the attack and predicted its success.[80] For the two grieving fathers, the assault fulfilled their obligation to avenge their lost sons.

American observers did not share this view. To their minds, the attack was an unjustified display of savagery. It prompted renewed cries of Indian malevolence, as well as claims that it proved the failure of the Peace Policy. For American Quakers, the attack triggered a crisis. The alleged Kiowa perpetrators were from "their" reservation. Agent Tatum's response would be crucial as Quakers sought to justify themselves to outside observers who questioned the Society's role in federal Indian policy.[81]

In the immediate aftermath of the attack, Tatum struggled between what his fellow Friends would approve and his conviction that only strong punishment would deter future Indian raids. In late May 1871, Tatum wrote Enoch Hoag, his Quaker supervisor, with news of the attack. The agent argued that he could not see why Indian assailants would be treated differently than other Americans guilty of murder. He asked for Hoag's view. Did he approve of Tatum having the attackers arrested at the reservation's headquarters, which would be a departure from expectations that soldiers had no authority there? Would he support Tatum in turning the guilty Indians over to the state of Texas for criminal trial?[82]

Hoag did not answer in time. Before he could write back, Sétthą́idé (White Bear) and the raid's other leaders, Sétągài (Sitting Bear) and Ádàuiétjè (Big Tree), arrived at the agency. Sétthą́idé admitted that he led the attack. According to a letter he wrote to Hoag, Tatum "immediately went ... to have them arrested, which General Sherman was more than willing to do."[83] Tatum reported that Sherman's men killed a Kiowa man in the process of arresting Sétthą́idé and the other two Kiowa leaders. He assumed Sherman would send the prisoners to Texas for trial. While his letter to Hoag merely narrated the events, Tatum's personal correspondence touched on his concern about the incident's aftermath. Writing the same day, Tatum asked his family to "trust that all will be over ruled for good." In a letter to his wife a few days later, Tatum reported that he had visited the Kiowa prisoners. He asked his family to pray that he act "prudently" under the circumstances.[84]

In early June, US officials arranged to transport the three prisoners to Texas for trial. While soldiers loaded the Kiowa men into a wagon, Sétągài claimed he would not go. Tatum declared that he began to sing his "death song." According to another Quaker who witnessed the transport, Sétągài also told Kiowas gathered around the wagon to prepare to retrieve his bones from along the roadside. He then rose from his seat in the wagon and began to "speak to God." Tatum claimed that Sétągài somehow took off his shackles, withdrew a hidden butcher knife from his sleeve, and attacked the wagon's driver. Within seconds, soldiers shot and killed him. From the Quakers' point of view, Sétągài exhibited his warlike propensity and heathen religion right up to the end.[85]

Years later, a Kiowa woman offered a different account of Sétągài's death. Her son transcribed it and wrote a literal translation, calling it the "chiefs they then imprisoned story."[86] According to it, Kiowas who led the wagon train attack were summoned to the "soldier's place" with a request to "council." But the Americans deceived them. Upon the men's arrival, troops surrounded the men. They tried to run, but soldiers raised their guns and detained them. The transport wagon for the journey to Texas came several days later. Once seated in the wagon, Sétągài sang his "Kiowa war order song" and gave a "war cry." He then addressed his son who had recently died. "You place ... in pipe the tobacco," Sétągài said, "and we together shall smoke this very day." Pointing to a tree ahead of the wagon, he proclaimed that there "I am to die." Sétągài produced a knife, attacked the driver, and soldiers shot him dead. According to other Kiowa accounts, the knife's appearance could be explained by Sétɑ̃gài's power. He had long been known for his ability to swallow a feather and cough up a knife.[87] Kiowa accounts of Sétɑ̃gài's death emphasize his grief over a lost son. His attack on the guard and death at American hands resulted not from his innate violence, but functioned as an escape and reunion made possible by sacred power. Indeed, one Kiowa calendar features an image of Sétɑ̃gài with shackled arms, moments before he freed himself.[88]

In death, Sétɑ̃gài found reunion with his deceased son. He also left a void among his living family and friends. Another of Sétɑ̃gài's sons buried his brother's bones, as well as his father's shield. He and his relatives discussed whether or not, according to custom, they should kill Sétɑ̃gài's favorite horse. They entered a period of mourning. That solemn feeling extended to the entire nation as Kiowas entered their second summer with no *Tɑ̃imé* keeper named to replace the long-serving Àunsójèqàptàu (Old Man Foot). Calendar entries not only document the lack of a summer gathering, but also the events surrounding Sétɑ̃gài's death.[89]

Concerned about the aftermath of the wagon train attack, including its implications for the Peace Policy, Tatum and other Quakers on the reservation hardly noticed the Kiowas' failure to gather for a Sun Dance. For several weeks, it seems, Tatum was unclear about what his Quaker supervisors expected him to do about Kiowas and Comanches who left the reservation without permission. Tatum implored Hoag: "Please give special instructions on the subject or I shall be compelled to act on my own judgments."[90] If Quaker leaders seemed reluctant to act, the federal government was not. Interior Department officials initiated a change in approach. They ordered Tatum to withhold rations from any Indian families outside reservation boundaries.[91] More important, they also granted the military power to come onto the reservation, overriding the strict separation between civilian and military leadership at the policy's core.[92]

The press lauded this tough approach to Kiowas and other "wild" Indians. The *New York Times* printed a letter from General Sherman saying Indians from the "Tatum Reservation" were on the warpath and "the Government should cease to care for them, and sequestrate [*sic*] their lands and punish them as their enormities deserve."[93] To some readers' surprise, the *Times* also claimed that Agent Tatum, his Quakerism notwithstanding, supported the military and government's tough approach to the Kiowa offenders.[94] The paper had acquired the agent's letter to General Sherman, written just days after the Kiowas' arrest. "Permit me to urge," Tatum wrote, "independent of my conscientious views against capital punishment, as a matter of policy it would be best for the inhabitants of Texas that they be not executed for some time, and probably not at all." "If they are kept as prisoners," Tatum continued, "the Indians will hope to have them released, and thus have a restricting influence on their actions; but if they are executed, the Kiowas will be very likely to seek revenge in a wholesale murder of the white people."[95] Tatum's Quaker colleagues initially balked at the agent's support for the government's stricter approach to the Kiowas. Hoag asked him to stop calling for arrests, and another Quaker leader entreated him reconsider his actions.[96]

Responses from Hoag and other Society leaders revealed their discomfort with Tatum's actions. They supported Tatum's calls for commuting the death sentence. They often repeated his claims that the death penalty would incite war. But unlike Tatum's more practical arguments, they emphasized the humanity, benevolence, and distinct "Quakerness" of their position. In a letter sent to the president and widely reprinted in Society publications, leaders claimed that their "opposition to the sacrifice of human life" was the primary reason for their intercessions.[97]

The Quaker leaders' nod to their anti-capital punishment convictions fell flat before a public seeking the Kiowa leaders' execution and the Peace Policy's demise. Referencing the wagon train attack, a San Francisco paper mocked the Society's response. "Let [the Quaker commissioners] come with their olive branches."[98] Other writers connected recent Indian raids with the perceived laxness of the Peace Policy. An Arkansas paper reported on a Cheyenne wagon train attack and the torture of its inhabitants under the headline, "Horrible Barbarity: Results of Quaker Policy."[99]

Despite his supervisors' emphasis on the benevolence and pacifism that inspired Grant's Peace Policy, Tatum continued to withhold rations and work closely with the military. He also called for arrests and continued surveillance of Kiowa people. After the unexplained death of two settlers near the reservation, Tatum withheld a quarter of *all* Kiowa rations and threatened to keep back more unless the people surrendered the perpetrators. He asked Fort Sill's commander to arrest four men who would not return stolen mules. Punitive actions became central to Tatum's Indian work. He wrote a letter claiming that Séttháidé's (White Bear) arrest and imprisonment had worked to keep the "whole tribe in check" and that troop movements in the region had prompted more Indians to come into the reservation.[100]

Tatum's actions signaled a change in how Americans dealt with Indians they identified as "friendly" and "hostile." According to those involved in Indian affairs, "friendlies" accepted at least some Anglo-American cultural practices, committed no violence, and kept their promises even when Americans failed to keep theirs. "Hostiles," on the other hand, resisted settled living and other American cultural practices, acted aggressively for reasons of economic gain or self-defense, and failed to keep treaty promises. To be sure, Americans had referred to some Native people as "friendly" in a relatively stable way for a few decades.[101] But during the Peace Policy years, the designation came to include more demands. In order for Indians to be counted as "friends" to Americans, they had to persuade their hostile relatives to cease their misbehavior.[102] Tatum went further, withholding rations from all Kiowas and thereby treating them all as hostile. He promised to restore full rations, which were guaranteed to Kiowas in the Medicine Lodge treaty, only when the people turned in those suspected of breaking the law.

The Quaker Indian committee struggled to come to terms with Tatum's actions. At their meeting a few months after the wagon train attack, they noted that Tatum had counseled Kiowas to choose peace and meet with US leaders. The Indians had been wrong to decline. They also observed that Tatum faced the prospect that leniency might lead to more raiding and murder. To be sure, the committee admitted that Tatum interacted with the army in ways they had not anticipated when the Peace Policy was first established. "Lawrie Tatum called upon the military to make the arrest," Society leaders wrote, "but there was no other authority in existence in the section." Further, the committee emphasized, Tatum's request for arrests seemed to have worked. Kiowas had not raided since their leaders were taken away. Some interactions with the military, the leaders averred, a kind of "cordial co-operation," might be necessary.[103]

On the reservation, Tatum celebrated Kiowas' changed behavior. He wrote to Hoag that increased troop movements in the area had prompted many to stay on the reservation rather than face attack. He warned Indians that leaders of any future raids would be arrested. The prospect of prison, Tatum claimed, filled the people with "dread." The agent also acted to disrupt Kiowa forms of political organization. Starting in the late summer of 1871, he stopped recognizing Kiowa leaders he considered hostile. He would not council with them or distribute rations through them to their followers. His actions bore fruit. In a letter to his wife, Tatum rejoiced that Kiowas were "nearer subdued than they ever were before."[104]

With Kiowas restrained, Tatum turned to their Indian allies. Some Comanches continued to raid into Texas and Mexico. The agent recommended arrests and surveillance to bring them to heel. Military officials in the region agreed. In 1872, General Mackenzie attacked a Comanche village, taking more than one hundred women and children captive. In order to get them back, Comanches followed American prescriptions. Tatum reported in a Society periodical that Comanches were "more docile and peaceable than they ever were before" because their women and children were being held as prisoners.[105]

Other Quaker leaders began to voice their support for Tatum's approach. One announced in a Philadelphia newspaper that Kiowas had "waked up" at their leaders' arrest.[106] In response to chastening, Indians made peace. Society officials also insisted that Tatum's unanticipated actions were peaceful, even as the agent supported and cooperated with the military. In a report published in a popular Society periodical, members of the Indian committee "den[ied] totally that [Tatum's action] is any evidence whatever of the failure of the peace policy."[107]

Other Protestant "friends of the Indian" concurred. The BIC, which still included no Catholic member, met to evaluate the Peace Policy and offer suggestions to the federal Indian office. Board members extolled President Grant's support, the "liberality" of Congress, and the American people's "humane sensibilities." The Peace Policy was working, they claimed. Through it, the United States fulfilled its moral duty as a leading nation. And to any skeptics, the board hoped they would someday understand the "uniform kindness and patience" that inspired the president's policy. Once realized, concerns about the policy would fall away, just like the "old hatred against freedom" that perpetuated slavery. "Friends of the Indian" cast the Peace Policy, enforced by armies and enabled by prisons, as freedom's harbinger.[108]

4

1872 to 1875

⌒──

WHEN AMERICAN SOLDIERS took Sétthạ̈idé (White Bear) and Ádàuiétjè (Big Tree) to Texas, Kiowas had no idea when or if they would ever return. A Texas court convicted the men and condemned them to hang. Their sentences were eventually commuted, but it was unclear if they would ever leave prison. Back on the reservation, Kiowa leaders approached their Quaker agent, Lawrie Tatum, to inquire about the prisoners' future.[1] Thènéàungópjè (Kicking Bird), a leader known for his good relations with the Americans, asked Tatum to appeal to Washington for the men's eventual release.[2] Clearly, the Kiowa leaders' imprisonment caused distress beyond their immediate families. The entire people wondered what they had to do for their men to be returned.

While American officials said little about the prisoners' prospects for release, they stated their expectations for Kiowas clearly. They insisted that Kiowas must not move outside the reservation's boundaries. Beyond that, they expected a transition toward settled living, farming, and schooling. Officially, President Grant's Peace Policy remained in place. Religious representatives administered reservations and worked to transform Native cultural practices by modeling Anglo-American alternatives. But violence between Indians and settlers across the West prompted criticism of Grant's policy, as well as renewed calls for a military solution to the "Indian problem." In response to arguments for the use of force, Protestant "friends of the Indian" defended reservations as spaces for Indian separation, the Peace Policy as the nation's best chance for ending frontier violence, and education as the critical factor in Native peoples' cultural transformation.

These debates over Native lands and peoples, insofar as they raised questions about a marginalized population's place in a democracy and the role of violence in achieving American aims, paralleled the national conversation about African Americans who were formerly enslaved. During Reconstruction, Protestant ministers, reformers, and missionaries from the North advocated a vast program of "racial uplift" for black people across the South. They partnered with the federally established Freedman's Bureau to provide food, employment, and education to African Americans making their way as newly independent workers in a wage economy. Because powerful white Southerners opposed black freedom and equality, the president sent troops to state capitals throughout the South to ensure African Americans' political participation. With massive civilizing programs enforced by military presence, the South's Reconstruction and Indian Country's Peace Policy revealed the "era of Citizenship" to be a period of conflict and coercion.[3]

Protestant "friends of the Indian" who worked on the Kiowa, Comanche, and Apache (KCA) Reservation continued to champion the Peace Policy. Hoping not only to avoid settler–Indian violence, but also to initiate the transformation of Native cultures, they asked for increased federal support of Indian schools. While these funds went to some government-run schools, they were also channeled to institutions run by missionaries. Protestant "friends of the Indian" encouraged this arrangement until Catholics mounted a campaign to receive federal funds to open schools as well. Facing opposition, Catholic leaders increased their presence in Washington, D.C., and confronted government workers unwilling to accept them as Peace Policy participants. Indeed, some officials were openly hostile to them. In response, Catholics crafted a distinctive understanding about how to be "friends of the Indian." They positioned themselves as protectors of Native people's "religious freedom," arguing that the Constitution guaranteed Catholic Indians' right to choose and have access to Catholic schools.[4]

While Catholics and Protestants bickered about which schools were best for Native people and how the government should fund them, Kiowas wondered if they should send their children to school at all. During their leaders' incarceration, Kiowas struggled against American efforts to constrain their movement and force cultural change. They also faced food shortages, illness, and transitions in internal leadership.[5] Despite these difficulties, Kiowas continued their practices for engaging sacred power. They dreamed and healed. They gathered for Sun Dances. But as tensions increased on the southern plains and some Indians considered defensive action against the Americans, new ritual specialists emerged. And in the summer of 1874, some Kiowas went to war.

SCHOOLING THE INDIAN COUNTRY

After Sétthăidé and Ádàuiétjè's extradition, Kiowas felt increased pressure to follow American directives with the hope that compliance might hasten their relatives' return. School was one option that Kiowas considered. Schools were not entirely new to them. Josiah Butler, a Quaker and former freedmen's schoolteacher, had arrived on the reservation in 1870 and had opened a school near Fort Sill. He initially concentrated his efforts Caddos and Comanches. Kiowas hesitated to send their children to Butler's unknown institution. Occasionally they dispatched leaders to observe the Quaker teacher and his Indian students. Butler's reports on the school, which detailed his methods for cutting children's hair, replacing their traditional clothes, and removing their "various gaudy ornaments," detail some aspects of school life to which Kiowas likely objected.[6]

Parents started to show some willingness to consider schooling when another Quaker teacher, Thomas Battey, offered to live and teach in a Kiowa camp. Battey ran a successful school for Wichita children, but could not escape the feeling he ought to be elsewhere. He wondered if he should go among the Kiowa, whom he considered the "most fierce and desperately bloodthirsty tribe of the Indian Territory." Just as Battey considered his future, Tẖę́néàungópjè (Kicking Bird) arrived at his home and ate with him. According to Battey, the Kiowa leader asked him to come among his people and act like a father to his little girl. The Quaker saw the hand of providence in Thęnéàungópjè's invitation to live and teach among his band. Sensing the Christian God's leading, Battey "yield[ed]" himself to work among the "wild and roving Kiowas."[7]

As a leader trying to maintain good relations with the reservation's Quaker agent, Thęnéàungópjè had good reason to invite Battey to teach within his camp. As the first Kiowa leader to allow children to attend school, he could gain Agent Tatum's favor and expect courtesies in return. He might also have been motivated by concern for his only living child's future. According to Battey, Thęnéàungópjè and his wife had lost five young children to disease. Securing a relationship between Battey and his young daughter could have offered Thęnéàungópjè more options for ensuring his child's welfare.[8]

If sending children to school offered prospects, it also presented potential threats. Some Kiowa mothers were indignant about Battey's proposal. They did not like the idea of Battey teaching their children "to do the things that white people do."[9] Other Indians saw danger in Battey's presence. Some Caddoes warned Thęnéàungópjè about having the teacher among them. They suspected that attending school had made their children sick. When Battey began classes in January 1873, he not only had 22 Kiowa children in attendance, but also "many young and old [Kiowa] men" who came to ensure their children's safety.[10]

The new schools on the KCA Reservation reflected a national trend. Treaties signed in the late 1860s usually included monies for Indian education. After 1870, the federal government funded the opening of dozens of new schools, usually under the direction of the religious representatives serving as reservation agents. This focus on education reflected the popular mood, as seen in John Gast's popular print, "American Progress" (Figure 4.1). In it, the woman leading settlers into the West bears a book in her right hand. Schools, then, were central to American ideas about inhabiting and settling the region.[11]

Protestant "friends of the Indian" applauded federal support for more schools, except when it went to those run by Catholics. Some Protestant reservation agents went so far as to bar priests from entering and forbade the use of reservation buildings for Catholic schools. Others made arguments that Catholics were unfit to participate in Grant's policy. On the Umatilla Reservation in Oregon, for instance, the agent called Jesuit teachers inadequate because they did not focus enough on manual labor, force children to speak English, or require American dress.[12] The agent's criticism reflected widely

FIGURE 4.1. John Gast's 1872 "American Progress." In this widely disseminated print, Native people and buffalo herds flee in the face of settlers, trains, farmers, and a looming female figure bearing a "school book" in one hand and an electric cable in the other.
Credit: Library of Congress Prints and Photographs Division, LC-DIG-ppmsca-09855

held Protestant concerns that Catholic schools failed to properly "Americanize" students. Even the commissioner of Indian Affairs claimed that Catholics used their role in the Peace Policy for the purposes of "church propagation," rather than moving Indians toward citizenship.[13]

This struggle over reservation schools composed one part of a national debate about religion's place in public education and Catholics' presence in American civic life. In 1869, a local struggle over Bible reading in Ohio schools prompted what came to be called the Cincinnati Bible Wars.[14] As with earlier conflicts, the debate focused on whether or not Protestant forms of Bible reading, prayer, and teaching were nonsectarian and amenable to all citizens, as opposed to Catholic practices, which Protestant Americans considered "sectarian" and therefore ineligible for government support. As the Cincinnati conflict unfolded before a national audience, some Protestants involved in the resulting court case wondered if Jesuits had orchestrated the conflict as part of their plan to undermine Protestant institutions and replace them with their own. These fears reflected a broader climate of anticlerical prejudice and anxiety about Catholic public activity.

Protestant resistance to Catholic influence on schooling regulations and their participation in the Peace Policy hardly resulted in Catholic withdrawal from political activity. On the contrary, Catholics initiated significant political engagement in order to secure the opportunity to run reservations and Indian schools. Many Catholic leaders were still outraged at the small number of reservations the federal government had assigned them. In late 1872, Catholics administered only seven reservations, while Protestants ran seventy-seven.[15] They also resented Protestant leaders who snubbed them at meetings with federal officials and organizations involved in the Peace Policy. To be sure, some Catholic leaders worried that lobbying would only increase Protestant opposition. But others argued that having representation in Washington earlier might have secured them a BIC seat and more reservation assignments. Ready to take action, Baltimore's arch-bishop asked General Charles Ewing, an attorney and Civil War veteran, to represent Catholic interests in Washington. Father John Baptiste Brouillet, a Canadian priest who had long served Indian missions in the Pacific Northwest, joined Ewing in Washington to advance the cause of Catholic Indian missions and schools.[16]

Ewing and Brouillet's roles were formalized in early 1874, when the church named Ewing the commissioner of Catholic Indian Missions, soon renamed the Bureau of Catholic Indian Missions (BCIM).[17] The two men publicized Catholic Indian mission work to Catholic leaders and laypeople. They focused not only on the number of baptized Indian Catholics, which they numbered at 100,000, but also on examples of Protestant reservation agents who restricted Indian Catholics' religious freedom. Bigoted agents, Ewing argued, kept priests from providing sacraments and education to Catholic Indians. The situation exposed the American government's tyrannical power over Indian nations. Native people could not control where they lived, Ewing complained. They faced military assault if they disobeyed. The government enriched itself by selling their land. Articulating a distinctive understanding of what it meant to be a "friend of the Indian," Ewing called on his coreligionists to defend "their Catholic brethren on the plains." "The religious liberty of the Indian" was at stake. Echoing broader Catholic discussions about parental authority, Ewing argued that Catholic Indians had the right to "educate [their] children to know and worship [God], free from all control or interference on the part of any secular power."[18]

Ewing and Brouillet's effort was broad in scope. They asked American Catholics to contribute funds to Indian missions and schools. They called on government officials to assign priests and Catholic schoolteachers to reservations in need. Their work marked a new direction in North American Catholic missions. As noted in earlier chapters, European Catholics had long supported missions to American Indians. Jesuits and Benedictines from Germany, France, Belgium, and Italy served in these far-flung venues. Funds for their work were provided by the Vatican's Society for the Propagation of the Faith, as well as mission societies created in various countries. Ewing now called on American Catholics to give and the American government to recognize Catholics' dis-tinctive contribution to Indian missions. Like American Protestants before him, Ewing often publicized Indians' "Macedonian call" for evangelization. Native people, he insisted, were begging for Catholic instruction. He claimed that "40,000 heathen Sioux" had called on Catholics to assist them.[19] He also encouraged delegations during which Indians asked federal officials to let priests work among them.[20] According to Ewing,

Catholics functioned as "friends of the Indian" by supporting missions and schools, as well as lobbying to protect Indians from Protestant-dominated federal agencies.

Ewing's was an uphill battle. Catholics had no seat on the BIC.[21] Further, President Grant expressed hostility toward "sectarian," meaning Catholic, education. In 1875, the president called for an amendment banning aid to religious schools. In a speech filled with vocabulary from anti-Catholic discourse, Grant argued that public schools should be devoid of all religion. True education, he insisted, resulted in patriotism rather than "superstition" and fostered ambition instead of "ignorance."[22]

Arguments between Catholics and Protestants who supported the Peace Policy did nothing to dispel the clamor of voices against it. Conflicts between soldiers, settlers, and Native people continued in Arizona and the Pacific Northwest. Angry Texans claimed that soldiers were needed because Indians, whom they referred to as the "Quakers' bloody pets," had not stopped raiding their northern settlements.[23] White Southerners expressed outrage that American troops were deployed in their communities rather than on the frontier. As one editorialist argued, "mawkish humanity" privileged a "few hundred worthless savages" over "white security."[24] Soldiers were needed to save American lives in the West, the writer opined, not to patrol Southern capitals.

Against voices clamoring for military action, Protestant and Catholic "friends of the Indian" continued their call for a peaceful approach based on modeling American cultural habits and educating Indian children. Even as they worked in direct competition with each other, they shared an emphasis on schooling. Increasingly, these "friends of the Indian" argued that removing children from their parents provided the best chance for ensuring a transformative environment. Quaker teacher Thomas Battey insisted that day schools were not ideal because Indian children had to be taken away from "home influences" in order to be improved and civilized. Agent Tatum claimed that boarding schools were the preferable means for raising Kiowas from their "degraded position." It was the only way to overcome the power of the "wigwam." The commissioner of Indian Affairs concurred and circulated these ideas through Grant's administration.[25]

According to "friends of the Indian," indigenous parents' "superstition" prompted their hesitation about, if not resistance to, school.[26] This idea promulgated by Protestant "friends of the Indian" influenced policy discussions at the federal level. In his report on the nearly 100,000 still "wild and scarcely tractable" Native people living in the United States in 1874, the commissioner of Indian Affairs declared that education was nearly impossible because "superstition" kept Indian parents from enrolling their children in school.[27]

SACRED POWER IN THE CLOSED LAND

While American officials and "friends of the Indian" bemoaned Kiowas' heathen religion, they also acknowledged how little contact Kiowa people had with Christian evangelists. No missionaries worked among the Kiowa. The Quaker agent could barely keep up with reservation administration, let alone organize Christian worship and education. The two Quaker schoolteachers certainly offered religious lessons as part of their curriculum, but had contact with only a few dozen Kiowa children.

Quaker workers also observed what they perceived as the stubborn persistence of Kiowa ritual practices. During a spell of dry weather, Thomas Battey witnessed Kiowas performing what he called a "Wild Apache Medicine Dance" in order to bring rain to the region. Several months later, the teacher accompanied a Kiowa leader named Fáitàlyì (Sun Boy) to his tipi. Outside it stood a tripod holding his shield. According to Battey, Fáitàlyì told him to take off the shield's cover. The Quaker did so, although he felt nervous handling "those things [the Indians] regard as sacred." Battey found a second cover underneath. It featured a sun with rays of color streaming from it. Below that cover, he found items attached to the shield, a bone whistle and raven feathers. The Quaker teacher touched the small objects, wondering why Fáitàlyì had asked him to do so. He soon got his answer. Fáitàlyì had engaged in an act of discernment and power seeking. He brought Battey before the shield to see if the object's "spirit" would become angry at the Quaker's presence. According to Fáitàlyì, it had not. The shield, therefore, now enveloped Battey with its protective power. Fáitàlyì said the teacher would be safe from bullets and arrows from those who did not trust him.[28]

Kiowas also continued their communal rites of power seeking. The 1873 Sun Dance gathering, which is detailed in the book's opening pages, speaks to this continuity. Kiowas and their allies gathered under the direction of Jòhéjè (Without Moccasins), the recently named *Táimé* keeper. The ceremonials included actions the people had performed for decades: hunting for a bison bull, cutting down a cottonwood tree, building a central lodge, performing an idealized buffalo hunt with costumed people, making offerings to the *Táimé* and other objects, fasting and dancing, and socializing through feasting and visiting. In many respects, the gathering mirrored decades of ritual action.

But details about the 1873 Sun Dance also reveal the Kiowas' difficult situation. To ensure distance from soldiers and safety from attack, they built their ritual encampment 150 miles away from the reservation agency and military post. Because the site offered the possibility for pan-Indian celebration, as well as political deliberation, Kiowas hosted many Indian neighbors at the event. An estimated 500 Comanches attended, as well as many Cheyenne and Arapahos from their neighboring reservation. As noted in the Introduction, Kiowas also hosted an American at their Sun Dance. Thomas Battey attended. During the lengthy gathering, leaders from several Indian nations, as well as Battey, considered how Kiowas might respond to American surveillance, arrests, and imprisonment.

At the Sun Dance, Kiowas also discussed a new reservation agent's recent arrival. Lawrie Tatum had resigned in the spring. The Society of Friends nominated James Haworth, a former Methodist and Civil War veteran turned Quaker, to replace him. Haworth arrived on the reservation with much of the optimism Tatum once evinced. Hoping to build trust with Kiowas and other Indians, he immediately removed the soldiers guarding the ration house. Haworth also gave a speech, telling the Indians he wanted a "peaceable country" with no raiding and stealing. Unlike Tatum, Haworth did not incentivize compliance by threatening to withhold rations. He wrote to federal officials of his hope. Quoting the prophet Isaiah, he claimed the Indians' spears would someday be turned into pruning hooks and "the art of war no longer learned." He envisioned a total transformation, claiming that Indians would someday live in permanent houses and love the "sweet name of Jesus."[29]

Haworth arrived at an opportune moment for rebuilding trust. Federal authorities were planning to release Sétthāidé (White Bear) and Ā dàuiétjè (Big Tree), who had been in a Texas prison for nearly two years. Haworth knew of Kiowas' desire to have their leaders returned. He reported to federal officials that Kiowas had fulfilled the government's demands and wanted, in return, to see their men. When he received news a few weeks later that the release was imminent, Haworth reported Kiowas' joy. Their "hearts were laughing," he said. Haworth's Quaker colleagues shared his view that the prisoners' release would yield positive results. But some of them also pondered the repercussions if the release was for some reason delayed. One leader penned a letter to the commissioner of Indian Affairs stating that the government's failure to release the prisoners after the Kiowas' recent record of compliance would likely cause an "Indian war."[30]

The writer's fears were realized by news of events hundreds of miles away. In early April 1873, Modoc Indians in the Pacific Northwest attacked American commissioners sent to negotiate peace with them.[31] The assault fueled anti-Indian sentiment across the nation. Federal and state officials balked at the prospect of releasing Sétthāidé and Ā dàuiétjè, who were guilty of killing Americans, in such a political climate. Quakers working on the Kiowa reservation responded vigorously. Battey called the decision "unjustifiable" as the "Kiowas had never even heard of the Modocs."[32]

The situation was all the more painful for Kiowas as their Comanche allies were reunited with more than one hundred women and children whom the army had imprisoned the summer before.[33] Quaker teacher Josiah Butler witnessed a "day of rejoicing" as Comanches wept at the sight of their returned relatives.[34] Agent Haworth wrote to his supervisors of the strong affections shown by reunited family members.[35] Drawing parallels to Kiowas who continued to wait for their leaders' release, Haworth noted the Comanches' "anxiety for their kindred" was genuine and needed to be taken seriously. The agent also cautioned that Kiowas would soon be holding their "Medicine Dance," a setting in which political decisions were often made. Time was precious, Haworth wrote. Releasing Sétthāidé and Ā dàuiétjè prior to the ceremonials could have great effect. Waiting too long, he warned, could have devastating consequences.

Haworth was right. At the Sun Dance, Kiowas discussed the possibility of going to war and pushing the Americans out of their lands for good. While they decided against armed resistance for the moment, they signaled their displeasure to Quakers working on the reservation. When the ceremony ended, several Kiowa parents withdrew their children from Battey's school, claiming they would not let students return until the government fulfilled its promise to release their leaders. Kiowas continued to wait over the summer, even as rumors circulated that troops would soon surround them and compel them to surrender their horses and arms. Haworth admitted that Kiowa leaders struggled to keep young men from raiding in the face of these rumors, especially in the midst of a crop-killing drought and periods of delayed ration deliveries. Kiowas also balked as surveyors, accompanied by soldiers, entered the reservation to complete a government study. Haworth struggled to explain the survey's purpose and implored federal officials to postpone it. With the hope of improving relations, he invited Kiowas and their allies to council in October. But some said they would not come. The council, they claimed, was a trap designed so that soldiers could take away their resources and leave them, as one Comanche chief put it, "sitting like poor dogs on the prairie." In response to these ongoing frustrations, a few Comanche young men began raiding into Texas.[36]

STRUGGLE IN THE CLOSED LAND

Kiowas, however, did not join them. They stayed on the reservation in anticipation of the leaders' return, which finally occurred in early September. A few weeks later, they attended a council to negotiate the terms of Sétthą́idé (Sitting Bear) and Ā́dàuiétjè's (Big Tree) release. Haworth and other Quaker officials organized the meeting. Officials from Washington, D.C., and Texas also attended. The Texas governor wanted to impose several restrictions, including the distribution of only one day's worth of rations at a time and Sétthą́idé and Ā́dàuiétjè's ongoing detention at Fort Sill. Even Kiowas who had good relations with the Americans, namely Thę̀néàungópjè (Kicking Bird), were let down when federal officials failed to challenge the Texans. Leaders who had always been skeptical of the Americans, especially Cûifä́gàui (Lone Wolf the Elder), felt further alienated and claimed there was nothing left but war. "I know that war with Washington means the extinction of my people," he claimed, "but we are driven to it: we had rather die than live." Haworth scrambled to save the proceedings. Although Texas officials eventually softened their terms, Kiowas emerged from the council facing a daily accounting to ensure their presence on the reservation. Failure to appear would lead to Sétthą́idé and Ā́dàuiétjè's rearrest and imprisonment.[37]

The officials' tough approach reflected shifts in the federal Indian office.[38] Administrators evidenced a growing impatience with how the Peace Policy addressed "hostile" Indians such as the Kiowa. In his 1873 report, the commissioner broke with the custom of proclaiming full support for Grant's policy and said, instead, he would "access" it.[39] He also noted his desire to encourage the allotment of lands and to change the format for annuity payments, actions that would constitute treaty violations, he admitted. But these changes were necessary, the commissioner reasoned, because they would instill notions of work and individual property rights among Indian people. Quakers objected to federal officials' changing approach, reiterating that they—as opposed to the military and its federal supporters—were true "friends of the Indian." Battey wrote to his family that his work would be easier if there were no soldiers at all. Employing rhetoric from the Peace Policy's early days, he declared that Americans had committed countless offenses against the Indians and that the Christian God surely kept a "record" of them.[40]

The increasingly tough American approach paralleled the harsh conditions on the southern plains that fall and winter. Rations did not arrive on time. Buffalo were increasingly scarce as American hunters illegally poached on reservation lands. Government officials refused to stop them, believing the herds' decline would force Indians to farm.[41] Native people across the region took to killing and eating their ponies to avoid starvation. Sickness spread among vulnerable children. In the camp Battey accompanied, an infant died and relatives wailed and cut their arms in mourning.[42]

Meanwhile, more Comanches raided into Texas and the commissioner of Indian Affairs threatened to turn the entire Comanche nation over to military supervision unless they surrendered the guilty men.[43] This threat put Indians on the reservation, as well as off, in danger. Agent Haworth worried that Comanches would not be able to turn in the raiders by the deadline and would, instead, prepare to defend themselves against an American assault. In an effort to forestall an armed conflict, Haworth wrote a lengthy letter to the secretary of the Interior detailing American offenses against the Comanches. He argued that they far outweighed those committed by a few Indian raiders.[44] He also worked to keep frustrated Kiowas from joining Comanches on the brink of war. He sent Thomas Battey out to the camps to discuss the government's ultimatum and to solicit Kiowa responses.[45]

Cûifǎgàui, who had considered war inevitable after the fall council, sent his reply. In it, he made clear that the army had no right to patrol reservation lands. If soldiers killed young Indian men while raiding in Texas, Cûifǎgàui said, then so be it. But the "father at Washington" had signed treaties making the reservation a place for Kiowas to live and hunt buffalo. Soldiers had no place in their "country of peace." Thẹ̀néàungópjè also replied. He, too, emphasized that reservation lands stretching from the Arkansas to the Red Rivers were set aside for Indian people. Troops had no authority to enter their lands. The government had no right to dispatch surveyors to make lines in it. Both leaders, then, argued that Americans had no right by treaty to come into their lands, divide it into segments, or arrest Indian people abiding there.[46]

While Cûifǎgàui and Thẹ̀néàungópjè supported their claims by referencing treaties, they ended their speeches with allusions to sacred power. Cûifǎgàui told the Americans of another Kiowa leader who had been severely ill. He had joined other powerful men to make "medicine" and heal him. Now the man was strong and hunting buffalo. Cûifǎgàui implied that he had the power to renew and strengthen things that appeared weak. Thẹ̀néàungópjè went even further. Considering the commissioner's threat, he ventured that even the strong "white man" could not kill all the Indians in one year. It would take at least two and perhaps four. And if Americans managed to kill them all, an apocalypse would ensue. "Then the world will turn to water or burn up," he said. "[The world] can't live when the Indians are all dead."[47]

Cûifágàui's words about young men off the reservation being killed soon came to pass. One of his sons joined a raiding party into Coahuila, Mexico. Nine Kiowa men were killed, including Cûifágàui's son and nephew. Calendar entries for this winter note their deaths. In his grief at losing a second son in just a few years, Cûifágàui withdrew from his conversations with the Americans.[48]

The Quakers tried to address the Indians' myriad concerns—delayed rations, surveyors, and disastrous raids—by calling a council for Indians across the southern plains. The situation seemed grim as Quaker agents provided only half-rations due to delayed American deliveries. Surveying continued. Several leaders from the Society's Indian committee in Philadelphia traveled to the reservation. One opened the council, reminding his listeners that Quakers were "true friends of the Indian." Another leader followed with words about settler mistreatment of Native people, as well as a rejoinder that Indians had often responded poorly to these offenses. He mentioned rumors that officials in Washington wanted to replace Quaker agents with soldiers. "Instead of your good agent and his friends . . . with his schools for the instruction of your children; with his mill, and ploughs, and wagons," he said, "you will be turned over to the soldiers, with their swords, guns, and drums." Whenever soldiers are in charge, he continued, we know that the Indians are sooner or later "harassed and destroyed." He called on Indians to let the "Great Spirit" change their hearts and stop doing displeasing things. Other Quaker speakers were more specific. One stepped to the front and begged the Indians to stop raiding as a response to settler misdeeds.[49] As historians have noted, American perceptions of raiding reflected ideas about innate Indian violence, rather than an understanding of the practice's role in a colonial borderlands economy.[50] The Indians replied that they raided far less then they once had. They also claimed that terrible conditions made it difficult to keep young men from going out to secure resources. The Quakers, while feeling that they had done their best to communicate their friendship, acknowledged the difficulties Indians faced.

While many Indians on the reservation attended the Quakers' council, Kiowas stayed away. When some finally arrived a few days later, they were without Cûifágàui, who was still in mourning. After lengthy discussions, thirty leading men agreed to be "friendly" and to try to keep raiding at bay.[51] In return, they asked the government to grant Cûifágàui permission to retrieve his son and nephew's bodies. The Quakers took up the request in earnest. One committee member insisted that Cûifágàui's request was no "transient caprice," but an "immemorial custom" the Americans should honor. Another wrote to the commissioner of Indian Affairs, proposing a military escort for a small number of Kiowas to retrieve the young men's bones. The Quakers urged a quick answer as Kiowas were waiting, rations were slow, and warm weather would soon open what had traditionally been raiding season. While the Friends tried to persuade themselves and officials that Kiowas intended peace, at least some of them admitted that they could not be sure. In a letter to his family, Battey referred to his effort to discern their future actions, which could not be known before Kiowas decided it themselves at their "Great Medicine Dance."[52]

WAR IN THE INDIAN COUNTRY

While Kiowas waited, their Comanche allies did not. In early May, Agent Haworth received news that Comanches would soon hold their own "medicine dance." A "new medicine man" had emerged among them. The young man, Isatai (Coyote Droppings), was a reputable warrior and had recently lost a relative during a raid. He also had a record of accessing and displaying *puha*, the Comanche word for sacred power. A year earlier, he had predicted a comet's path and a blizzard's arrival. But in the spring of 1874, he made new claims. He announced that he could rectify the imbalance of power between Indians and Americans by rendering fighters bulletproof, raising people from the dead, and producing an endless supply of ammunition from his stomach. Haworth's Comanche informant said that the upcoming dance would likely result in an attack on the reservation's headquarters and fort. Haworth knew that most Comanches were hesitant to make war on the Americans, but he wondered what impact the new ritual leader and his group of followers might have. He hoped that a resupply of rations would calm the potential storm.[53]

News about the Comanches' powerful new leader spread to the Kiowas. They told Thomas Battey about the powerful acts he was said to perform, as well the origins of his power.[54] Isatai, they said, had ascended into the sky, where he conversed with the "Great Spirit." Some Comanches had seen him rise into the air. His power was substantial and his followers maintained that "in no respect is [Isatai] inferior to the Great Spirit." Filled with this power, Isatai told Comanches that he could provide all the ammunition needed for a war against the Americans. He claimed to have "medicine" that would make them invulnerable to American assault. Some Comanches, as well as neighboring Cheyennes, agreed to follow him into war. They planned to start with their Indian enemies, the Tonkawas, who had killed so many buffalo in the area that Comanches and other Indians were left with little food.[55]

Kiowas, however, hesitated to join them and concentrated on their own affairs. They needed rations and pledged to keep the peace in order to get them. One Kiowa, however, could no longer abide by American rules. Cûifâgàui (Lone Wolf the Elder) could not leave his son's body unattended. Without permission, he left the reservation and told his friends to let Agent Haworth know what he had done. "It [is] the Kiowa road to get their dead and bury them." Upon finding his son's body, Cûifâgàui is said to have kneeled beside it and vowed to avenge his death by killing a white man. He came back in early June, just as the Comanche's "medicine dance" ended. With Cûifâgàui's return, Kiowas planned to hold their Sun Dance. Leading men told Haworth about the upcoming ceremonial. The agent trusted that Kiowas intended to keep the peace, insisting in his letters to Quaker officials that they would make "good medicine." In contrast to his understanding of Isatai's dance among the Comanches, Haworth reasoned that the Kiowa ceremonials would confirm their status as "friendly" Indians. He hoped their "good medicine" might convince other Indian nations to scrap their plans for war.[56]

Jòhéjè (Without Moccasins), the *Táimé* keeper, called for a Sun Dance shortly after Cûifágàui's return. The people traveled toward a fork of the Red River to build their encampment. But not all arrived or stayed. Some Kiowa men joined a group of several hundred Comanche, Cheyenne, and Arapaho warriors. They smoked, performed ritual preparations, and listened to speeches. They painted themselves and took up their warbonnets and shields. The next day they attacked an outpost of American buffalo hunters at Adobe Walls in the Texas Panhandle. One man, likely Isatai, was seen painted yellow and watching from afar as the Indians attacked. The battle stretched over several hours. When a Comanche leader suffered a gunshot wound, some fighters questioned Isatai's power. Others wondered if someone had broken a taboo and sabotaged their effort. The battle ended in a draw. After a long standoff, the Americans abandoned the outpost. The Indians burned it down and headed back toward the reservation.[57]

The Kiowa fighters returned to the Sun Dance encampment in the midst of ritual practice as well as discussions about going to war against the Americans.[58] Some Comanches and Cheyennes joined them. Kiowas listened to the fighters' claims that American demands must be resisted. Many, however, chose to go into the reservation agency after the Sun Dance, declaring themselves peaceful with the hope that their people might survive.[59] While it was no surprise that some leaders, such as Thènéàungópjè (Kicking Bird), decided to report to the agency, some Kiowa men who had once been warriors also planned to join them. Séttháidé (White Bear), who had long fought the Americans and served time in prison, decided not to fight. As men gathered for a meeting and dance, he appeared with his *zebat*, or medicine lance, as well as his "no-retreat" sash. While men danced around him, Séttháidé gave these powerful items away, the former to a distant relative and the latter to his beloved son, Ôlpàu (Bison Bird). After the dance, Séttháidé went to Fort Sill and registered as friendly, or "neutral."[60]

But Séttháidé's gift of powerful objects for warfare signaled that even some Kiowas who registered as neutral had sympathy for those preparing to fight. After receiving these powerful objects, the two young men were also given "medicine bags" to tie to their scalp locks. Older men helped them apply red paint to their bodies. They fasted and danced until the Sun Dance ended. Then they left on a war party.[61] They were among the men who supported Cûifágàui's call to battle. Cûifágàui's contingent, guided by Cáumâmájè's (Goose Flying Overhead) dreams and directions, joined the pan-Indian fighters. As with his earlier activity among Kiowas, Cáumâmájè promised to protect fighters and predict battle outcomes. Again, men painted their bodies, as well as their horses. They took up their warbonnets and shields. They joined the Comanches, whose ritual specialists also encouraged the fighters. As one Comanche reported to Thomas Battey, Isatai "made medicine so strong" that white soldiers' bullets could not harm them.[62]

Not long after the Sun Dance, Quaker leaders met in Kansas. They discussed the possibility of war and bemoaned Kiowa "religion." As they considered the many obstacles to Indian civilization, members mentioned "superstition or unenlightened religiousness." According to one speaker, Native people struggled to see the "infinite love of the Great Spirit through Jesus Christ." In their blindness, he claimed, Indians affirmed "dreams as prophecies" and "meaningless forms" in worship. According to the Quakers, Isatai's "medicine" and Cáumâmâjè's dreams kept Kiowas and Comanches at odds with those who could help them.[63]

Quakers serving in Indian Country tried to encourage Kiowas to avoid confrontation with the military by coming into the reservation headquarters. Agent Haworth wrote to his supervisor that he considered most Kiowas to be "friendly." Only a few leading men had joined the belligerents. But even dealing with "friendlies" proved challenging for Quaker agents. Officials from Fort Sill placed Indians in what amounted to house arrest. Haworth, who was trying to convince Indians to come in, worried about his role, especially after his supervisors advised him to help prosecute Native people off the reservation. By the end of July, the Americans announced their plans to make war on any southern plains Indians outside reservations boundaries after August 3. Five cavalry columns spread across the region. Their aim was to force the final surrender of all "hostile" Indians.[64]

In an effort to delineate friendlies and hostiles, Americans called for an Indian census on the KCA Reservation. According to Haworth, many Kiowas expressed fear they would be killed after adding their names to the census list. Their concern grew when soldiers arrived to assist the process. Kiowa leaders told Haworth that their people would rather forgo rations and leave the reservation's relative safety rather than be enrolled. Army officials were undeterred. On August 9, they announced that the census was finished. No more Indians could come in unless Agent Haworth dismounted, disarmed, and received them as "prisoners of war." American officials also insisted that Quakers could no longer council with Indians. This was no time for "peace promises," the official wrote. This was a time for "serious war talk."[65]

Hoping to avoid war, members of the Society of Friends' Indian committee debated whether removing Kiowas from the plains might provide a better solution. They looked to the lands occupied by more "civilized" tribes to the east. Meeting minutes and letters exchanged by committee members show that they agreed about the benefits of moving Kiowas away from the buffalo herds. They disagreed, however, about how to do it. Some insisted that removal must be voluntary.[66] Others considered methods for relocating Kiowas who refused to move. Some argued that Kiowas were "subdued" enough that even those who refused could be managed by the government in order to affect change.[67] Others pressed further, claiming that force could be used given the benefits that a move offered and the likelihood of war if the Kiowas stayed on their lands.[68]

Quakers working on the nearby Cheyenne and Arapaho Reservation also found themselves in a difficult situation. The agent, John D. Miles, proved unsuccessful in convincing Indians from heading out to fight on the plains. Like Lawrie Tatum after the 1871 wagon train attack, Miles called on troops for support. Society leaders rebuked Miles for his response and called for his resignation. Miles refused to comply, arguing that he would be guilty of "criminal negligence" if he did not try to stop the killing of innocent settlers. When troops headed out to force an Indian surrender, Miles accompanied them.[69]

In late August, violence erupted at the nearby reservation headquarters for Wichita Indians. As with other historical incidents of Indian–American violence, there is little clarity about what started the battle. Some Comanches had come into the reservation to surrender. While American soldiers disarmed them, a cry was heard. Some thought one man was calling out to another. Others heard a "war whoop." Americans fired. Comanches fired back. Runners scattered to tell other nearby Indians. Some Kiowas, including Cûifãgàui and his band, arrived to join the ongoing battle. Before the day ended, Kiowas and Comanches burned down the reservation school, storehouse, and some permanent homes. Worried about the army's reaction, many fled onto the plains. Years later, Kiowas recalled the frantic nature of this period as they camped in new places every night and soldiers came at them from many directions. Some remembered wandering the plains, finding no buffalo, and experiencing terrible hunger. As Kiowas scrambled to stay ahead of the cavalry, Zépcàuiétjè (Big Bow) suggested they head for the Texas Panhandle and camp in Palo Duro Canyon. Cạumâmâjè used his power to speak to owls and received a message that soldiers would not find them in the canyon's steep recesses.[70]

But Cạumâmâjè was wrong. On September 28, American troops made a surprise early morning attack on Kiowas, Comanches, and Cheyennes camped at Palo Duro. At the sound of gunfire, Indians scrambled from their tipis. Women and children ran for cover near the canyon walls. Men grabbed their guns and tried to protect their fleeing relatives. No match for the Americans' firepower, Kiowas and other Indians fled the canyon. After securing the encampment, the soldiers burned more than 200 lodges and destroyed more than a thousand horses and mules. Coming into winter, Kiowas now lacked crucial supplies. Without shelter or resources, many made their way to the reservation to surrender.[71]

The losses at Palo Duro were many. Cạumâmâjè's prediction had failed.[72] Many Kiowas surrendered. Those still on the plains had few supplies and scattered in the hope of evading soldiers. But Kiowas also remembered ways that protective powers had worked on their behalf, even on a day of loss. Descendants of Páutáuljè (Lean Bison Bull) tell of his bravery as he tried to protect his wives and children from American bullets.[73] He sang his warrior society song as he held off soldiers and his family ran to safety. Others tell of a Kiowa man calling on powerful beings to aid their escape. He told the people to listen for an owl who would lead them safely out of the canyon. Survivors recalled hearing the bird's voice as they escaped. Even at a time of despair, some powers, it seemed, continued to protect them.

TORN FROM THE LAND

The battles that came to be known as the Red River War crushed Kiowa armed resistance to American occupation. It also presented Americans with a stark choice concerning the nation's Indian policy. As one prominent Quaker wrote, buffalo hunters, cattle thieves, and whiskey peddlers caused problems when they refused to respect Indians as well as reservation boundaries.[74] Native people had been driven to war by white aggression. Counter voices sounded loud in the American press. The *New York Times* ran headlines about Kiowa and Comanche "treachery." A civilian scout serving among the American forces offered his assessment in print as well. His newspaper columns identified Indian fighters as "redskins" and "savages." While emphasizing Native peoples' capacity for cruelty, the scout also detailed American actions after battles, noting dead Indians' heads on gateposts at Adobe Walls. The writer also claimed that Indian "religion" played a part in the armed resistance. They make lodges, he wrote, to "hold their councils, make medicine, have war dances, and gloat over the number of white men they have murdered."[75]

If many Americans read accounts that emphasized Indians' propensity for violence, Kiowas and their allies found that their capacity for armed resistance had faded by the end of 1874. In early October, American troops attacked another Indian encampment and burned hundreds of lodges. After the New Year, military officials requested assistance from detained Kiowas. They called on them to convince the last few hundred Indians to surrender. Zépcàuiétjè (Big Bow) agreed and persuaded several leaders and their bands to come in. When the Indians arrived at Fort Sill, soldiers put them in irons. As spring approached, only a few Native people remained free on the southern plains. American officials decided that at least some of the fighters required punishment and incarceration. They turned to Indian leaders to create lists of men to send to a military prison.

Thẹ̀néàungópjè (Kicking Bird) created the list of Kiowa prisoners.[76] And while Kiowas played a smaller role in the Red River War than their Cheyenne and Comanche allies, military officers sought out the most prisoners from among them. In all, seventy-two southern plains warriors were sent to Fort Marion, a Florida military prison. Twenty-seven were Kiowa. Thẹ̀néàungópjè's list included some, like Cûifàgàui (Lone Wolf the Elder) and Cạumâmájè (Goose Flying Overhead), who played leading roles in the fighting. But most of the prisoners were young men who had participated in the war, but were hardly leaders or men of prominence. In late April, American soldiers placed the shackled men in wagons to begin their journey to prison (Figure 4.2). Oheltoint (Charlie Buffalo), a young warrior, remembered the experience vividly. Kiowa women wailed and made war cries. One Comanche woman, along with her young child, jumped into the transport wagon beside her husband and refused to get out. Cûifàgàui's daughter also tried to climb in, saying she would rather die than see her father leave. As the wagons pulled away, the women followed. Oheltoint heard his mother crying. "We feel so bad," he remembered, "jus' sittin' there in chains."[77]

FIGURE 4.2. Zótâm's drawing of Plains Indian prisoners of war rounded up before their transfer to a military prison in Florida. The men, still wear Native clothing, are shown in great detail. Behind them stands Fort Sill, marked by an American flag and a chapel with a cross.

Credit: Dickinson Research Center, National Cowboy & Western Heritage Museum, Oklahoma City, Oklahoma

Thềnéàungópjè approached the departing wagons, reminding the prisoners that he had told them not to fight and now they must accept their punishment.[78] Cầumâmȃjè, whose power from owls had prevailed in some battles and disappointed in others, looked back at Thềnéàungópjè. "You must die for this deed," Cầumâmȃjè said to him. "You see me in chains, in this wagon—look good—at us all, for it is your last time to see us before you die." That evening, Oheltoint and the other prisoners overheard Cầumâmȃjè talking to an owl. The next morning, an army officer told them that Thềnéàungópjè was dead. Cầumâmȃjè admitted that he must forfeit his life for using his power to harm a fellow Kiowa. A few days later, he gathered his fellow prisoners around him and told them he was going to sleep. He never woke up.[79]

In 1867, Kiowa men had hunted and raided across lands that stretched from current-day Colorado and Kansas all the way to central Mexico. By the spring of 1875, some were confined in prison, while their relatives and friends lived under soldiers' watch on the reservation. They had struggled against many of the changes that federal officials and "friends of the Indian" had tried to introduce. Ritual power seeking, including new leaders claiming powers related to war, played a part in this struggle. But the Red River War marked the end of Kiowa armed resistance. In the conflict's aftermath, the people lived within the reservation's confines and turned their attention toward maintaining their communal ties and threatened lands.

Protestant "friends of the Indian" were also changed by Kiowa resistance to civilizing programs enacted on reservations—Quakers especially so. They confronted internal divisions about the meaning of their peace testimony.[80] They argued about their representatives in Indian Country, including reservation agent John Miles, who accompanied military forces as they went out to arrest Indians. Despite these internal struggles, the Society presented itself as the Peace Policy's truest representatives. They positioned themselves and their Protestant allies as "friends of the Indian," in contrast to military leaders and War Department officials. But this position became more difficult to maintain as conflicts between Indians, settlers, and soldiers continued. Soon enough, the Peace Policy fell out of favor. Not long after troops withdrew from the American South, they came in great numbers to the plains to subdue populations who had not yet yielded.

If these years marked America's "era of Citizenship," the story from Indian Country provides another angle on the ways in which both race and religion figured in the formation of national belonging. As scholars of Reconstruction and its aftermath have shown, re-establishing unity among white Americans came at the cost of black equality.[81] Overcoming sectional division involved depicting African Americans as unable to meet— if not biologically incompatible with—the demands of democratic citizenship. Many Americans, including supporters of the Peace Policy, also deemed Indians unworthy of such inclusion. Crucially, they saw this as a temporary incapacity. Kiowas and other Native peoples simply needed to progress along the spectrum of civilizational development. In this way, "friends of the Indian" imagined Native people's destiny in ways similar to a few of the Protestant evangelists working among Chinese immigrants laboring in the western gold fields and railroad lines.[82] Racial otherness did not figure as insurmountable. It was culture, including "heathen religion," that blocked Indians' progress toward civilization. As a result, many Americans assumed that inclusion in the body politic required Native people to throw off their cultural and religious practices. Citizenship lay before them if they relinquished what tied them to each other.

Protestant "friends of the Indian" assumed that the offer of individual land and wealth might finally prompt Native people to make this choice. Kiowas, however, already faced the disheartening situation of living on bounded lands and enduring separation from their relatives in prison. They were not about break down the bonds they had left. In the coming years, they found new ways of engaging sacred power to help them stay together.

5

1875 to 1881

SITTING IN A military prison, Zótâm (Driftwood) picked up a pencil and drew images of his exile from Indian Country. One of his drawing books features Native prisoners of war crammed together at Fort Sill, the military post on the Kiowa reservation. The pages show army officers selecting men for transport and scenes from the eight-day wagon trip over the plains to a train station. Zótâm drew the bridge he crossed by rail in Saint Louis, the curious onlookers who gathered when their train stopped in Indianapolis, and the boat that took him to his final destination of Fort Marion, an old Spanish fort converted into an Indian prison.[1]

His fellow prisoners also drew the trains, boats, and wagons that carried them on their journey, but Zótâm's work referenced some of the trip's more frightening episodes.[2] Native people on the southern plains had no practice of incarcerating prisoners of war. The Indian fighters rounded up at Fort Sill had no idea where their American captors might take them. They did not know if they would live or die. Zótâm's notebook depicts their responses to the confusing journey to Florida. Near Nashville, a desperate prisoner stabbed two guards and then turned the knife on himself. Outside Macon, another tried to escape by jumping out a train window. Zótâm sketched the guards chasing the man and shooting him down. Zótâm also rendered the Indian prisoners newly arrived at Fort Marion (Figure 5.1). Still wearing colorful blankets and sporting long hair, the inmates stood on the parapet awaiting an unknown future.[3]

The Red River War's cessation in the spring of 1875 marked the end of Kiowa efforts to expel American invaders. It also prompted an unprecedented rupture among the people. As Kiowas and other southern plains Indians surrendered, hundreds were taken into custody. Seventy-two Indian men—twenty-seven of them Kiowa—were selected for exile and imprisonment. As American soldiers loaded the shackled men into wagons for transport, one officer observed that Kiowa mothers, wives, and daughters wailed with grief. They, too, had no idea where their kin were going or if they would ever return.

The prisoners' exile was hardly the only crisis Kiowas experienced after the war. American officials on the reservation, many of them from Christian groups participating in President Grant's Peace Policy, initiated plans to change nearly everything about the Kiowa way of life. These self-described "friends of the Indian" tried to end nomadic living by settling the people around fields for crop cultivation. They worked to retrain young people and disrupt family relations by expanding schools for Kiowa children. They also scrutinized and tightly regulated Kiowa communal practices, including buffalo hunting and Sun Dances. Their goal was Indian assimilation into national life through the adoption of Anglo-American cultural practices, especially productive labor. While "friends of the Indian" worked toward these goals on dozens of reservations, they also began to register their displeasure with these particular spaces. Indians living within them were not changing fast enough.

Kiowas responded to American efforts to promote and enforce their assimilation. They continued to see themselves as a distinct people tied to a particular place. They performed many of the rituals that had long reinforced their connections to place and each other. They also engaged new ritual options coming from within their community, from other Indian nations, and from the Americans. Throughout these years, Kiowas

FIGURE 5.1. Zótâm's rendering of Plains Indian prisoners standing on the parapet just after their arrival at Fort Marion. Soldiers watch them and cannons point toward them.

Credit: Dickinson Research Center, National Cowboy & Western Heritage Museum, Oklahoma City, Oklahoma

dealt with ruptures and challenges in multiple ways. Sometimes they took on cultural practices promoted by Americans. But when Americans required changes that threatened their connection to lands and people—and especially if these changes violated treaties—Kiowas resisted.

American efforts to promote Indian assimilation, as well as Kiowa responses to those pressures, occurred within the wider context of Reconstruction and post-Reconstruction debates about religious and racial difference.[4] As one historian has observed, Reconstruction was a "multiracial and multiregional process of national reimagining."[5] In the decades after the Civil War, American efforts to change Kiowa ways of living had connections to, but also differences from, modes by which white Protestant Americans adjudicated their relationships to a variety of marginalized populations. The Kiowa case was not unique insofar as Protestants were key players in debates about Native people's destiny, but it uniquely shows how their rhetoric obscured the coercion and violence that fueled assimilation programs and the dispossession of Indian lands.

CIVILIZING THE INDIAN COUNTRY

On the Kiowa, Comanche, and Apache (KCA) Reservation, American officials and Protestant "friends of the Indian" with whom they partnered tried to change nearly every aspect Kiowa life. Crucially, they focused on land. As noted in the previous chapter, Quakers had sought to relocate Kiowas from their reservation in the western part of the territory to the eastern side, more than 150 miles away. They advocated this dramatic and costly plan because it would remove Kiowas from the buffalo herds, as well as the Texas Panhandle settlements they sometimes raided. They argued that the move would hasten the transition to economic self-sufficiency as the eastern side of the Indian Territory also boasted better farmland. Throughout 1874, the plan had found backers in the Indian Office, as well as Congress. But the Red River War caused potential allies to balk, and resettlement prospects died by 1875.[6]

Despite this defeat, Quakers and federal officials considered moves on a smaller scale. At the very least, they wanted to keep Kiowas away from Fort Sill and its soldiers who drank and exhibited other vices. They proposed a move to centralize Kiowas around Mount Scott, where the people could be settled in houses around fields for cultivation.[7] Quakers hoped that farming would decrease reliance on hunting. As one official stated in his report to the Friends Indian committee, ample buffalo guaranteed that Kiowas "will be roving Indians, whom no appliances of Christian civilization can effectively reach."[8]

Concerns about buffalo hunting prompted Agent Haworth, the Quaker serving at the KCA Reservation since 1873, to increase restrictions on the practice after the war ended. He required troops from Fort Sill to accompany Kiowas on longer buffalo hunting expeditions. He ordered Indians to stay within reservation boundaries on these outings. Haworth sometimes prohibited hunting altogether.[9] Kiowa calendars noted these changes to traditional practices. Keepers recalled one of the last authorized buffalo expeditions in the winter of 1876–1877.[10]

Restrictions on hunting meant that Kiowas relied heavily on government rations to sustain their diet. Agent Haworth noted numerous occasions when Kiowas complained that rations simply did not provide adequate nutrition without the protein supplemented by hunting. He later informed the federal Indian office that Kiowas suffered significantly from hunger and malnutrition. Government officials could not be swayed. They sought progress toward assimilation and argued that more rations discouraged Indians from making the transition to self-sufficient farming.[11]

Federal officials and their Quaker partners also discouraged Kiowa ritual practices. After the war ended, Agent Haworth required soldiers to monitor the Sun Dance. Some calendar entries for the summer of 1875 feature uniformed men, likely American soldiers, near the medicine lodge pole.[12] Surveillance continued in the coming years. Officials paired the oversight of Kiowa rituals with encouragement to participate in new Christian activities. By the fall of 1875, Agent Haworth reported that the agency doctor hosted weekly religious meetings.[13] By the spring of 1877, the gospel seemed to be moving forward as Indian children attended religious meetings some Sunday mornings.[14] In the afternoons, Agent Haworth spoke at Indian camps. He mentioned that well over 100 Indians attended a recent Sunday afternoon session. According to the agent, some of the Indians felt the presence of Jesus.

Even as Haworth celebrated what he considered to be evidence of assimilation, he worried about ongoing challenges. Quakers had worked among Kiowas since 1869, but the reservation had no organized church or permanent missionary. Further, competitors moved closer to Kiowa country. In 1876, American Catholic bishops appointed a prefect for Indian Territory. A year later, Benedictines established a mission among the Potawatomi on the territory's eastern side. These Catholic missionaries, mostly from France and Belgium, traveled west to identify potential mission and school sites among several Plains Indian nations, including the Kiowa. The Catholics were coming.[15]

So were the Mormons. If Haworth and other Protestant proponents of the Peace Policy harbored concerns about Catholics, they felt outright disdain for the Mormons. Their fear of Mormons was realized in the fall of 1877, when three men claiming to be from the Latter-day Saints' headquarters in Salt Lake City arrived at the reservation headquarters. Haworth's panicked assistant shot off a letter to federal officials after denying the missionaries access to Indian camps. "In view of the very great difference in the doctrine and practices of the Mormon Church, together with the attitude that it has always held in relations to government," the assistant decided to bar their entry.[16] His hesitancy mirrored the government's. The Indian office consistently denied Mormon requests to administer reservations through the Peace Policy. Mormons' theological difference and stormy relations with Washington resulted in their estrangement from privileges open to other Christian groups.[17]

Haworth approved his assistant's actions. He wrote to his Quaker supervisor that he harbored suspicions that the Mormon missionaries had come not to evangelize Kiowas, but to gain Indian "allies" for an impending "rupture between their Church and the Authorities." The supervisor forwarded the warnings to the government, amplifying Haworth's claim that regulating missions was necessary to forestall "an alliance of these South Western Indians with the Mormon Church." This suspicion reflected American concerns about possible Mormon-Indian co-conspiracy dating back to the 1840s.[18]

Establishing "true religion" on the reservations became important to Quakers and other Protestant "friends of the Indian," not only to bring Native people to the proper faith, but also to keep undesirable competitors at bay. With only a small church led by laymen, reservation officials hoped that schools would introduce Kiowas to Christianity. But as noted in previous chapters, getting Kiowas to enroll their children was no small task. They had shown little interest in the government school near the reservation's head-quarters at Fort Sill or Thomas Battey's lessons at Thèné àungópjè's (Kicking Bird) camp. But after the war ended, Quakers noticed increasing Kiowa interest in school enrollment. To them, growing attendance signaled Kiowas' willingness to assimilate.

To the Friends' surprise, school enrollment surged after the war. As the conflict ended, only twenty Kiowa children attended school.[19] Two years later, Haworth claimed, "Kiowas [were] well represented" in the school population.[20] Schools seemed to be working at last. Students learned rudimentary English, along with manual and domestic skills. And teachers could introduce Kiowas to Protestant Christianity.

Finally feeling successful, Haworth summarized the vision he shared with many Protestant "friends of the Indian." He planned to resettle Kiowas in permanent houses near fields for farming. He advocated school attendance. He restricted practices, including buffalo hunting and Sun Dancing, which worked against his goals. Further, Haworth and other Protestant reformers modeled Anglo-American civilizational practices with the hope of persuading Native people about the benefits of assimilation. Kiowas, it seemed, finally responded. In his 1877 report, Haworth claimed that many Indians "evinced a willingness to cast aside many of the customs which characterize the wild Indian, and assume in their stead those of the white man."[21]

Haworth's emphasis on persuasion and modeling obscured the coercive methods that Quakers and other "friends of the Indian" sometimes employed. As noted in the previous chapter, Society leaders debated whether "forcible removal" was an ethical way to relo-cate Kiowas to the other side of Indian Territory. They continued to consider the possi-bility of using coercion, even as most of their reports emphasized Indian willingness to adopt new cultural practices. At the end of Haworth's glowing 1877 report, he added one last recommendation. Some parents still kept their children from school, he admitted. He recommended that federal officials *require* all Indian children to attend school, re-gardless of their parents' wishes.[22]

PLATE 1. Gùhâudè's (Stripping Off of a Rib Cage) drawing of a crier bringing news about an upcoming Sun Dance. Gùhâudè was known by Americans as Wohaw.

Credit: Missouri History Museum, St. Louis, image no. 1882-018-0030

PLATE 2. Gùhâudè's rendition of a Sun Dance lodge, *Tą́imé* keeper, *Tą́imé*, and natural elements such as the crescent moon, morning star, and thunderbirds. Note the line, signifying sacred power, connecting the thunderbird and *Tą́imé*.

Credit: Missouri History Museum, St. Louis, image no. 1882-018-0046

PLATE 3. Replica of Páuthòcáui's (White-Faced Bison Bull) painted shield, featuring animal hair, feathers, and yarn.

Credit: Department of Anthropology, American Museum of Natural History, catalog no. E229892

PLATE 4. George Catlin's *The Last Race, Mandan O-kee-pa Ceremony*, in which he depicted his understanding of a Mandan ceremony similar to the Kiowa Sun Dance.

Credit: Smithsonian American Art Museum, Gift of Mrs. Joseph Harrison, Jr.

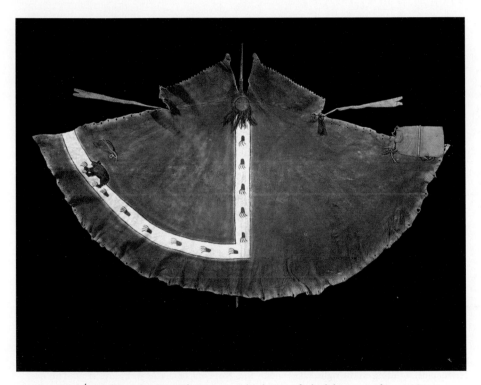

PLATE 5. Sétbấujè's (Bear Bringing It) tipi cover, the design of which he received in a vision.

Credit: Department of Anthropology, National Museum of Natural History, image no. 245023

PLATE 6. Hầugû's (Silver Horn) rendering of Sétjáuáuidè's (Many Bears) battle with Utes. Sétjáuáuidè, standing on the right, takes enemy fire. Note one of the *Tậimé* figures around his neck. He also wore war paint and carried a painted shield into the ultimately unsuccessful fight.

Credit: Museum of Fine Arts, Boston

PLATE 7. Gùhâudè's image of leading Kiowa men in front of an arbor with painted tipis and feathered lances. Note the detail in the men's dress and headwear.

Credit: George W. Fox Collection of American Indian Ledger Drawings and Photographs, Yale Collection of Western Americana, Beinecke Rare Book and Manuscript Library, Yale University

PLATE 8. Bad Eye's drawing of his wife carrying their child's hand-decorated cradleboard.
Credit: Fairbanks Museum & Planetarium

STRUGGLE IN THE CLOSED LANDS

Haworth and others interpreted Kiowa school enrollment as one of several signs that Indians on the southern plains were headlong into a process of assimilation. Kiowa decisions about education, however, must be read in light of the devastating ruptures and losses they experienced after the war. With a portion of their men exiled and perhaps never to return, as well as facing pressure to enroll their children in school, Kiowas recognized Americans' willingness to break apart their communal bonds. In the years after the war, Kiowas acted in a variety of ways to maintain land connections, family ties, and ritual practices in the face of these pressures.

To be sure, the most dramatic rupture in this period was the exile and imprisonment of twenty-seven Kiowa men. While relatives left behind initially assumed that their loved ones would be killed, they eventually realized that they were incarcerated for an undetermined length of time. At that point, Kiowas and other Indians with incarcerated relatives sought ways to connect with prisoners. Observers at Fort Marion in Florida commented that Native inmates received a variety of items from their families, including letters "written in a picture language."[23] One noticed that prisoners' wives sent them handmade moccasins.[24] Kiowas and other Indians remaining on the reservation asked the Quaker agent to help them communicate with their relatives. A Cheyenne prisoner's wife approached her agent with a picture letter for her husband.[25] The drawing included symbols with news of three children born, three deaths in the community, and assurances about their relations' good health. Other glyphs note her son's desire to see his exiled father and her own pledge of commitment to her exiled husband.

Not only did Kiowas and other Indians communicate with imprisoned relatives, they also petitioned for their release. Beginning in the summer of 1876, Kiowas regularly approached Agent Haworth to send their petitions to President Grant. In their initial statement, two dozen Kiowa leaders emphasized that they had complied with the government's demands. They had ended violent engagements with soldiers, sent their children to school, moved to places the agent demanded, and planted corn fields. "We have done as Washington has asked us," the headmen argued. They also emphasized their attachment to their imprisoned kin. "Our people are anxiously waiting and watching for the return of our kindred, towards whom our feelings of attachment are as strong as those of the white man for his kindred." They asked the president to send their loved ones home and agreed to obey government demands regarding land, farming, and schools as the price of their return.[26]

In early 1877, federal officials responded by sending home a sick Kiowa prisoner, along with another inmate to accompany him.[27] With stories from these returned relations, Kiowas made more specific demands in their petitions to Washington. At the next meeting of Kiowa leaders with Agent Haworth, Fáitàlyì (Sun Boy) declared that "all the Kiowas are doing right . . . and we think Washington is glad for that." Fáitàlyì expected Washington to act in return. "We move quickly and we ask you to move quickly and send out friends back to us." Sétèmqíà (Bear That Runs Over Them) concurred: "We have been doing whatever Washington and the agent have asked of us." In response, he demanded that Washington listen to them and let the prisoners come back "to their wives and children, who are crying for them, and who love them." Māyítèndè (Woman's Heart), who had accompanied the sick Kiowa prisoner home, also spoke at the meeting to draft the petition. He emphasized how much Kiowas had changed during his forced absence. He noted that they followed Agent Haworth's demands. He wanted something in return. The agent must "work hard to get the rest of the people back," he declared.[28]

The petitions show that Kiowas expected their Quaker agent, the federal Indian office, and the president to respond. Kiowas had started to settle in houses, to farm, and to send their children to school. The government ought to acknowledge these actions by returning their relatives. Even Haworth seemed persuaded, writing to his supervisor that Kiowas were doing well. He claimed that establishing an end date for the prisoners' incarceration would help Kiowas progress toward civilization.[29]

If Haworth applauded some changes in Kiowa living, he still worried about Sun Dances. In the years after the war, Kiowas performed this ritual under surveillance by troops from Fort Sill. Several Kiowa calendars noted the controlled environment that began in the summer of 1875. Cûitònqì's (Wolf Tail) calendar entry, for example, shows the medicine lodge pole with offerings and the *Táimé* keeper in yellow paint beside it (Figure 5.2). Underneath the pole stands another figure wearing what looks like a soldier's hat. The following summer, Kiowas faced an internal challenge to Sun Dancing: the *Táimé* keeper died. In previous cases of a keeper's death, Kiowas often postponed the ritual gathering for a year or more. But even with the stresses of 1877, the people quickly named a new leader and celebrated under the watch of soldiers. The challenges continued, however, at the next year's gathering. Kiowa calendars note a Sun Dance during a measles epidemic. Under the strains of family separation, sickness, and death, as well as pressures to settle, farm, and go to school, Kiowas gathered for rituals that connected them to sacred power, the land, and each other.[30]

In light of these many efforts to stay connected as a people, Kiowa school attendance can be seen in a new light. If Quakers considered it a signal of the people's willingness to assimilate, Kiowas seemed to have viewed it as a way to secure their children's futures while staying connected to them. As early as June 1876, Kiowas sent one of their leading men, Thènézélbé (Fierce Eagle), to keep watch over events at the reservation school. When one Quaker official visited a year later, he reported that Thènézélbé's presence "satisfy[ed] the parents that their children were well treated."[31] Haworth claimed that Kiowa parents came to visit their children every day.[32] Clearly, Kiowas did not allow school attendance to cut them off from their children. Further, Kiowas emphasized to observers that they allowed attendance at American-style schools and lived in American-style houses "for their children's benefit."[33]

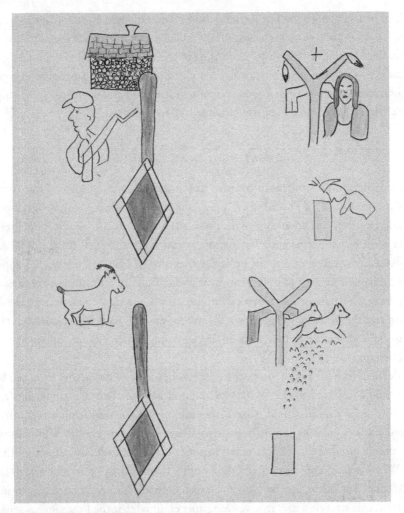

FIGURE 5.2. Cûitònqî's calendar entries for the winter of 1874–1875 through the summer of 1876. The images at the upper right depict the Sun Dance of 1875, including the outline of an American soldier below the central pole.

Credit: National Anthropological Archives, Smithsonian Institution, Manuscript 2002-27

Even as Kiowas lived with increasingly tight strictures regulating their cultural practices, they articulated clear reasons for complying with some American demands. They wanted their imprisoned family members back. They desired to stay connected to their children and to secure their future. They defended their status as a distinct community tied to a particular place. These actions and statements, even as they appear in documents mostly penned by Americans, offer a different interpretation from those put forward by Protestant "friends of the Indian." As a writer in the *Methodist Quarterly Review* put it, Kiowas had been "the wildest and most barbarous of all the Indians in the Indian Territory." Their move toward civilization was a sign that "the whole Indian

world, so to speak, is crying out for schools, for permanent homes, for houses and fur-
niture, for cattle and sheep, for agricultural implements, for lands in severalty, and some
of them for American citizenship." According to the writer, the Kiowa example signaled,
"the Indian wars are evidently drawing to a close." Modeling and persuasion were the
most humane and effective methods. Indian acculturation and eventual citizenship, the
writer affirmed, will "end all our troublesome Indian questions."[34]

DEBATING INDIAN POLICY

While this Methodist author anticipated a smooth transition from Indian wars to peaceful
assimilation through the Peace Policy, some Americans disagreed. Several developments
portended the eventual unraveling of the president's program. Most important, President
Grant's term was about to end. The nation would go to the polls in late 1876. A new
chief executive could continue the policy or overturn it. The new president's approach
would probably hinge on popular sentiment about Indians. Continuing episodes of violence between Indians and Americans, especially Custer's 1876 defeat at the Little
Bighorn and the Nez Perce flight toward Canada, dashed many Americans' hopes for a
peaceful solution to the Indian problem. It also brought Peace Policy opponents out of
the woodwork.[35]

As detailed in previous chapters, the Peace Policy had its detractors from the beginning. Often connected to the military or situated west of the Mississippi, they argued
that only coercive means could make Plains Indian nations transition away from their
raid and trade economies. Some opponents went further, arguing that Indians would
never submit and that extermination was inevitable. For Peace Policy detractors, the Red
River War was one more example of the policy's failures. Listing it, along with the recent Modoc War in the Pacific Northwest and General Crook's campaigns to subdue
Indians in Arizona, one writer in a western paper claimed that the Peace Policy generated
"annoyance, expense, suffering, and discord."[36] Many throughout the American West
shared his opinion.

But Quakers and other "friends of the Indian" objected. Despite ongoing violent
episodes between soldiers and Indians, they continued to claim the humanity, effectiveness, and lower costs of Grant's policy. Even after the Little Bighorn, Protestant
newspapers defended it. An Episcopal bishop active in Indian affairs argued that the
policy's opponents wanted to exterminate Indians. They failed to see the progress that
Native people had made. Would these opponents exterminate Indian people who "cultivate more than 300,000 acres of land, produce 2 million bushels of corn, have more
than 300 schools with 11,000 students, and more than 22,000 members of Christian
churches?"[37] Still others made explicit moral claims, calling a militarized approach to
Indians "an enormous outrage upon human rights."[38]

Promoters of the Peace Policy faced an uphill battle after Rutherford Hayes's 1876
election and what has come to be known as the Compromise of 1877. Hayes, of course,

is best known for issuing orders to withdraw troops from the American South, ending Reconstruction and federal protection of African Americans' civil rights. He also oversaw dramatic changes at the federal Indian office as military leaders pressured him to end religious groups' involvement in Indian affairs and return the office to the War Department.[39]

Quakers worried about the presidential transition even before the inauguration. They were already having trouble as Congress often failed to approve their nominations for reservation agents. At the spring 1876 Quaker Indian committee meeting, one leader reported that Congress was "no longer happy with the president's plan to let religious bodies nominate these positions." Some Friends connected these troubles to conflicts over Reconstruction. In the handwritten meeting notes, the secretary commented that Congress was obsessed with military presence in the South. "Everything is political," he complained.[40]

So it was. Quakers approached Hayes soon after his inauguration. They also sent him a long letter detailing their successes at the reservations they administered.[41] But relations between Friends and the president quickly soured. Hayes appointed officials who voiced skepticism about religious denominations' involvement in Indian work. With Grant out of office, Society leaders struggled to keep the Peace Policy going.

As Quakers and other Protestant "friends of the Indian" faced resistance, their Catholic counterparts hit their stride. As noted in the previous chapter, Catholics were furious when President Grant gave them only a handful of reservations to administer under the Peace Policy. They opened an office in Washington, D.C. to advocate for reservation assignments, as well as secure federal funding for Catholic schools on reservations. Facing both popular and government opposition, BCIM leaders tapped into the laity's resentment about Protestant public dominance. They asked American Catholics to support efforts to "secure the religious liberty of the Indian." They argued that Catholics, whether Indian or not, had the right to worship their God and to educate their children free from governmental interference.[42]

Catholic laywomen answered the appeal. In October 1875, several women in Washington, D.C., formed the Ladies' Catholic Indian Missionary Association.[43] It was the first of many Catholic lay groups to raise funds to support Indian missions. Members voiced their concern for heathen Indians in need of salvation, as well as Catholic Indians oppressed by the nation's Protestant majority. The capital chapter's most prominent member, the wife of General William Tecumseh Sherman, laid out these arguments in an appeal to American Catholic laywomen. Jesus, she wrote, had suffered and died for "the conversion of heathen nations to the end of the world." He also called his followers, through the great commission, to evangelize. If Catholic laywomen could not be missionaries, they could "pray and labor for the conversion of souls." Hoping to bring more Catholic women into the movement, BCIM officials sought papal support. In a summer 1876 meeting with Pius IX, administrators received the pope's blessing for all who supported American Indian missions and schools. The pope also offered a seven-year plenary indulgence for female members of Indian mission associations and wrote a prayer for their use in daily devotions.[44]

The women's funds supported the growing number of Catholic schools on reservations. This expansion signaled Catholics' change of course as the Peace Policy fell out of favor. Rather than fight for reservation assignments, BCIM officials focused on defending their right to build Catholic schools for Indians.[45] This work included expanding their presence in Indian Territory. The region's prefect, along with the French and Belgian Benedictines who had worked there since 1877, made plans for missions and schools among the Kiowa.

THE CIVILIZING PRISON

If Catholics surged in this period, there was at least one place where Protestant dominance continued unchecked: the prison at Fort Marion. Seventy-two Indian prisoners from the southern plains had arrived in May 1875. They were supervised by Captain Richard Pratt, a Civil War veteran who participated in Kit Carson's 1868 attack on the Cheyenne, as well as the Red River War. While Pratt's assignment took place within fortified prison walls, he considered it a program of Indian assimilation. His approach soon garnered supporters and accolades from Protestant "friends of the Indian" around the country.

Pratt's prison experiment was inspired by his distaste for reservations. He argued that bounded reservations where Indians lived apart from other Americans constituted "reservation prisons." At Fort Marion, Pratt aimed to solve the separation problem, as well as ongoing Indian resistance to assimilation. He *required* prisoners to undergo cultural transformation. He *situated* prisoners so they made contact with non-Indians. He also hoped to convince others of reservations' many problems.[46]

Once he arrived in St. Augustine with his Native charges, Pratt quickly departed from earlier American practices for imprisoning Indians. He insisted that inmates cut their hair and wear American-style clothes. He engaged prisoners in military-inspired marching drills and prescribed work assignments, reflecting a wider Protestant emphasis on work in Christian life.[47] Pratt also brought in local Protestant women to teach reading and language classes. He used the fort's chapel for worship services. At every opportunity, Pratt required Indian prisoners to engage in American cultural practices. He aimed to reform Indians' bodily habits of labor, discipline, and dress. He introduced new forms of education and religious ritual to his captive audience.

Pratt also engineered numerous contacts between St. Augustine residents and the Native prisoners. He encouraged tourists to visit the prison, at times offering performances of Indian dances and hunts to draw in crowds. The engagement also went the other way. Pratt took inmates into the local community. He arranged for Indian prisoners to work at a variety of jobs, such as carrying luggage and selling handmade objects to tourists. He brought inmates to services at local churches. Pratt also sponsored "outings" to nearby islands, where the Native men camped in tents and hunted sharks. He encouraged tourists to come out in boats to watch the Indian prisoners on their "outings."

Visitors to Fort Marion testified to the transformative power of Pratt's strategies. One early observer wrote to a popular literary magazine that Indian inmates "with their shuffling chains and strange tongues and barbaric gestures" now moved about the prison freely during the day and engaged in the work of trade.[48] Another commented on the Indians' "exemplary patience" as they sat through a service in the gallery section of the St. Augustine Presbyterian Church.[49] Prominent reformer Harriet Beecher Stowe offered some of the strongest accolades for Pratt's transformative program. Her account began in the spring of 1875 with her sighting of the Native prisoners as they traveled from Indian Territory to Florida. They were the "wildest, most dangerous, and the most untamable of the tribes." Thankfully, the nation's "conscience and Christianity" prompted their imprisonment rather than execution. Fort Marion's results, according to Beecher Stowe, were nothing short of miraculous. "We found no savages," she told readers. The Indian men were clean, wore uniforms, attended reading lessons, participated in trade, wrote letters to their families, and attended prayer meetings. For Beecher Stowe, these new activities signaled a deeper transformation. The Indians had "use of a new set of faculties." Pratt's program achieved what decades of reservation life had failed to do.[50]

Some of the most powerful testimonies about Fort Marion came in visual form. Pratt used photographs to emphasize his program's transformative potential. Reflecting broader trends in photography, Pratt used side-by-side, "before and after" images to "prove" the Native men's improvement through cultural practices associated with white Americans.[51] The photographs also obscured coercive practices and the militarized setting. In the "before" image (Figure 5.3), Indian prisoners appeared as "savages." The "after" image (Figure 5.4) of neat and clean Indians ready for American life offered no details about the means Pratt employed to secure this transformation.

With prominent citizens such as Harriet Beecher Stowe as allies, along with photographs providing dramatic visual testimony to how Indians had changed under his care, Pratt promoted his program and continued his criticism of "reservation prisons." Reservations, he affirmed, kept Indians separate from other Americans. They allowed Indians to continue their unreconstructed ways: moving their lodges, hunting buffalo, and raising their children in camps. His program changed all that. He had found a way to change Indian dress, labor, education, and religion. Pratt publicized Fort Marion as the new solution to the "Indian problem."

Pratt's supporters made big claims, even if the captain himself sometimes acknowledged the difficulties he faced at Fort Marion. He knew the Indian prisoners opposed the changes he enforced. For instance, when some inmates cut up their uniforms to fashion traditional leggings, Pratt called for "immediate correction."[52] Pratt relied on the fort's strong walls and American guards to maintain the program. At the same time, he counted

FIGURE 5.3. Stereographic print of Kiowa prisoners at Fort Marion soon after their arrival.

Credit: Richard Henry Pratt Papers, Yale Collection of Western Americana. Beinecke Rare Book and Manuscript Library, Yale University

FIGURE 5.4. Stereographic print entitled "The Company," featuring Kiowa prisoners after American officials cut their hair and issued them military-style uniforms.

Credit: Richard Henry Pratt Papers, Yale Collection of Western Americana. Beinecke Rare Book and Manuscript Library, Yale University

on his supporters, who typically overlooked the use of coercive practices, as well as the program's setting in a military prison.

KIOWAS IN EXILE

Onlookers' accolades could easily overwhelm any effort to consider Kiowa perspectives on their incarceration. But documentary sources by white Americans, as well as visual materials created by prisoners, allow us some sense of Kiowa responses. These sources show how inmates experienced separation from their families and Fort Marion's program of enforced assimilation. In these materials, incarcerated Kiowas reflected on their lands, their people, and their ritual practices in light of their exile.

Kiowa responses were apparent already on the trip to Florida. Pratt's memoir includes some clues. Reflecting back on the journey, he remembered that the train ride unsettled the Indian prisoners, and some pulled blankets over their heads rather than watch the landscape whizzing by. Pratt recalled a Cheyenne prisoner who attempted suicide early in the trip. Pratt also wrote of a prisoner who asked him how he would feel if chained up and removed from his family. The man later jumped from the train. Guards shot him. The Cheyennes' interpreter told Pratt that the man had wanted to die ever since being taken from his family.[53]

Pratt also wrote about episodes of Indian resistance after arriving at Fort Marion. The Cheyenne man who attempted suicide on the train began a hunger strike and later died. Chẹ̀thàidè (White Horse), a Kiowa prisoner, plotted to escape. Pratt became suspicious about Chẹ̀thàidè's request to go to a nearby dune to "perform some religious ceremony." The captain had Chẹ̀thàidè followed. He also demanded that the other prisoners reveal any knowledge they had of a plot. Some Kiowas revealed their escape plans. They told Pratt they had vowed not to be taken alive. When Chẹ̀thàidè returned and saw his plot was foiled, he asked Pratt to kill him. Instead, Pratt gathered the "ringleaders," drugged them, and lectured the rest that escape was impossible. Pratt kept Chẹ̀thàidè and his co-conspirators in the guardhouse for weeks. Despite such episodes, Pratt and his supporters emphasized his program's reliance on "kindly persuasion." But Kiowas and other prisoners certainly faced threats and violence when they resisted Pratt's reformative program.[54]

Over time, inmates relinquished plans for escape and focused instead on finding ways to make life bearable and connecting with family in Indian Territory. Just a few months after arriving, with the duration of their imprisonment unknown prisoners asked if their wives could join them. The request filtered through the Indian office to the White House and back to the reservation. But when Agent Haworth asked the women to go, they demurred. According to Haworth, they were afraid. They had no idea where their husbands were and if they would ever return. They did not want to meet the same fate.[55]

With their wives unwilling to travel to Florida, Kiowa inmates devised other ways to connect to their families from afar. One American visitor wrote that prisoners sent letters to their families and included money they earned from jobs and selling handmade objects.[56] She also observed that inmates wore handmade items sent by their families, including a Kiowa prisoner who wore his child's moccasin on a cord around his neck. The Indian inmates also cared for the most vulnerable among them. In October 1875, Zébàutéfèą̀ (Comes Along Straightening An Arrow) died of consumption. Kiowas asked Pratt if they could take charge of the prisoner's burial and death rites. Pratt allowed them to take Zébàutéfèą̀'s body and bury him "according to their customs."[57] Even in documents from white observers, then, we see traces of Kiowa efforts to connect with loved ones at home and to care for kin held at Fort Marion.

While American sources offer details about Indian experiences of Fort Marion, materials left by the prisoners themselves provide a rich archive.[58] Kiowas and other Indian prisoners made scores of drawings in which they transformed artistic traditions from the southern plains into a new form of visual expression. As discussed in the Introduction, Kiowa drawings during the Fort Marion years emerged from rock art and buffalo hide-painting traditions. While incarcerated, the prisoners innovated in both form and content. They used new materials such as paper, notebooks, colored pencils, and watercolors. They also drew new subject matter.

While there are multiple ways to approach Kiowa drawings produced at Fort Marion, their work offers particular insight into how prisoners experienced exile from family and homeland, as well as the ways in which they understood what was happening to them at Fort Marion. Kiowas depicted places, people, and rituals as they remembered them in their homeland and encountered them during their incarceration. They used these visual strategies to maintain their identity as a distinct people tied to a particular place.[59]

At least ten separate Kiowa artists produced work at Fort Marion. Some of them made images of their native land.[60] Landscape drawing was a significant departure from earlier Kiowa artistic practices. Neither painted tipis nor shields depicted the southern plains landscape. But the prisoner-artists at Fort Marion frequently drew the plains in general, as well as specific sites important to their people. Éttàlyìdònmàui (We Are Seeking Boys), for instance, drew many of the region's natural features, such as small mountains and rivers, as well as the buffalo and elk that populated it. He also depicted Kiowas' place within the landscape, noting how their lodges fit into the bends of rivers and rested below the Wichita Mountains (Figure 5.5). Éttàlyìdònmàui often depicted his people in positions of strength as they interacted with the land, including images of men in their finest clothing, engaging in hunting and war, carrying weapons, and riding upon beauti-fully painted horses.[61]

But Éttàlyìdònmàui's Fort Marion notebooks also detail how Kiowas' relationship to the land had changed. He drew Fort Sill, the American fort established to oversee Kiowas and their Indian allies.[62] He depicted ration and annuity distribution, signaling Kiowas' altered ability to provide for themselves once they lived on bounded lands.[63] Éttàlyìdònmàui also drew the landscapes of his exile. He sketched the cities he passed through by train and boat, as well as images of Fort Marion and Saint Augustine

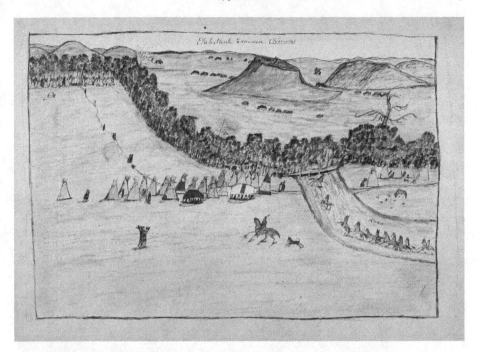

FIGURE 5.5. Éttàlyìdònmàui's (We Are Seeking Boys) drawing of Kiowa lands, including encampments with painted tipis, men hunting and holding council, and buffalo herds. Éttàlyìdònmàui made the image while working for the Smithsonian.

Credit: National Anthropological Archives, Smithsonian Institution, manuscript 290.844-290.845

(Figure 5.6). In them, Éttàlyìdònmàui included great detail, such as the trees surrounding St. Augustine's central plaza and windows in the buildings. For this exiled prisoner, drawing landscapes both reminded him of home and allowed him to consider the vastly different place he now inhabited.

The Kiowa prisoner-artists also depicted people, both their relatives at home and Americans they encountered during their exile. Gùhâudè (Stripping Off Of A Rib Cage), another Kiowa prisoner, made many images of his people. His incarceration mandated separation from his wife. Gùhâudè's notebooks feature several images of courtship and marriage, including the traditional courting practice in which couples were wrapped together in a blanket.[64] He also illustrated gatherings of prominent Kiowa men.[65] Like Éttàlyìdònmàui, Gùhâudè's images of his people in their homelands communicated strength, as in Plate 7, depicting men in council sitting before lavishly decorated tipis.

Gùhâudè's notebooks also included Americans he encountered on the reservation and during his exile from it. One drawing shows white people visiting a Kiowa village.[66] While it is impossible to identify the situation precisely, the drawing possibly depicts the reservation's Quaker employees. Gùhâudè also drew soldiers from Fort Sill.[67] Some of Gùhâudè's work shows Americans, including women, who taught Kiowa prisoners

FIGURE 5.6. Éttàlyìdònmàui's rendering of St. Augustine's main plaza, including intricate detail of the cathedral and a building with an American flag.
Credit: Richard Henry Pratt Papers, Yale Collection of Western Americana. Beinecke Rare Book and Manuscript Library, Yale University

at Fort Marion. Figure 5.7 depicts Captain Pratt leading an evening prayer service for Indian prisoners. It also features the American women who sometimes attended chapel. Another drawing shows Indian prisoners giving archery lessons to the women who taught their reading and language classes.[68] In Gùhâudè's work, American women engaged Indian prisoners in archery lessons, while others looked on at the spectacle. If his images of Kiowa people in their lands recall family relations and political activity designed to strengthen the nation, his representations of interactions with Americans depict outsiders with the power to disrupt Kiowa ties.

The Kiowa prisoner-artists drew peoples and lands both familiar and strange. They followed a similar pattern in depicting ritual practice. Zótâm (Driftwood), whose images of his forced journey opened the chapter, offers a particularly helpful example. Zótâm chronicled many aspects of Kiowa life in Indian Country, including their engagements with powerful beings through ritual practice. At least one drawing appears to include a sacred thunderbird. In it, men in matching regalia process around a painted tipi. A rainbow curves overhead and a colorful bird exchanges a pipe with one of the men. The image likely depicts someone's vision.[69]

FIGURE 5.7. Gùhâudè's drawing of Colonel Richard Henry Pratt preaching to Indian prisoners in Fort Marion's chapel. American women look on from the side.

Credit: George W. Fox Collection of American Indian Ledger Drawings and Photographs, Yale Collection of Western Americana. Beinecke Rare Book and Manuscript Library, Yale University

Zótâm's drawings also depict the Sun Dance. Born in 1853, Zótâm could recall at least some Sun Dance celebrations prior to the reservation's 1867 establishment. He witnessed ceremonials at favored locations that stood out in Kiowa memory. He observed Kiowas' effort to maintain ritual obligations in difficult situations. He lived through the period when Utes captured the smaller *Tâimé* figures and the *Tâimé* keeper of many years died.[70]

Zótâm's drawings show many moments from Sun Dance ceremonials. He depicted strong men cutting down the cottonwood tree to serve as the central lodge's pole.[71] He showed women cooperating to erect the pole and construct the lodge over several days. These events, along with the calling of the buffalo, were among many that involved a host of Kiowa people. In his work, Zótâm depicted times when the people had no struggles gathering or finding the materials they needed to celebrate their central ritual act.

Zótâm's notebooks contain many drawings of the central lodge and the ritual practices that took place inside it. As the Introduction detailed, Sun Dance activities moved toward a four-day central event, led by the *Tâimé* keeper, in which men who had made vows

FIGURE 5.8. Zótâm's rendering of the Sun Dance lodge, including Kiowas dressed as buffalo gathered inside and onlookers watching from outside.
Credit: Collection of the Colorado Springs Fine Arts Center, gift of the Debutante Ball Purchase Fund and Carlton Trust, TM 1983.1, photographed by Ross Frank

performed acts of suffering and sacrifice. In the lodge, the leader kept a cedar fire burning and led the men as they stood before the pole adorned with sacred objects and offerings, as well as the sun burning through the lodge's roof opening, for four days without food or water. Zótâm made at least two drawings of male devotees inside the lodge with other Kiowa people gathered to look upon their ritual work (Figure 5.8).[72] Even if Sun Dance practices had been difficult among his people during his lifetime, Zótâm drew them in their idealized form: when buffalo could be found for the central offering, the people could gather without restriction, and neither disease nor death disrupted their ceremonial practice.[73]

Of course, Zótâm had experienced the ultimate disruption: exile and imprisonment in Fort Marion. Under Pratt's program, he encountered religious practices promoted by his American captors. His initial encounters with Christianity came through recitation of the Lord's Prayer in classes taught by local women.[74] Zótâm also attended evening prayer services led by Pratt and probably attended church in the St. Augustine community.[75] In contrast to the communal autonomy and empowerment revealed in his Sun Dance depictions, Zótâm's drawings of encounters with Christian practices show Kiowa inmates dressed in American clothes, seated close together on benches, and lectured by

American men and women. His first encounters with Christianity came alongside multiple forms of disempowerment.

LOSS IN THE CLOSED LANDS

By early 1878, neither Kiowa prisoners nor their families knew when, if ever, they would be released. During their exile, several of the prisoner-artists drew the rituals that had kept their people together. They could not have known that the Sun Dance was in a precarious position, not only because soldiers monitored the ritual and another *Táimé* keeper had died. Rather, something central to the ritual was in danger of disappearing. The medicine lodge needed a buffalo hide procured in the traditional fashion. By 1878, buffalo herds were difficult to find.

In February 1878, Kiowa headmen and younger men asked Agent Haworth to transcribe a petition concerning the buffalo. They wanted him to send it to Washington. Haworth's letter attests to the situation's seriousness. First, old and young men came together to make the request, bridging a divide that sometimes kept Kiowas and other Indian nations from presenting a unified voice in negotiations with Americans. Further, Haworth noted that the "medicine smoke" preceding the speeches, an event typical to such occasions, was in this instance marked by "gravity" and "reverential feeling." While we have no record of this meeting from Kiowa perspectives and have the speeches only in translation, the American taking notes sensed the people's urgency.[76]

Zépcàuiétjè (Big Bow) opened the time for speeches. As with earlier petitions, he began by noting that Kiowas had complied with Washington's demands. In turn, they brought their "great sorrow" and a request. "We wish you to understand," Zépcàuiétjè said, "that we consider ourselves passing away, as our buffalo are passing away." Only the government, he claimed, had the power to stop the herds' decline. "We ask Washington to make mercy on us and stop the killing of the buffalo, if not it will be useless to release our people in Florida and send them home to us, for we shall be dead and they will be dead." Ending his speech, Zépcàuiétjè claimed that Washington must act so "that our children may live."[77]

Càuáufìjáu (Crow [Feathered Sheathed] Lance), the next speaker, further explained relations between Kiowas and the buffalo. The president, he claimed, desired to protect Kiowas. "But we think he does not realize the situation, that when the buffalo are gone we cannot live." This was not simply for lack of food. The problem, Càuáufìjáu explained, was cosmic. "The Great Spirit gave us the buffalo when he placed us here, and at that time we received information that we should exist only as long as the buffalo lived." Government officials allowed for the herds' slaughter because they did not understand that "when they [are] dead we should die too, just as two brothers die." With Càuáufìjáu's speech, Kiowas communicated to Washington the dimensions of "this terrible calamity."[78]

Páutáuljè (Lean Bison Bull) then rose to speak. Like Zépcàuiétjè, he opened by reminding Washington that Kiowas complied with their demands. "Now we are going to talk and we want Washington to listen," he said. "The buffalo killing may be stopped and we may have a long life." Washington could do something. Páutáuljè also recalled the many petitions they made for their imprisoned kin. "We used to think we would see our people in prison again . . . we have concluded there is no use in making further talk about them. We shall never see them again. The buffalo are nearly gone; their days are numbered, as the days of all the Kiowas are numbered and gloom and death is upon us all." As Páutáuljè finished his remarks, more Kiowa headmen followed with similar arguments. Kiowas had listened to Washington. It was time for Washington to listen to them. Their very survival was at stake.[79]

It could be easy to read the petition in a way that reinforces what some scholars have called the myth of the "ecological Indian" and the particular romantic notion that Plains Indians hunted only as much buffalo as they needed.[80] Historians have dispelled these myths by showing that Plains Indians made strategic choices to develop mounted horse cultures that relied almost exclusively on the buffalo herds.[81] Some Plains Indians hunted in excess in order to trade for desired items made available through expanded markets. Emphasizing Indian activity, however, has not led historians to downplay the devastating role that American hunters and merchants played in the herds' demise. Rather, their work prompts a closer look at Indian actions and choices as one part of a much greater ecological collapse. The Kiowas' petition, then, need not be read as the manifesto of ecological Indians in harmony with nature. Instead, it helps reveal the particular way in which Kiowa interactions with the buffalo had changed and to what end. As one Native Studies scholar has argued, many Plains Indian nations understood their peoplehood to include other-than-human animals such as the buffalo.[82] If Kiowas had overhunted for market purposes in the past, they were certainly not doing so by 1878. Their concerns in the petition speak to their precarious situation. Without decent herds, Kiowa could neither feed themselves adequately nor maintain ritual practices that had bound them together for several generations. Claiming their relationship with the buffalo was one way Kiowas continued to regard themselves as a distinct people in the face of American pressures to acculturate.

The Kiowa speakers persuaded Agent Haworth. In his introductory statement to the petitions, he recommended that officials arrange for a Kiowa delegation to Washington. He encouraged the Indian office to treat the matter carefully. This, he wrote, is "a matter involving their traditional religious belief." Something must be done, he recommended, "to take them safely over the time of suspense which seems to be gathering over them." Despite his willingness to designate the Kiowas' relation to the buffalo as "religious," what Haworth envisioned is unclear.[83] Should the government heed their call and stop the slaughter? Or should they help Kiowas transition to a world with no buffalo? Haworth took no clear position, transmitting the petition with only an emphasis on the situation's gravity.

CIVILIZING REGIMES

The years after the Red River War marked a turning point for both Americans and Kiowas. Assuming that further Kiowa armed resistance was unlikely, and bolstered by the perceived success of Pratt's program at Fort Marion, Americans pressed their assimilation agenda through massive efforts at Indian schooling and calls for changing land policy. Pratt's prison experiment provided the template for assimilation strategies, as well as the rhetorical habit of obscuring coercion and force. For Kiowas, the coming years brought further assaults on their ability to remain bound to each other in a particular place. Their petition to save the buffalo herds was one of many efforts to counteract American efforts to dismantle their community. They tried to maintain Sun Dance rituals in the face of increasingly insurmountable obstacles. As more Kiowas encountered Christianity, they struggled to determine a response to Americans' message about a new source of sacred power. Would Jesus exacerbate the unequal power relations they experienced in Fort Marion's chapel? Or did he offer something that could somehow be harnessed for Kiowas' good?

The Americans' program for Indian assimilation coincided with national debates in which race and religion served as key issues in the consideration of citizenship and national belonging. Religious difference continued to register as a potentially insurmountable obstacle to national inclusion. In early 1879, the Supreme Court ruled against a Mormon practitioner of plural marriage. Claiming that Congress had no right to legislate religious opinion but had every duty to suppress unacceptable religious practice, the court claimed no sympathy for Mormons who broke bigamy laws. Congress followed with increasingly restrictive laws against and punishments for plural marriage.[84]

Racial difference also occupied the center of national debates about citizenship and freedom. In the years following Reconstruction's dismantling, white Southern leaders responded in earnest to their new ability to limit black citizens. Tennessee enacted the first legal restrictions, or Jim Crow laws, in 1881. Other states followed with legislation designed to restrict voting rights and segregate public spaces. As one historian has observed, Northern Christians failed to stop their Southern counterparts, and a series of Protestant revivals and interdenominational activities smoothed the path to reunion for North and South at the expense of African Americans.[85]

Further west, white leaders focused on racial and religious difference as they sought to solidify their political power. In California, anti-immigrant and anti-Indian leaders argued for laws that excluded Chinese workers and restricted Native Americans due to their religious status as heathens. In 1879, California leaders passed Article 19 of the state constitution, banning employment for Chinese workers. Although defended as an effort to stop "Asiatic coolieism" as a "form of human slavery," anti-Chinese politicians promoted the amendment with the hope of driving immigrants from the state. These attitudes were hardly limited to California, as both major political parties boasted anti-Chinese planks in 1876. Throughout the United States, citizens debated the implications of religious and racial difference for citizenship. Kiowas were one of many communities contending with what one historian has called the "religio-racial vision of white male Christian supremacy" that emerged in the post–Civil War period.[86]

Kiowas felt even more pressure to assimilate in 1877 after Agent Haworth resigned. Federal officials did not wait for Quakers to nominate a replacement. Instead, they appointed P. B. Hunt, a Civil War veteran and former Internal Revenue Service (IRS) employee. Hunt approached his new position with every intention to change Kiowa ways of living and even less reluctance to use troops in the process. He began his service with an effort to enforce recent federal prohibitions on communal buffalo hunting.[87] Kiowas balked at his action, citing particular articles of the Treaty of Medicine Lodge guaranteeing their hunting rights. Hunt realized that young Kiowa men might rebel if he enforced federal orders. Even after the Indian office granted a hunting exception, Kiowas continued to push Agent Hunt to honor treaty obligations. Just a few months later, they demanded that an expedition go to the reservation's western border, which Kiowas claimed had been illegally established so as to reduce Indian landholdings promised at Medicine Lodge.[88]

Despite Kiowa efforts to convince him of their treaty rights, Agent Hunt quickly took a strong hand with them on other matters. During the summer of 1878, he refused permission for a Sun Dance celebration until the school year was finished. He also authorized troops from Fort Sill to oversee the ritual celebration. Hunt's report at the end of the summer offered his perspective on how to quicken the pace of Kiowa assimilation. He looked upon the declining buffalo herds with approval as he considered the animals' disappearance as a "factor" in Indians' move toward civilized living. He applauded recent changes in federal policy that allowed agents to withhold sugar, coffee, and tobacco rations from Indians who would not work, even though treaties guaranteed these supplies as compensation for land. Hunt also noted that he hoped to get increasingly younger children enrolled in school. These more pliable children would be easier to work with, Hunt affirmed. "The next generation can be made whatever we desire to make them."[89]

Hunt combined his effort to restrict hunting, compel labor, and require more school enrollment with the previously considered plan to move Kiowas to another section of the reservation. In September 1878, the federal Indian office consolidated what had once been two separate headquarters on the reservation and relocated the new unified agency further east.[90] The move meant a change in the distribution point for rations and annuities. Kiowas felt compelled to move closer to the new headquarters. Hunt hoped the move would further disrupt traditional modes of political authority in which leading Indian men made decisions about movement and food distribution. By asserting the government's authority over where and to whom rations were distributed, Agent Hunt affirmed his desire to "break up [Kiowa] bands," which if undisrupted allowed Indians to maintain "their savage rites and customs."[91]

In his desire to restrict communal practices, disrupt relationships to land and leaders, and require an American education for Kiowa children, Hunt shared priorities with Protestant "friends of the Indian." For many Americans, Pratt's experiment at Fort Marion, which drew to a close in the spring of 1878, fueled visions of expanded Indian education and evangelization. As one historian has noted, the years leading up to 1880 witnessed a renewed confidence in the possibility of Indian assimilation into American life.[92] Based on the "success" at Fort Marion, Americans created new sites of Indian assimilation, ranging from distant boarding schools and private homes, to schools for formerly enslaved persons and the farm fields of white families. To support these new efforts, Americans argued not only that Fort Marion benefited Indians, but also that the imposition of labor, drills, classes, and new bodily habits were, in fact, a "kindness" made possible because their architect, Captain Pratt, exemplified a spirit of Christian service.

As Pratt planned for the release of his Indian prisoners, Americans praised the effectiveness of his transformative program. Numerous small magazines and denominational papers ran positive stories about Fort Marion, but promotion also came in widely popular magazines such as *Harper's Weekly*. A May 1878 article emphasized the Christian nature and transformative possibilities of Pratt's experiment. The Indian prisoners had arrived as "dirty, greasy, unkempt savages." But "kindly treatment" changed them inside and out. Many of the prisoners had become "good, earnest Christians." The author praised Pratt and the "worthy ladies" who taught the inmates.[93]

Over time, religious groups continued to evoke Fort Marion as the ideal form of Indian education and evangelization. A writer in *The Independent* claimed that Pratt and "noble Christian ladies" had transformed "savages" into true believers. During chapel, the Indian prisoners sang revival hymns, recited the Lord's Prayer, and begged God to forgive their sins.[94] Quaker leaders, who had worked for decades to secure a humane method of Indian transformation through the Peace Policy, agreed. They extolled Pratt's "labor of love" at Fort Marion and argued that it brought about change "nothing short of the mighty transforming power of God."[95]

SCHOOLING AND POWER

Pratt's program had wide public support, but he needed real places to continue his program of Indian transformation once his work at Fort Marion ended. Most of the prisoners chose to go home to Indian Territory. But Pratt offered other options to those who would stay in the East. Some men agreed. In the months before the inmates' release, Pratt found new venues in private homes, as well as a recently founded school. Pratt's initial efforts focused on Hampton Institute, a manual labor school for formerly enslaved African Americans.[96] In the spring of 1878, he arrived with sixteen former prisoners. He arranged for them to take classes and learn industrial skills. To promote his new project, Pratt wrote news reports about an "Indian Raid on Hampton Institute." Relying on readers' surprise at the headline, Pratt then assured his audience that the Indian prisoners from Fort Marion proved to be model students.[97]

The Hampton experiment paid off for Pratt. The school's promotional newspaper printed glowing reports about Indian students. Pratt went on to recruit dozens of Indian young people from the northern plains. Native students featured prominently at the May 1879 commencement ceremonies. A popular evangelical newspaper reported the "progress made in teaching and civilizing the sixty-six Indians who are now students here." Several Indian students, including one Kiowa, gave speeches. Booker T. Washington, a Hampton graduate, offered the commencement address. Government officials, including the secretary of the Interior, praised the experiment in which Indians had been "taught the industrial arts" and were "elevated so as to be worthy of citizenship." The writer offered a hopeful conclusion to his readers: "Hampton Institute is evidently working out successfully both the Negro and the Indian problems."[98]

While most of the Indian prisoners who stayed in the East went to Hampton, a few went further north. They played a part in another of Pratt's experiments, this one placing Indian men in private Christian homes under the combined oversight of an Episcopal bishop, a minister, and an active laywoman. The program was the brainchild of Mary Burnham, a longtime supporter of Indian missions.[99] In 1876 her Episcopal diocese had "set her apart" as a deaconess involved in supporting Native missions. Soon after, Burnham had visited St. Augustine and heard about the Indian inmates at Fort Marion. In her later writings, she described her amazement when she heard uniformed prisoners sing a Christian hymn and recite scripture. She suspected that Indian prisoners would benefit not only from education, but also from homestays with Christian families.[100] She soon gained support from her bishop, as well as Captain Pratt.

Two Kiowas were among the Indian inmates released to Burnham's care in October 1878. Zótâm (Driftwood) and Sétqópjè (Mountain Bear) lived with local families. That same month, the bishop baptized four Indian men, including Zótâm, giving him the baptismal name Paul Caryl Zotom. In his remarks, the bishop claimed the Indian converts had "entered upon a greater warfare than they had ever known, as soldiers and servants of the Lord Jesus Christ." Two weeks later, the bishop confirmed the four men. His sermon contrasted the conferees' past, wearing rude clothing and fulfilling vengeful instincts, with their new situation in which they received the knowledge of the Christian God "like little children" in order to pass it on to their kinsmen still "sitting in the darkness."[101]

The Indian men attended school in the mornings, performed farm labor in the afternoons, and attended prayer meetings with a local minister, the Rev. Wicks, most evenings. Burnham worked with Wicks, preparing the Indian men to return to their reservations as missionaries. She coordinated her efforts with Pratt, who settled just south of her in central Pennsylvania, where he had acquired a former military barracks to use as the first off-reservation Indian boarding school.

Pratt opened the Carlisle Indian Industrial School in November 1879 with former Indian prisoners as his first students. Pratt's project to assimilate Native people became known by his oft-quoted motto: "Kill the Indian in him and save the man." Carlisle mirrored many of Fort Marion's daily routines. When new students arrived, they were quickly subjected to strenuous baths, dressed in American clothes, and had their hair cut short. Speaking Native languages was strictly forbidden. Daily routines included lessons in English and arithmetic, military-style drills and exercises, followed by manual and domestic labor. Also like Fort Marion, students attended chapel services and received instruction based on Protestant catechetical materials.[102]

The Carlisle curriculum also mirrored Fort Marion's emphasis on getting Indians out of the institution and engaged with white Americans. Pratt initiated an outing program in which Native students lived with American families over holiday and summer breaks. These were hardly respites, however. Most students who participated in the outing program performed manual labor for the families that hosted them. Boys worked on farms and girls did domestic chores.[103]

Pratt had used photography to promote Fort Marion's transformative power. He used a similar technique at Carlisle. He hired John Choate, who took thousands of photographs of Carlisle students. Choate's postcards featuring images of students upon arrival and months or years later became immensely popular. Pratt used a photograph of Tom Torlino, a Navaho student, to promote the school's transformative program (Figure 5.9). The "before" image epitomized Americans' definition of savagery. Torlino's hair is long.

TOM TORLINO—NAVAJO

As He Entered the School in 1882.   As He Appeared Three Years Later.

FIGURE 5.9. John Choate's photographs of Carlisle Indian Industrial School student, Tom Torlino. School boosters staged before-and-after photos like this to garner public support. The juxtaposed images highlighted students' physical transformation.

Credit: Carlisle Indian School Digital Resource Center

He is clothed in a blanket and wears jewelry. The "after" image includes no sign of his former of savagery. Torlino's hair is shorn. His brass adornments are stripped. His blanket is replaced by American-style clothes. As one scholar has noted, Choat even manipulated the studio lighting to make Torlino's skin look lighter. Pratt sent copies to members of Congress and sold them to raise money for the school.[104]

Americans loved Carlisle. In February 1880, the Department of the Interior issued a report praising Carlisle's transformative program. Students arrived from reservations across the plains "filthy, vermin covered, and dressed in their Native garb," like "wild beasts," the report's author claimed. Then a transformation occurred. Students attended classes, learned practical skills, and attended chapel. The writer marveled at the students' progress and attributed the success to Pratt's benevolent aim: "It is not necessary to say that a mild, kind, firm, but sympathetic Christian influence pervades the whole atmosphere of the place and every part of the management." Protestant leaders, including Quakers, also praised Carlisle. In 1880, *Friends' Intelligencer* proclaimed Carlisle a success. The following year, an article in *The Friend* boasted of Carlisle's nearly 200 Indian students who successfully learned English, acquired manual skills, and lived with white families over summer vacation. The Society proved to be some of the most vocal advocates of Pratt's program.[105]

Quakers and other "friends of the Indian" supported Carlisle as the Peace Policy fell further out of favor. As noted earlier, Friends struggled in their early engagements with President Hayes and his appointees. In the spring of 1879, Friends working in Washington reported that the commissioner of Indian Affairs was unsympathetic to their request to continue administering reservations on behalf of the nation. Soon after, committee members decided they had no option but "to resign the charge committed to us by the Government." While "friends of the Indian" bemoaned the Peace Policy's demise, it's unclear whether Kiowas or other Native people ever recognized what supporters insisted was their distinctively "humane" approach. There is no documentary evidence to show that Kiowas registered the changes that came with the Hayes administration.[106]

But citizens debating the "Indian problem" did notice. While some Americans objected to the Peace Policy from the beginning, the Friends' eventual departure could be attributed to a growing distrust in the reservation system. Public opinion was moving from support for Indian separation to a new emphasis on assimilation achieved through contact with Americans. On- and off-reservation boarding schools became the new focus of federal policy and public hopes for solving the Indian problem.

Pratt's experiment at Fort Marion, then, initiated a number of changes. Religious groups involved in the Peace Policy found that the government and the public were more willing to support their work in schools than their partnerships in reservation administration. Indeed, many Protestant "friends of the Indian" began to argue against the reservation altogether. The perceived success of Pratt's outing programs persuaded many that segregating Indians on reservations had been misguided. They wanted methods focused on assimilating Indians into the general population. Kiowas and their allies on the reservation, however, hesitated to accept the idea of off-reservation schools. When Pratt sent Indian representatives to recruit there, Kiowas showed little interest. They also defended their reservation as it had been assured to them by treaty. Even as they heard about reformers' early calls to dissolve reservations and settlers' claims that Indian Territory should be opened for settlement, Kiowas denied that the government had the authority to break apart their lands or their community. They had a treaty and they planned to see it upheld.

REUNITED IN THE CLOSED LANDS

There are few accounts of the moment in May 1878 when Kiowa prisoners reunited with their families. The former inmates had written letters and sent money to their relatives. They had received updates about life from letters sent by family. But these could hardly have prepared them for the changes that occurred during their three-year absence. Many Kiowas had settled in new parts of the reservation due to consolidation and the agent's push to locate Kiowa encampments around fields for cultivation. Soldiers now accompanied the people on hunts and ritual celebrations. More Kiowas had wooden houses on their property and wore American-style clothes. More children attended school. Agent Hunt wrote to his superiors that he expected the returned prisoners to help accelerate the pace of change. They will be "useful in teaching the wild Indians how to work," he wrote to his superiors.[107] Even as they changed some cultural practices, however, Kiowas rejected some of the agent's directives. They argued that their current situation left them in a state of near starvation. Soon after the prisoners' return, Kiowas informed Agent Hunt that limits on hunting and poor crop yields left them hungry. Government rations did not fill the void. Complaints about hunger continued in the coming years. These conditions made for an increasingly unhealthy environment. Kiowas soon recorded their first deaths from tuberculosis and observers noted the "frightful mortality" of Kiowa children under the age of four.[108]

In the face of these challenges, Kiowas sought empowerment and healing through their Sun Dance rites. The summer the prisoners returned, Kiowa calendars depict two Sun Dance lodges. Rather then two separate encampments, this observance simply extended the ceremony by a few days. Such celebrations typically occurred when more than one man vowed to sponsor one upon receiving a particular blessing or protection. Perhaps relatives had vowed to sponsor the ritual if and when the prisoners came home? The next few summers, however, involved significant obstacles to the ritual's performance. In 1879, Kiowas celebrated the Sun Dance, but had so little food they resorted to eating some of their horses during the ritual encampment. Calendars entries for 1880 show no Sun Dance celebration that summer, although there is no clear reason indicated.[109]

Just as Kiowas experienced many obstacles to celebrating their central ritual, one of their own returned and represented a new source of sacred power. It was Zótâm (Driftwood), the artist and former Fort Marion prisoner. He had lived in upstate New York under Mary Burnham's supervision. While there is no evidence that Zótâm continued drawing there, he did write some letters in English. He corresponded with Sétqópjè (Mountain Bear), his fellow Kiowa in Burnham's care, on several occasions.[110] He also made a few entries in a journal kept by Rev. Wicks, the local minister who oversaw his education.[111] Zótâm wrote about a typical weekday in New York: school in the morning, farm work in the afternoon, and visits with American friends once work was done.

Zótâm's letters and journal provide hints about the religious education he received. In one entry, he noted his attendance at a prayer meeting. If his schedule was anything like Sétqópjè's, whose more extensive journal has survived, we can assume he attended prayer meetings several nights a week. In letters to Captain Pratt, Zótâm reported that his hosts told him about Jesus, Rev. Wicks implored him to have only one God, and the bishop was planning to baptize him.[112] Of course, it is impossible to know what Zótâm might have thought about these new experiences. We have only the words he offered to the local minister who supervised his education and the man who once imprisoned him. He presented himself to these Americans as a person seeking transformation. "I very want be pure in heart and holy man," he wrote to Pratt.[113] "I think about Jesus and all night I pray about God."[114] Zótâm also thought about his Kiowa friends. In his letters to Pratt, he asked the captain to remember him to his relatives and friends at Hampton Institute. He asked that they not forget him.

Mary Burnham kept Pratt abreast of Zótâm and the other Indians' development. She praised their manual skills, writing that the "boys" were as sought after for farm work as any "white laborers." By summer 1881, Wicks and Burnham determined it was time for their Indian charges to return home. Once again, the bishop arrived. He ordained Paul Caryl Zotom and David Pendleton Oakerhater, a Cheyenne, to the diaconate. During the service, Zótâm read the gospel. Burnham's glowing account of the proceedings noted that Christian teaching had changed a man once "so perverse and insubordinate." At a sending service later that day, the bishop reminded the new deacons that New York Christians had prayed for three years in support of their impending mission to "their perishing people." Like so many Protestant "friends of the Indian," Burnham attributed the new momentum to Pratt. Considering the Native nations that would soon receive the Indian missionaries, Burnham wrote to Pratt that they "are redeemed through your work in Florida."[115]

The two deacons and Rev. Wicks traveled to Indian Country. The minister boasted he was about to confront 10,000 souls "in heathen darkness."[116] They first arrived at the Cheyenne and Arapaho Reservation, which was already served by at least two white missionaries. As the Indians were already familiar with missionaries, Wicks had little problem drawing a crowd for his first service.[117] The KCA Reservation, however, was a different story. Agency staff organized Sunday meetings for worship, but the gatherings mostly drew white employees. No permanent minister or missionary served there.

Wicks and Zótâm struggled to find any interested Indians.[118] The minister began by meeting with some of the headmen. He quickly returned to the Cheyenne and Arapaho Reservation, leaving Zótâm to begin his ministry just as the people gathered for the Sun Dance.

If the summer of 1880 had been a ritual disappointment, Kiowas came back with new vitality in 1881. Calendars recall many lodges for sweats and purification. Agent Hunt's report confirmed the uptick in activity. After his successful effort to suppress the ritual the previous summer, Hunt was dismayed to hear "the medicine men have been unusually active." The agent complained that despite Kiowas' changes in housing, farming, dress, and education, "the Indian holds to no one of his savage beliefs and customs so tenaciously as he does to his belief in the power of his medicine men and their ceremonies for making medicine."[119]

Zótâm was apparently drawn in. His fellow Cheyenne deacon heard about it and wrote to Burnham, claiming that he had attended the "big Medicine heathen dance" despite Wicks's admonition against it.[120] Wicks apparently got wind of the letter and dashed off a clarification.[121] Zótâm, Wicks explained, was simply homesick for his people who were staying in the ritual encampment. Zótâm went to see them, but "preserved his character as a Christian man and minister." While we cannot know exactly what transpired, it is clear from the correspondence that both Wicks and the Cheyenne deacon believed that Christian Indians should reject the Sun Dance. Wicks decided to return to the KCA Reservation in September and keep a closer eye on Paul Zótâm.[122]

After the Sun Dance, Zótâm found formats for spreading the Christian message and garnered some Kiowa followers. He taught catechism and led prayers at the agency school. On Sundays, he offered sermons to those who gathered to hear him. According to Wicks, some of Paul's adult relatives showed interest in Christianity. In late October, Wicks baptized seventeen Kiowas between the ages of ten and eighteen. After the baptisms, Wick's letters to Burnham contained a new urgency about the mission's potential. This reservation, he wrote, is "one of the most important missions that our church has engaged in within the borders of our own country." He seemed incredulous that so many people, mostly Indian but also some whites, lived in a part of the United States untouched by Christian mission efforts. It is, he wrote, "as though they were living in the heart of Africa."[123]

But Kiowas hardly lived in Africa. They resided in territory ruled by the United States. They made their lodges and houses on lands increasingly coveted by white settlers. Rumors abounded about the future of Indians' communal landholding. Protestant "friends of the Indian," among others, increasingly called for lands in severalty, meaning the replacement of tribal landholding with individual land ownership.[124] Severalty, also known as allotment, would dramatically disrupt communal practices among Indian nations. When the Quaker agent for the Cheyenne and Arapaho spoke at the Friends Indian committee in the spring of 1881, he argued that "one of the greatest drawbacks to permanent work of any kind at this Agency is the uncertainty of their land title." The same was true on the Kiowas' reservation. From the agent's perspective, Indians would not put resources and energy into constructing wood houses and cultivating fields if the reservation could be broken into separate parts with the "surplus" sold off to white settlers.[125]

If a nearby Quaker agent worried about allotment, Wicks saw it as an opportunity. The reservation's potential breakup and opening to settlers could encourage Indians to act now by selecting plots and settling near the church and school he planned to build. It was beautiful land, he reasoned. It "eventually will be densely populated." The railroads would soon carve their way through the region. A forward-thinking missionary could

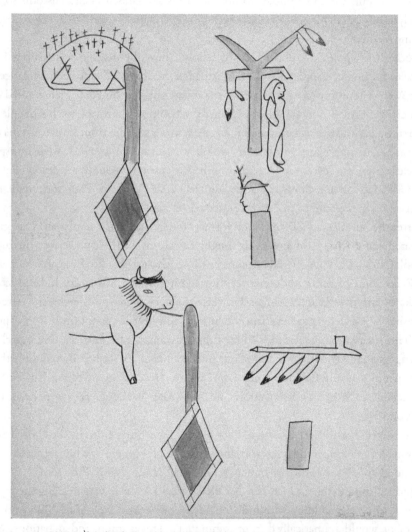

FIGURE 5.10. Cûitònqi's calendar entries for the winter of 1882–1883 through the summer of 1884. The image at the upper left depicts the large encampment of Páutépjè's (Bison Bull Emerging) followers.

establish a building and convince individual Indians to follow his example. The severalty threat could prompt Indians to secure plots and advance civilized living through individual landholding.[126]

But Kiowas denied that white people—whether missionaries, settlers, or railroad men—had any rights to their reservation lands. They had a binding agreement with the federal government, the Treaty of Medicine Lodge, which deemed these lands as their communal possession until at least 1898. The reservation was theirs. But Kiowas knew the threats. Some invoked sacred power to rectify the situation. As winter settled onto the plains in 1881, word spread of a new man of power. Jáudèkáu (Retained His Name A Long Time) claimed he could bring back the buffalo herds. He said the people's medicine bundles had appeared to him in a vision. He took a new name, Páutépjè, which means Bison Bull Emerging. He built a lodge and called people to join him. Many did. Páutépjè asked them to affirm his power to bring back the buffalo and re-establish their nation's health. Calendar makers and artists recalled his effort and the people who responded (Figure 5.10). When no buffalo appeared, Páutépjè lost his followers. His effort to revitalize the herds was the first of several to follow.[127]

Some efforts at empowerment took quieter forms. One new option made its way into some Kiowa lives by the 1880s. It was a gift from Indian neighbors. Under their guidance, Kiowas learned about this spiny cactus that could be ingested when dried into buttons or ground into powder. Many became convinced of its potential to heal and guide. While peyote played a much larger role in Kiowa ritual life in the mid-1880s, scholars date its slow introduction already in the early 1870s. Over time, more people would seek it out.[128]

As Kiowas entered the new decade, they struggled to hold on to their most cherished rituals. Against many odds, they gathered for Sun Dance rites. At the same time, they considered Zótâm's message about Jesus, Páutépjè's promise to rectify their situation, and peyote's potential for healing. Kiowas searched for sacred power as they struggled against forces aimed at their assimilation. They did not want to be subsumed into the wider population. They did not want to occupy land the way other Americans did. They considered themselves a distinctive people. They cherished and defended their place on the southern plains.

Protestant "friends of the Indian," however, pushed even harder for policies aimed at Indian assimilation. Pratt's program at Fort Marion, as well as his new effort at Carlisle, persuaded them that Native people could be citizens if they simply shed their tribal connections and ways of living. More than ever, Americans sponsored schools to facilitate this transition. In the 1880s, Catholics would join these efforts in new and unprecedented ways. The 1880s would also bring more arguments for lands in severalty. American efforts to assimilate Indians found expression not only in boarding school classrooms, but also in the process of dismantling communal landholding and reservation life across the American West. Indian separation would be a thing of the past.

FIGURE 5.11. Ellen Smoky, a Kiowa girl, standing next to an infant in a handmade cradleboard.
Credit: Museum of the Great Plains, Tingley Historical Collection, 1993-P008:247

Schools and farms would make them citizens of the future. Missionaries would make them Christians.

In the face of more missionaries and civilizing programs, Kiowas underwent their own transformation. They sought new powers in new forms in order to remain a people. These efforts reflected Kiowa understandings of how power circulated through the universe, in what forms it could be known, and what sorts of transformation it could initiate. But Kiowas also engaged in smaller acts that reinforced communal ties. In the reservation years, which included illness, child mortality, and separation from children in school, Kiowa women put new energies into making cradleboards for their babies (Figure 5.11).[129] They sewed intricate bead designs that represented family ties. They prayed before making them and had them smoked and blessed once they were complete. The family connections expressed through cradleboards stretched far afield from Indian Country. One Kiowa prisoner, whose first son was born during his incarceration, drew pictures of his wife and the cradleboard she made to carry their child (Plate 8).[130] From new sources of sacred power to new ways of holding their children close, Kiowas confronted "friends of the Indian" and the colonial powers that tried to break them apart.

PART THREE
Divided Lands

6

1882 to 1892

~———————————————————————————————————

IN HER CALENDAR entry for the summer of 1882, Cáulánàundáumà (Standing In The Footprints Of Bison) drew a bear with an American-style hat, a name glyph for Bear's Hat.[1] Underneath the image, an unknown person later wrote, "The son of Woman Heart still continued in this summer to make his claim good. He had for a helper Bear Hat, who died at this time." The son in this reference was Páutépjè (Bison Bull Emerging), the man who claimed power to restore the buffalo. But the herds did not come. Páutépjè's followers disbanded.

By 1882, Kiowas faced Americans' unrelenting effort to sever their ties to their lands and to each other. The dwindling buffalo herds threatened ritual observation as well as basic nutrition. Drought undermined efforts to farm. Worried that rations caused dependency, officials did not increase them, despite the food scarcity. Bouts of whooping cough and malaria plagued the people.[2] Infant mortality rose. Children attending reservation day schools returned to their families in the evenings, but Americans increased recruiting efforts for off-reservation boarding schools. For Kiowas, American presence in their homeland threatened their very survival. Páutépjè provided one sort of ritual response. It was one of many options Kiowas pursued to protect both land and community in an increasingly dire situation.

Americans had a different view of what troubled Indian nations and what the solution might be. By 1882, the Peace Policy ended and government officials returned to posts as reservation agents. Following Richard Pratt's lead, Protestant "friends of the Indian" proclaimed that reservations had failed to assimilate Indians.[3] They sought new ways to speed Indians' absorption into American life. Through efforts that sometimes paralleled and at other times diverged from campaigns to assimilate African Americans, Chinese laborers, immigrants, and Mormons, Protestant "friends of the Indian" proposed laws and policies to break down Native ties and encourage individual land ownership, productive labor, and middle-class consumption. In Indian Country, they focused on land and schools. They advocated allotment of reservations, which divided communally held lands into plots owned by individuals. To shape Indian attitudes toward ownership, reformers supported a massive system of Indian schools to teach both civilized habits and Christian practice.[4]

While some of these policies depended upon Native peoples' willingness to participate, others did not. To be sure, Protestant "friends of the Indian" continued to scorn those who proposed military solutions to the "Indian problem." But they emphasized their benevolence, even as they encouraged a wave of sometimes coercive policies and institutions aimed at dismantling Native communities and cultures.[5]

Sweeping religious changes resulted as Kiowas felt pressure to relinquish their lands and educate their children in American-style schools. The people considered new sources for healing, protection, and empowerment. On the surface, their struggles to continue older practices such as the Sun Dance looked significantly different from new ritual experiences such as Methodist camp meetings and what has come to be called the Ghost Dance. But even as Kiowas experimented with new sources of power and modes for accessing them, their practices reflected a consistent concern for their connection to land and each other.

CONFRONTING THE GODS OF INDIAN COUNTRY

The early 1880s continued a trend, introduced in the previous chapter, toward a post-Reconstruction hardening of legal restrictions on and extra-legal actions against racial and religious minorities. In 1883, the Supreme Court handed down a series of decisions that undermined civil rights legislation created to ensure black political participation. Across the South, white citizens created legal barriers to freedom and used lynching to terrorize African Americans.[6] In 1882, President Chester Arthur signed the Chinese Exclusion Act. The debate about this unprecedented immigration restriction invoked Chinese racial difference and "heathenism" as dangerous to the American republic.[7] That same year, Congress passed the Edmunds Anti-Polygamy Act as part of an ongoing effort to bring Mormons to heel. The law made polygamy a felony and barred those engaged in it, as well as those who affirmed it as a religious practice, from voting, serving on juries, and holding political office.[8]

American officials employed similarly restrictive measures to address the ongoing "Indian problem." In 1882, the federal Indian office published its "Code of Indian Offenses." The code criminalized rituals such as Sun Dances and peyote practices, as well as communal dancing, polygamy, the work of "medicine men," and property destruction as an expression of mourning. The code also established reservation-based courts to punish offenders. Reservation agents were directed to support the courts and carry out punishments such as withholding rations and, for repeat violators, incarceration. Agents on reservations in the southern plains did not enforce the code with as much vigor as their colleagues among the Sioux. But Kiowas felt some pressure to curtail communal rites and individual practices. For example, an agent arrested a Kiowa woman who claimed to have power from snakes. He threatened her with jail if she did not stop her healing work.[9]

Officials acted not only against cultural and ritual practices they sought to eliminate, but also Indian sovereignty. After an 1883 court case that upheld tribal leaders' ability to deal with offenses between Native people on Indian lands, Congress passed the Major Crimes Act of 1885, bringing some reservation disputes under federal jurisdiction. In 1884, the court decided *Elk v. Wilkins*, a voting rights case that held Indians could not pass the allegiance test and therefore had no access to citizenship or the franchise.[10] Like other racial and religious minorities, Native people experienced significant legal pressures in the early 1880s. While African Americans and Chinese laborers felt these measures as exclusively restrictive, Mormons and Indians faced policies that made assimilation the price of political inclusion.[11]

Parallel to these legal pressures on Native people, Protestant "friends of the Indian" advanced programs for Indian cultural transformation. The 1880s saw the creation of several organizations for this purpose. The Indian Rights Association (IRA) advocated for Indian inclusion in American political life and founded their claims on the possibility of Native peoples' assimilation.[12] A Quaker involved in Indian affairs founded the Lake Mohonk Conference of Friends of the Indian and Other Dependent Peoples (LMC), an association of like-minded Protestant reformers.[13] Leading citizens who gathered annually at Lake Mohonk collaborated on work to "uplift" Native and African Americans. For both populations, they recommended individualism, industry, property ownership, education, and economic ambition.[14] To be sure, historians have shown that these two powerful reform groups did not represent all interested voices, and their policy proposals were hardly inevitable.[15] Counter voices, including the National Indian Defense Association, attempted a different vision of reform, one that worked harder to highlight Indian voices and priorities. Even so, the IRA and LMC had substantial influence on Indian policy and shaped popular sentiment about solutions to the "Indian problem."

American Catholics, who had fought for inclusion in the Peace Policy and federal Indian school budgets, also stepped up. Two developments propelled their increased presence in Indian Country. At the 1884 Third Plenary Council, the American bishops established an annual appeal to support African American and Native American evangelization. The work of the Bureau of Catholic Indian Missions (BCIM) and its lay supporters increased afterward. Support from heiress and nun Katherine Drexel also fueled the Church's work on reservations.[16] Catholic activity continued to irk Protestant "friends of the Indian," who remained dubious of their ability to properly Americanize Native people.

BCIM leaders, both priests and laymen, persisted in their calls for Indians' religious freedom as they sought federal funds for reservation schools. Referring to years of struggle against agents who represented Protestant denominations during Grant's Peace Policy, Father Jean Baptiste Brouillet argued that Indians' freedom of conscience was at stake. In a pamphlet designed to generate lay support for missions, he wrote, "These [Catholic] Indians want their church to have the control of their agency, to train them and their children in the faith they have adopted, and to direct their civilization."[17] With these arguments, Brouillet and other Catholics redefined what it meant to be "friends of the Indian." They asserted the importance of protecting Native people's constitutionally guaranteed right to practice Catholicism. Throughout the 1880s, this rhetoric accompanied their expanding network of reservation schools and raised the ire of Protestants who deemed their efforts purely sectarian.[18]

Protestant "friends of the Indian" faced more than just their Catholic competitors. They also confronted a public sphere teeming with nativist rhetoric.[19] In response, they strongly affirmed Indians' ability to assimilate. But theirs was not necessarily a popular sentiment. The reading public encountered a barrage of negative assessments about the citizenship capacities of African Americans, Chinese workers, immigrants, and Mormons. In 1885, social gospel minister Josiah Strong published a manifesto calling for Anglo-Saxon dominance over potentially destructive counterforces in American life.[20] His book, *Our Country*, sold nearly 200,000 copies and predicted that Anglo-Saxon Christianity and civilization would someday conquer the world. That same year, John Fiske published "Manifest Destiny" in *Harper's Monthly*. Like Strong, Fiske proclaimed that civilized societies would prevail as barbarians succumbed. Americans, Fiske argued, would inevitably colonize less civilized parts of the globe.[21] Citizens debating the "Indian problem" operated within this larger climate of nativist sentiment. To be sure, there were serious disagreements and competing rhetoric. But a common thread ran through it all: the presumption that Native people must assimilate and must do it soon.

THE GODS LIVING IN THE LAND

Decisions and policies enacted in the nation's capital made an increasingly significant impact on the Kiowa, Comanche, and Apache (KCA) Reservation. In 1882, most Kiowas still lived in small bands in tipis scattered across the reservation. Some attempted farming.[22] Some wore American-style clothes. Some sent their children to reservation day schools. A few attended Captain Pratt's Indian boarding school in Carlisle, Pennsylvania.[23] Only one missionary worked on the reservation at the time, although more would arrive over the course of the decade. These Christian evangelists brought with them more pressures to settle, farm, and attend school.

Kiowas still gathered for the Sun Dance despite physical obstacles and the ritual's criminalization in the Code of Indian Offenses. In the spring of 1883, the *Táimé* keeper died. But Kiowas named a new one in time for the summer observation. Hunters found a buffalo to offer, and Kiowas celebrated with visitors from a Nez Perce delegation. Difficulties finding buffalo, as well as challenges from an unsympathetic agent, however, undercut Kiowa efforts to continue the practice. They held no Sun Dance in 1884 or 1886. In 1887,

Kiowas resorted to buying a buffalo hide from a Texas rancher. When they began to build the medicine lodge, their agent informed them that this year would be their last.[24]

The agent worried not only about the Sun Dance, but also peyote. Historians posit that neighboring Indian nations brought peyote to the Kiowas in the 1870s, but few details have survived about the practice prior to 1880. Considering peyote a powerful medicine, Kiowas sought physical healing and guidance from ritual peyote leaders. Accounts from the 1880s detail all-night ceremonies in which practitioners gathered around a crescent-shaped altar to sing, pray, ingest peyote, and experience its healing and guidance. While certain elements of ritual peyote ingestion were new to Kiowas, others reflected older power-seeking traditions. Some Kiowas reported that they came to peyote after receiving guidance in dreams. Others continued inheritance practices similar to those for bundles and shields. Fathers passed on their "father peyote," the large button placed on a crescent altar, to their sons. By the mid-1880s, ritual peyote ingestion spread enough to worry reservation agents. Without exception, government officials and missionaries viewed peyote practices as a drug habit or a new form of nature worship. Agents tried to use Courts of Indian Offenses to stop peyote meetings.[25]

Christian missionaries hoped to replace older traditions such as the Sun Dance, as well as newer ones like the peyote road, with Christian civilization. When Quaker agents and teachers departed as the Peace Policy ended, a variety of missionaries arrived to establish churches and schools. As noted in the previous chapter, Episcopal priest J. B. Wicks started his mission work in 1881. Others soon arrived with equally ambitious plans to evangelize, educate, and civilize. In 1885, Hilary Cassal, a French Benedictine living in the eastern part of Indian Territory, made his first trip to the Kiowa reservation. Soon after, Catholics missionaries planned for a permanent mission among the Kiowas. The Methodist Episcopal Church-South (MECS) also considered an expansion into western portions of the territory. Baptists, who had long been active among the "civilized tribes" settled to the east, planned to move west to work with "wild" Indians. In 1883, the Baptists sent George Washington Hicks, a Cherokee preacher trained at the University of Rochester, to evangelize Wichitas and Caddoes living on the KCA Reservation. Soon after, a Baptist carpenter began to visit Kiowa encampments, preaching and establishing relations with leading Kiowa men, including Cûifágàui (Lone Wolf the Younger), nephew of the elder Cûifágàui. These first missionary labors were followed by a steady stream of religious workers representing the nationwide effort to assimilate Indian peoples.[26]

Kiowas played central, if perhaps ambiguous roles in these early mission efforts. As detailed in the previous chapter, Rev. Wicks had taken five former Fort Marion prisoners to upstate New York to train them as missionaries. One of them, Zótâm (Driftwood), arrived on the reservation in 1881 after being baptized and ordained a deacon. But Zótâm's path took an unexpected turn, at least to Wicks, upon arrival in Indian Territory. While Zótâm worked with Wicks for several months, his service was short-lived. He disappeared, for a time, from any record of the mission. Wicks reportedly baptized two

Kiowa children in March 1882. The same source reported, without explanation, that Zótâm no longer engaged in missionary effort.[27]

Zótâm's kinsman in upstate New York, Sétqópjè (Mountain Bear), offers another example of how Kiowas responded to Christian missionaries, as well as other new options available on the reservation in the 1880s. Unlike Zótâm, Sétqópjè was not ordained in New York. He had contracted tuberculosis in Florida and was frequently ill once he traveled north. While he attended some church services, he was often too sick to participate. In January 1879, Sétqópjè underwent examination for church membership by five Presbyterian elders.[28] He received baptism and a new name, Paul Caruthers. His diary from three years in New York faithfully records the prayer meetings, Bible study, and church activities that constituted his new life there.

The diary also details his ongoing connection to his people. Like Zótâm, Sétqópjè sought connection with Kiowas on the east coast as well as back on the reservation. He wrote and received many letters from former Fort Marion inmates. Sétqópjè must have contacted the Kiowa reservation agent because he received a response with an update about his mother. Sétqópjè also maintained some Kiowa cultural practices. In his diary, he noted the nights he stayed up singing in his native tongue. He also made bows and arrows in a traditional manner. When he became increasingly ill in 1882, Sétqópjè asked if he could return home to die. Rev. Wicks obliged.[29]

According to a later account, Sétqópjè arrived at the reservation in terrible condition. In response, his friends urged him to seek healing in a peyote meeting. He did. Sétqópjè's situation and his friends' response mirrored older Kiowa healing practices. Terribly ill, he sought out a source of power, along with men who could doctor him with it.[30] Later in life, Sétqópjè affirmed that peyote brought him "speedy relief." As a result, he continued the practice and served as a leader in the peyote movement for many years.[31]

Both Zótâm and Sétqópjè showed a willingness to experiment with Christian practices and learn the new religion's tenets. Both also continued to feel connected to Kiowa friends and relations, as well as certain customs. Their encounters with missionaries show the various ways in which Kiowas engaged Christianity as it was introduced on the reservation. Throughout the 1880s, then, Kiowas exhibited flexibility in their ritual lives, demonstrated by ongoing efforts to practice the Sun Dance, even if it meant buying a buffalo hide from a Texas rancher. Some followed the peyote road, which, according to at least one historian, was practiced widely on the reservation by 1887. This flexibility in the face of colonial power, as well as the ongoing commitment to land and community, became increasingly important as Kiowas faced a new challenge: allotment.

DIVIDING THE LAND

Allotment, or the legal process of establishing individual Indian landowning on what had been communally held reservation lands, was a long-desired goal of American policymakers. One historian has traced its beginnings to 1789, when the Secretary of War commented that Indians needed to acquire a sense of "exclusive property."[32] Most treaties negotiated in the 1850s and 1860s included terms for eventual allotment. The process involved not only breaking apart commonly held lands into 160-acre plots owned by individuals, but also the overall reduction of tribal landholdings, as "surplus" acreage became available for sale to white Americans. By the 1870s, population growth in the states and territories surrounding Indian Territory prompted settlers and their representatives to call for allotment, and thus the opening of vast Indian lands to American buyers.[33]

Government officials and "friends of the Indian" argued that allotment would solve several vexing problems. It offered a method for breaking down tribal relations by undermining communal landholding.[34] Owning individual plots of land would spur Indian efforts at farming and economic self-sufficiency. In effect, allotment served as another strategy within a broader program for Indian assimilation.[35] In the early 1880s, Protestant "friends of the Indian" pursued allotment with great energy. Prominent preacher Lyman Abbott led the way, calling for the abolition of reservations altogether.[36]

Reformers and officials typically framed their support for allotment in the language of Indian protection and American benevolence. They focused on the accompanying social programs established for Indian people while downplaying the fact that allotment violated some treaties.[37] Senator Henry Dawes, whose name became synonymous with allotment, began promoting the process in 1882.[38] He submitted a petition to Congress purportedly to address settlers illegally taking lands in Indian Territory. The petition encouraged Congress to protect Indian rights under the law, fulfill treaty obligations, and provide more funds for schools. It also called for allotment so that individual Indians could gain the rights of citizenship and the protections afforded to landowners.

Like reformers from the Lake Mohonk Conference, Protestants working on the Kiowa reservation threw their support behind allotment. In an update on Episcopal missions to Indians, Rev. Wicks informed readers that "the tribal relation" stood as an impediment to progress. Lands in "severalty," meaning individually owned, were needed. Without allotment, Wicks opined, Indians could not move from "childhood" to "manhood," from "wild life" to "civilization." Property rights, he wrote, would "inspire and bless [the Indian man]."[39]

A few American reformers and religious leaders did not agree. Representatives from the National Indian Defense Association argued that Indians would suffer if tribal relations were imminently dissolved by allotment. They asked that Native people be granted more time to transition toward individual landholding.[40] Even strong supporters of eventual land cessation and assimilation, such as Richard Pratt, worried about pushing the process too fast. He contended that more Indian education was needed before individual landownership could be successful.[41] Such voices, at least among American citizens, were few.

Indians across the West, including Kiowas, resisted allotment, especially as it violated treaties they had with the American government. The Treaty of Medicine Lodge had established peace, laid out reservation boundaries, and provided a variety of forms of compensation and government support for a term of thirty years.[42] It also provided that future land cessations would require the affirmation of three-quarters of the reservation's male population. Because of their treaty, Kiowas assumed they could not be forced to negotiate an allotment deal before 1897.

But allotment advocates pushed ahead. In 1886, Senator Dawes introduced the Sioux land bill.[43] Protestant "friends of the Indian" and other powerful interests supported it, arguing that it offered a way to allot Indian lands without breaking treaties.[44] The combined social and political power of Senator Dawes, the federal Indian office, and Protestant "friends of the Indian" overwhelmed the bill's critics. Dawes then moved forward with allotment legislation. In February 1887, President Grover Cleveland signed the Dawes Allotment Act. It called for a government commission to negotiate with tribal authorities across the West. It promised citizenship to Indians willing to accept allotment.[45]

With so many Americans convinced of allotment's benefits, few recognized that Indians might have opposing views. Thomas Battey, a Quaker schoolteacher who had served on the Kiowa reservation, took to a Society newspaper to explain. "[The Indian] regards the division of the land into parcels and appropriating it to individuals, as so nearly approaching sacrilege as to be utterly intolerable." Battey was not necessarily against allotment, but he insisted that Indians first needed Christian instruction to change their views about land. Allotment prior to that transition would be "certainly unkind if not cruel and unjust."[46]

According to Kiowas, allotment violated the Treaty of Medicine Lodge, which promised them thirty years of annuities and rations. Starting in 1887, the Kiowas' agent regularly reported to federal officials that the Indians opposed allotment.[47] By the early 1890s, Kiowas informed their agent that they desired to keep the time frame established in the Medicine Lodge treaty. Allotment could not begin before 1897.[48]

Kiowas reiterated their opposition as government officials sought to expedite allotment on reservations across the west. In 1888, federal representatives traveled to the Lakota (Sioux) reservations to recommend significant land cessations. In March 1889, Congress passed the Springer Amendment, which organized the Oklahoma Territory and created a commission to negotiate with Indians about buying "surplus" lands. The commissioners arrived at the nearby Cheyenne and Arapaho Reservation. In a deal that Cheyenne and Arapahos later protested, commissioners divided their reservation into individual plots and provided $55 a person for tens of thousands of acres of "leftover" land. In 1892, settlers participated in a land run to claim the surplus. Despite Kiowa protests, allotment was coming.[49]

FEARING THE GODS OF INDIAN COUNTRY

So were more missionaries and schoolteachers. The most influential early missionary among Kiowas, J. J. Methvin, arrived in late 1887. He represented the Methodist Episcopal Church South (MECS), which maintained significant missions in the eastern part of

Indian Territory. The region's Methodist bishop claimed that Kiowas, like non-Christian peoples known to the apostle Paul, had made a modern-day Macedonian call by asking for Christian missionaries. The bishop appointed Methvin to begin work among the "wild tribes." Imitating Methodist missions further east, Methvin planned to evangelize Indian camps, start a school, and teach Christian civilization.[50]

Methvin arrived as Kiowas struggled to sustain their Sun Dance practice and attempted, once again, to reinvigorate the buffalo herds. Similar to Páutépjè's (Bison Bull Emerging) effort in the early 1880s, a new ritual specialist promised a supernatural transformation of Kiowas' increasingly desperate situation. Vạuigài (In The Middle) came from an eminent Kiowa family. His father, Sétạgài (Sitting Bear), had been a legendary warrior who raided into Texas and Mexico, fought Americans, and was killed only after being taken into custody and mysteriously producing a weapon to attack his army captors. Vạuigài claimed to be Páutépjè's successor, but with even greater power.[51] He gathered followers at an encampment. According to the Rev. Methvin, Vạuigài said he could raise the dead, kill enemies with a single glance, and stand immune to bullets. Like earlier Native leaders who promised to rectify disastrous colonial situations, he asked his followers to purge practices borrowed from whites.[52] He warned that tornadoes and lightning would destroy those who did not follow these new instructions. Vạuigài said that white people, along with their reservation buildings and schools, would be obliterated.[53]

Kiowa responses to Vạuigài were mixed. Many gathered around him. Some took their children out of school to join the crowds. Some of his male followers banded together, calling themselves the Sons of the Sun and shunning those who rejected the message. Others were skeptical, including Vạuigài's own brother, Joshua Givens. When the movement began, the nervous reservation agent asked Givens, who had recently returned from boarding school, to intervene. The Rev. Methvin claimed Givens's effort, which included challenging Vạuigài's power, was critical to the movement's eventual decline. According to some American observers, the agent requested troops from Fort Sill to stop Vạuigài's progress. Clearly rattled by the situation, the agent also took further steps to suppress ritual power seeking through the Sun Dance and ritual peyote ingestion.[54]

Joshua Givens, though Vạuigài's brother and Sétạgài's son, had been raised by an American doctor after his father was killed. He learned English at a reservation school and then continued his studies at Carlisle and Lincoln University. He became a member of a Presbyterian church and studied theology. The Presbytery of Carlisle licensed him to preach and sent him back to the reservation in 1888. Once there, he not only battled rectification movements such as the one promulgated by his brother, but helped the newly arrived Presbyterian missionary, Silas Fait, in opening a church and school. Like many of the American missionaries, Givens encountered his share of conflicts concerning the Christian church he represented.[55]

Rev. Methvin also became involved in ongoing disputes over Kiowa ritual practices. He wrote of an 1889 encounter with Ádàuiétjè (Big Tree), a Kiowa headman incensed that the federal Indian office had forbidden the Sun Dance. Ádàuiétjè accused Methvin of informing the government about plans for the ceremonial. He threatened to fight rather than capitulate to the ban. Methvin denied the accusation, as well as admonished Ádàuiétjè against violence. When rumors of Ádàuiétjè's statement spread, the agent again sent for troops from Fort Sill. He did the same the next summer when Kiowas began Sun Dance preparations.[56]

Kiowa calendar makers registered the people's efforts to perform rituals despite difficult circumstances and American opposition. One calendar depicts the 1887 medicine lodge pole, adorned with a buffalo hide purchased from the Texas rancher. Entries for summer of 1888 recall Vą́uigài's activity and feature no Sun Dance references. Drawings about the summer of 1890 depict an interrupted ritual, with central poles lacking offerings or incomplete lodges. According to oral accounts and other sources, 1890 marked the last attempted Sun Dance in Kiowa history.[57]

As Kiowas struggled to sustain their traditions, Methvin established new ones. In the summer of 1890, he hosted his first camp meeting. His plans reflected a perennial missionary strategy: perform Christian rituals at sites that once hosted indigenous practices. In his memoirs, Methvin delighted in the "strategic spot" where Kiowas once held their "medicine dances" and made their "preparations for the warpath." The minister remarked on the site's beauty. He hoped his camp meeting would "redeem the surroundings from the wild orgies of pagan worship to consecrated ground for the worship of God."[58]

Methvin's account of the camp meeting's proceedings proved equally dramatic. He read scriptures and preached to "half-naked Indians" with painted faces. The Indians listened to him patiently. But Methvin struggled to interpret their response to his message. His hopes for the meeting's potential, however, were confirmed when a Comanche woman "converted" on the final evening. After this initial success, Methvin planned for annual camp meetings in the auspicious location.[59]

Methvin's camp meetings were not the only new ritual practices on the reservation. That same summer, several Kiowa men visited the nearby Cheyenne and Arapaho Reservation after hearing news about a Paiute man of power. According to interviews with descendants, Páutáuljè (Lean Bison Bull) led the delegation and brought back a favorable report, as well as red paint provided by this new figure.[60] The delegation comprised Kiowas' first contact with Wovoka and the Ghost Dance movement he inspired. Scholars have wrestled with interpreting Wovoka and the many Indian nations that affirmed his message and adapted it to their contexts. Their work offers important suggestions for understanding the movement. They advise attending to the particular epistemologies and histories of each Native nation involved, tracking how participants sought health and prosperity on Native terms in a rapidly changing world, and considering it as a direct response to American colonialism.[61]

Some Kiowas joined the Ghost Dance movement. They eventually called it the Feather Dance, from *amacunga*, a Kiowa name for the dance that referenced the single feather worn by each dancer.[62] After visiting the Cheyenne and Arapaho, Páutáuljè came back and shared what he had heard. He provided instructions for dancing. He promised that followers would experience reunion with dead relatives, the return of the buffalo, the Americans' disappearance, and a renewed world. As Wovoka's message spread, Kiowas established a large encampment and began to dance. They composed their own songs to accompany their movement. They painted their bodies and clothes. Calendar makers recalled dancers wearing feathers and other markers of the movement (Figure 6.1).[63]

By 1890, Kiowas were at a turning point in their ritual power seeking. American soldiers blocked Sun Dances several years in a row, and the reservation agent insisted it would never be celebrated again. The agent also threatened to withhold rations from practitioners of ritual peyote ingestion. The first long-term missionary on the reservation, Rev. Methvin, searched out Kiowa sacred sites and claimed them for Christian worship. The buffalo were nearly gone. Infant mortality was high. More and more children departed from their families to attend on-reservation, and some even to off-reservation boarding schools. In the face of significant loss and dramatic change, the Feather Dance offered Kiowas a world in which their primary obstacles were removed and their primary joys were restored.

Americans, however, were worried about the new movement. Rumors about the Ghost Dance spread rapidly across the southern plains. An officer at Fort Sill reported what settlers were saying.[64] The Indians believed that Jesus was coming back to earth, specifically to them, because white men had killed him during his first visitation long ago. Other rumors told of Indians preaching Jesus's imminent inauguration of a new age. Whites would be removed from the plains and thrown into the sea. The stories were hardly limited to Indian Territory. The officer's report echoed settler rumors across the West. In a

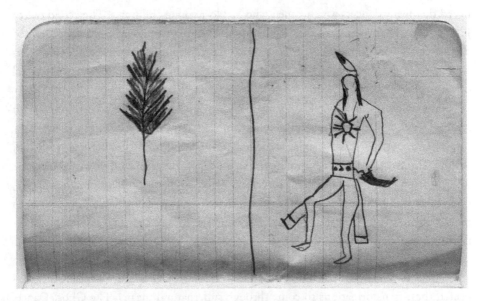

FIGURE 6.1. Black Bear's calendar entry for the summer of 1896 with a Kiowa Feather Dancer (Ghost Dancer) wearing a feather in his hair and a sun painted on his shirt.
Credit: American Museum of Natural History, catalog no. 50.1/6208 A37

short time, Wovoka's movement had been translated into local forms by Native peoples from Nevada to North Dakota to Indian Territory. Throughout the nation, Americans heard stories, some true and some outrageous, about the pan-Indian phenomenon.[65]

Americans in the West did not view the varieties of Plains Indian Ghost Dancing as a search for sacred power designed to rectify a terrible situation. They saw it, instead, as a threat to white safety and settlement. By November 1890, the Indian office's acting commissioner directed the Kiowas' agent to pay attention to the "threatening excitement" reported across the plains. He asked the agent for updates so he could suppress possible "outbreaks." Acknowledging dramatic newspaper coverage of Sioux Ghost Dancing, the commissioner warned the agent not to be sensational, but to act quickly if he heard of any "spirit of disobedience to orders." [66]

The Kiowas' agent continued to hear nearby settlers' and soldiers' reports about Ghost Dance activity. In December 1890, a local trader wrote that a new "medicine man" proclaimed a message "against civilization" because Jesus was coming soon.[67] The commander at nearby Fort Sill wondered if a pan-Indian revolt was in the works. "Are your Indians excited about the coming Messiah?" he asked the agent. "Have any runners been visiting them from the Northern Indians?" Like journalists, settlers, and military men across the West, the commander wondered if the Ghost Dancers were "likely to give any trouble."[68]

Some of our most detailed accounts of the Feather Dance come from an army officer, Hugh Scott, who was relatively sympathetic to Indian concerns and culture. Unlike many military figures, Scott did not see the movement as a precursor to armed uprising. His accounts of Ghost Dance activity emphasized Kiowa anxieties about family and land. He noted that many dancers were women who had lost young children.[69] They cried out to Jesus to bring back their dead children and protect others from dying. He also described the variety of Kiowa opinions on Jesus' potential return. Some were skeptical. Others expected the imminent return of dead relatives and the buffalo, along with the removal of white people.[70]

Scott's observations about Kiowa references to Jesus or a Messiah correspond with scholars' findings. Kiowas' emerging conceptions of Jesus operated within their established framework for how people interacted with great powers. Connecting with him was not limited to those with experience accessing *dwdw,* or sacred power. Rather, he was a protective and powerful being directly available to everyone. In the Feather Dance, then, Kiowa women implored Jesus to act positively on their behalf. They asked him to reunite them with their lost children. They implored him to restore the buffalo and remove the threatening Americans.[71]

In this way, Captain Scott did not see the dance as a prelude to war. Neither did he attribute it to the work of an Indian charlatan. Rather, he emphasized that Kiowas expected these transformations to come through supernatural means. The Ghost Dance, then, did not greatly concern him, but he was practically alone in this view. This was late December 1890. Kiowas were lucky enough to have a sympathetic officer in their midst;

other Indian nations who took up the Ghost Dance were not. Further north, in Lakota country, army officers surrounded a band of Ghost Dancers making their way to the reservation. In one of the most notorious assaults in American history, the Seventh Cavalry opened fire on Lakotas. At the Wounded Knee massacre, soldiers killed more than 300 people, many of them women and children.[72]

Ghost Dance excitement among the Kiowas soon flagged. Wounded Knee prompted a period of despair for Wovoka, along with a new direction to his message. Soon after, Áfîtàu (Wooden Lance), a leading Kiowa headman, boarded a train bound for the Paiute Reservation. Meeting Wovoka, however, disappointed him. Áfîtàu had recently lost a child and hoped he might be reunited with him. Wovoka told him it would not happen. After his visit, Áfîtàu mailed a negative letter about Wovoka to the Kiowa Reservation. He gave his account in person upon his return in February 1891. Áfîtàu argued against those who proclaimed the movement's power. After his denunciation, Kiowas' interest in the dance seemed to fade.[73]

HELP FROM THE GODS IN THE LAND

But Kiowa concerns, particularly about their children's vulnerability, continued. Throughout the 1880s, Americans had expanded efforts to achieve Indian assimilation through education. As noted earlier, networks of Indian schools grew in this period. In 1880, 4,651 Native children were enrolled in school. By 1890, there were 12,232. Federal appropriations for Indian education increased eighteen-fold during the same period. School expansion on the KCA Reservation began slowly. In the early 1880s, there were only two government-operated schools, one of which served Kiowa students. Some Kiowa young people attended Carlisle in Pennsylvania. After 1884, a few others traveled to the Chilocco boarding school in northern Indian Territory.[74]

Representations of and appearances by Native students bolstered the belief of many "friends of the Indian" that boarding school provided the best path to Indian assimilation and citizenship. Captain Pratt toured the East with Carlisle students. At an 1887 appearance at New York's Academy of Music, Pratt brought 140 students to play music, demonstrate their manual labor skills, recite sections of the Constitution, and debate— in front of a white audience—whether or not Indians ought to be exterminated. By this time, Joshua Givens, son of Sétágài (Sitting Bear) and brother to Vàuigài (In The Middle), was among Pratt's star students. At the New York event, Givens gave a speech in which he told of his "savage" childhood and implored his listeners to support Indian education. Givens also expressed his desire for citizenship, highlighting the irony that the government denied Indians this privilege even as they offered it to immigrants from Europe.[75]

More often, Americans encountered images of Indian students through photography. As noted in the previous chapter, Pratt had created dramatic images of Indian prisoners upon arrival at Fort Marion and juxtaposed them with pictures taken once they had been issued uniforms and had their hair cut. As noted earlier, Pratt expanded this strategy at Carlisle. Americans eagerly consumed the "before and after" prints. One writer raved upon seeing the Indian "originals," "half-clothed, repulsive, miserable, squalid, painted creatures," contrasted with the "fine looking stalwart young fellows" they became at school.[76]

Changing Indian children's appearance was only the beginning of the desired transformation. Boarding schools were more totalizing institutions than Indian day schools. Whether on-reservation or off, they had more extensive offerings and the capacity to oversee every aspect of Indian children's lives. As Methodist minister and superintendent of Indian schools Daniel Dorchester acknowledged, schools offered a basic academic curriculum and supplemented it with manual labor and industrial education.[77]

Schools also provided Indian children with narratives about their place in civilized society generally and the contemporary United States of America in particular. School boosters shared with many Americans a sense that Indians occupied a lower place in the hierarchy of civilizations. The commissioner of Indian Affairs argued that schools provided a "bridge over . . . the dreary chasm of a thousand years of tedious evolution." Indian students received messages about their people's inferiority and marginality in a variety of forms. Geography lessons refigured students' understanding of land. Instead of a place with their own people at the center, lessons about land used maps with American political boundaries. Students learned US history through standardized textbooks, as well as mandated celebrations on Columbus Day, Thanksgiving, and the Fourth of July.[78]

School supporters argued that boarding schools were best, as they separated Native students from their families and tribal communities. Day school teachers constantly complained that their efforts were undone when students returned to their homes every evening. To the teachers' chagrin, older family members spoke Native languages, practicing "uncivilized" habits of living, and shared their goods "recklessly." They did not foster Indian children's independence. In 1888, the federal superintendent of Indian schools argued that students needed to be "wean[ed]" from "the degrading communism of the tribal-reservation system."[79]

When Kiowas enrolled their children, they preferred nearby day schools and kept a close eye on them. In the 1890s, options for having their children in school nearby increased. The Rev. Methvin opened his school in spring 1890. The reservation agent noted plans by a Presbyterian missionary to open another school with the help of Joshua Givens. The agent also responded to Kiowa demands to stay in contact with their children. He informed his superiors that schools needed to be well run. Indian families paid attention. The agent and teachers felt they were "constantly watched and studied by the old [Indian] people." Indian parents also occasionally removed students from school. Some brought them home during ritual activity that promised imminent change. The agent reported such removals during Váuigài's activities in 1887. While the agent claimed that the Ghost Dance did not affect school attendance, at least one family recalled their son all the way from Carlisle.[80]

At times, Kiowa students and their parents experienced school as dangerous to child health and welfare. In January 1891, three boys ran away from the agency school after being punished. A blizzard blew in and the boys became lost as darkness fell. They froze to death. Americans on the reservation reported Kiowas' anger, especially at the abusive schoolteacher who prompted the boys to flee from school. Some whites worried about potential unrest. A Presbyterian missionary described her fear after the boys died. "The Indians declared war on the teacher and all the whites," she wrote in her memoir.[81] The agent sent for troops and fired the offending teacher. "Soldiers finally averted what came nearly being an awful tragedy," the missionary wrote. While Americans registered their concerns about potential violence, Kiowa calendar makers focused on the three dead boys. Several calendars feature them in entries for the winter of 1891.

Relations between Kiowas and school workers deteriorated further during a measles outbreak the next spring. To be sure, Kiowas were no strangers to devastating epidemics. They had suffered from smallpox, cholera, and measles in the past. But on this occasion, schools were implicated in the epidemic's high toll. A school superintendent sent infected children back to their homes rather than nursing them at the schools. The disease, to which Kiowas had no immunity, quickly spread through the camps. Some claimed that more than 200 Kiowas, mostly children, died. Methvin maintained it was more than 300. Again, calendar keepers recalled the devastation in their entries for 1892 (Figure 6.2).[82]

So much sickness and familial loss provoked controversy regarding both healing and proper rituals for the dead. With sick children returned to their homes, parents turned to Kiowa healers who employed sweats, cold water, and suction as part of treatment. Methvin recalled their efforts with disgust: the "medicine men" were "grunting like a hog or bellowing like a bull, trying to scare the evil away." Methvin blamed the high number of deaths on the healers' improper treatment.[83]

With so many dead, Kiowas were overwhelmed with the responsibilities of ritual burial. The epidemic was described as "the most terrible calamity that has befallen the tribe for years." According to some observers, "Every family lost relatives." Kiowas performed their deathways, which included female family members cutting their bodies, destruction of the deceased's belongings, and sometimes burial with gifts. One witness claimed "thousands of dollars' worth of property, in the form of horses, wagons, and blankets, etc., was destroyed at the graves." Methvin wrote that the cemetery looked like a "junk yard."[84]

Methvin, who had been evangelizing for a few years, sought to perform Christian burial for the victims whose families attended his church. When his son died, Sétèmqíà (Bear That Runs Over Them) approached Methvin and asked for a burial service that included the minister's rites as well as Kiowa elements. According to the minister, Sétèmqíà wanted the "benefit" of both ritual forms. Methvin replied that he "could not mix idolatrous worship with Christian faith and hope." Sétèmqíà allowed him to go ahead with

FIGURE 6.2. Detail from Hául̥gúʼs calendar entries for the winter of 1891–1892 through the summer of 1893. The image depicts the measles epidemic of 1892.
Credit: National Anthropological Archives, Smithsonian Institution, manuscript 2531

the service, which Methvin made "as impressive as possible" as an "opportunity to teach." The minister conceded on one issue and watched as the family buried gifts with their son. Sétèmqíà then asked him to leave. As Methvin walked away, he turned around to see the family take their son's horse, slit its throat, and let the blood pour out over the new grave.[85]

At least some Kiowas responded to the epidemic with renewed interest in the Feather Dance. In the middle of the outbreak, the acting commissioner at the federal Indian office heard rumors about dancing. He telegrammed the Kiowas' reservation agent and demanded that dancers stop or he would dispatch troops.[86] The agent, however, knew the struggles that Kiowas faced. In the summer of 1892, he reported to superiors that Kiowas suffered from whooping cough, pneumonia, and measles.[87] He informed officials that promised annuities from the government arrived late, leaving families with little food. Further, the agent reported, Kiowas wanted no part in the impending delegation from Washington coming to discuss allotment.

TAKING THE INDIAN COUNTRY

In September 1892, American commissioners arrived at the KCA Reservation to negotiate allotment. Under the Dawes Act, commissioners conceivably had the power to enforce allotment without Kiowas' consent.[88] Even so, government representatives told the Indians that they preferred to reach an agreement about a timeline and a payment amount for "surplus" land. Negotiations lasted nearly a month, beginning at Fort Sill with a large number of Indians settled on the southern part of the reservation and later moving north to the agency headquarters at Anadarko. During that time, discussions went from cordial to tense. According to English transcriptions from the meetings, Kiowas increasingly employed language about sacred power to support their anti-allotment arguments.

Kiowa representatives expressed hesitancy from the beginning of talks with American commissioners. David Jerome, the head commissioner, began by presenting the government's position.[89] He rehearsed popular arguments about the reservation's failure. It had not moved Indians toward self-sufficiency or assimilation. It was time for a change. Indians needed to farm their own land. Congress passed the allotment law to encourage the transition from nomadic Indian to settled farmer-citizen. The United States would compensate Indians for the transfer of "surplus" lands to American ownership.

Kiowas responded with references to the Treaty of Medicine Lodge, which guaranteed their occupation of reservations without interference. Sétèmqíą̀ (Bear That Runs Over Them), who had been present at the 1867 negotiations, asked why the government attempted allotment before the treaty expired or the people agreed to the process. Kiowa speakers involved in these early negotiations expressed concern that immediate allotment violated their treaty and jeopardized their community. Ádàuiétjè (Big Tree) noted their Cheyenne and Arapaho neighbors' disastrous experience with allotment. "We saw tears in their eyes," he said. "We saw that they had nothing to their name."[90]

As the meetings progressed, Kiowas repeatedly asked commissioners to return when the treaty expired. Cûifâgàui (Lone Wolf the Younger), a respected headman, invited them to come back in four years.[91] A few days later, as the negotiations continued, Páutáuljè (Lean Bison Bull) referred to Medicine Lodge as a "road" from which he would not deviate.[92] As negotiations continued, Kiowas evoked their fathers and grandfathers who had made the treaty. Jòhâusàn II (Little Bluff), a relative of longtime leader Jòhâusàn, referred to the land's importance in Kiowa life. "My father told me not to give up my country to the whites."[93]

As the negotiations continued, Kiowas expressed confusion over the actual terms of the commissioners' offer. This uncertainty was hardly surprising given that the conversations involved three languages and multiple interpreters. Despite the questions and lack of clarity, commissioners pressed the Indian men to sign the proposed agreement. Some did. Several Kiowas claimed that they signed under the impression that allotment would not occur before the treaty's expiration, at least four years away. Some blamed the confusion on Joshua Givens, the Kiowa interpreter. Angry about their translator's possibly intentional obfuscation, some Kiowas asked to have their signatures struck from the agreement. The commissioners refused.[94]

With some signatures secured, the commissioners left Fort Sill and traveled to the agency headquarters at Anadarko. There they met with another large group of Indians.

The confusion and disagreement surrounding the earlier meetings was well known by this point. Kiowa leaders again focused on the Medicine Lodge treaty, emphasizing its status as a sacred agreement.⁹⁵ Áf̃tą̀u (Wooden Lance) declared that the treaty was "written upon my heart" and a solemn obligation before the "Great Spirit." Another Kiowa man pressed further, arguing that both Kiowas and Americans ought to respect the treaty's sacred status. "I was told when a boy that white people as a race had great respect for the Great Spirit and . . . that whatever they told the Great Spirit they would do." As negotiations progressed and confusion ensued, conversation turned from treaty dates and the practical problems of Indian farming to concerns that Americans broke promises made before their god.⁹⁶

Commissioner Jerome tried to keep the negotiations from dissolving into chaos. But by mid-October, he insisted that Kiowas misunderstood the 1867 treaty and that the president had the power to enforce allotment. At a subsequent meeting, he barred long-time leader Ádàuiétjè's (Big Tree) effort to speak. Outraged, Áf̃tą̀u interjected and called out the American officials: "You have missed the good road and cheated." The meeting fell apart as Kiowas walked out. Before leaving, another Kiowa representative told the commissioners that Kiowas had no present interest in an allotment agreement or further negotiations. "They feel that they have not been listened to," he declared. The commissioners seemed unfazed. They had some signatures. They planned to take them back to Congress and push for ratification.⁹⁷

Before the commissioners left the KCA Reservation, Kiowas headed for Methvin's church. They asked the Methodist minister to transcribe a protest petition.⁹⁸ In the document, Kiowas declared that they had been misinformed of the agreement's terms and tricked into immediate allotment and sale of their lands. They also accused their interpreter, Joshua Givens, of misleading them. Methvin took the petition to Jerome and the other commissioners, but they refused to accept it. The minister then gave the document to the reservation agent, asking him to forward it to the Department of the Interior. Methvin admitted his discomfort with his role in the process. He "did not wish to become involved in [Kiowas'] political affairs or quarrels." In his unpublished autobiography, however, he explained why he helped. He "refused to deceive the Indians." To be sure, Methvin supported allotment and had often told Kiowas that Jesus wanted them to farm and live in houses. But he could not condone the commissioners' use of deceptive measures.⁹⁹

The agent never forwarded the Kiowa petition. It remained in a desk drawer. But Kiowas were only beginning their allotment resistance. Over the next several years, Cûifágàui (Lone Wolf the Younger) emerged as the movement's leader. Kiowa calendars note the meetings he organized and the trips he took to Washington to advocate against the Jerome Agreement's ratification.¹⁰⁰ But even as his name became attached to one of the most important Native land disputes in American history, he also served as a central character in American Christians' stories about missions to "wild Indians."

GODS IN THE DIVIDED LANDS

The story was first told by a Baptist layman in 1889. He worked as the reservation carpenter. Hoping to spread the gospel, he and his wife opened a school in Cûifágàui's (Lone Wolf the Younger) camp. According to church leaders, Cûifágàui asked for more missionaries. When he called, Baptists answered. George Washington Hicks, a Cherokee missionary to other Indian nations, arrived at Cûifágàui's camp in the summer of 1892. Marietta Reeside, a student at a Baptist missionary training school, read that Oklahoma's "blanket Indians" were "begging for help," especially from Christian women. According to the pamphlet, the Indians wanted to be taught "the ways of white women." She and her missionary partner Lauretta Ballew came to Cûifágàui's camp in late 1892. Soon, these workers had a few Baptist missions up and running across the KCA Reservation.[101]

Even as the story of "Lone Wolf's appeal" gained traction among Baptists, Catholics circulated stories about him as well. As noted earlier, French and Belgian Benedictines had been active in the eastern part of Indian Territory for many years. Allotment and land runs made the national church take note of a region they previously left in the hands of Benedictine brothers. In 1891, Bishop Theophile Meerschaert was appointed Vicar Apostolic for the territory. That same year in Philadelphia, Mother Katharine Drexel founded the Sisters of the Blessed Sacrament for Indians and Colored People. Heiress to a huge fortune, Drexel's order infused Indian missions and schools with funds and teachers over the next several decades. With more national attention on the region, Benedictines quickly sent one of their own, French-born Isadore Ricklin, to start a mission among KCA Indians.[102] Within a year, he opened a school with Drexel's money and staffed it with mostly Irish nuns from the Sisters of St. Francis in Philadelphia.[103] Meerschaert arrived to bless the school. According to later accounts, "Old Chief Lone Wolf" came to the bishop's celebratory mass. Cûifágàui bowed before the cross and thanked the "Great Spirit" for sending a "great spiritual man" to teach them about Jesus.[104] A Comanche leader continued by asking the "pale face medicine man [to] heal the sick, to procure abundant food, and grant them better luck with their ponies and pastures." Cûifágàui stood at the center of both Catholic and Protestant accounts of Christian presence in Kiowa country.

The Cûifágàui/Lone Wolf story was one of many that Catholics in Indian Country circulated to generate lay support for missions. Through a new publication, *The Indian Advocate*, Benedictines joined the Jesuits in presenting Indian missions as part of a broader global project, rather than a particularly American one. They pointed to their founder, the sixth-century Saint Benedict, who brought Christianity to "barbarians" in France, Germany, and England, as well as to the Slavic peoples.[105] The Benedictine authors also highlighted Catholic presence on the continent long before the US founding. "The first missionary who touched the soil of America was a son of Saint Benedict," the writer recalled.[106] It was now lay Catholics' obligation to support ongoing mission efforts through prayer and financial offerings.

As missionaries founded new churches and schools, Kiowas continued to engage in peyote practices and the Feather Dance. James Mooney, a Smithsonian ethnologist living among Kiowas, observed peyote meetings during his research on the reservation.[107] He got to know Háugú (Silver Horn), a budding Kiowa artist from a prominent family. Mooney asked him to create images of some of the peyote rites that Mooney had observed.[108] Háugú drew ritual preparations, the interior of a tipi with its altar and fire, ritual implements, and practitioners in ceremonial dress (Figure 6.3). During the period, the number of Kiowas participating in ritual peyote ingestion grew steadily.

In mid-1891, even after Áfîtāu's (Wooden Lance) disavowal of Wovoka had discouraged many Kiowas from participating, the agent reported that the Ghost Dance was a "disturbing occurrence throughout the year." Not long after, he complained that the "Messiah craze" prompted some Kiowas to stop farming. Some of this excitement can be attributed to Mooney's visit to Wovoka early 1892. Upon his return, Mooney reported on Wovoka's new teachings and the ethnologist distributed red paint to the movement's followers. If Kiowa dancing had subsided to some degree, neighboring Cheyenne and Arapahos had not. They also visited Wovoka and brought back messages and sacred items. They claimed that Wovoka now spoke of Jesus coming to back earth. They gathered for dances. At least some Kiowas showed interest in the evolving movement. Mooney gathered stories from some of them, including Fíqí (Eater). A long-time healer,

FIGURE 6.3. Háugú's drawing of a peyote meeting, featuring a leader and implements such as feathers and a rattle.

Credit: Dickinson Research Center, National Cowboy & Western Heritage Museum, Oklahoma City, Oklahoma

Fíqí took on a new name, meaning Messenger, during his participation in the Feather Dance. He claimed a vision in which he visited the village of the dead and saw deceased relatives, painted tipis, and buffalo. He encouraged others to join him so that they could also be reunited with lost loved ones.[109]

Mooney also asked Fíqí to draw about his experiences with sacred power. Fíqí obliged and produced four drawings. They feature men on horses, encampments of painted tipis, stars, rainbows, and lines representing the transfer of power. The last one includes a circle, representing a formation of Feather Dancers, connected to three figures in the sky above them. The central figure, a bearded man, wears a colorful robe and crown. On each side, two men on crosses look at him (Figure 6.4). In his Feather Dance vision, Fíqí saw Jesus. Like so many powerful Kiowa men in the past, Fíqí sought out blessing and protection for his people. But in his case, Feather Dancing provided access to Jesus and his power.[110]

From 1882 to 1892, Kiowas experienced a host of changes, including major revisions to their ritual practices for seeking power. Though they tried to sustain the Sun Dance, environmental conditions and American suppression proved overwhelming. Kiowas talked of "putting away" the ceremony.[111] Some Kiowas had tried to rectify their situation by bringing back the buffalo through supernatural means. Others ingested peyote. Some

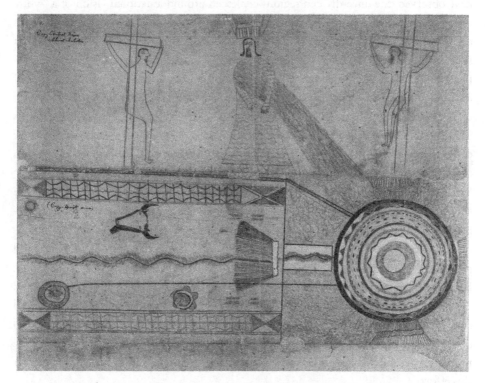

FIGURE 6.4. Fíqí's (Eater) rendering of his Feather Dance (Ghost Dance) vision. Jesus, surrounded by the two thieves on crosses, connects to a Feather Dance circle by a line denoting sacred power.
Credit: National Anthropological Archives, Smithsonian Institution, manuscript 2538

listened to Christian preachers, both American and Indian, who hoped to evangelize them. When word came that a new movement promised reunion with dead loved ones and a world renewed, some of them danced. In a period of great change and unrelenting threat, Kiowas attempted a series of new ritual practices aimed at maintaining community in a beloved place.

THE CIVILIZING FARMSTEAD

Kiowas experienced these changes as Americans applied new measures to transform Indians into civilized Christians through education and individual property ownership. Marginal populations across the nation felt the weight of similarly coercive pressures. Chinese workers no longer had legal options for immigration. African Americans faced white supremacists working to constrain political rights and to terrify through lynching and other forms of violence. Like Mormons, Indians faced a situation in which their legal protection and civic inclusion demanded giving up cherished ways of life and connections to people and place.[112]

In the post–Civil War era, Americans sought a unified North and South. As historians have observed, the once-divided regions coalesced around a national vision of a "white republic" with Protestant Christianity at its core.[113] Other scholars have extended this argument, showing how white Americans in places like Reconstruction-era California shared a similar vision and enacted it by excluding Chinese immigrants and Native peoples from legal rights.[114] Developments in Indian Country, in which white Americans of differing politics collaborated to take Native land, confirm these earlier findings.

These episodes demand close inspection of the material strategies that white citizens used to extend their claim on power and resources, all the while insisting upon their project's moral rectitude. Lyman Beecher's 1835 *Plea for the West* imagined the region developing under the Christian God's providential eye. Even so, it also required Anglo-Saxon Protestant efforts to overcome Catholics and others ill suited for liberty. To secure the West, white Protestants needed to control the region's politics, economics, and religious life. To do so, they opposed Catholic expansion, suppressed Mormon religious practice, restricted Chinese immigration, controlled African American mobility, and prescribed Indian assimilation through land appropriation and compulsory education. Protestant "friends of the Indian" presented these strategies as gifts to Indian peoples and evidence of American benevolence. They failed, however, to consider that Kiowas would continue to raise up new ritual leaders and defend their treaty rights. Kiowas remained determined to keep their people alive on an increasingly small stretch of land. In the 1890s, they employed a variety of new ritual practices and legal maneuvers to empower this effort.

7

1893 to 1903

IN 1898, MORE than two and a half million Americans visited the Trans-Mississippi and International Exposition in Omaha. The event celebrated the history and peoples of the American West. Promotional displays extolled agriculture and mining, horticulture and fine arts. Modeled on the 1893 World's Fair in Chicago, the exposition also included international simulations, such as a Chinese village, a German town, and a "street of all nations." Processions, including a flower parade, delighted spectators throughout the exhibit period. Some of these processions signaled Americans' interest in traditional societies around the world. The "Parade of All Nations" featured Egyptians on camels and Mexican villagers on donkeys. A parade also opened the exposition's Indian Congress. American Indians from thirty-five nations wore traditional dress as they processed through the Omaha streets.

The Trans-Mississippi Exposition highlighted the nation's changes over the course of the nineteenth century. The West, once outside the country's borders and later a wild frontier, by the 1890s had a rapidly expanding settler population and contributed enormously to the American economy. The exposition's exhibits featured non-white and non-Christian populations from around the world, indicating many white Americans' fascination with the nation's newest international contacts. They also reflected the growing religious, racial, and ethnic diversity at home. During the 1890s, a surge in immigration from southern and eastern Europe brought tens of thousands of Catholics and Jews to the eastern seaboard. Increased immigration from Mexico to the American Southwest also contributed to a growing Catholic population.[1]

White Protestants noted these trends. For some, these shifts registered not as something to celebrate with parades, but as a threat to national identity. Throughout the decade, some sought to restrict the cultural influence and legal protections of religious as well as racial and ethnic minorities. Anti-immigrant advocates and other nativists founded the

Immigration Restriction League and other related organizations. They produced reams of literature warning readers about problems associated with ethnic groups arriving from around the world. They also stressed the perils resulting from growing numbers of Catholics, Jews, and Mormons. Populations deemed racially different fared even worse in this period. Chinese workers continued to be barred from entry due to immigration restrictions put in place in the 1880s. African Americans were subjected to ongoing efforts to restrict their post–Civil War freedoms. White supremacists across the South used lynching and other forms of intimidation to terrorize black communities. The Supreme Court proved an ineffective protector of black freedom, especially with its 1896 *Plessy v. Fergusen* decision upholding the legality of segregated public transportation.[2]

Efforts to limit the legal rights and economic opportunities of domestic racial and religious minorities paralleled some Americans' desire to wield similar power in territories overseas.[3] In January 1893, American capitalists began their takeover of Hawaii. With the help of American marines, the businessmen successfully deposed Hawaii's leader and eventually secured the island's annexation by the United States. The 1898 Trans-Mississippi Exposition's most distinguished visitor, President William McKinley, visited the celebration while embroiled in the Spanish-American War. To be sure, citizens strenuously debated the nation's imperial actions after 1890. But the last decade of the century ushered in an era in which America's long struggles over the rights and freedoms of domestic minorities resonated in new global settings.[4]

Ongoing concerns about religious and racial difference, as well as the control of material resources both at home and abroad, shaped how American policymakers and Protestant "friends of the Indian" understood their work during the 1890s.[5] Extending allotment and schooling policies from the 1880s, these powerful players cast the breakup of communally held lands and the creation of coercive education policies as gifts that enabled Native people's freedom. Increasingly, they exported their impulse to affect Indian transformation through land policy and school expansion to peoples and places around the world.

On the reservation, Kiowas and their allies felt these overwhelming pressures and strategized to maintain their ties to the land and each other. Rituals for invoking sacred power, in ways both old and new, were integral to their labor. In their drawings, texts, and material creations, Kiowas recorded their efforts to protect land and community, as well as preserve memories of past practices. Kiowas, both individually and collectively, engaged in a variety of practices and affiliations—including Feather (Ghost) Dancing, peyote rites, and Christianity—in order to preserve their people's place in the Kiowa homeland.

WHOSE GOD IN INDIAN COUNTRY?

Protestant "friends of the Indian," especially participants in the Lake Mohonk Conference (LMC), supported government policies to allot land and enforce Indian education. As noted in the previous chapter, LMC members celebrated the 1887 passage of the Dawes

Allotment Act and lobbied for its swift enactment afterward. From their perspective, allotment broke down the stifling hold of tribal relations and granted Indian people the rights and responsibilities of eventual American citizenship.[6] As Captain Richard Pratt, founder of the Carlisle boarding school, argued before conference attendees in 1893, "To end the Indian problem, the Indian masses must be broken up, distributed and assimilated."[7] Throughout the decade, the LMC annual platform called for allotment and dissolving tribal governments.

Pratt and other Protestant "friends of the Indian" insisted that the smooth transition to individual landholding depended on a robust system of Indian schools.[8] They argued that educating Indian children away from their parents provided the best chance at teaching the skills necessary for landownership and citizenship. They viewed Indian parents as obstacles to their children's assimilation. Commissioner of Indian Affairs and Baptist minister Thomas J. Morgan argued that the government should consider overruling Indian parents' rights. "Shall we say that, after having made this abundant provision [for schools] and having offered to the children, we will allow those who are still savages in their instincts, barbarians in their habits, rooted in conservativism,—that we will allow them to keep their children out of these institutions of learning, in order that they may be prevented from becoming like white men and women?" Morgan asked. "I say, NO," he answered.[9]

While LMC attendees emphasized that education was necessary for Indian citizenship, the schooling issue continued to present conflicts as American Catholics grew in numbers and increased their political engagement.[10] By 1895, Catholics ran thirty-six boarding and fifteen day schools for Indian children.[11] Many of these schools, like their Protestant counterparts, were funded through a contract system that allowed government money, gained from the sale of Indian lands, to support Indian education. For many years, Protestants had received contracts for schools, as well as salaries for government positions related to Indian affairs. But as Catholics became major players in the competition for Indian school contracts, federal officials and Protestant "friends of the Indian" balked.

LMC attendees voiced their concerns in two ways. First, they decried the practice of religious organizations accepting government money to fund any religious schools. In 1893, social reformer and minister Lyman Abbott told the LMC that Protestant denominations, unlike Catholics, had stopped taking public funds for their Indians schools. He paraphrased evangelist Dwight L. Moody to argue, "If you want to do the Lord's work you should use the Lord's money."[12] The LMC also criticized Catholic Indian schools as inherently sectarian, unlike their own schools, which they considered purveyors of a non-specific and generic Christianity. As the Unitarians' representative to the 1894 LMC meeting reported, "We are not trying to make [Indian] children Unitarians." Referring to the teachers' use of hymns, prayer, and Sunday school lessons, the speaker continued, "What we are trying to do is to make them Christians."[13]

According to members of the LMC, Protestant school efforts stood in marked contrast to Catholics, who pursued Indian school contracts only to grow the ranks of "Romanists." Throughout the 1890s, leaders at the Bureau of Catholic Indian Missions (BCIM) responded in earnest. They reminded their critics that private funds reserved for Indian nations, rather than public ones, supported several of their Indian schools. They noted that some Indian nations requested Catholic schools and ought to have the freedom to make such choices. This advocacy proved central to Catholic understandings of their particular relationship to Native people. For instance, a visiting bishop told Congress that Catholics were "friends of the Indian" insofar as they advocated for equal funding of Catholic reservation schools.[14] Being the Indian's friend, then, included the work of transforming Native people into Christians, but more important, it entailed a battle against Protestant dominance. The bishop and other BCIM leaders regularly argued that Protestants sought to end the contract system less out of concern about Indian education and more from their desire to restrict Catholic freedom.[15]

Catholic arguments about Indian religious freedom and anti-Catholic discrimination were hardly new, but one aspect of their argument was an innovation. In the 1890s, BCIM officials began to emphasize that their schools advanced the nation's interest by assimilating Indians. Money from Mother Katharine Drexel, along with annual collections taken for Indian missions, could be used in tandem with government money to achieve "beneficent results," namely the "civilizing and Christianizing [of] Indian children."[16] Catholic leaders made this case to the public, as well as to political leaders. In a petition to Congress, James Cardinal Gibbons of Baltimore claimed that Catholics had been "laboring in the cause of the civilization of the Indian" since the continent's discovery. Protestant denominations had simply followed the Catholics' lead. Government contracts to run Indian schools, Gibbon reasoned, were simply the most recent arrangement within which Catholics performed their "duty" as Americans to improve Indian people.[17]

Protestant "friends of the Indian" disagreed. They insisted that only their Indian schools provided a nonsectarian "Christian" message best suited for American citizenship. When Rev. James M. King took the LMC podium to speak on the school contract issue, he scoffed at Catholic complaints that Protestant mission schools were also "sectarian" because they used Protestant Bibles and gospel hymns. "In this Columbian year," he replied, "it becomes us to remember that our civilization is not Latin, because God did not permit North America to be settled and controlled by that civilization. The Huguenot, the Hollander, and the Puritan created our civilization." According to King, Protestant practices were inherently American.[18]

However eager LMC members might have been to educate Indian children, the school contract question prompted fears of rising Catholic power and the possible decline of Anglo-Protestant influence. The debate continued as the nation's northeastern cities surged with new Catholic arrivals from Europe. Protestant "friends of the Indian" sought to prove the wisdom of their Indian policies for reasons well beyond Native communities. Indian policy was as an index of their ability to direct the nation's future in line with their sense of the nation's Protestant identity.

SACRED POWER IN DIVIDED LANDS

If Kiowas failed to register the particular anxieties that informed Lake Mohonk reformers' vision of Indian citizenship, they certainly felt the pressure of government policies aimed at breaking apart their communal lands, tribal bonds, and ritual practices. By 1892, Kiowas faced overwhelming opposition to their Sun Dance traditions. As noted in the previous chapter, reservation agents had repeatedly called on troops from nearby Fort Sill to stop their summertime gatherings. After 1890, Kiowas no longer attempted the ritual. During the 1890s, Kiowa experimentation with new ritual forms expanded. Some continued to follow ritual peyote specialists and seek healing and empowerment in all-night peyote meetings.[19] Though the 1890–1891 Feather Dance, the Kiowa version of the Ghost Dance, had not maintained a lasting following, it was not gone for good, and the movement continued into the twentieth century. Finally, some Kiowas engaged with Christian missionaries, both American and Native. In these encounters, Kiowas heard sermons in their encampments, attended tent meetings and revivals, and considered enrolling their children in mission schools. Throughout the 1890s, Kiowas engaged in a range of ritual alternatives in the face of allotment, school expansion, and eventually, the opening of their reservation to white settlement.

The Christian missions and schools that had started in the late 1880s expanded rapidly over the next decade.[20] Energized by their successful push for allotment legislation, new missionaries made their way to Indian Country. The Baptists, especially, increased their presence. As noted in the previous chapter, George Washington Hicks, a Cherokee Baptist minister, led worship services and a few tent meetings in the late 1880s. Marietta Reeside and Lauretta Ballew had arrived by the fall of 1892. Hicks and his wife established a chapel on the reservation's western side. Reeside and Ballew worked with Kiowas living further east. Baptist work expanded again in 1896, when Isabel Crawford established a new mission further south. Crawford spent many years among the Kiowa, becoming proficient in Plains Indian sign language in an effort to communicate with Native people across the reservation.[21]

Rev. J. J. Methvin, who had represented the Methodist Episcopal Church-South (MECS) on the reservation since 1887, also expanded his work. He had organized camp meetings, founded a school near the reservation agency, and assisted the Kiowa drafters of the initial protest against allotment. In the 1890s, he initiated new Kiowa house churches and increased the number of students at his school.[22] Methvin also helped newly arrived Presbyterian missionaries, Silas and Anna Fait, when they founded a church and later a school in Anadarko.[23]

While Protestant missionaries bemoaned it, Roman Catholic presence on the reservation also increased.[24] As noted in the previous chapter, French Benedictine Isadore Ricklin established St. Patrick's mission in 1891. Having lived in a Comanche camp for several months, Ricklin spoke basic Comanche and became proficient in Plains Indian sign language.[25] With the support of his new benefactor, the heiress and nun Mother Katherine Drexel, Ricklin opened a school near the reservation agency. He welcomed several nuns from the Sisters of St. Francis in Philadelphia to run it. Soon, St. Patrick's was the largest school on the KCA Reservation.[26] With the influx of Catholic and Protestant missionaries, the reservation's religious landscape changed dramatically. In 1885, Kiowas had no full-time missions or religious schools. By the mid-1890s there were at least a half dozen fledgling missions holding regular services and almost as many denominational schools.

Along with the schools, missionaries employed a range of strategies to reach Kiowas and other Indians on the reservation. Silas Fait's Presbyterian mission welcomed some Native people to their church, which served mostly white Americans living at the reservation agency. Session records show that Fait expected Indian converts to affirm Presbyterian teaching and fully renounce Kiowa ritual forms and sacred power. Early in 1890, for example, the session rejected an "Indian named Emma" because she insisted that her acceptance of Christ "must not interfere with her own gods."[27] Four years later, Fait found the kind of Indian convert he wanted. "On examination, Annie Aone Jones, a full blood Kiowa Indian, was received into membership of the church. This is the first Indian to unite with the church on confession of faith. There can be no question of her fitness for church membership."[28] While Jones and some other Indians were baptized, few other examples of Indian participation can be found in church records.

Unlike the Faits, other missionaries regularly visited Indian camps and attempted more informal teaching and preaching. Father Ricklin and the Franciscan sisters frequently called on encampments near St. Patrick's. One sister, Aemiliana, reported that she and her fellow sisters concentrated on connecting with sick children and their parents. She found that Indians who received medical attention were likely to respond by visiting the parish and school.[29] Native participation at St. Patrick's services grew quickly. Father Ricklin reported that more than 300 "blanket Indians" attended mass on Christmas Day 1892. Fifteen received Holy Communion.[30]

Methodist and Baptist missionaries also visited and evangelized Kiowa camps, but considered large camp meetings central to evangelization. Not only did this strategy suit their denominations' histories, but it also allowed them to engage large numbers of Kiowas gathered for ration distribution. As noted in the previous chapter, missionaries sought out sites of religious significance to Kiowas. Methvin, for instance, delighted to hold camp meetings at places that once hosted Sun Dances. Baptist missionaries, who began holding camp meetings in 1893, shared Methvin's sentiments. Writing about a June 1894 camp meeting, Marietta Reeside rejoiced that "God's Israel set up their standards" on what once was a "favorite place in the old times for sun dances and war councils."[31] When missionary Isabel Crawford hosted a camp meeting in 1897, she marveled that Kiowas who had once built arbors near Sun Dance lodges now built "arbor[s] for Jesus."[32]

As with earlier evangelization efforts on the reservation, Native people played key roles. Missionaries initially sought out these partnerships because they needed interpreters, but the relationships often developed in unexpected ways. Methvin, for instance, began working around 1889 with Ándálé, a Mexican captive raised among the Kiowa. Ándálé worked at Methvin's school and served as a translator at Methodist services. In his recounting of Ándálé's life, Methvin acknowledged the crucial role his Kiowa colleague played. He recalled an early camp meeting in which Kiowas gathered with a "threatening attitude." He asked them to be quiet and listen to scripture, but could not control the audience. According to Methvin, Ándálé began to speak and the "whole crowd fell before him with cries and supplications." While readers of missionary literature will recognize Methvin's flair for the dramatic, the minister's willingness to acknowledge his dependence on an Indian associate is striking.[33]

The Baptists also formed crucial partnerships with Kiowas. Hicks attributed the beginnings of the Elk Creek mission to Paddlety, a Kiowa man who visited a mission church for baptism.[34] Paddlety then went back to his own camp at Elk Creek and initiated Sunday gatherings in which he fed people and told them about Jesus. The female missionaries at the Rainy Mountain mission hired former Carlisle Indian School student Julia Givens as their assistant and interpreter. Givens's work was so useful that the missionaries eventually secured an appointment and salary for her from the Baptist mission board.[35]

At the Saddle Mountain Baptist mission, Isabel Crawford formed a long-lasting partnership with another former Carlisle student, Lucius Aitsan (Etsanti). He moved quickly from being Crawford's translator to her co-leader and, eventually, the congregation's choice for pastor.[36] Crawford also had dealings with Zótâm (Driftwood), the artist and Fort Marion prisoner who had returned to the reservation as an Episcopal deacon in the late 1870s. While Zótâm's relationship with his Episcopal bishop ended on tense terms, he had amicable relations with Crawford.[37]

Several of these early Kiowa Christians lacked strong kinship connections and might have seen prospects for relationship and support by affiliating with missions. Ándálé, for instance, had been adopted into a Kiowa family after being taken captive as a child. As an adult, he returned to his family of origin in New Mexico, only to come back to the Kiowa four years later. In meeting Methvin, Andele found a supportive friend and a good job at the Methodist school.[38] Julia Givens also had tenuous family connections. She was the daughter of the renowned Kiowa warrior Sétágài (Sitting Bear), who died in 1871. Her mother died soon after. Essentially orphaned, Givens traveled to the Carlisle school at age nine. Her enrollment card includes a blank space where her family should have been listed.[39] Lucius Aitsan's father was a captive adopted by Kiowas. When Aitsan's mother died, his father struggled to care for him. Aitsan entered boarding school.[40] From a marginal family, Aitsan was one of the first Kiowa children to attend Carlisle. Upon his return, he got married and baptized. He tried his hand at farming, interpreting, and serving in the Indian cavalry unit. In partnering with Crawford, Aitsan found work and community that previously had eluded him.[41] Along with marginal kinship ties, several early Kiowa Christians also had experiences in boarding schools. Missionaries hoped that school enrollment would produce this exact result.

Kiowa parents recognized the potential for separation and alienation. As a result, they preferred on-reservation schools. They embraced boys' opportunity to receive industrial education and girls' training in the domestic arts. Kiowa parents did not, however, support school policies without question. They resisted missionary efforts to secure the choicest land for school buildings, as well as government restrictions on rations and annuities for families who kept their children out of school. Parents also balked when school administrators tried to restrict their visits, eliminate school breaks at Christmas and summer, and enroll very young children. Because they privileged being near their children, some Kiowa parents simply moved their encampments close to schools once they had been established.[42]

As Kiowa parents considered whether or not to send their children to school, missionaries fought with each other and government officials as they competed for enrollments. As noted earlier, the 1890s hosted feuds at the national level about Indian schooling. Missionaries on the reservation expressed their concern that the agent encouraged, if not forced, Indian parents to choose government schools, which they considered harmfully secular. They also competed between themselves for enrollments. Father Ricklin, for example, worried that Protestant missionaries were at "war against" him. Sister Aemiliana wrote to her funders that Protestants worked constantly against the Catholic school.[43]

While the missionaries perceived differences between themselves, as well as between religious and government schools, their programs were remarkably similar. School enrollment involved physical transformation when teachers bathed children, dressed them in American-style clothes, and cut their hair. Most Native students received non-Indian names and were forbidden to speak their Native languages.[44] Curricula included some work toward English literacy and basic competency in a few other academic skills, but focused on manual labor training. Missionaries approved these offerings and sometimes sacralized them. Isabel Crawford, for instance, wrote that Indians knew the English word "work" and that she wanted them to "associate it with religion."[45]

Like missionaries throughout the United States and around the globe, evangelists and teachers on the reservation reported enough success to make the effort seem promising, but not so easy as to lose support from Americans willing to send money. For Catholic readers of *The Indian Advocate*, Father Ricklin described how the sisters "scrub[bed] the little Indian girls from head to foot" and worked hard each day to bring more students to St. Patrick's.[46] Readers of the Protestant *New York Evangelist* received periodic updates about Rev. Fait's Presbyterian mission and school. The minister reported that he had convinced many Kiowas to shun "medicine men." But the work was not yet done, according to Fait, as not every Indian child attended school.⁴⁷

Baptist missionaries also balanced the successes they reported with ongoing obstacles. Maryetta Reeside spoke about her work among the Kiowa at an 1893 mission conference, a speech later published in a promotional book. Reeside detailed her methods, including her use of "large colored pictures to illustrate our simple story of Jesus and his love and death for us." She told of tent meetings held at large Indian encampments. At these events, she reported, missionaries got their first Kiowa converts and performed their first baptisms. Reeside also noted the struggles. She visited camps and could hear Kiowas "shaking the medicine gourd and singing in their weird way." Traditional death practices, such as destroying belongings and cutting the body, prevailed. Reeside reported decent progress, continued adversity, and the need for ongoing financial support.⁴⁸

Missionary accounts include many stories of Kiowas affiliating with missions by attending services, professing faith, receiving baptism, and participating in communion. Coming from missionary perspectives, these accounts of Kiowa activity demand critical examination. As noted earlier, missionary texts bear the marks of not only American Christians' assumption that Indians denounce all former religious ideas and practices, but also their mission boards' expectation that the work take place on the border between impending success and terrific difficulty. Missionary texts, then, are often dramatic and require careful handling. This is especially true for narratives that portray ideal Indian converts making a total turn from their former ritual observance.⁴⁹

These reports about Indian Christians can be read in tandem with material culture that Native people produced. Some Kiowas affiliated with Christian missions created drawings that depicted past ritual practices, as well as their current activities in churches. Qódèbọ̀hòn, who lived through the reservation's creation, witnessed the Red River War, and experienced increased American pressure to assimilate, is one such example. Like many young men, Qódèbọ̀hòn drew scenes from his life (Figures 7.1, 7.2, and 7.3). His drawings included images of his wives, his traditional weapons and shield, and the painted tipi he had inherited. His notebook also detailed Qódèbọ̀hòn's participation in Sun Dance and peyote rites. The last drawing in the notebook shows Qódèbọ̀hòn wearing American clothes and pointing to a cross. Qódèbọ̀hòn, known to Americans as Gotebo, received baptism and joined the Rainy Mountain Kiowa Indian Baptist Church in 1893. An accompanying note, likely written by a Baptist missionary, states, "These drawings represent a chronological self-portraiture of Gotebo's life, primarily in terms of his religious activities."⁵⁰

The missionary insisted that the drawings detailed Qódèbọ̀hòn's total transformation from heathenism to Christianity.⁵¹ To be sure, Qódèbọ̀hòn served as a church deacon and hymn writer for the rest of his life. But this is not to say that his Christian affiliation required renunciation of his Kiowa identity or posture toward sacred power. Kiowa viewers of the drawings would know that Qódèbọ̀hòn once held prominence as a bustle

FIGURE 7.1. Qódèbǫhòn's drawing of his experience as a supplicant in the Sun Dance. A Baptist minister later added the typed captions about Gotebo, the name by which many Americans knew Qódèbǫhòn.
Credit: College of the Ozarks

keeper for the Ohomo Society, a prominent men's organization.[52] The early pictures offer important details about Qódèbǫhòn's social position: his wives, who represent his family connections; his tipi designs, received from his father and his second wife's father; his weapons, which speak to his role defending Kiowa people; and his shield, which he would have received either from an elder or through a vision. We also know that even after his affiliation with the Baptists, Qódèbǫhòn continued to hold close some Kiowa traditions. While he had a wooden house on his property, he offered it to the missionaries and continued to live in his tipi. His work as a deacon focused on visiting the sick and connecting them with missionaries and medical care. He also composed several hymns in Kiowa, one of the key ways the language survived despite missionaries' and teachers' efforts to enforce English use in schools.[53]

Missionary documents also reveal concerns about land, including ways Kiowas hoped that Christian affiliation might help protect their homeland. Isabel Crawford's writings include stories about Kiowas who questioned how Jesus, as a new source of power, could help as they faced the expanding settler population. Crawford noted that Kiowas asked

FIGURE 7.2. Qódèbòhòn's rendering of his participation in peyote rites, including several elements integral to its ritual ingestion, such as the crescent-shaped altar, feather fan, and rattle.
Credit: College of the Ozarks

what "the Jesus Book," or Bible, had to say about carrying revolvers, which many were doing as more Americans trespassed on the reservation. Another responded to Crawford's doggedness about Kiowa farming that he had never heard it was Jesus who wanted him to plow. He had always thought it was the white man, which is why he had not done it. These accounts, while certainly written from missionaries' position of power, offer some details about Kiowa engagement with Christian ideas and practices, as well as the Americans who brought them.[54]

Sources from this period, produced by Kiowas and Americans, also speak to pressing concerns about life, death, and family connection. Indeed, Kiowa engagements with Christianity often focused on how Jesus affected life after death. We can see this, especially, in missionary accounts of Kiowas who made professions prior to baptism.[55] In 1894, Marietta Reeside recorded that an old Kiowa woman requested baptism because she wanted to see Jesus when she died.[56] Isabel Crawford recounted the story of an Indian man who came to church and declared his hope that Jesus would seek out his dead parents and bring them to heaven.[57] Lucius Aitsan, the Kiowa co-leader at Saddle Mountain, reflected on the Christian burial of a young girl, emphasizing the comfort he

FIGURE 7.3. Qôdèbòhòn's drawing of himself wearing American-style clothes and pointing to a cross.
Credit: College of the Ozarks

found in her burial at the church cemetery as well as the knowledge that "our sister is safe at home with Jesus."[58]

While some accounts depicted Kiowa comforted by reunion with relatives in a Christian afterlife, missionaries also encountered Kiowas who questioned their assumptions about death. As noted in previous chapters, Kiowa deathways included wailing, bodily cutting, and the destruction of the deceased's property. Crawford's memoirs are full of stories in which she tried to offer a Christian alternative. Even some who attended church refused her. Soon after arriving at Saddle Mountain, Crawford received a visit from parents seeking healing for their child suffering from consumption. She had no way of treating the illness and the child soon died. In her memoir, Crawford wrote of her effort to minister to the grieving parents. "Jesus has taken your child to sit with Him," she told them using sign language. In an effort to transform Kiowa death customs, she continued, "He does not want you to cut off your fingers." Crawford felt sure that the "wonderful resurrection story was signed into the heart." The parents, however, did not follow Crawford's plans for the funeral. Rather than quietly suffer, they "wailed." Despite Crawford's protestation against burial objects, the parents placed all their child's belongings in the grave. Just days later, Crawford reported on another family who brought their dying child to her. After burial, the parents cut their hair, burned their tipi, and wailed all night long.[59]

Kiowa calendars and other drawings feature the people's struggle with infant and childhood death in this period. Keepers of one calendar drew small figures to memorialize the summer of 1892, images that descendants have suggested recall a child's death during a smallpox outbreak.[60] Háugú (Silver Horn), who began keeping a calendar in the 1890s, began to note children's births. This record marked a departure from older calendar-keeping practices, which highlighted the deeds and deaths of prominent men. Háugú's entry for the winter of 1897–1898 includes a cradleboard to recall the birth of a child named Old Peyote.[61] In 1903, Háugú drew three cradleboards, marking the births of three children, including his son. At a moment when disease struck their children with frequency, and schooling, even on the reservation, caused painful separation, artists revised calendar practices to register Kiowas' ongoing concern for their children.

The network of Christian missions and schools expanded as several conditions made Sun Dance practice less relevant, if not impossible, and as Kiowas faced American efforts to sever their ties to land and to each other. Kiowas struggled to secure their children's futures through schooling without losing touch with them entirely. They sought assistance from missionaries, particularly in the areas of healing, as diseases and malnutrition continued to plague their nation. Within this context, some Kiowas affiliated with particular missionaries. They also sought blessings directly from Jesus. Many of the requests they brought to this new power, as least as we have them recorded in missionary texts and some Kiowa drawings, reveal the ongoing importance of maintaining family and tribal connections. But Christian affiliation was not the only way Kiowas sought empowerment in this period.

PEYOTE AND DANCE

Missionaries focused on Indian affiliation with missions, but their writings also noted ongoing participation in practices they deemed improper, including ritual peyote ingestion. As noted in earlier chapters, neighboring Native peoples introduced peyote to Kiowas sometime in the 1870s. As a result, government workers throughout the 1880s identified it as a problem.[62] Despite national and local efforts to penalize peyote rituals, some Kiowas continued.[63]

American observers recorded details about evolving Kiowa peyote rites. Sétqópjè (Mountain Bear), who credited peyote with saving his life after he contracted tubercu- losis while at Fort Marion, later reported on his experience of healing. In conversations with an army officer, he claimed that peyote was good for weak lungs and other sicknesses. "It keeps me alive," he claimed. Sétqópjè also provided details about an 1897 peyote meeting. He referred to the sage and cedar used to prepare the lodge and the crescent- shaped altar holding the "Father *wakoare*," or father peyote. Beside the button rested an eagle bone whistle, similar to those used in Sun Dances, as well as two prayer books ac- quired from missionaries. During the meeting, the leader spoke to the father peyote on the altar, directing prayers for health and power, as well as appeals related to "anybody who work[s] and decide[s] about this country." According to Sétqópjè, Kiowas mostly brought personal concerns to their encounter with father peyote. But they also spoke of political processes that threatened their tribal lands.[64]

Firm numbers about participation in peyote rites are difficult to generate, but many Kiowa sources refer to gatherings. Calendar makers in the 1890s made several references. Háugú (Silver Horn), who was among the practitioners, noted meetings and the deaths of ritual leaders in his calendars.[65] Cáukị (Ten), a calendar maker who led a Methodist house church, memorialized peyote rites in his work. His calendar (Figure 7.4), organ- ized with crosses marking every Sunday, includes a figure bearing a gourd rattle common in peyote rites. Oral histories also abound with peyote stories. Kiowas recall episodes when their relatives sought healing or when they themselves participated in ritual peyote ingestion and received a cure.[66]

Missionaries urged the reservation agent to suppress peyote rites. In 1892, Methvin called for a "wholesome law" against peyote ingestion. In 1896, the agent consulted with missionaries "regarding the best methods for breaking up . . . [peyote rites] . . . and other kindred evils." Missionaries publicized their concerns in denominational newspapers. They warned readers of the popular *New York Evangelist* that peyote prompted visions akin to "forms of insanity." But peyote's "dangers" also proved enthralling when

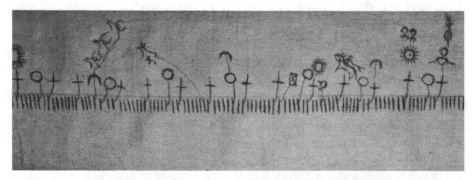

FIGURE 7.4. Detail from Cáukị's (Ten) calendar section for June 1893. The right-hand side features a peyote leader with a gourd rattle above him.
Credit: Panhandle-Plains Historical Museum, Canyon, Texas, photograph by Candace Greene

missionaries claimed the gospel's power to overcome it. A Baptist worker recounted a Kiowa deacon interrupting a peyote meeting, preaching about Jesus, and convincing the practitioners to disband. Another publication named peyote the "greatest curse resting upon the Blanket Indians," but offered readers reassurance with accounts of Kiowa Christians who had given it up for the "Jesus Road."⁶⁷

Along with peyote, missionaries considered the Ghost Dance to be among the "kindred evils" that persisted in Kiowa life. The broader Ghost Dance movement had come to the Kiowas in 1889. Participants adapted it to local conditions, calling it the Feather Dance. But as noted in the previous chapter, the movement seemed to have lost momentum by late 1890. Ethnologist James Mooney, who had studied Ghost Dance practices across the plains, reported its revival among the Kiowa in 1894. He attributed the activity to two men, Fíqí (Eater) and Páutáuljè (Lean Bison Bull). Mooney wrote that dancers composed songs in the Kiowa language. Leaders carried feathers considered to have renewing power. They sometimes brought the people's medicine bundles to their dance circle. Participants wore shirts decorated with moons, stars, and crosses. Agency correspondence from that summer confirms that reservation staff heard about Feather Dance gatherings and nervously monitored the situation.⁶⁸

Examination of Kiowa calendars and notebooks, however, suggests some possibility that Kiowas maintained an interest in Feather Dancing even after what seemed like the movement's earlier dissipation. Cûitònqì's (Wolf Tail) calendar, whose entries prior to 1890 rarely feature figures adorned with feathers, includes men wearing them for all but one of the entries between the winters of 1892–1893 and 1895–1896. Cáukì's (Ten) calendar includes feathers, as well as men holding feathers to recall spring 1892, summer 1893, and spring 1894. At least one American minister, writing in January 1892, detected ongoing interest in the dance during his preaching tour to Kiowa camps.⁶⁹

By 1894, other missionaries also noticed and responded in earnest. Maryetta Reeside wrote to the reservation agent about Ghost Dancers near her mission.⁷⁰ She reported that Sétáfètjàui (Afraid Of The Bear) regarded himself as a "Messiah," went into trances, and claimed to communicate with Jesus. He told listeners that Jesus said that white people were Kiowas' enemies. They had "hemmed them in a small reservation" and brought them a book-based religion intended only for white people. As with earlier rectification movements, Sétáfètjàui promised that Kiowas would soon have a "home" with plenty of land and buffalo. Reeside worried that the dance "paralyzed" her work to encourage Indians' civilization. In desperation, she implored the agent "to do all in [his] power to blot out this great evil." Letters like Reeside's arrived in the agent's office regularly.⁷¹ In the fall of 1895, the agent called on troops. He hoped a show of force would deter the Ghost Dancers.⁷²

Missionary Isabel Crawford worried so much about the Ghost Dance that she decided to attend one herself. In April 1896, she accompanied her Kiowa interpreter to a tipi full of the movement's participants. According to her memoir, Crawford felt unnerved by the "weird singing" and "excessive weeping." Crawford later witnessed a second, all-night meeting in which numerous Kiowa women went into "trances." Once awake, they told of "wonderful things seen, their dead children, the buffalo, Jesus." Like Reeside, Crawford also reported that dancers believed white people had a religion of the book, whereas Indians had been given dance.[73]

While missionaries fretted about Ghost Dancers receiving negative messages about white people and Christianity, Kiowas affiliated with Christian missions focused on different concerns. For instance, Ádàuiétjè (Big Tree) argued that the Feather Dance was the "wrong road" because it led his people away from farming and education, skills they would need for survival once the reservation opened to white settlement. He asked the agent to talk to the movement's leader—the word "messiah" does not appear in his communication—in order to convince him of the dance's harm. Ádàuiétjè's tone was strikingly different from Reeside's. He focused on the movement's potential to derail Kiowa efforts at community survival. He asked for the agent's "help" in getting his people back "into the right way."[74]

Other accounts of Kiowa Christian responses to Feather Dancing reveal a similar concern for community survival. In her memoir, Isabel Crawford recalled Domot's speech at a council called to determine if she could build a house nearby. At earlier meetings, Domot made clear that he was not a Christian and that most Saddle Mountain Kiowas unconnected to the church hesitated to have a missionary's house among them. Even so, Domot argued that Crawford had been kind to his family and "helped the Indians." The Feather Dance leaders, on the other hand, had not. Like Ádàuiétjè, Domot allowed for Crawford's presence and even acknowledged her appeal as her work benefited his people.[75]

Kiowas, then, tried new ritual forms for securing protection and blessing. At the same time, their ritual revisions reflected their long-held posture toward sacred power. As in their Sun Dance days, they came to Jesus, the father peyote, and Feather Dancing to ask for pity, health, and long life. For some, peyote rites offered the healing and guidance necessary for such perilous times. Others, especially those who had lost their children to illness, found fulfillment in the Feather Dance's promise of reunion with deceased loved ones. For still others, affiliation with missions offered a "good road" to walk with Jesus, as well as material support and education provided by missionaries.

Although it troubled missionaries, some Kiowas participated in more than one of these ritual options or refigured Christian theology and practice so that it might bear a resemblance to their older Sun Dance practices. An example of the former comes from a Kiowa man who recalled that his grandmother, who was affiliated with the Baptists and regularly attendeded church, sought out a peyote meeting upon falling ill. Exploring multiple ritual options did not trouble her. She persisted despite her pastor's threat to remove her from the church roster.[76] As an example of the latter, missionary Isabel Crawford recalled a feast held by a Kiowa woman named Cáulánàundáumà (Standing In The Footprints Of Bison). While Kiowas ate beef from the cow she butchered, Cáulánàundáumà stood up to speak. "When I was sick last winter I told Jesus if He would make me well I would kill a beef and call in all the Christians," she said. "Jesus made me better and I had the meeting today to thank Him and to give ten cents a piece for each of my children, for my husband, my son-in-law, and my grandchildren."[77]

As with Kiowa rites in the past, Cáulánàundáumà killed an animal to feed many people. She admitted her helplessness and dependence on sacred power. She made an offering that beseeched this power not only on her own behalf, but also for her extended family. Missionaries said Kiowas needed to turn away from older ritual practices and worship Jesus only. They asked them to stop sharing everything and start managing their resources individually. But they faced a people who differed in their approach to sacred power. Mirroring ritual postures developed in the Sun Dance, Kiowas made vows at evangelistic camp meetings and asked Jesus to pity them.[78] They looked to Him for help to live well on their land.

FROM INDIAN COUNTRY TO THE WIDER WORLD

Missionaries among Kiowas recognized the complicated local dynamics shaping Native ritual activity. Even so, these religious workers tried to connect their programs for civilizing Indians to new sites of US global occupation. The Ladies Industrial Mission (LIM) at Silas Fait's Presbyterian mission to Kiowas provides a useful example. Their work illustrates how Protestant "friends of the Indian" viewed both foreign and domestic populations. As one historian has observed, groups of white women employed the rhetoric of colonization to justify their presence on indigenous lands and efforts to transform indigenous societies.[79] The LIM, which formed in 1889, formed part of a network of American Protestant women circulating stories about Native people within a larger conversation about populations around the globe.

The LIM encouraged socializing as well as good works among its members. Other than Anna Fait, the pastor's wife, most participants were married to staff, traders, and merchants working on the reservation. The women met monthly to sew quilts for Fait's Indian school and raise funds for mission efforts in the United States and abroad. Over time, the LIM focused less on the nearby Indian school and more on educating members about people around the globe in need of religious and economic transformation.[80] At their monthly meetings, the women learned about foreign missions in China, Syria, Guatemala, and parts of Africa. They paired these discussions with materials about domestic concerns, including outreach to freedmen and women, Native Americans, Mexican workers in the United States, and immigrants from Asia.[81]

The LIM used educational materials in the Presbyterian *Home Mission Monthly*, which closely followed political concerns about marginal populations at home and abroad. In the wake of legal cases that forced an end to sanctioned plural marriages among Mormons, the LIM discussed the need for further anti-polygamy activism. Members also considered "Romanism" and its compatibility with American citizenship. They learned of Catholics' growing electoral influence in the American Southwest and read excerpts from Josiah

Strong's anti-Catholic polemic, *Our Country*. The women's political discussions eventually took an international turn. In the fall of 1898, members considered the imminent need for new missions in "territory acquired by the Spanish-American War" and at the war's end considered the religious needs of "our Island Possessions." They also had a lesson on Chinese missions in the wake of Western nations' entry onto the mainland and later discussed the Boxer Rebellion.[82]

Clearly, national conversations about racial and religious difference, as well as political developments both at home and abroad, shaped experiences of missionaries and their families living on the KCA Reservation. These Americans then completed the feedback loop as they reported on Native people to denominational audiences and, sometimes, the mainstream press. As the 1890s progressed, missionaries spoke about the reservation's most serious issue: land allotment and Kiowas' resistance to it.

Congress had passed the 1887 Dawes Allotment Act, which mandated breaking up reservations into individual plots of 160 acres. It deemed that leftover or "surplus" lands be made available for sale to settlers. Government officials, in a body popularly called the Jerome Commission, had arrived at the KCA in 1892 to discuss how allotment would proceed.[83] As noted in the previous chapter, negotiations with the Jerome Commission descended into chaos, and Kiowas worked with Methvin to draft a petition asking Congress to reject the proposed agreement. The petition marked the beginning of a decade-long protest that eventually took Kiowas to the US Supreme Court.[84] The struggle also shaped how Kiowas navigated their ritual options in the 1890s.

Several factors affecting Kiowa reactions to allotment also merit mention. They engaged in the legal battle with their Comanche allies, including some who had financial and legal support from American cattlemen who leased grazing lands on the reservation.[85] Some Americans involved in the allotment debate at the time attributed Indians' resistance solely to the issue of cattle leasing. To be sure, leasing brought important financial benefits. But Kiowas had many reasons for resisting allotment. Most important, they had a relationship to the lands on which they lived. As missionary Isabel Crawford recounted when rumors about the reservation's opening circulated, "The Indians are running everywhere gathering up the bones of their dead and bringing them to the different missions."[86] Dividing lands into individual plots, as well as losing "surplus" lands to white settlers, prompted panic about community maintenance, economic viability, and beloved places where Kiowas had made their homes, celebrated rites, and buried their dead.

Because reservation agents proved unsympathetic to their efforts to resist the Jerome Commission, Kiowas coordinated with other Native people, interested cattlemen, and a few Indian policy reformers in the East. Kiowas also relied on their relationships with sympathetic whites to publicize their opposition. Ethnologist James Mooney, who had lived among Kiowas for many years, spoke against the Jerome Agreement's ratification. In a Quaker periodical, he quoted Áf îtàu (Wooden Lance), an early leader in the Kiowa anti-allotment movement. "We are standing now on a little island," Áf îtàu reportedly said, "and the water is all around us and coming higher."[87]

Áfî̱tą̀u and other Kiowas who opposed allotment argued that the government had only one legal method for allotting their reservation before the Medicine Lodge treaty expired. Officials needed signatures from three-quarters of the male population. Kiowas maintained that the Jerome Commission's claim to have secured enough was fraudulent. In October 1893, they sent their first petition to Congress, decrying the commissioners' trickery and emphasizing the "sacredness of the promises" made in the original Medicine Lodge treaty. In June 1894, they penned another petition citing the government's failure to stop white intruders from trespassing on reservation lands. They sent more petitions over the next several years. They also tried to negotiate in other ways. Some Kiowa parents kept their children from school with the hope of winning concessions from the government.[88]

With the help of the cattlemen, Kiowas and their Native allies sent delegations to Washington, D.C., every year between 1892 and 1900.[89] The makeup of these groups shows that, unlike experiences in some other Indian nations, differences in ritual practice did not preclude a coordinated effort to defend their political autonomy. Áfî̱tą̀u, who participated in the 1894 and 1900 delegations, was known as a leader among peyote practitioners. Some delegates had relationships to, if not membership in, mission churches. Others had experience with multiple ritual forms. Zépcàuiétjè (Big Bow) was among the earliest peyote practitioners among the Kiowa. Not long after one of the delegations, a Baptist missionary reported on his baptism. Cûifágàui (Lone Wolf the Younger), another delegate, had relationships with both Baptist and Catholic missions. His nephew, Delos Lonewolf, took over the legal battle against allotment. He attended the Carlisle boarding school and returned to the reservation, where he served as a Methodist minister and a leading peyote man. The anti-allotment leaders, therefore, participated in a range of ritual practice even as they united to resist allotment.[90]

A similar variety of ritual practice can be found in the lists of Kiowa anti-allotment petitioners. The initial 1893 petition includes Feather Dance participants such as Páutáuljè (Lean Bison Bull) and Gùhâudè (Stripping Off Of A Rib Cage).[91] Because we have little documentary evidence by or about Feather Dancers, it is hard to know how Kiowas understood these practices in relation to their anti-allotment efforts. It is clear, however, that their search for a renewed world did not preclude political activity. At least some Feather Dancers connected with sacred power while entranced, and signed petitions and organized with their community at other times.[92]

Documentary limits also affect what we can know about peyote practitioners who joined the anti-allotment effort. American documents refer to ritual peyote ingestion as a problem akin to drug addiction, which it is not. Missionaries assumed that peyote would make Indians too lazy to farm and unable to succeed on individual plots of land. But peyote practitioners, including Áfî̱tą̀u, Delos Lonewolf, and several others, put great efforts into the legal struggle surrounding allotment.[93]

Because American missionaries created so many documents, we know a bit more about the allotment struggle among Kiowas affiliated with missions.[94] Letters and memoirs tell of Kiowas considering allotment in light of the Bible. For instance, Isabel Crawford recounted one Kiowa man's reflection on the Garden of Eden. He claimed the story was actually about white people stealing land and receiving the just punishment of exile from the garden. Another man asked if the "Jesus book" said anything about living on 160-acre plots of land. In a speech before the congregation, he then replied that Jesus said no such thing. Only white people did. He then called on the missionaries to support Kiowas in fighting allotment. "The Great Father made the land and put us on it," he said. "We love the land our Great Father gave us."[95]

Kiowas also worked with missionaries to secure land once allotment began.[96] In 1898, Kiowas living near Saddle Mountain met to choose land for a church building. Isabel Crawford celebrated the occasion and the "land promised [to] Jesus." Kiowa speakers at the meeting, some of whom were not affiliated with the mission, announced their expectations for this gift of land. Domot spoke on behalf of the non-Christian Kiowas at Saddle Mountain. He acknowledged Crawford's assistance of many in the community. He also noted the impending arrival of white settlers to scoop up "surplus" land. "We must hurry up and look for land for Jesus and put his brand on it . . . Maybe so after us old men pass away [the white men] will come in here and drive our children out of the Jesus House and worship the Great Spirit in it themselves. We want you [Crawford] to get paper and ink and draw up a road that will make this an Indian church forever." To build a church, then, offered the prospect that this piece of land might stay in Kiowa hands. It also secured the sanctity of their ancestors' burial sites as Saddle Mountain Kiowas selected land for the church adjacent to their cemetery.[97]

As noted earlier, variation in ritual practice did not result in community fracture, at least in the work of responding to external threats.[98] This is significant not only as it differs from episodes in some other Indian nations, but also because it suggests that Native affiliation with Christianity had within it the possibility of anti-colonial activity. Kiowas had long attachments to places and the sacred power that dwelled among them. At least some Kiowas who affiliated with Christianity looked to Jesus as a power who could bless their way of life and the Bible as a book with a potential anti-allotment message.

Protestant "friends of the Indian" also agreed about allotment, although they were strongly in favor of it. They published editorials in denominational newspapers extolling the benefits of dissolving reservations. The Women's Board of Home Missions, which supported Presbyterian mission work among the Kiowa, created educational materials calling for well-funded schools that could aid the government's work of breaking down reservations, settling Indians on individual plots, and "making citizens out of them."[99] For these women and other Protestant "friends of the Indian," allotment was crucial to Native peoples' complete and final transformation. Participants in the Lake Mohonk conferences also overwhelmingly supported allotment. Speakers' transcripts and the organization's platform, which were published after every annual conference, called for allotment throughout the 1890s.[100]

Catholics, on the other hand, were less unified about allotment for a number of reasons. Most important, BCIM leaders focused on their struggle to fund Catholic schools for Indian children. They faced powerful political adversaries and lobbied hard to keep their schools intact. Indeed, there is little evidence that Catholic leaders and missionaries had strong opinions about allotment legislation. To be sure, some felt that individual Indian landholding would benefit Native people.[101] But others questioned the government's tactics. One Jesuit missionary compared allotment of Indian lands to losses the Irish had suffered at the hands of British colonizers.[102]

In the end, the national clamor for opening Indian lands overwhelmed Kiowa petitions and delegations. In June 1900, the Senate ratified a version of the Jerome Agreement, and President McKinley announced that the KCA Reservation would be opened to white settlement a year later.[103] The opening would go ahead even as Kiowas disagreed about how to move forward. Some, including Áfîtàu, resigned themselves to it. Others, especially Cûifàgàui (Lone Wolf the Younger), considered a potential legal fight and initiated a case that would end eventually up in the US Supreme Court. But the legal battle could not stop the scheduled opening. As with other parts of the Oklahoma and Indian Territories, the KCA Reservation was about to have a land run.

CLAIMING THE INDIAN COUNTRY

The Indian Territory hosted its first land run in 1889. Fifty thousand settlers raced across the plains to stake their claims on "surplus" Indian land. As the government sent commissioners to negotiate allotment with Native nations throughout the territory, it took possession of hundreds of thousands of acres and made them available for more land runs in the coming years. Newly arrived settlers pushed for formal status, which they achieved with the 1890 creation of the Oklahoma Territory. Kiowas heard about land runs in other parts of the region. They also watched as federal officials allotted the neighboring Cheyenne and Arapaho Reservation and opened three and a half million acres of "surplus" lands to settlement. In April 1892, more than 20,000 people arrived for a run on Cheyenne and Arapaho lands.

Since Congress had finally authorized the Jerome Agreement, allotment and a land run seemed inevitable for the Kiowa. The reservation agent reported the people's dismay. "Distress" over allotment prompted many to give up farming.[104] The reservation's imminent opening also encouraged the entry of whites who stole Indian horses and cattle, as well as merchants who peddled illegal whiskey. Laura Pedrick, a Kiowa woman who taught domestic skills to Indian women, reported her own work upended by the reservation's pending dissolution. She emphasized the people's worry, as well as her efforts to help Kiowas select plots of land. Pedrick recognized that "white people, who have come amongst [the Kiowas] to remain," meant a whole new world for her people. She reported to government authorities that she expected her work among "my people" to be difficult in the coming years.[105]

Missionaries also noted the distress about the opening. Isabel Crawford's memoir includes a June 1900 entry about the pending land run. "Now for the tug of war," she wrote sadly. In September 1900, she included a letter from Lucius Aitsan (Etsanti). "We are all troubled about our land," he told Crawford. At this point, Kiowas living near Saddle Mountain had selected land for a church, but had not started construction. They worried that designating the "land for Jesus" would not hold back white settlers, who might be stopped only by the sight of an actual church building.[106]

Aitsan brought his concerns about the land run to Jesus. According to Crawford, Aitsan asked for help selecting a plot of land. "I can do nothing without you, Jesus," he prayed. "Choose the land for me and don't let me make any mistakes." Even as Aitsan turned to Jesus, his prayer paralleled older forms of Kiowa petitions to sacred power. "I want my cows to have calves and when I get money I will give you some," Aitsan proclaimed. As in so many exchanges throughout Kiowa history, Aitsan made a vow. If great powers helped him, he would respond with an appropriate action and offering.

Aitsan hoped that he and his family would simply survive the allotment to come. American settlers, on the other hand, hoped for much greater things. Railroad companies cultivated big expectations. In a pamphlet on "The Oklahoma Opportunity," the Rock Island and Pacific Railroad claimed that the nearly three million acres to be opened on the KCA Reservation were "the new white man's country." The land, the writer claimed, was "rich and beautiful" and excellent for farming. Most of the Indians, the pamphlet assured, were "detribalized," making them "pleasant and polite." Here was one of Americans' last chances to scoop up government land, the writer declared. And it was rumored to have petroleum. Land in Oklahoma, he told eager readers, equaled "prosperity and money."[107]

With such riches close at hand, settlers and prospectors trespassed on the reservation prior to its opening, distressing Indian people as they tried to secure plots before the land run. Settlers spread rumors that the Wichita Mountains were full of gold and silver. Concerned that thousands of prospectors had illegally entered the mountains, the reservation agent called on troops from Fort Sill. The soldiers could do nothing, however, as the prospectors outnumbered them.[108]

Even as the government scheduled a land run for the KCA, some Kiowas and their allies kept up their legal battle. In 1901, Cûifấgàui (Lone Wolf the Younger) visited Washington, D.C., to make a last-ditch appeal.[109] He returned to the reservation to gather signatures for yet another anti-allotment petition. Newspapers around the country followed the Kiowas' ongoing protest.[110] Cûifấgàui gained nearly one hundred signatures to keep the fight going. He filed a lawsuit against the secretary of the Interior. Arguing that the federal government had no right to violate the Treaty of Medicine Lodge, Cûifấgàui and his fellow plaintiffs sought to keep the land run at bay.

But they could not. More than 150,000 settlers registered for the lottery organized for the land run. In early August 1901, the winners raced across the plains to claim 13,000 new homesteads.[111] In a single day, Kiowas and their allies lost two million acres of treaty-guaranteed lands. Calendar makers memorialized the event with rectangles and squares denoting their land broken into plots and their practice of tribal ownership undone (Figure 7.5).[112]

Kiowas struggled in the period immediately after the land run. The land was not their only loss. That year, the government failed to appropriate money for rations. It also stopped allowing rations to be distributed at mission schools. Cattle thieves beset Kiowas who raised stock on their new farmsteads. During this period of strained food resources, smallpox spread through the region. While Kiowas did not lose as many people as their Comanche neighbors, the epidemic still hit them hard. In response, Kiowas tried to make their new situation viable. Some leased their lands for grazing. Others leased their houses

FIGURE 7.5. Cûitònqî's calendar entries for the winter of 1900–1901 through the summer of 1902. The image on the upper right notes the reservation's 1901 allotment and land run.

Credit: National Anthropological Archives, Smithsonian Institution, manuscript 2002-27

and moved back into tipis. They also considered their ritual options. Kiowas continued to attend peyote rites, perform the Feather Dance, and go to church.

The women of the Presbyterian LIM also continued to meet, although they had little to say about Indians. Their gatherings included discussions about Puerto Rico, America's most recent imperial experiment. They took up the question of Mormon political activity and rumors that polygamy continued. They considered the future of immigrant populations, such as the Chinese, Japanese, and Mexicans living in the United States. LIM members, living still in the heart of a dissolved reservation, followed the direction of their denominational materials. They turned their eyes to other populations in need of transformation.[113]

Other Protestant "friends of the Indian," especially those who continued to gather for the Lake Mohonk Conference, followed suit. As their 1903 platform proclaimed, "The Indian problem is approaching its solution, leaving us confronting the larger problem of our duties toward the people who have recently become subject to our Government and dependent on our care." As free citizens like any other, Indians needed to attend state and territorial schools, participate in the open market, and deal with disputes in the regular system of courts. Rev. S. J. Barrows added his perspective, arguing that the United States was in a new phase of Indian relations, one of "benevolent absorption." "We say to the Indian," Barrows declared, "join our life, enter into its opportunities and obligations, be one of us and with us." And while Barrows referred to the Indians' place in the United States, the Lake Mohonk platform announced that the nation had new dependent populations to consider. Their 1903 meeting included discussions of what to do about people living in America's new holdings: Hawaii and Puerto Rico.[114]

PERSISTING ON THE LAND

In February 1903, the Supreme Court ruled in *Lonewolf v. Hitchcock*. A year and a half after the reservation's land run, the justices unanimously found in favor of the government. They decided that Kiowas could not hold Congress to the Treaty of Medicine Lodge's provisions. Further, the court claimed that Congress had the constitutional authority to abrogate Indian treaties whenever it deemed such action necessary. The *Lonewolf* case, then, was a loss not only for Kiowas and other Indians from their reservation, but all Native people who called on Congress to fulfill its treaty obligations.[115]

The *Lonewolf* decision coincided with the nation's celebration of the Louisiana Purchase's centennial. Commemorative events took place around the country. An exposition in St. Louis served as the premier location. Protestant leaders joined in. The Baptists dedicated an entire issue of their *Home Mission Monthly* to the ways the purchase had shaped America, Protestant Christianity, and the kingdom of God.[116] Prior to the acquisition, wrote one minister, French Catholics had not allowed Protestants to enter the territory. But one hundred years later it contained 40,000 Protestant churches, and 85 percent of the region's residents were Protestant. This growth, the writer claimed, was astounding given Catholic efforts to take the West for themselves. But Jefferson's deal allowed for Protestant entry into the West. "We think it not too much to say," he concluded, "that the Purchase saved our American Christianity."[117] If in the 1840s, Americans naturalized and militarized expansion through talk of manifest destiny, they used centennial celebrations to sacralize it.

The same issue of *Home Mission Monthly* contained an update on Kiowa missions. It told of Paddlety's effort to preach and build a church.[118] The paper also provided details about mission work with children at the Rainy Mountain School.[119] An image

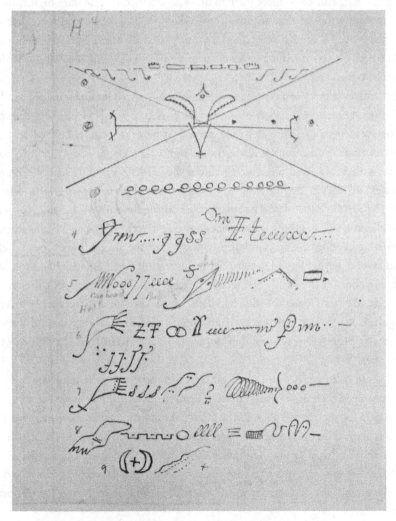

FIGURE 7.6. Letter to Belo Cozad, a student at the Carlisle Indian boarding school, from his family on the Kiowa reservation. The letter delivers news about family, as well as references to Jesus's presence in Kiowa lands and relatives' peyote practices.

Credit: Dickinson Research Center, National Cowboy & Western Heritage Museum, Oklahoma City, Oklahoma, Arthur and & Shifra Silberman Native American Art Collection, photograph by Jennifer Graber

accompanied the article, a picture of a Kiowa infant nestled in a handmade cradleboard. The editors referred to the tiny child as a "new Indian junior," another Native child waiting to be transformed into a Christian citizen.

Kiowa calendars also featured children in 1903. As noted earlier, Hầugữ's (Silver Horn) entry for that summer included three cradleboards, celebrating the births of babies among the people. Despite their diminished land holdings, Kiowas remained in their homeland and highlighted their connections to one another in calendars and cradleboards, as well as in their ritual work. That spring, Kiowas affiliated with the Saddle Mountain mission built a new church. When their children arrived from school in time for the Easter service, their parents rushed to meet them. They also decided to celebrate their own "Jesus Eat," or communion service, without the leadership of a white male member of the Baptist ministry.[120] Some Kiowas gathered for peyote rites, where they sought healing for their children. Others met for Feather Dances, hoping to experience reunion with their children who had died.

In this ritual variety, Kiowas sustained themselves as a people connected to their homeland. Colonial pressures not only prompted these new ways of relating to sacred power, but also new formats for addressing their altered situation. Consider how relatives found a way to translate the motions of Plains Indian sign language onto paper in order to communicate with Belo Cozad, a Kiowa student at the Carlisle boarding school (Figure 7.6). The circles and lines in the third line assure Cozad that everything is all right. Why? The line above provides an answer. The triangles stand for the tipis of Indian Country. The "X" proclaims that something is over that country, stretching out to the four directions. It is Jesus, signaled by the crosses pointing down and the angel wings. Cozad's relatives also had several pieces of good news to deliver in their letter. A relative had a job hauling freight. Members of the family had recently gathered for a big meal. But the letter also contained bad news. Cozad's brother had died. He was buried on a hillside. In this period of struggle, Cozad's family encouraged him to pray to Jesus. At the same time, they noted other rituals options. One relative, they wrote, had gone out many nights in a row to sing peyote songs.[121]

In all these contexts, Kiowas asked great powers to come near them and pity them. They announced their desire to stay in their homelands. And they made vows in order to heal and care for their loved ones. In the face of American dispossession, Kiowas faced a future in a nation that assumed they were now detribalized. To be sure, allotment took a great portion of their lands and undermined communal ownership. But Kiowas, like other Native people who survived allotment, had other kinds of connections to one another. The gods of Indian Country would continue to play a crucial role in their ongoing communal life.

Epilogue

DESPITE EFFORTS BY Protestant and Catholic "friends of the Indian," as well as other Americans who devised solutions to the "Indian problem," Kiowas persisted. They cultivated a sense of themselves as a distinct people connected to a particular place. Ritual practices that engaged sacred power played a crucial role in that persistence. Kiowas came to churches, peyote meetings, and Feather Dance circles. They drew near to the gods of Indian Country. They asked to be sustained within, if not delivered from, an increasingly perilous situation.

Self-described "friends of the Indian" also persisted. In the early twentieth century, they continued to advocate for Native people's assimilation. Beginning in the 1930s, some sought Indians' "preservation" through programs that paralleled the Department of the Interior's "Indian New Deal." By the 1960s and 1970s, Americans who had long dominated the public sphere faced protests from people of color, women, workers, and sexual minorities. Native people also protested, referring often to the federal government's history of land dispossession and environmental degradation. Some Native American activists also addressed the legacy of Christian missions. They told painful stories about the role that missionaries, reformers, and church-supported schools played in their people's histories. Non-Indian Christian leaders, however, often failed to hear their voices.

In time, some American Christians began to express sympathy with Native Americans and their accounts of historic injustices. The 1992 celebration of the five hundredth anniversary of Columbus's North American voyage prompted some acknowledgment of the role Christians had played in the continent's colonization and its destructive effects on indigenous people. More recently, some American Christians have expressed not only concern for, but also solidarity with Native people protesting the Dakota Access pipeline and other threats to water, land, and the larger environment. While these developments are significant, they are not necessarily widespread.

Whether newly sympathetic or not, contemporary American Protestant and Catholic churches populated by non-Indians have a different relationship to Native people than their nineteenth-century forebears. Churches no longer feature white reformers and missionaries dedicated to "Americanizing" Indians through boarding schools or long-term missions. More likely, they have one of three forms of engagement with Native Americans. Perhaps it is a short-term mission trip, likely a youth group seeking to serve on an impoverished reservation. Or it might be curious baby boomers dabbling in Native "spirituality" to remedy their disaffection with monotheism. Most likely, though, American Christians outside Indian communities have no contact with and not much interest in contemporary Native Americans at all.

That does not mean that the impulse to be "friends of the Indian" has disappeared or even faded. On the contrary, it has simply transferred to other bodies in other places. In the early part of the twentieth century, as noted in Chapter 7, American Christians who had once been dedicated to Indian assimilation turned their attention to America's new overseas holdings. They embarked on a "civilizing mission" in the Philippines and expressed surprise when Filipinos resisted. Again, Americans were divided on the question of using force to transform an indigenous population. But they all, even the Filipino's "friends," agreed that the island's people were backward and required training before they could be ready for democracy. Perhaps the latest instantiation of the "friends of the Indian" can be found among those who would civilize the people of Afghanistan and other majority Muslim nations. Who claims the mantle of the Afghan woman's friend more than those who assume that a military occupation will liberate her? The "friends of the Indian" took the Christian God to Indian Country. Now they take their God abroad.

As Americans turned their eyes away from the southern plains, Kiowas continued the work of caring for each other and the land, even as the community faced forces that would impoverish them. As with earlier incidents of disease, occupation, and attempts at cultural genocide, neither poverty nor isolation has destroyed them. And as I noted in the book's last few chapters, many Kiowas raised their children with knowledge of their people's history and cultural practices. That effort continues. It's been my great privilege to meet Kiowas working at the tribal museum and to learn about their classes on beading, traditional flute playing, singing in Kiowa language, and even tipi making. I've also witnessed these efforts outside the museum's purview. At Rainy Mountain Kiowa Indian Baptist Church, congregants old and young sing hymns in Kiowa. In conversations with Kiowa elders, I've listened to men talk about putting up tipis for peyote meetings. At a birthday party for a young girl, I watched a naming ceremony. An elder came forward, gave the child a Kiowa name, and explained its meaning. The parents offered gifts in return. Everyone offered blessings.

Finally, in an experience that I will be old before I fully understand, I attended a celebration of the Kiowa Black Leggings, a warrior society. I could tell you about the historic Tipi with Battle Pictures pitched on the dance grounds. I could describe the men and women dressed in red. I could detail the two days of dancing, singing, drumming, socializing, and eating. But I leave you, instead, with my wonder at the role Kiowa children played at the gathering. I watched as a baby was carefully placed in a cradleboard made by his great-grandmother. The baby's father, now in his twenties, was also once placed in the same cradle. I saw little girls adorned in beautiful clothes, learning Kiowa dances from their mothers. And when a high point in the proceedings arrived, I sat beside a father who quickly urged his ten-year-old son to get up and join the singers around the drum. The boy looked up at his father, his face betraying a little reluctance. "Why?" he asked. "Because these are Kiowa songs," His father answered. "These are our songs."

Appendix

KIOWA NAMES

⌒⌒——

Kiowa names can be difficult to track in historical records for several reasons. First, Kiowas were sometimes known by multiple names over the course of a lifetime. Along with a name given in infancy, a person could be given different names later in life. Older people could give their name to younger people and go by a different name themselves afterward. Second, because there is no standard form of written Kiowa, names have been rendered a number of ways. When possible, I provide the spelling suggested by Parker McKenzie or William Meadows. (See Meadows, "Kiowa Names and Naming Practices.") For readers interested in exploring the historical documents or more recent scholarship, I also list other renderings of the Kiowa names and their English translations. Finally, Americans often attempted to translate Kiowa names. Sometimes these efforts turned out to be close to the original. Others, at times, bordered on the comic. Some translations are so far off that determining whom they referred to is nearly impossible.

In this list, I provide the name I use in the text and follow it with other possible Kiowa spellings and English translations that appear in both historical documents and later scholarship.

Ácàą̀ (Going Into The Timber)—Richard Henry Pratt used Ah-Ke-Ah in Fort Marion records and posited an alias of Pah-oh-ka, which his translator rendered as Coming to the Grove.

Ádàuiétjè (Big Tree)—This name is rendered variously in historical documents and scholarship as Ado-Eete, A'do-eete, Adoetti, A-do-ete, Ado-eetti.

Áfîtą̀u (Wooden Lance)—In American documents, this name appears as Apitan, Apiatan, and Ah-Peah-Tone. Greene uses Ahpeahtone. Meadows offers Spear as another possible translation.

Áisèáuidè (Many Camp Smokes)—Áisèáuidè is listed as Tahbonemah in some census records. He enlisted in a troop of Indian scouts under the name I-See-O. That name appears as Iseeo and Isseo in many documents from the period.

Ándálé—He came to the Kiowa as a captive from New Mexico. His name was originally José Andrés Martínez. Ándálé is the Kiowa pronunciation of Andrés. His name often appeared in American records as Andele.

Annie Aone Jones—This name appears in Presbyterian church records and almost certainly refers to a woman often referred to "Kiowa Annie," who eventually married and took the last name Berry.

Ȧthàuhȧuiqȉ (Warbonnet Man)—Mooney renders his Kiowa name as Ä'-tahá-ik'í and writes that he was also called Sét-k'-ódalte, meaning Bear Neck.

Ȧunsójèqàptȧu (Old Man Foot)—In her list of *Ṭáimé* keepers, Marriott spells this name Ansote and Anso-gia-ny. Mooney suggests Ánsogíani.

Càuáufȉjȧu (Crow [Feathered Sheathed] Lance)—This person appears as Heidsick in many historical documents penned by Americans. Alternate translations are Crow Lance and Feathered Lance.

Cȧukȉ (Ten)—This name appears in many forms in the historical documents and archived collections, including Gawky, Gawkey, and Gaukein. Mooney renders this name Ga'kiñâte. Meadows adds that Cȧukȉ was also known as Kȧuqígàcùthè, which means Return From Battle Marks.

Cáulánàundáumȧ (Standing In The Footprints Of Bison)—Historical documents often refer to her as Ananthy Odlepaugh. Silberman uses Anati, An-an-ti, and Anate in his research notes. He rendered her name as Kawlahnohndaumah and translated it as Footprints of a Buffalo. Corwin spells her name A-nan-thy, Ananthy, and A-Nanthy in his articles about her calendar.

Cȧumâmȧjè (Goose Flying Overhead)—According to Meadows, Cȧumâmȧjè was popularly known as Mamanti. He was also known as Doy-hau-ty, which translates as Walks on a Cloud. Other sources translated Cȧumâmȧjè as Swan or Screaming on High.

Chálkǫgái (Black Goose)—Historical sources list this name as Chaddle-kaungy-ky, Chatlekaungky, and Tsadalkonkya.

Chȩthȧidè (White Horse)—McKenzie writes that White Horse's name in Kiowa, which has often been given as Isa-tah, would be better realized as Tsa-tah.

Cómȧjè (Friendship Tree)—Cómȧjè's name appears as Komalty, Comalty, Komalte, Komulta, Komalta, and Goma'te in American documents. He was also sometimes known as Big Head.

Cûifȧgàui (Lone Wolf the Elder)—This English rendering appears in documents from the period and in many scholarly works. Mooney referred to this person as Gu'i-pägo.

Cûifȧgàui (Lone Wolf the Younger)—Lone Wolf the Elder passed on his name to him. He was also known as Mammadety.

Cûiqáuje (Wolf Lying Down)—Mooney renders this name as Guikate. Alternate translations include Wolf Emerging and Wolf Appearing.

Cûitònqȉ (Wolf Tail)—Cûitònqȉ, also known as Jimmy Quitone or Quoe-tone, created a calendar known as the Quitone Kiowa Calendar.

Cûjòkǫgai (Black Eagle)—Mooney rendered the Kiowa as Gu'ato-ko'ñkya. On the Medicine Lodge treaty, Cûjòkǫgai's name appears as Wah-toh-konk.

Delos Lonewolf—He was nephew of Cûifȧgàui (Lone Wolf the Younger) and was christened as Delos Knowles.

Domot—This name appears in missionary writings from the period. This man was also a member of Troop L, a unit of Indian soldiers at Fort Sill.

Éàunhâfàui (Trailing The Enemy)—This name appears in sources as Eonah-Pah, Eonhapa-a, E-one-ah. Nye and Hardoff offer Trails The Enemy as a translation.

Éttàlyìdònmàui (We Are Seeking Boys)—This name, often rendered as Etahdleuh Doanmoe and translated as Boy or Boy Hunting, was spelled a variety of ways by American officials. Some sources refer to him as Et-ta-lyi-don-maui.

Fáitàlyì (Sun Boy)—Mooney renders his Kiowa name as Paí-tälyí.

Fíqí (Eater)—This named has also been rendered as Bi'ank'i, Biäñki, and Bi'äñki. Once he began participating in the Feather Dance, Fíqíí received the name Asatitola (or Asa'tito'la), which has been translated as Messenger.

Gùhâudè (Stripping Off Of A Rib Cage)—American officials knew Gùhâudè as Wohaw, which they translated as Beef.

Gǔkáulê (Lump On The Rib Cage)—Ewers renders the Kiowa name as Guakale and offers Tumor or Swelling Inside as possible translations.

Hǎugǔ (Silver Horn)—Hǎugǔ's name is also rendered as Hangun and Haungooah. Meadows offers Metal Horn as a possible translation.

Isatai—He was a Comanche man of power in the 1870s. Scholars offer several alternative spellings, including Isa-tai, Eschiti, and Ishatai. It is alternately translated as Wolf Shit and Coyote Droppings.

Jáudèkǎu (Retained His Name A Long Time)—*See* Pǎutépjè (Bison Bull Emerging).

Jèhân—He was taken as a captive and lived with the Kiowa. His name is the Kiowa pronunciation of the Spanish "Tejano."

Jòhâusàn (Little Bluff)—According to Greene, the man known as Jòhâu first went by Aanonte and later received the name Jòhâusàn from his father. Scholars use a number of different spellings, including Tohausen, Tohasan, and Dohausen. His nephew later received his name and is often designated in sources as Jòhâusàn the Younger.

Jòhéjè (Without Moccasins)—This name appears as Dohente, Dó-héñte, and Tòhéjè in historical documents and scholarly sources. English translations include Barefoot, No Shoes, and Got No Moccasins. Jòhéjè also went by the names Plenty Stars and Napewat.

Joshua Givens—Joshua received his American name from a doctor who raised him after his father, Sétǎgài (Sitting Bear), died. This name appears in school and missionary records. His last name sometimes appeared as Given.

Julia Givens—Julia also received her name from the American doctor who raised her after her father's death. This name appears in school and church records and also sometimes appears as Given. One source provides Odle-Tay-Die as her Kiowa name and Spliced Hair as a translation.

Lucius Aitsan (Etsanti)—The name Lucius Aitsan appears in Kiowa agency records, as well as in several documents penned by missionaries. Meadows renders his Kiowa name as Etsanti or Éxànhólǎ, which means Killed Them By Tricking Them.

Mǎyítèndè (Woman's Heart)—This name appears as Manyi-ten on the Medicine Lodge treaty. Mooney offered two different spellings of the Kiowa name: Man'nyi'-te'n and Ma'nyi-ten. It also appears in sources as Maientende.

Mokeen—Americans used this name to refer to a Kiowa taken captive from Mexico. Meadows suggests the spelling Màucîn, a Kiowa pronunciation of the name Joachin.

Oheltoint (Charlie Buffalo)—Palmer renders the Kiowa name as Ó:èljǿi, which translates as Speaks With A Big Voice. His records from Carlisle list his name as Charles Oheltoint. His last name shows up as Ohettoint and Ohetoint in historical sources. It appears that he was known as Charlie Buffalo later in life.

Ôlpàu (Bison Bird)—This name appears as Odlepaugh in missionary accounts and other reservation-era sources.

O-Tank (White Bird)—This name appears in American records of 1860s treaty negotiations. It does not, however, appear in other records. Nor does it have the root words for "white" or "bird." It is difficult to know who the speaker might have been.

Paddlety—This man was associated with Kiowas living near Redstone and was affiliated with a mission near there. His name appears in American sources as Padlety and Paudlety, the latter of which can lead to confusion with another Kiowa man of that name.

Páugų̀héjè (Hornless Bison Bull)—Mooney offers Pá-guñhéñte as a rendering of his Kiowa name. Kracht uses Pagunhente.

Páutáuljè (Lean Bison Bull)—This name appears as Phi-tal-ti in the 1867 Medicine Lodge treaty. Mooney uses Pátádal. Several sources use a variation, Patadel, on Mooney's spelling. Jordan renders it as Pautaudletay. The most common translation is Poor Buffalo.

Páutépjè (Bison Bull Emerging)—Páutépjè took this name as he began a movement to restore the buffalo herds. Prior to that, he was known as Jáudèkáu, meaning Retained His Name A Long Time. Historical sources and scholarship often cite his earliest name as Datekan and new name as Patepte. Mooney translates the latter as Buffalo Bull Coming Out.

Páuthòcáui (White-Faced Bison Bull)—Meadows suggests two names that this person was known by: Jòhâudè (Recess In The Side Of A Cliff) and Páuthòcáui (White-Faced Bison Bull). McCoy renders the latter as Pa-dogai. Greene uses Padogai.

Qódèbọ̀hòn—This name appears as Gotebo in most American sources. Qódèbọ̀hòn was first known by the name Dáuàuiqí, or Many Wounds. In the reservation period, he became known as Qódèbọ̀hòn, which Americans began to pronounce as Gotebo. Later in life he was known as Bónhàqaptàu, meaning Bent or Hunchbacked Old Man.

Qóichégàu (Dog Society)—The society for Kiowas' warrior elite. The society's name has been rendered a number of ways, most often as Koitsenko, in American sources.

Sétáfètjàui (Afraid Of The Bear)—This name is also rendered as Set-apeto and Sit-ah-pa-tah and translated as Afraid Of Bears and Even The Bears Are Afraid Of Him. Kracht offers Setzepetoi as a possible spelling.

Sétá̧gài (Sitting Bear)—Several scholars use Satanke in their work. American documents often render the name as Satank.

Sétbáujè (Bear Bringing It)—Ewers offers Setbati.

Sétbọ̀hon (Bear's Hat)—Cáulánàundáumà's (Standing In The Footprints Of Bison) calendar contains a caption, possibly provided by Lucius Aitsan, about Bear's Hat assisting Páutépjè's (Bison Bull Emerging) rectification effort.

Sétèmqíą̀ (Bear That Runs Over Them)—This name appeared as Set-im-kia on the 1867 Medicine Lodge treaty. In many American sources, the name is translated as Stumbling Bear. Mooney spelled it Set-īmki'a and provided Pushing Bear as a translation.

Sétjáúáuidè (Many Bears)—Palmer offers this rendering and translation. Other options are Setdayaite and Set-Daya-Ite. Other possible translations include Heap of Bears and Plenty Bears.

Sétqópjè (Mountain Bear)—American sources from the period often spelled this name as Setkopti, including Sétqópjè's handwritten diary at the National Anthropological Archives.

Mooney rendered his name Se't-k'o'pte and translated it as Mountain Bear. Petersen used Tsaitkopeta in her early work on Kiowa drawing. Tash Smith uses Tsaitcopte. Sétqópjè was also known as Paul.

Séttàun (Little Bear)—Séttàun's calendar was central to James Mooney's major work on Kiowa historical memory. Mooney referred to him as Sett'an. Another option is Settan.

Sétthàidé (White Bear)—There are a variety of renderings of this Kiowa name in historical documents, as well as in the scholarship. They included Satanta, Set-tainte, and Setthaide.

Thènéàungópjè (Kicking Bird)—Many sources from the period offer Kicking Bird as a translation, although some offer Kicking Eagle and Striking Eagle as options. Mooney writes that the name Ton-a-en-ko appears for Kicking Bird on treaty documents. He provides T'ene'-ango'pte as a Kiowa rendering. Meadows translates the name as Eagle Striking With Talons. Kicking Bird's nephew later took his name and was often referred to as Kicking Bird the Younger.

Thènébáudài (Bird Appearing)—Mooney used T'ene'-badai' and translated it as Bird Appearing. Kracht offers Tenebwde. Greene uses Tenebati and adds Eagle Emerging as another possible translation.

Thènézélbé (Fierce Eagle)—Mooney provided Gu'ato-ze'dalbe as a Kiowa rendering with Dangerous Bird as a translation. Quaker sources list this man as Dangerous Eagle.

Tòhàlmà (Limping Woman)—Sources render her Kiowa name in several ways, including T'owyhawlmah, Tonhadal, and Tone-haddle-mah. Another translation offered is Broken Leg. She was given the name Laura at school. She acquired the last name Doanmoe after marrying Éttàlyìdònmàui (We Are Seeking Boys), also known as Etahdleuh Doanmoe. After his death, she married an American with the last name Pedrick.

Tónàuqàut (Snapping Turtle)—Meadows also translates it as Rough-Tailed.

Vàuigài (In The Middle)—This name appears as Paingya in several historical sources and in scholarship.

Zébàutéfèà (Comes Along Straightening An Arrow)—Ih-Pa-Yah is the rendering of this name in documents from Fort Marion. Pratt offered a Straightening An Arrow as a translation.

Zépcàuiétjè (Big Bow)—This name appears as Zepko-eeta in the 1867 Medicine Lodge treaty and Sa-aunt on allotment records. Mooney uses Zépko-eéte. At other times in his life, Zépcàuiétjè went by other names, including Say-au-day, Belfa, or Johegi. Say-au-day can be translated as One Who Gave Peyote.

Zótâm (Driftwood)—Some English sources spell his name Zotom, Zotum, Zontom, or Zo-tam and provide the translation Biter. McKenzie suggests a second name by which he was known among Kiowas: Fóláuljè (sometimes spelled Podal-adalte), which means Snake Rattle Hair Ornament or Snake Head, a name that likely derived from a relative who wore a snake head charm as a form of personal medicine. Upon baptism, Zótâm received the name Paul Caryl Zotom.

NOTES

INTRODUCTION

1. On *dwdw* and its embodiment in natural phenomenon, see Kracht, "Kiowa Religion: An Ethnohistorical Analysis," 80–83; Kracht, "Kiowa Religion in Historical Perspective," 16. Some aspects of *dwdw* overlap with other Plains Indian concepts of power, such as the Siouan concept of *wakan*. As such, *dwdw* differentiates the human and superhuman (or suprahuman), rather than the natural and supernatural. Further, *dwdw* and *wakan* do not designate pantheons of gods, but are ways to classify the "distribution and function of power in the universe." See DeMallie and Lavenda, "Wakan," 153, 155. My account of the 1873 Sun Dance is drawn from several sources, which I cite throughout the chapter. Works that shape my discussion of Kiowa engagement of sacred power include Fowles, *An Archeology of Doings*; Orsi, *History and Presence*; Wenger, *We Have a Religion*; and King, *Orientalism and Religion*.

2. On variations of the Sun Dance among Plains Indian nations, see Archambault, "Sun Dance," 983–984.

3. Levy, "Kiowa," 907. Kiowas' Tanoan language means that in their deeper history they were related either to Puebloans in the Southwest or Athapaskan-speaking Avonlea hunters in the Big Horn Basin of what is now Wyoming. See Calloway, *One Vast Winter Count*, 59.

4. Calloway dates this migration to the fourteenth or fifteenth centuries. See *One Vast Winter Count*, 59–60. Most other historians, if they date the move at all, put it somewhat later. Calloway also explains the cultural transition to horses. See *One Vast Winter Count*, Chapter 6.

5. On Kiowas' southern migration, see Mooney, *Calendar History*, 157–162. On Native peoples making places for themselves in new lands, see Basso, *Wisdom Sits in Places*, 5–7.

6. Meadows, "Black Goose's Map," 265–282. There is no standardized form of written Kiowa. When I use Kiowa names for people and places, I provide it in one form, typically the Parker McKenzie version, followed by one possible English translation. In the appendix I detail other possible Kiowa spellings and English translations.

7. Voget, *The Shoshoni-Crow Sun Dance*, 78.

8. Kracht, "Kiowa Religion: An Ethnohistorical Analysis," 168–172.

9. I will discuss this image and other Kiowa drawings later in the Introduction.

10. On the *Táimé* keeper's actions and bison hunting for the Sun Dance, see Scott, "Notes on the Kado," 356; Kracht, "Kiowa Religion: An Ethnohistorical Analysis," 258, 280–281. On the ritual importance of idealized hunts, see Smith, "The Bare Facts of Ritual," 112–127.

11. Scott, "Notes on the Kado," 359.

12. Marriott, *The Ten Grandmothers*, 100; Kracht, "Kiowa Religion: An Ethnohistorical Analysis," 305.

13. On pipes and smoking, Marriott, *The Ten Grandmothers*, 98–99; Battey, *The Life and Adventures of a Quaker*, 167; Winter, *Tobacco Use by Native North Americans*, 3, 9. On the *Táimé* keeper, see Marriott, *The Ten Grandmothers*, 101. On the general mood, see Battey, *The Life and Adventures of a Quaker*, 167–168.

14. Battey, *The Life and Adventures of a Quaker*, 172; Kracht, "Kiowa Religion: An Ethnohistorical Analysis," 315–318.

15. Greene uses the language of "medicine complex" to describe traditions with combinations of components. See "Buffalo and Longhorn," 45.

16. Battey, *The Life and Adventures of a Quaker*, 171–172.

17. Kracht, "Kiowa Religion in Historical Perspective," 16–17. On a similar overlap between men with access to sacred power and military honors, see Kavanaugh, *Comanche Political History*, 28.

18. Scott, "Notes on the Kado," 349–350.

19. On the dancers and their vows, see Kracht, "Kiowa Religion: An Ethnohistorical Analysis," 324, 331; Battey, *The Life and Adventures of a Quaker*, 175. On the *Táimé* as a kind of mediator between the sun and the people, see "Kiowa Religion: An Ethnohistorical Analysis," 168. On the *Táimé* keeper's role, see Scott, "Notes on the Kado," 367. On the role of Kiowa relatives, see "Kiowa Religion: An Ethnohistorical Analysis," 336.

20. Some anthropologists referred to these bundles as the Ten Grandmothers. This led some to conclude that Kiowas related to, if not worshipped, ten separate gods residing within the bundles. Many Kiowas objected to this presentation. See James Silverhorn, interview by Julia A. Jordan, June 6, 1969, interview T-18, OFLC, M452, Box 5, Folder 2, WHC, UO. On the emergence of medicine bundles among Plains nations, see Fowler, "The Great Plains," 10–11. On overlaps with other Plains Indian nations, see DeMallie and Lavenda, "Wakan," 157.

21. Meadows, *Through Indian Sign Language*, 177.

22. On the bundles' powerful attributes, see Kracht, "Kiowa Religion: An Ethnohistorical Analysis," 152–153. On men coming to them before raids, see Guy Quetone, interview by Julia A. Jordan, March 30, 1971, interview T-638, OFLC, M452, Box 5, Folder 2, WHC, UO; Cecil and Jenny Horse, interview by Julia A. Jordan, October 10, 1968, interview T-324, OFLC, M452, Box 5, Folder 2, WHC, UO; Cecil and Jenny Horse, interview by Julia A. Jordan, October 2, 1968, interview T-326, OFLC, M452, Box 5, Folder 2, WHC, UO. On the bundles within Sun Dance practices, see Marriott, *The Ten Grandmothers*, 106; Nye, *Bad Medicine and Good*, 58–59.

23. Marriott, *The Ten Grandmothers*, 107.

24. Scott, "Notes on the Kado," 365.

25. I use the word "present" in the way Robert Orsi discusses "gods truly present." See Orsi, *History and Presence*. I see Kiowa practices of declaration and engagement in the way Severin Fowles describes "doings" in his work on the Pueblo. See Fowles, *An Archeology of Doings*.

26. I will discuss these new alliances in Chapters 1 through 3.

27. See Note on Terms for designations for Quakers or the Society of Friends.

28. Battey and other American observers used the terms "savage" and "barbaric" to describe cultural practices they considered uncivilized. They employed the words "heathen" and "pagan" to denote non-Christian religious practice. See DuVal, "Debating Identity, Sovereignty, and Civilization," 26.

29. Battey, *The Life and Adventures of a Quaker*, 182. Battey maintained this negative view of Kiowa rituals for the rest of his life. The appendix of his memoir characterized Kiowa "religion" as lacking accountability, enthralled to "medicine men," and steeped in practices of witchcraft and sorcery. See *The Life and Adventures of a Quaker*, 330–332.

30. On the concept of "true religion" in nineteenth-century America, see Modern, *Secularism in Antebellum America*, Introduction and Chapter 1. As Fluhman notes, American Protestants' efforts to delineate "true religion" often involved identifying groups outside it, namely the Latter-day Saints. See *A Peculiar People*, 9.

31. Battey, *The Life and Adventures of a Quaker*, 183.

32. See the section on terms for the phrase "friends of the Indian." On the construction of benevolent identities, see Ryan, *The Grammar of Good Intentions*, 4–8.

33. Nineteenth-century Americans identified a number of "problems" they faced, the "Indian problem" being only one of them. See Dippie, *The Vanishing American*; Brantlinger, *Dark Vanishings*.

34. On civilizing missions, see Conroy-Krtuz, *Christian Imperialism*; Hutchison, *Errand to the World*; Chang, *Citizens of a Christian Nation*; Liebersohn, "Introduction: The Civilizing Mission," 384–387.

35. Battey, *The Life and Adventures of a Quaker*, 183.

36. Several historians have shown the federal government's interest and support for the development of the American West. For its particular role in regard to Indian nations, see Rockwell, *Indian Affairs and the Administrative State*.

37. Battey's assignment, along with many other posts held by representatives from religious groups in this period, was a particular program under President Grant. I detail this program in Chapters 3 and 4. Other kinds of partnership, which included federal support for religious workers living within Indian communities, existed throughout the century and are detailed in the book's chapters.

38. Ned Blackhawk writes about patterns of pre-colonial and colonial-era violence. See *Violence over the Land*.

39. Chapter 3 includes a full discussion of these events.

40. On the broader context of religious social reform, see Mintz, *Moralists and Modernizers*. On the violence that accompanied these benevolent movements, see Ryan, *The Grammar of Good Intentions*, 26.

41. Jacki Thompson Rand also discusses the colonial collision between Kiowas and Americans. She argues that Kiowa "tribalism expressed their social values and humanity." I am interested in

how old and new rituals were a part of this effort. See *Kiowa Humanity and the Invasion of the State*, 6, 152.

42. I use language about Native "affiliation" with Christian churches, as opposed to a conjecturing about Indian "conversion." See Fisher, *The Indian Great Awakening*, Chapter 4.

43. According to Robert Orsi, these "gods" are "truly present" and act "with, to, for, and against humans." See *History and Presence*, 4.

44. Asad, *Genealogies of Religion*; Masuzawa, *The Invention of World Religions*. On the implications of this category's history for American religious history, see Lofton, "Religious History as Religious Studies."

45. Long, "Religion, Discourse, and Hermeneutics," 185.

46. See Altman, *Heathen, Hindoo, Hindu*; Fluhman, *A Peculiar People*; Paddison, *American Heathens*; Pinhiero, *Missionaries of Republicanism*; McGreevy, *Catholicism and American Freedom*; Jacobsen, *Whiteness of a Different Color*.

47. As such, "religion" functioned as an instrument of colonial knowledge and power, similar to what David Chidester observed in colonial South Africa. See Chidester, *Savage Systems*.

48. Wenger, *We Have a Religion*.

49. On framing Indian defenses of land in terms of sovereignty, see Wilkins and Lomawaima, *Uneven Ground*, 4–5.

50. Ryan notes that benevolent work among Indians and other populations provided both a format for whites to identify with non-white peoples, as well as language for articulating those populations' differences and needs. See *The Grammar of Good Intentions*, 5, 19.

51. Those that cover the nineteenth century include McNally, *Ojibwe Singers*; Martin, *Sacred Revolt*; Pesantubbee, *Choctaw Women in a Chaotic World*; Holler, *Black Elk's Religion*; Irwin, *Coming Down from Above*; Niezen, *Spirit Wars*; Christensen, *Sagwich*.

52. See Fisher, *The Indian Great Awakening*; Silverman, *Red Brethren*; Pointer, *Encounters of the Spirit*. Writers of more synthetic accounts of American religion in the colonial period also make Native people a crucial part of their narratives. See, for instance, Butler, Wacker, and Balmer, *Religion in American Life*.

53. Major works on the early nineteenth century reflect this trend. Hatch's *The Democratization of American Christianity* has almost nothing on Native people. Butler opens with an intriguing mention of Indian missions and then drops the issue. See *Awash in a Sea of Faith*. For a focus on missions, see McLoughlin, *Champions of the Cherokee* and *Cherokees and Christianity*. One important exception is Marty's *Righteous Empire*, which opens its section on the nineteenth century with the Indian removals of the 1830s. On the significance of Marty's use of "empire," see Graber, "The Imperial Angle."

54. For an example of this focus on missions and Ghost Dancing, see Butler, Wacker, and Balmer, *Religion in American Life*. For a critique of standard works in American history that focus on the Ghost Dance and Wounded Knee as episodes of anti-modern Indian activity, see Warren, *God's Red Son*, 368.

55. I suspect that focusing on Native peoples and lands would complicate and undermine a literature that remains strongly exceptionalist in its focus on America's "triumph" over slavery and the growth of evangelicalism as signs of political freedom.

56. Callahan, *New Territories, New Perspectives*, 1–7; Slotkin, *The Fatal Environment*, 111. Haselby argues that the period after the revolution, in which Americans faced questions of how to govern themselves, acquire lands for a growing population, and deal with Indian nations, was

the real cauldron in which American identity was formed. See Haselby, *The Origins of American Religious Nationalism*.

57. Shoemaker, "How Indians Got to Be Red"; Goldschmidt and McAlister, eds., *Race, Nation, and Religion in the Americas*; Prentiss, ed., *Religion and the Creation of Race and Ethnicity*.

58. While my focus is on Indian lands, I am cognizant that the struggle to maintain these lands often involved Native people leaving them. As scholars of American Indian history have emphasized, Native people showed up in all sorts of "unexpected places" as they engaged colonial power and defended their lands. The story I tell is no exception. See Deloria, *Indians in Unexpected Places*.

59. The works that have most influenced my thinking about settler colonialism include Jacobs, *White Mother to a Dark Race*; Johnson, *African-American Religions*; Ostler, *The Plains Sioux and U.S. Colonialism from Lewis and Clark to Wounded Knee*; and Adelman and Aron, "From Borderlands to Borders." On the nineteenth-century surge of English-speaking settler expansion, see Belich, *Replenishing the Earth*.

60. Several scholars have influenced my thinking about the critical study of empire. They include Kramer, "Power and Connection;" Chidester, *Empire of Religion*; Hall, *Civilising Subjects*; Jacoby, "Indigenous Empires and Native Nations;" Kaplan, "Manifest Domesticity;" and Lincoln, *Religion, Empire, and Torture*.

61. On attachment to homelands among migrating Native people, see Warren, *The Worlds the Shawnee Made*.

62. Due to their size and prominence in this period, the Comanches have generated a substantial bibliography. See Hämäläinen, *The Comanche Empire*; Delay, *War of a Thousand Deserts*, and Anderson, *The Conquest of Texas*.

63. Boone and Mignolo, *Writing without Words*; Brander Rassmussen, *Queequeg's Coffin*. On Kiowa material culture, see Tone-Pah-Hote, "Envisioning Nationhood."

64. Keyser, *Art of the Warriors*.

65. Greene, *One Hundred Summers*; Greene and Thornton, *The Year the Stars Fell*.

66. See Wiedman and Greene, "Early Kiowa Peyote Ritual and Symbolism"; Schmittou and Logan, "Fluidity of Meaning"; Greene, "Bison Robes to Ledgers"; Meadows and Harragarra, "The Kiowa Drawings of Gotebo"; Greene, *Silver Horn*.

67. Major works include Petersen, *Plains Indian Art from Fort Marion*; Berlo, *Plains Indian Drawings*; Szabo, *Howling Wolf and the History of Ledger Art*; Szabo, "Shields and Lodges, Warriors and Chiefs."

CHAPTER I

1. On the purchase, see Kastor, "What Are the Advantages of Acquisition?" 1013; Wood, *Empire of Liberty*, 368–369. On removal ideas in the early republic, see Rockwell, *Indian Affairs and the Administrative State*, 174; Banner, *How the Indians Lost Their Land*, 193; Guyatt, *Bind Us Apart*, 232, 235.

2. On some Americans' view that Indians forfeited all claims due to their participation in the revolution, see Horseman, "The Indian Policy of an 'Empire of Liberty,'" 37–39. On the long history of removal (or ostensibly voluntary emigration) prompted by treaties, see Banner, *How the Indians Lost Their Land*, 191–192. On Washington and Knox's use of treaties, see Rockwell,

Indian Affairs and the Administrative State, 54–56. On "limited" notions of discovery, see Wilkins and Lomawaima, *Uneven Ground*, 20–28, 37–47.

3. On federal support for civilizing projects, see Rockwell, *Indian Affairs and the Administrative State*, 58–59. On notions of civilization in the early republic, see Conroy-Krutz, *Christian Imperialism*, 14–15; Horseman, *Race and Manifest Destiny*, 97, 107; Johnson, "Religion and American Empire," 41–42.

4. Some historians focus on Enlightenment ideas that shaped notions of civilization. Religious reformers were certainly shaped by Enlightenment ideas, but I also consider their theological commitments, ideas about ethical living, and views about worship and ritual. While I focus on Protestant activities at this point, Roman Catholics are also part of the story.

5. On the SPG and New York missions, see Franklin, "America's Missions," 33–37, 134, 137. On Quaker missions in New York, see Wallace, *The Death and Rebirth of the Seneca*; Dennis, *Seneca Possessed*. Richter found that Quakers desired to teach not just any mode of farming, but specifically Euro-American agricultural methods that used more tools and relied on mostly male labor. See Richter, " 'Believing That Many of the Red People Suffer,' " 601–628. On federal funding for missions, see Rockwell, *Indian Affairs and the Administrative State*, 59–60.

6. Tiro, " 'We Wish To Do You Good,' " 355, 370–372.

7. Prucha, *The Great Father*, 183.

8. Guyatt, *Bind Us Apart*, 4–6, 88.

9. On Jefferson's views on African Americans and Native Americans, see Wood, *Empire of Liberty*, 395. On widely held views about Native people's future, see Duval, "Debating Identity," 26, 49–50.

10. Hämäläinen, *The Comanche Empire*, 161.

11. Brooks, *Captives and Cousins*, 170; John, "An Earlier Chapter in Kiowa History," 387; Nye, *Bad Medicine and Good*, 3–14; Hämäläinen, *The Comanche Empire*, 161–162; Kavanaugh, *Comanche Political History*, 145–148.

12. Hyde, *Empire, Nations, Families*, 290–293; Anderson, *The Indian Southwest*, 178. Brooks describes the emergence of this market in the 1780s. See *Captives and Cousins*, 160. Hämäläinen describes the nature of Comanche domination of the region: "Their aim was not to conquer and colonize, but to coexist, control, and exploit." See *The Comanche Empire*, 2.

13. Hämäläinen, *The Comanche Empire*, 172.

14. On horses, fighting, and ritual lives of Indian men, see Hoig, *Tribal Wars of the Southern Plains*, 20, 25–26.

15. McCoy, "A Shield To Help You Through Life," 70–81.

16. McCoy, "A Shield To Help You Through Life," 80. Fair Hair Old Man also received his shield, with a bird design, in this period. See McCoy, "I Have a Mysterious Way," 70–74.

17. Guyatt argues that Quakers and other self-designated "friends of the Indian" promoted a kind of "providential nationalism" in regard to Native people and American expansion. See *Bind Us Apart*, 3, 14–15, 234, 280. While Protestants dominated early American missions, Roman Catholics also played a part. Indeed, George Washington wrote a note of thanks to Bishop John Carroll for Catholic work to teach Indians. See Franklin, "America's Missions," 128.

18. Delay, *War of a Thousand Deserts*, 40.

19. Brooks, *Captives and Cousins*, 3, 9; Zappia, *Traders and Raiders*, 1–6.

20. Delay, *War of a Thousand Deserts*, 16, 182.

21. On Pike, see Delay, *War of a Thousand Deserts*, 10; Baird, *Oklahoma: A History*, 48. On the later American expedition, see Anderson, *The Indian Southwest*, 195. On mapping the region, see Kastor, "What Are the Advantages of Acquisition?" 1005, 1019, 1022.

22. Guyatt, *Bind Us Apart*, 281; Baird, *Oklahoma: A History*, 56; Hyde, *Empires, Nations, Families*, 257.

23. In the words of Adelman and Aron, the North American interior went from a borderland to a bordered land in which Americans could now treat Indians as subjects. See "Borderlands to Borders," 816, 821–823, 829.

24. On debates about Native people's fitness for citizenship, see Dippie, *The Vanishing American*, 6; Guyatt, *Bind Us Apart*, 6, 108, 145; Horseman, *Race and Manifest Destiny*, 109. On religious reformers' responses, see Guyatt, *Bind Us Apart*, 108–110.

25. On the ABCFM see, Hutchison, *Errand to the World*; Kling, "The New Divinity and the Origins of the American Board of Commissioners for Foreign Missions"; and Conroy-Krutz, *Christian Imperialism*.

26. Mission workers celebrated the occasions when this occurred. See Baird, "Cyrus Byington and the Presbyterian Choctaw Mission," 7.

27. On Monroe's approach, see Guyatt, *Bind Us Apart*, 287–288; Rockwell, *Indian Affairs and the Administrative State*, 87. On the Civilization Fund, see Prucha, *Documents of United States Indian Policy*, 33; Guyatt, *Bind Us Apart*, 281–282.

28. On Native people moving west, see Rockwell, *Indian Affairs and the Administrative State*, 177, 182–183. On Kiowa and Comanche responses, see Delay, *War of a Thousand Deserts*, 41, 48; Hämäläinen, *The Comanche Empire*, 220.

29. Long, *Account of an Expedition*, 502. On the expedition, see Smallwood, "Major Stephen Harriman Long's Account."

30. Long, *Account of an Expedition*, 268–272, 276, 357. On accusations of human sacrifice in colonial discourse, see Watson, *Insatiable Appetites*, Chapter 5. On colonial comparative religion, see Chidester, *Empire of Religion*.

31. Morse, *Report to the Secretary of War*, 9, 34, 66, 75, 79–80. Morse founded a group called the Civilization Society. On Morse's assignment and background, see Hyde, *Empires, Nations, Families*, 281–283; Conroy-Krutz, *Christian Imperialism*, 135.

32. Morse, *Report to the Secretary of War*, 80, 85, 159, 285.

33. Morse, *Report to the Secretary of War*, 100–101, 106.

34. Delay, *War of a Thousand Deserts*, 10. At the same time, Americans also assumed this desert and void would someday be filled. See Corrigan, *Emptiness*, 90–92.

35. Morse, "Indian Improvement," *Missionary Herald* (March 1822). Morse promoted his new society in other religious periodicals as well. See "View of Public Affairs: The United States," *Christian Spectator* (March 1, 1822); "Indian Improvement," *Religious Intelligencer* (March 9, 1822); "Dr. Morse's Report," *Columbian Star* (March 23, 1822).

36. Wilkins and Lomawaima, *Uneven Ground*, 52–54; Watson, *Buying America from the Indians*, 318–319; Banner, *How the Indians Lost Their Land*, 150.

37. On Adams's administration, see Guyatt, *Bind Us Apart*, 293; Delay, *War of a Thousand Deserts*, 4; Horseman, *Race and Manifest Destiny*, 197–199.

38. On Tecumseh and Tenskwatawa, see Dowd, *A Spirited Resistance*, xvii–xx; Irwin, *Coming Down From Above*, 4–6, 133, 177–194; Cave, *Prophets of the Great Spirit*, 91–139. On Creek resistance, see Martin, *Sacred Revolt*, 1–6, 77; Dowd, *A Spirited Resistance*, 187–189.

39. On Jackson and removal, see Prucha, *The Great Father*, 191; Rockwell, *Indian Affairs and the Administrative State*, 139–141; Hausdoerffer, *Catlin's Lament*, 6. On War Department statements and other federal responses, see *ARCIA 1826–1839*, 172, 174, 180. On Jackson's humanitarian framing, see Rockwell, *Indian Affairs and the Administrative State*, 159–162.

40. Perdue and Green, *The Cherokee Nation and the Trail of Tears*, 66; Dippie, *The Vanishing American*, 65. On language of civilization and savagery in the removal bill debate, see Bowes, "American Indian Removal Beyond the Removal Act," 65–66.

41. Rockwell, *Indian Affairs and the Administrative State*, 142–144.

42. On laypeople's responses, see Hershberger, "Mobilizing Women, Anticipating Abolition," 15, 20, 25–28, 35–40.

43. Prucha, "Introduction," 9, 10, 18. See also Prucha, *The Great Father*, 201–207; Andrew, *From Revivals to Removal*.

44. Evarts, *Cherokee Removal*, 49–51.

45. White, "Memorial in Behalf of the Cherokees," *The Friend*, January 23, 1830; "Indian Statistics," *The Friend*, March 13, 1830. Friends continued this emphasis through the removal period. See "Memorial in Behalf of the Cherokees," *The Friend*, April 7, 1838; "The Oppression of the Cherokees," *The Friend*, April 28, 1838; "Report," *The Friend*, August 18, 1838.

46. On Jackson's supporters, see Banner, *How the Indians Lost Their Land*, 209; Ryan, *The Grammar of Good Intentions*, 28–40. On McCoy, see Untitled article, *United States' Telegraph* 34 (February 10, 1830); Dippie, *The Vanishing Indian*, 51. On the opposition, see "National Journal: In the Senate," *Daily National Journal* 1973 (April 7, 1830); "The Indian Question," *Observer and Telegraph* 16 (June 17, 1830).

47. Kerber, "The Abolitionist Perception of the Indian," 271–295.

48. Hyde, *Empires, Nations, Families*, 277. See also Kavanaugh, *Comanche Political History*, 234–235.

49. Warde, "Alternative Perspectives on the Battle of Wolf Creek of 1838," 4; Hämäläinen, *The Comanche Empire*, 164–165; Delay, *War of a Thousand Deserts*, 41.

50. Greene, *One Hundred Summers*, 45.

51. Brooks, *Captives and Cousins*, 195–197.

52. McCoy, "A Shield to Help You through Life," 75.

53. Ewers, *Murals in the Round*, 21–22.

54. As Ute Hüsken notes, we must be careful about claiming that a ritual has failed. Deviation and change are not necessarily mistakes or failures. Instead, she recommends attending to what matters to the community performing the ritual. In this case, Kiowa ritual efforts did not secure them from devastating attack. See "Ritual Dynamics and Ritual Failure," 337–339.

55. This account was given in 1967 by Akaudona (b. 1878) in the Kiowa language to her son, Parker McKenzie. McKenzie translated and transcribed her story. See "Events Surrounding the So-Called Cutthroat Massacre of Kiowa Indians by Osage Warriors in Early Summer of 1833," Box 28, Folder 12, PMP, OHS. There are other accounts from Kiowas available. See Mooney, *Calendar History*, 257–260; Corwin, *The Kiowa Indians*, 17–18.

56. Details in this paragraph come from "Events Surrounding the So-Called Cutthroat Massacre" and Corwin, *The Kiowa Indians*, 18–19. Kiowa maps depict the attack as well. See Meadows, "Black Goose's Map," 272.

57. Mooney, *Calendar History*, 259.

58. Hyde, *Empires, Nations, Families*, 224.

59. For other Native American visual accounts of the meteor shower, see Greene, *The Year the Stars Fell*.

60. Mooney, *Calendar History*, 261.

61. On Catlin in Indian Country, see Dippie, *The Vanishing American*. On his Indian writings in eastern newspapers, see Coward, *The Newspaper Indian*, Chapter 2. Scholars have long debated the veracity of Catlin's account of the O-kee-pa. Elizabeth A. Fenn considers a range of documents related to the Mandans' central ritual. See *Encounters at the Heart of the World*, 99, 120–130.

62. On romantic, yet fearful attitudes about Native people, see Slotkin, *Regeneration through Violence*, 33. On Catlin's call for the nation's duty toward Indians, see "The Red Kings Beyond the Frontiers," *North American Magazine* (October 1833): 387. On viewers of his paintings, see Untitled article, *North American Magazine* (November 1833): 65.

63. On Catlin's conflicted feelings about Indian extinction and American aggression, see John, "Cultural Nationalism," 175–203. On popular attitudes about Indians' extinction, see Horseman, *Race and Manifest Destiny*, 190–191.

64. Eisler, *The Red Man's Bones*, Chapter 15.

65. Hyde, *Empires, Nations, Families*, 296; Kavanaugh, *Comanche Political History*, 237–239.

66. Agnew, "Leavenworth and Dodge," 97; Viola, *Diplomats in Buckskin*, 25–26. Brooks, *Captives and Cousins*, 262. According to Delay, the Wichita village was not in US territory, but in the Republic of Texas. See *War of a Thousand Deserts*, 65–66.

67. Catlin, *Illustrations of the Manners*, 74. Catlin included these characterizations about civilization in an appendix to his *Letters and Notes* in 1844. See Dippie, *The Vanishing American*, 28.

68. Catlin, *Illustrations of the Manners*, 82.

69. Pratt, *Imperial Eyes*, 60.

70. Hausdoerffer, *Catlin's Lament*, 68.

71. Hausdoerffer, *Catlin's Lament*, 68–69.

72. Chidester, *Savage Systems*, 3, 16–17, 28. Baptist missionary Isaac McCoy followed this pattern exactly in his introduction to Native cultures for Baptist readers. He claimed that Indians did not have "religion" because their "precarious habits prevent the concocting of systems of mythology or the organization of the priesthood." Instead, Indian people had superstition and witchcraft. See McCoy, *History of Baptist Indian Missions*, 13, 303.

73. Catlin, *An Account of an Annual Religious Ceremony*, 12, 37, 34. In terms of anti-Catholic comparison, Catlin wrote of "medicine men" who were "haranguing" villagers (8), a "medicine man's . . . secret" transactions (18), ritual practices that seemed to be "torture" (20), and traditions so ancient that Indians had no knowledge of their meaning (63–64).

74. "Red Pipe Mountain," *Christian Advocate and Journal* (November 18, 1836): 49; "Red Pipe Mountain," *The Friend* (November 19, 1836): 52; "Red Pipe Mountain," *Christian Secretary* (January 21, 1837): 8; "Correspondence of the New York Commercial Advertiser," *Catholic Telegraph* (December 8, 1836): 2.

75. On the meeting, see Hyde, *Empires, Nations, Families*, 296–297. On alternate accounts of the girl's return, see *Calendar History*, 261–262; LaVere, *Contrary Neighbors*, 76–77. Several calendars commemorate the captive's return. See Green, *One Hundred Summers*, 261–269. On the trip toward Fort Gibson, which became complicated for a number of reasons, see Kavanagh, *Comanche Political History*, 239–240; Viola, *Diplomats in Buckskin*, 26.

76. *ARCIA 1835*, 240; US Congress, House of Representatives, Committee, "Regulating the Indian Department," 81.

77. US Congress, House of Representatives, Committee, "Regulating the Indian Department," 2, 7, 17–18.

78. Horseman discusses the increasingly popular idea that "inferior races" would either be absorbed or excluded from political participation. See *Race and Manifest Destiny*, 189.

79. US Congress, House of Representatives, Committee, "Regulating the Indian Department," 18, 76, 85–86.

80. US Congress, House of Representatives, Committee, "Regulating the Indian Department," 76–77, 85–86; *ARCIA 1835*, 239.

81. On the ongoing use of monies from the Civilization Fund during and after the fight over removal, see Rockwell, *Indian Affairs and the Administrative State*, 150–152. Jackson reduced Civilization Fund support for some of his most vocal opponents, including the ABCFM.

82. *ARCIA 1835*, 241.

83. Beecher, *Plea for the West*, 8–9, 11, 32. On similar concerns about religious developments west of the Mississippi, see Pasquier, "Introduction," 3–5.

84. Beecher, *Plea for the West*, 13, 51, 56–57, 61–63, 128. On rising anti-Catholicism in the 1830s, see McGreevy, *Catholicism and American Freedom*, 11–13. On concerns about Catholicism's incompatibility with democracy, see Green, *The Second Disestablishment*, 266–268.

85. Bunson, *Faith in the Wilderness*, 71.

86. Dichtl, *Frontiers of Faith*, 1, 10; Pasquier, *Fathers on the Frontier*, 15.

87. Pasquier, *Fathers on the Frontier*, 5, 90–91, 114–116.

88. Dichtl, *Frontiers of Faith*, 86; Pasquier, *Fathers on the Frontier*, 91–92, 107, 121–122.

89. O'Daniel, *The Right Rev. Edward Dominic Fenwick*, 389–390, 396, 403; Rahill, *The Catholic Indian Missions*, 9–13.

90. Mooney, *Calendar History*, 259. For another account, see LaVere, *Contrary Neighbors*, 77.

91. Mooney, *Calendar History*, 269–270.

92. Parsons, *Kiowa Tales*, 109, 124.

93. Eugenia Mausape, interview by Julia A. Jordan, September 6, 1967, interview T-37, OFLC, M452, Box 5, Folder 2 WHC, OU; Guy Quetone, interview with Julia A. Jordan, July 12, 1967, interview T-22, OFLC, M452, Box 5, Folder 2 WHC, OU; Guy Quetone, interview with Julia A. Jordan, July 19, 1967, interview T-23, OFLC, M452, Box 5, Folder 2 WHC, OU; Guy Quetone, interview with Julia A. Jordan, June 14, 1967, interview T-28, OFLC, M452, Box 5, Folder 2 WHC, OU. Some Kiowa accounts put reception of the buffalo medicine when the people still lived on the northern plains. See Meadows, *Through Indian Sign Language*, 159.

94. Kracht, "Kiowa Religion in Historical Perspective," 90, 122–128. DeMallie and Lavenda note parallels in other Plains Indian nations, namely Native people attesting to physically humbling situations that led sacred powers to send an animal with instruction and special objects. See "Wakan," 157.

95. Delay, *War of a Thousand Deserts*, 61.

96. Greene, "Exploring the Three Little Bluffs of the Kiowa," 224. The exact date of this raid is contested and some sources put it in 1839. Details about the Comanches' arrival also differ in other versions. See Meadows, *Through Indian Sign Language*, 124.

97. Nye, *Bad Medicine and Good*, 41–44.

98. Anderson describes this process as ethnogenesis. See *The Indian Southwest*, 4. Other authors, however, use this term to describe the formation of altogether new ethnic groups.

99. Delay, *War of a Thousand Deserts*, 60.

100. Klassen, "Spiritual Jurisdictions." For another helpful resource on how Native nations approached councils and the treaties that followed, see DeMallie, "Touching the Pen."

101. DeMallie, "Early Kiowa and Comanche Treaties," 16–21. For more on the history of Indian-Texan relations, see Anderson, *The Conquest of Texas*, 6–7, 15.

102. According to Delay, it became increasingly difficult for older Kiowa leaders to control raiding by young men. See *War of a Thousand Deserts*, 96–99. Leaders of forcibly removed Indian nations had similar difficulty getting their men to stop hunting on Kiowa and Comanche lands, which also jeopardized the treaty. See Brooks, *Captives and Cousins*, 260.

103. DeMallie, "Early Kiowa and Comanche Treaties," 18.

104. McCoy, *History of Baptist Indian Missions*, 586.

CHAPTER 2

1. On the surge in press coverage about Indian affairs as Americans migrated to Oregon, Texas, and California, see Rockwell, *Indian Affairs and the Administrative State*, 220.

2. Hyde, *Empires, Nations, Families*, 409; Banner, *How the Indians Lost Their Land*, 228.

3. Accounts of the battle, usually referred to as the Battle of Wolf Creek, can be found in Nye, *Bad Medicine and Good*, xi; Mooney, *Calendar History*, 273–274; Warde, "Alternative Perspectives on the Battle of Wolf Creek of 1838," 3–14. On effects on the Sun Dance, see Mooney, *Calendar History*; Silver Horn Pictorial Calendar, MS 2531, Volume 7, NAA, SI. On Cûiqáuje and ritual abandonment of shields, see McCoy, "'A Shield to Help You through Life,'" 75; McCoy, "I Have a Mysterious Way," 75.

4. Brooks, *Captives and Cousins*, 262–264; Delay, *War of a Thousand Deserts*, 80; Hyde, *Empires, Nations, and Families*, 298; Kavanagh, *Comanche Political History*, 248; Comer, *Ritual Ground*, 124–125.

5. On the uptick in raiding, see Delay, *War of a Thousand Deserts*, 83, 93, 109, 113, 214; Brooks, *Captives and Cousins*, 266. On deaths of prominent men between 1841 and 1844, see Greene, *One Hundred Summers*, 59; Mooney, *Calendar History*, 277–281; Quitone Kiowa Calendar, MS 2002–27, NAA, SI; Silver Horn Pictorial Calendar. On dreams as a possible prompt for vowing a Sun Dance, see Mooney, *Calendar History*, 279.

6. On the raid, see Mooney, *Calendar History*, 282. On the shield design, see McCoy, "'A Shield to Help You Through Life,'" 77–80.

7. On the epidemic in the late 1830s, see Hyde, *Empires, Nations, Families*, 330; Brooks, *Captives and Cousins*, 265; Delay, *War of a Thousand Deserts*, 79. For calendar entries denoting smallpox in 1839–1840, see Quitone Kiowa Calendar; Greene, *One Hundred Summers*, 55–57; Mooney, *Calendar History*, 274–275. For entries about measles, see Greene, *One Hundred Summers*, 65; Quitone Kiowa Calendar.

8. Ewers, *Murals in the Round*, 26.

9. On the Texas creation myth, see Delay, *War of a Thousand Deserts*, 227–231. On American racialist thinking during the conflict with Mexico, see Horseman, *Race and Manifest Destiny*, 210–213, 229. On Texans' decades of fighting with Mexicans and American Indians, see Anderson, *The Conquest of Texas*, 3–16. Pinheiro argues that this view of Mexicans' inability to settle its northern frontier drew on and also contributed to American anti-Catholicism. See *Missionaries of Republicanism*, 2.

10. *ARCIA 1837*, 37–38; *ARCIA 1844*, 5, 137; *ARCIA 1845*, 455, 537–538.

11. For calls for troops, see *ARCIA 1838*, 507, 516; *ARCIA 1841*, 317; *ARCIA 1844*, 137. On the debate about troops, see Rockwell, *Indian Affairs and the Administrative State*, 227. Five companies of the Missouri Volunteers were sent to protect the Santa Fe Trail in 1847. See Kavanagh, *Comanche Political History*, 317–19.

12. On other Indian nations as examples, see *ARCIA 1838*, 441, 450. On the bison, see *ARCIA 1841*, 316; *ARCIA 1842*, 455. For calls for more education, see *ARCIA 1838*, 450, 513; *ARCIA 1839*, 343–344; *ARCIA 1840*, 242; *ARCIA 1841*, 240–241; *ARCIA 1842*, 379; *ARCIA 1844*, 11; *ARCIA 1845*, 453.

13. *ARCIA 1845*, 455. On the transition from borderlands to "bordered lands," as well as the impact of such transitions on Native people, see Adelman and Aron, "From Borderlands to Borders," 814–841.

14. Rockwell, *Indian Affairs and the Administrative State*, 218.

15. Catlin, *Letters and Notes on the Manners*, 121, 131–132. For a review of the book, see "Letters and Notes on the Manners," *North American Review*, April 1842.

16. As noted in Chapter 1, scholars have questioned Catlin's account of Mandan ritual activities.

17. Catlin, *Letters and Notes on the Manners*, 155–176.

18. "Letters and Notes on the Manners," *North American Review*, April 1842. On similar comparisons to Muslims and Arabs, what Timothy Marr calls "domestic orientalism," see *The Cultural Roots of American Islamism*, 11, 17–19.

19. For McCoy's observations, see *History of Baptist Indian Missions*, 13; 457–458. For the other missionary's view, see "Letter from Mr. Bliss, January 18, 1844," *Missionary Herald*, 93–94.

20. "Letter from Mr. Bliss, January 18, 1844," *Missionary Herald*, 93–94.

21. "Indian Missions: A Hoax," *Boston Investigator*, August 21, 1844. On ideas about some populations' inability to assimilate, see Horseman, *Race and Manifest Destiny*, 229. Rockwell notes the ironies of easterners who called for Indian removal (at great expense) and later withdrew support for programs in Indian Territory. See *Indian Affairs and the Administrative State*, 215, 227–228.

22. On Quaker efforts, see "Report on Indian Concerns to Baltimore Yearly Meeting," *The Friend*, November 21, 1840; "The Indian Race," *The Friend*, January 10, 1846; "Indian Disturbances," *The Friend*, June 10, 1848; "Alas for the Poor Indian!" *The Friend*, September 2, 1848. On Baptist calls for support, see McCoy, *History of Baptist Indian Missions*, 586–587.

23. McGreevy, *American Jesuits and the World*, 2; McKevitt, *Brokers of Culture*, 8, 120.

24. For the connection between missionaries in the United States and Catholics in Europe, see De Smet's *Western Missions and Missionaries*.

25. On Marian devotion in this period, see McGreevy, *American Jesuits and the World*, 17; McKevitt, *Brokers of Culture*, 92–93, 137. On Jesuit activity in the Pacific Northwest, including visual representations of Native people and mission life, see Buckley, "Overland with Optimism," 9, 21–23; Rochford, "Father Nicolas Point," 53; Point, *Wilderness Kingdom*.

26. White and St. Laurent, "Mysterious Journey," 72, 83; Thiel, "Catholic Ladders and Native Evangelization," 53–56; Vescey, "The Good News in Print," 10.

27. On ultramontane Catholicism in this era, see McGreevy, *Catholicism and American Freedom*, 12–13. On Protestant ladders, see Thiel, "Catholic Ladders and Native Evangelization," 58–59; Addis, "The Whitman Massacre," 239.

28. Indeed, De Smet's writings proved popular around the globe. His books were translated into five languages and frequently reprinted. It's estimated that his appeals drew in more than a quarter million dollars. See Carriker, "Admiring Advocate of the Great Plains," 254.

29. De Smet, *Western Missions and Missionaries*, 51, 55.

30. *ARCIA 1847*, 18.

31. See Rockwell, *Indian Affairs and the Administrative State*, 246–247.

32. Delay, *War of a Thousand Deserts*, 279.

33. *ARCIA 1847*, 129–131.

34. Addis, "The Whitman Massacre," 221–251; Horseman, *Race and Manifest Destiny*, 228.

35. *ARCIA 1847*, 13.

36. Delay, *War of a Thousand Deserts*, 227–235, 253–258.

37. Mooney, *Calendar History*, 287.

38. Meadows, *Kiowa Military Societies*, 215–246.

39. Hämäläinen notes a similar development among Comanches, claiming that in the late 1840s they were both at the height of their power and on the brink of collapse. See *Comanche Empire*, 293. Hyde claims epidemics, dwindling bison herds, drought, and overhunting made 1849 a terrible year on the southern plains. See *Empires, Nations, Families*, 344.

40. On Kiowas' experience of cholera, see Mooney, *Calendar History*, 289–290; Greene, *One Hundred Summers*, 69; Silver Horn Pictorial Calendar; Powers and Leiker, "Cholera among the Plains Indians," 321.

41. Mooney, *Calendar History*, 287–289.

42. Mooney, *Calendar History*, 289–290. Hyde also discusses the presence of cholera at the 1849 Sun Dance. See *Empires, Nations, Families*, 345.

43. Brooks, *Captives and Cousins*, 192–193.

44. Mooney, *Calendar History*, 294–295.

45. Silver Horn Pictorial Calendar. See the explanation of Mooney's remarks about this event in Greene, *One Hundred Summers*, 73.

46. For the American flag, see Greene, *One Hundred Summers*, 73. For the army caps, see Quitone Kiowa Calendar.

47. This should not to be confused with the 1868 Treaty of Fort Laramie, which ended Red Cloud's War and mandated that Americans stay out of the Powder River country.

48. De Smet, *Western Missions and Missionaries,* 101, 111.

49. On De Smet, see *Western Missions and Missionaries,* 102–103, 105; Carriker, "Admiring Advocate of the Great Plains," 254–255. On the treaty's impact, see DeMallie, "Teton," 795.

50. On calls for reservations, including different justifications for them, see *ARCIA 1848*, 386–387; Utley, *The Indian Frontier*, 46, 63; Rockwell, *Indian Affairs and the Administrative State*, 228, 256; Banner; *How the Indians Lost Their Land*, 232–238.

51. E. L. "North American Indians," *Friends' Review*, August 16, 1851: 755. See Chapter 1 on Quaker missions to the Seneca.

52. Evans, "Report to the Yearly Meeting of the Committee on Indian Affairs," *Friends' Review*, May 19, 1849: 549.

53. Treat, "Indian Missions," *Vermont Chronicle*, September 28, 1852. For another Protestant voice of support for reservations, see Loomis, *Scenes in the Indian Country*.

54. The demand also included attacks on Mexicans, which I discuss later.

55. DeMallie, *The Kiowa Treaty of 1853*; Kavanagh, *Comanche Political History*, 343–351.

56. DeMallie, *The Kiowa Treaty of 1853*, 15.

57. DeMallie, *The Kiowa Treaty of 1853*, 16–21. Banner explores the spectrum between voluntary and involuntary agreement to treaties, of which this is an example. See *How the Indians Lost Their Land*, 3–4.

58. DeMallie, *The Kiowa Treaty of 1853*, 29–30, 36. Congress ratified the amended treaty on April 12, 1854.

59. These thefts included an 1854 defeat by the Sauk, the Cheyenne theft of tipis and winter camp supplies in 1856–1857, and Pawnee stealing horses in 1857–1858. On Thẹ̀nébáudai's death, see Meadows, *Kiowa Military Societies*, 30. On calendar recollections of these episodes, see Mooney, *Calendar History*, 308; Quitone Kiowa calendar.

60. Mooney, *Calendar History*, 300.

61. Quitone Kiowa calendar.

62. See section on Tecumseh and Tenskwatawa in Chapter 1.

63. Smith, "A Pearl of Great Price and a Cargo of Yams," 1–19.

64. On Smohalla's movement, see Trafzer and Beach, "Smohalla," 309–324; Irwin, *Coming Down From Above*, 255–263.

65. *ARCIA 1857*, 157; DeMallie, "The Unratified Treaty," 1–2.

66. Comer, *Ritual Ground*, 14.

67. *ARCIA 1859*, 138.

68. "Indian Wars," *Friends' Review*, December 22, 1855.

69. Because the ABCFM resisted taking a strong stance on slavery, some supporters of Indian missions left it in 1846 and founded the American Missionary Association. See Kerber, "The Abolitionist Perception of the Indian," 283–285.

70. Of course, escape to the north had only ever guaranteed freedom from chattel slavery, not from a powerful climate of racism.

71. Drescher, *Abolition*, 327.

72. Gordon, *The Mormon Question*, 26–28, 49–55, 77, 81.

73. On failure to stop settlers, see "Indian Troubles in the West," *Friends' Review*, August 3, 1850; "North American Indians," *Friends' Review*, August 16, 1851.

74. They were among the many Americans who debated the "morality, values, and national purpose" of "public administration" before, during, and after the Civil War. See Rockwell, *Indian Affairs and the Administrative State*, 243. Rockwell also connects activists' concern about the protection of minorities in the aftermath of the Fugitive Slave Act with this uncertain point in Indian policymaking. See 243–244.

75. *Friends' Intelligencer*, January 14, 1860; "Extract from 'A Plea for the Indians,'" *Friends' Intelligencer*, March 19, 1859. On pre–Civil War speculation on the nation's damnation, see Gin Lum, *Damned Nation*, Chapter 5.

76. *ARCIA 1858*, 99.

77. Arensen and Graybill, *Civil War Wests*.

78. On the Civil War's impact on Native people, see Rockwell, *Indian Affairs and the Administration of the State*, 222; Gibson, "Native Americans and the Civil War," 385–410.

79. Gibson, "Native Americans and the Civil War," 385–410.

80. Viola, *Diplomats in Buckskin*, 89, 99–102.

81. Mooney, *Calendar History*, 89; Kavanagh, *Comanche Political History*, 398; Jordan, "Reclaiming the Past," 82–86.

82. Jordan, "Reclaiming the Past," 84–85.

83. This event should not be confused with the better-known Second Battle of Adobe Walls, which took place during the 1874–1875 Red River War.

84. Mooney, *Calendar History*, 315–317.

85. For a recent assessment of the massacre's aftermath, see Kelman, *A Misplaced Massacre*.

86. Graber, "From Drone War to Indian War," 93–96; Prucha, *American Indian Policy in Crisis*, 13.

87. *ARCIA 1865*, 387.

88. Mooney, *Calendar History*, 317

89. Marriott, *The Ten Grandmothers*, 53.

90. Marriott, *The Ten Grandmothers*, 55. One might be from the 1839 story.

91. Kracht claims that Àunsójèqàptàu made a new *Ṭ̇aimé* after the 1833 Osage attack. He also says that Poor Buffalo, also known as Páutáuljè (Lean Bison Bull), had an 1839 vision for a new figure. See "Kiowa Religion: An Ethnohistorical Analysis," 174–175.

92. DeMallie, *The Treaty on the Little Arkansas River*. On the treaty negotiations, also see Kavanagh, *Comanche Political History*, 399–404; Rockwell, *Indian Affairs and the Administrative State*, 294; Oman, "The Beginning of the End," 35–37. Banner writes that American efforts to present treaty negotiations in this period as consensual were a "sham." See *How the Indians Lost Their Land*, 229.

93. Klassen, "Spiritual Jurisdictions."

94. DeMallie, *The Treaty on the Little Arkansas River*, 23–24.

95. Banner, *How the Indians Lost Their Land*, 3–4.

96. DeMallie, *The Treaty of Medicine Lodge, 1867*, 5, 12–13. See also Kavanagh, *Comanche Political History*, 410–418.

97. DeMallie, *The Treaty of Medicine Lodge*, 13.

98. On the American public's interpretation of Indian speeches, see Eastman, "The Indian Censures the White Man," 535–564.

99. *Western Reserve Chronicle*, November 13, 1867.

100. DeMallie, *The Treaty of Medicine Lodge*, 57.

101. DeMallie, *The Treaty of Medicine Lodge*, 44–45.

102. Rockwell, *Indian Affairs and the Administrative State*, 236; DeMallie, *The Treaty of Medicine Lodge*, 40–41.

103. Janney, "Indian Affairs," *Friends' Intelligencer* (October 19, 1867): 513.

104. DeMallie, *The Treaty of Medicine Lodge*, 44.

CHAPTER 3

1. As Sarah Dees notes, E. B. Tylor's famous arguments about Zuni animism, which depended on an understanding of Native religions as primitive, came out in 1871. It coincided with Christian representatives expanding their work among Indian nations. See "The Scientific Study of Native American Religions," 1–5, 24–25, 44.

2. I will discuss the moniker "Peace Policy" later in the chapter.

3. Richardson, "North and West of Reconstruction," 69.

4. Foner, *Reconstruction*; Paddison, *American Heathens*, 4–8; Gordon, *The Mormon Question*, 111–114; Fluhman, *A Peculiar People*, 106, 110; Chang, *Citizens of a Christian Nation*, 4–9; Cahill, *Federal Fathers and Mothers*, 2–3. To be clear, most Native Americans were not eligible for citizenship in this period. In 1870, a Senate committee determined that the Fourteenth Amendment did not apply to Indians belonging to recognized tribes. See Kantrowitz, "Not Quite Constitutionalized," 83. Even so, federal officials and "friends of the Indian" discussed Native peoples' "fitness" for citizenship and their eventual attainment of that status.

5. Downs and Masur, "Echoes of War," 1. Eliot West has noted the concern over securing the West and calls this period a "Greater Reconstruction." See West, "Reconstructing Race."

6. Utley, *The Indian Frontier*, 118.

7. *ARCIA 1868*, iii.

8. *ARCIA 1868*, 10. Rockwell explores not only the estimates of the costs of fighting Indians, but also the federal government's desire to sell Indian land as a huge source of revenue. See *Indian Affairs and the Administrative State*, 225–226. Byler also notes concerns about costs, as well as the emerging idea that American society would evolve in ways that would make war obsolete, see *Civil-Military Relations*, 3, 25.

9. *ARCIA 1868*, 1–14. On concerns about the size and cost of maintaining a standing army after the Civil War, see Byler, *Civil-Military Relations*, xiii–xiv.

10. On Quaker action, see *Memorial of the Society of Friends in Regard to the Indians*, 2; Illick, "'Some of Our Best Indians Are Friends,'" 289. This committee was called the Associated Executive Committee of Friends on Indian Affairs. Because even the acronym for this organization is clumsy, I refer to it as the Society's "Indian committee." On Child's work, see Mielke, "The Evolution of Moving Encounters in Lydia Maria Child's American Indian Writings," 15–35. On the US Indian Commission, see Prucha, *American Indian Policy in Crisis*, 27–28, 34.

11. On Grant's conservatism and nativism, see Levine, "Indian Fighters and Indian Reformers"; Anbinder, "Ulysses S. Grant, Nativist."

12. Keller, *American Protestantism*, 9–24.

13. Hagan, *United States-Comanche Relations*, 57.

14. Prucha, *American Indian Policy in Crisis*, 31, 48–49.

15. *ARCIA 1869*, 4–5; Hagan, *United States-Comanche Relations*, 58.

16. Keller, *American Protestantism*, 72–73.

17. Rockwell, *Indian Affairs and the Administrative State*, 253.

18. Graber, "'If A War It May Be Called,'" 36–69.

19. Hagan, *United States-Comanche Relations*, 57.

20. Keller, *American Protestantism*, 1–2, 17, 18; Prucha, *American Indian Policy in Crisis*, 103. Chang argues that assimilation via cultural practices was also demanded of African Americans and Chinese immigrants in this period. See *Citizens of a Christian Nation*, 5, 23, 28–30. Johnson identifies a precedent for enclosed spaces deemed ideal for civilizing others in Mississippi's plantation missions. See "Religion and American Empire," 44–45.

21. Killoren, *"Come, Blackrobe,"* 340–341.

22. Mooney, *Calendar History*, 320–322; Ware Calendar, MS 7268, NAA.

23. Kiowa Calendar on Canvas, MS 2002–28, NAA, SI; Quitone Kiowa Calendar, MS 2002–27, NAA, SI.

24. Páug̱héjè (Hornless Bison Bull) had been initiated into the Q̱óichẹ́gàu (Dog Society) or Koitsenko in 1846. See Meadows, *Kiowa Military Societies*, 229. On the figures leaving the camp, see Kracht, "Kiowa Religion: An Ethnohistorical Analysis," 178–179.

25. Mooney, *Calendar History*, 322–325; Corwin, "The A-Nanthy Odle-Paugh Kiowa Calendar," (January 1971), 130–134; "The Legend of the Ṯạimé," FWP, Box 62, Folder 4, OHS; Meadows, *Through Indian Sign Language*, 176–177.

26. Mooney, *Calendar History of the Kiowa Indians*, 322; Quitone Kiowa Calendar.

27. The person who provided English captions for Anati Odlepaugh's calendar listed this warrior's name as "Date-Toe-Ay." See Corwin, "The A-Nanthy Odle-Paugh Kiowa Calendar" (January 1971), 134. As noted earlier, ritual abandonment was not uncommon in this sort of situation. See McCoy, "I Have a Mysterious Way," 75; Hüsken, "Ritual Dynamics and Ritual Failure," 337–339.

28. Rockwell, *Indian Affairs and the Administrative State*, 240; Smits, "The Frontier Army;" Grimsely, "Rebels and Redskins."

29. Killoren, *"Come, Blackrobe,"* 330–332; Genetin-Pilawa, "Ely Parker and the Contentious Peace Policy," 198.

30. Anderson, *The Conquest of Texas*, 351–352; Utley, *Indian Frontier*, 169; Hämäläinen, *The Comanche Empire*, 333.

31. Hardoff, *Washita Memories*, 9; Haley, *The Buffalo War*, 12; Kavanagh, *Comanche Political History*, 422.

32. Hardorff, *Washita Memories*, 21–26.

33. On the attack and Éàunhâfàui's participation, see Hardorff, *Washita Memories*, 345–348; Jordan, "Reclaiming the Past," 87–93. On calendar entries, see Greene, *One Hundred Summers*, 97, 227; Ware Calendar; Quitone Kiowa Calendar.

34. As noted in other chapters and the Note on Terms, I use Jonathan Z. Smith's work on rectification movements to consider what is often called Native American prophecy. See "A Pearl of Great Price and a Cargo of Yams," 1–19.

35. Hittman, "The 1870 Ghost Dance," 250–251; Irwin, *Coming Down From Above*, 284–291; Warren, *God's Red Son*, 91–93.

36. Christensen, *Sagwitch*, 81; Warren, *God's Red Son*, 96; Smoak, *Ghost Dances and Identity*, 80, 115. Smoak claims Shoshones might have experienced a similar figure in the 1850s. The new leader emerged among Bannocks, with whom Shoshones shared a reservation. He responded to the booming American population by claiming the distinct origin and identity of Indian peoples and counseling resistance to rituals advocated by missionaries. See Smoak, *Ghost Dances and Identity*, 75.

37. On C̱ạumâmạ́jè's (Goose Flying Overhead) tipi, see Ewers, *Murals in the Round*, 33–34; Greene, "Buffalo and Longhorn," 45–46. On the shield, see "Mamanti (Kiowa)," Box 1, Folder 65, JMND, NAA, SI.

38. On the owls, see Unnamed manuscript related to Big Bow's calendar, page 12, ASSNAA, Box 1, Folder 19, DRC; Kracht, "Kiowa Religion: An Ethnohistorical Analysis," 92. On the buffalo doctors and their particular expertise healing battle wounds, see Nye, *Bad Medicine and Good*, 222–223; Greene, "Buffalo and Longhorn," 45–46. On C̱ạumâmạ́jè's visit to the afterworld, see Nye, *Bad Medicine and Good*, 223–224.

39. Letters written by the reservation's agent confirm the problem with the crops and sickness. See Tatum to Parker, June 24, 1869, RG 75, M234, Roll 376, NA. On Cáumâmáje's (Goose Flying Overhead) experience while ill, which may or may not be the same vision where he visited the village of the dead, see Meadows, *Through Indian Sign Language*, 178–180. On the earlier vision, see McCoy, "I Have a Mysterious Way," 70–73.

40. Tatum diary, May 1869, LTP, SHSI. For Tatum's work on the KCA reservation, see Keller, *American Protestantism*, 132–137; Anderson, *The Conquest of Texas*, 352–353; Cutler, "Lawrie Tatum and the Kiowa Agency," 221–244; Hämäläinen, *The Comanche Empire*, 329.

41. Grant assigned two large sections of the plains to rival Quaker groups. Tatum's Orthodox Friends took assignments in the Central Superintendency, including reservations for the Kiowa and Comanche, as well as for the Cheyenne and Arapaho. Their Quaker rivals, the Hicksites, were assigned reservations in the Northern Superintendency.

42. Tatum to Parker, June 24, 1869, RG 75, M234, Roll 376, NA.

43. Tatum to Parker, June 24, 1869, RG 75, M234, Roll 376, NA.

44. *ARCIA 1869*, 361–362.

45. *ARCIA 1868*, 1. Fort Sill is an example of the scattered military outposts that Downs and Masur call the "Stockade State," a situation in which the federal government was sometimes capable of enforcing its will and was sometimes overpowered. See "Echoes of War," 6–7.

46. On Tatum, see *ARCIA 1869*, 386; Tatum to Hoag, October 16, 1869, M234, Roll 376, NA. On Hoag, see Hoag to Parker, October 16, 1869, M234, Roll 376, NA.

47. On responses to the Piegan massacre, see Byler, *Civil-Military Relations*, xviii, 32; Keller, *American Protestantism*, 31–32; Prucha, *American Indian Policy in Crisis*, 50; Killoren, *"Come, Blackrobe,"* 337–338. On concern about military posts, see Byler, *Civil-Military Relations*, 31. For examples from Western respondents, see "Opposition to Grant's Quaker Indian Policy," May 1, 1869, *Daily National Intelligencer*; Untitled article, May 6, 1869, *Daily Central City Register*.

48. Tatum, *Our Red Brothers*, 28–30.

49. *ARCIA 1869*, 385.

50. Mooney, *Calendar History*, 326.

51. Greene, *One Hundred Summers*, 97; Mooney, *Calendar History*, 326–327; Corwin, "The A-Nanthy Odle-Paugh Kiowa Calendar" (January 1971) 152; Quitone Kiowa Calendar, MS 2002–27, NAA, SI; Ware Calendar. Also see Marriott, *Kiowa Years*, 1–5, 6–22; Marriott, *Ten Grandmothers*, 100.

52. Butler, "Pioneer School Teaching at the Comanche-Kiowa Agency School," 495.

53. Ewers, *Murals in the Round*, 27; Meadows, *Kiowa, Apache, and Comanche Military Societies*, 37.

54. Marriott, *Kiowa Years*, 31–33.

55. On Àunsójèqàptàu's death, see Mooney, *Calendar History*, 328; Greene, *One Hundred Summers*, 99; Corwin, "The A-Nanthy Odle-Paugh Kiowa Calendar" (October 1971) 108; Ware Calendar. On political discussions at the Sun Dance, see Anderson, *The Conquest of Texas*, 353; Kavanagh, *Comanche Political History*, 426.

56. On Tatum's direction to leave, see Butler, "Pioneer School Teaching," 491–492. On Tatum's ongoing work, see Tatum to Hoag, May 14, 1870, M234, Roll 376, NA. On Mary Ann, see Mary Ann Tatum diary, May 1, 1870, SHSI; Mary Ann Tatum diary, July 4, 1870, SHSI; Tatum diary, June 26, 1870, SHSI.

57. Butler, "Pioneer School Teaching," 493.

58. Tatum to Hoag, June 22, 1870, M234, Roll 376, NA.

59. Tatum to Hoag, June 15, 1870, M234, Roll 376, NA; Mary Ann Tatum diary, June 18, 1870, SHSI.

60. On raiding, see Tatum to Hoag, July 1, 1870, M234, Roll 376, NA; Tatum diary, July 7, 1870, SHSI; Tatum diary, July 11, 1870, SHSI; Tatum diary, July 20, 1870, SHSI; Tatum to Hoag, July 22, 1870, M234, Roll 376, NA; Tatum to Hoag, July 29, 1870, M234, Roll 376, NA. On avoiding meetings, Tatum to Hoag, July 1, 1870, M234, Roll 376, NA. On rations, see Tatum diary, July 4, 1870, SHSI; Tatum diary, July 10, 1870, SHSI. On Tatum's ultimatums, see Tatum diary, July 14, 1870, SHSI; Tatum to Hoag, July 16, 1870, M234, Roll 376, NA.

61. On the meeting with weapons, see Tatum diary, August 10, 1870, SHSI; Tatum, *Our Red Brothers*, 40–43. On withholding rations, see Tatum to Parker, August 12, 1870, M234, Roll 376, NA; Tatum diary, August 18, 1870, SHSI; Tatum to Hoag, August 19, 1870, M234, Roll 376, NA; Tatum diary, September 2, 1870, SHSI; Hagan, *United States-Comanche Relations*, 72–74. On difficulties Kiowas faced, see *ARCIA 1870*, 260–263. On Tatum's insistence that Kiowa actions were unjustified, see *ARCIA 1870*, 264; "Lawrie Tatum's Letters," 52.

62. Tatum to Hoag, September 6, 1870, M234, Roll 376, NA.

63. Tatum diary, September 2, 1870, SHSI.

64. Tatum diary, September 2, 1870, SHSI.

65. Tatum to Hoag, September 6, 1870, M234, Roll 376, NA.

66. On Hoag and rations, see Hagan, *United States-Comanche Relations*, 74. On the committee's response to Tatum, see Tatum diary, November 27, 1870, SHSI. On Hoag's effort to reassure Quakers, see Hoag, "Western Indians," February 25, 1871, *The Friend*.

67. I detail protests registered by some Ohio Quakers. See Graber, " 'If a War It May Be Called.' "

68. "Missions and the Quaker Policy," *Vermont Chronicle*, June 11, 1870.

69. On the BIC, see *Second Annual Report of the Board of Indian Commissioners*, 4. On the Baptist response, see Smith, "Reminiscences of a Missionary Among South-West Wild Indians," JSMNAMC, WHC, UO. On Episcopalian response, see Botkin, "Indian Missions of the Episcopal Church in Oklahoma," 41.

70. On Catholic arguments, see Rahill, *The Catholic Indian Missions and Grant's Peace Policy*, 36–44. See Chapter 2 on the heated competition for Indian missions between Catholics and Methodists in the Oregon Territory.

71. Rahill, *The Catholic Indian Missions*, 46–54.

72. Blanchet and De Smet were invited as guests at these meetings, but were not included as board members. See Clatterbuck, *Demons, Saints, and Patriots*, 12, 36–37. Several Protestant members of the board had threatened to quit if any Catholics were named to it.

73. Keller, *American Protestantism*, 39.

74. On the Catholic-Protestant school struggles that stretched outside Indian reservations, in particular what has become known as the Cincinnati Bible wars in the late 1860s and early 1870s, see Green, *The Bible, The School, and the Constitution*, Chapters 2 and 3; Green, *The Second Disestablishment*, 276–287. For McGreevy's discussion of Jesuit involvement in the school funding issue, see *American Jesuits and the World*, 158. This period was not only a time of change for Catholicism in the United States, but also globally because of Vatican I, which met from 1869–1870.

75. On the man who grew crops, see Mary Ann Tatum diary, March 2, 1870, SHSI. See the Note on Terms for a discussion of the "Great Spirit," including translation issues, missionary use,

and Native people's responses to the popular phrase. On Cújòkọ́ģai (Black Eagle), see Tatum diary, July 14, 1870, SHSI.

76. Marriott, *The Ten Grandmothers*, 106–111.

77. On the end of treaty making, see Banner, *How the Indians Lost Their Land*, 251–252; Rockwell, *Indian Affairs and the Administrative State*, 40. On the language of wards and children, see *ARCIA 1868*, 13; Mary Ann Tatum diary, January 27, 1870, LTP, SHSI; Banner, *How the Indians Lost Their Land*, 250; Cahill, *Federal Fathers and Mothers*, 11, 17. On the Camp Grant massacre, see Jacoby, *Shadows at Dawn*.

78. On Sétágài (Sitting Bear) or Satanke, see Marriott, *The Ten Grandmothers*, 116–120. On Protestants' opposition to proposals to open Indian Territory to settlement, see *Second Annual Report of the Board of Indian Commissioners*, 137–141; "Minute Book," March 2, 1871, vol. 4 AAP, PYMICR, QSC, HC. On the hunters and depleted buffalo herds, see Haley, *The Buffalo War*, 21, 24; Anderson, *The Conquest of Texas*, 345–346.

79. Tatum, "Diary, December 7, 1870," LTP, SHSI.

80. Nye, *Bad Medicine and Good*, 188; Hoig, *Tribal Wars of the Southern Plains*, 272.

81. Keller, *American Protestantism*, 133–137.

82. Tatum to Hoag, May 25, 1871, LR, Roll 377, NA. Recall that under the Peace Policy soldiers could not come into the agency without invitation. Their authority was limited to Native people off reservation.

83. Tatum to Hoag, May 28, 1871, LR, Roll 377, NA.

84. "Lawrie Tatum's Letters," 60–61.

85. For Tatum's account, see Tatum to Hoag, June 10, 1871, M234, Roll 377, NA. The other account comes from Josiah Butler, a Quaker schoolteacher discussed later in the chapter. See Butler, "Pioneer School Teaching," 505–506. The incident was also covered in national newspapers. See "The Indians," June 10, 1871, *NYT*.

86. "Chiefs They Then Imprisoned Story," Box 28, Folder 13, PMP, OHS.

87. Marriott, *Kiowa Years*, 2–3, 39–40. Marriott discusses Sétágài's power to cough up knives in another work; see *The Ten Grandmothers*, 114.

88. Kiowa Calendar on Canvas.

89. Calendar keepers marked Sétágài's death with his name glyph and bullets. See Quitone Kiowa Calendar; Ware Calendar. Other calendars include all three arrested men. See unnamed manuscript related to Big Bow's calendar, page 26, ASSNAA, Box 1, Folder 19, DRC.

90. Tatum to Hoag, June 17, 1871, LR, Roll 377, NA.

91. Columbus Delano to Parker, June 20, 1871, LR, Roll 377, NA.

92. Byler, *Civil-Military Relations*, 108–110; Utley, *Indian Frontier*, 165.

93. "The Indians," *NYT*, June 20, 1871.

94. "Commissioner Tatum's Views of What Should Be Done with Satanta and Big Tree," *NYT*, June 29, 1871.

95. Tatum wrote letters to the judge, the Texas attorney general, and the Texas governor, arguing against the Kiowa defendants' execution based not on a principled objection to capital punishment, but rather that a sentence of life imprisonment would likely stave off a revenge-inspired, all-out war on the southern plains. See Lawrie Tatum to Mary Ann Tatum, July 17, 1871, LTP, Folder 2, SHSI; Tatum to Hoag, July 1, 1871, LR, Roll 377, NA. The *New York Times* reprinted Tatum's letter to the governor. See "The Indians," *NYT*, August 3, 1871.

96. Hoag to Tatum, June 26, 1871, LR, Roll 377, NA.

97. Untitled article, *The Friend*, August 26, 1871. Hoag included a similar letter to the president in his correspondence with Parker. See Hoag to Parker, July 19, 1871, LR, Roll 377, NA.

98. "Eminently Practical Suggestions to Quaker Indian Commissioners," *San Francisco Daily Evening Bulletin*, July 19, 1871.

99. "Horrible Barbarity: Results of Quaker Policy on the Indian," *Daily Arkansas Gazette*, July 28, 1871.

100. Tatum to Hoag, October 14, 1871, LR, Roll 377, NA; Lawrie Tatum to Mary Ann Tatum, October 14, 1871, LTP, Folder 2, SHSI; Tatum to Grierson, August 4, 1871, LR, Roll 377, NA; Tatum to Hazen, August 5, 1871, LR, Roll 377, NA.

101. See earlier references to "friendly bands of the Comanches" in *ARCIA 1848*, 573; a reference to "friendly" Kiowas in "Our Army and the Indians," August 31, 1854, *NYT*; and a characterization of Kiowas and Comanches as acting "friendly" in *ARCIA 1861*, 17.

102. Quaker Jonathan Richards argued that friendly Indians should use their influence with hostiles. See "The Indians," *NYT*, May 16, 1871.

103. The report comes from the minutes of an August 1871 Indian committee meeting. See Associated Executive Committee of Friends on Indian Affairs, "Minute Book, Volume 4, AA9," Philadelphia Yearly Meeting Indian Committee Records (PYMICR), QSC-HC. Selections from the minutes were reprinted for a wider Quaker audience. See "Extracts from the Second Annual Report of the Associated Executive Committee of Friends on Indian Affairs," *Friends' Review*, September 30, 1871.

104. Tatum to Hoag, August 5, 1871, NA; Tatum to Mary Ann Tatum, August 5, 1871, SHSI; Hoag to Pope, August 12, 1871, NA.

105. *ARCIA* 1871, 503; Tatum, untitled article, *Friends' Intelligencer*, March 29, 1873; Hagan, *United States-Comanche Relations*, 88.

106. Richardson, "Indian Affairs," *The Friend*, September 9, 1871.

107. "Extracts from the Second Annual Report of the Associated Executive Committee of Friends on Indian Affairs," September 30, 1871, *Friends' Review*.

108. *Annual Report of the Board of Commissioners*, 12.

CHAPTER 4

1. Tatum to Mary Ann Tatum, July 8, 1871, LTP, SHSI.

2. "General News by Telegraph: The Indians," *NYT*, August 26, 1871.

3. Richardson, "North and West of Reconstruction," 69; Chang, *Citizens of a Christian Nation*, 5.

4. Wenger discusses the Catholic effort to protect Indians' freedom to practice Catholicism, especially on Pueblo reservations. See *We Have a Religion*, 20.

5. On illness, see *ARCIA 1870*, 260; Tatum to Mary Ann Tatum, September 19, 1871, LTP, SHSI; Tatum to Mary Ann Tatum, October 14, 1871, LTP, SHSI; Battey, *The Life and Adventures of a Quaker*, 44, 82, 101, 118, 189–190; Butler, "Pioneer School Teaching," 498, 514.

6. On efforts to attract Kiowas to school, see *ARCIA 1871*, 475–476; Tatum to Mary Ann Tatum, September 10, 1871, LTP, SHSI; Butler, "Pioneer School Teaching," 484, 491, 498–500, 502–503; Hagan, *United States-Comanche Relations*, 74. Some Kiowas were so leery of schooling that they tried to convince Caddo parents to withdraw their children. See Butler, "Pioneer School Teaching," 507.

7. Battey, *The Life and Adventures of a Quaker*, 47, 59–63.

8. Battey, *The Life and Adventures of a Quaker*, 60.

9. Marriott, *Kiowa Years*, 21–22.

10. Battey, *The Life and Adventures of a Quaker*, 118.

11. *ARCIA 1868*, iii; Rockwell, *Indian Affairs and the Administrative State*, 268. Congress began appropriating funds specifically for Indian schools in 1877. See Adams, *Education for Extinction*, 26.

12. *Second Annual Report of the Board of Indian Commissioners*, 27. One historian of Catholic Indian missions sees some truth in the Protestants' critique. He claims Jesuit missionaries were far more likely to emphasize religious teaching, along with skills in trades and farming. They were less concerned with altering Native dress and teaching the English language. See McKevitt, *Brokers of Culture*, 151, 165.

13. *ARCIA 1875*, 22–23.

14. Green, *The Second Disestablishment*, 276–287.

15. *ARCIA 1872*, 73–74. Quakers had sixteen of the seventy-seven run by Protestant representatives.

16. Bunson, *Faith in the Wilderness*, 101; Rahill, *The Catholic Indian Missions*, 72–73, 81, 103–108; Prucha, *American Indian Policy in Crisis*, 57.

17. *Bureau of Catholic Indian Missions, 1874 to 1895*, 5–8; Clatterbuck, *Demons, Saints, and Patriots*, 13; Bunson, *Faith in the Wilderness*, 102–103.

18. *Circular of the Catholic Commissioner of Indian Missions*, 4–14.

19. *Manual: Catholic Indian Missionary Associations*, 8.

20. Rahill, *The Catholic Indian Missions*, 132–133.

21. Rahill, *The Catholic Indian Missions*, 144–145.

22. Green, *The Bible, The School, and the Constitution*, 187–195; McGreevy, *American Jesuits in the World*, 99.

23. Hagan, *United States-Comanche Relations*, 79.

24. "Grant's Quaker Policy Exploded," *Georgia Weekly Telegraph & Journal and Messenger*, September 17, 1872.

25. On Battey, see Battey, *The Life and Adventures of a Quaker*, 153. On Tatum, see Tatum to Mary Ann Tatum, September 19, 1871, LTP, SHSI; *ARCIA 1872*, 248. On the commissioner, see *ARCIA 1873*, 8.

26. Battey, *The Life and Adventures of a Quaker*, 142.

27. *ARCIA 1874*, 3–4.

28. Battey, *The Life and Adventures of a Quaker*, 127–129, 208–209. On Fáitàlyi's (Sun Boy) shield, see Greene, *Silver Horn*, 95.

29. On Haworth's approach, see Haworth to Hoag, April 7, 1873, M234, Roll 378, NA; *ARCIA 1873*, 219–220; Battey, *The Life and Adventures of a Quaker*, 141.

30. On the potential release, see Anderson, *The Conquest of Texas*, 357. On Haworth's reaction, see Haworth to Hoag, April 7, 1873, RG 75, M234, Roll 378, NA; Haworth to Hoag, April 24, 1873, RG 75, M234, Roll 378, NA; *ARCIA 1873*, 219. On concerns about a delay, see Beede to Smith, May 14, 1873, RG75, M234, Roll 378, NA.

31. Prucha, *American Indian Policy in Crisis*, 87; Byler, *Civil-Military Relations*, 10; Hagan, *United States-Comanche Relations*, 95; Utley, *Indian Frontier*, 170–172; Coward, *The Newspaper Indian*, 198–201.

32. Battey, *The Life and Adventures of a Quaker*, 156–157.

33. See Hagan, *United States-Comanche Relations*, 94; Battey, *The Life and Adventures of a Quaker*, 161–163.

34. Butler, "Frontier School Teaching," 527–528.

35. Haworth to Hoag, June 12, 1873, RG 75, M234, Roll 378, NA.

36. On discussions at the Sun Dance, see Mooney, *Calendar History*; Battey, *The Life and Adventures of a Quaker*, 164–184; Corwin, "The A-Nanthy Odle-Paugh Kiowa Calendar" (October 1971): 124. On parents and school, see Battey to Haworth, July 31, 1873, RG 75, M234, Roll 378, NA; Haworth to Hoag, August 2, 1873, RG 75, M234, Roll 378, NA. On rumors, see Haworth to Hoag, July 21, 1873, RG 75, M234, Roll 378, NA. On surveying, see Haworth to Hoag, July 31, 1873, RG 75, M234, Roll 378, NA; Battey, *The Life and Adventures of a Quaker*, 219, 225. On council invitations, see Beede to Smith, July 31, 1873, RG 75, M234, Roll 378, NA. On Comanche raiding, see Haworth to Hoag, August 21, 1873, RG 75, M234, Roll 378, NA; Haworth to Hoag, September 8, 1873, M234, Roll 378, NA.

37. On the release, see Haworth to Hoag, September 8, 1873, RG 75, M234, Roll 378, NA. On the officials and their demands, see Battey, *The Life and Adventures of a Quaker*, 195–204; Hagan, *United States-Comanche Relations*, 97–99; Kavanagh, *Comanche Political History*, 437–439.

38. Banner, *How the Indians Lost Their Land*, 253–256.

39. *ARCIA 1873*, 3–10.

40. Battey to family, February 17, 1874, TCBC, Box 1, Folder 15, WHC, UO.

41. Haley, *The Buffalo War*, 24, 37–38, 40; Hagan, *United States-Comanche Relations*, 104; Hubbard, "Buffalo Genocide in Nineteenth-Century North America," 293–294.

42. Battey, *The Life and Adventures of a Quaker*, 243.

43. Haworth to Smith, December 1, 1873, RG 75, M234, Roll 378, NA.

44. Haworth to Delano, December 15, 1873, RG 75, M234, Roll 378, NA.

45. Battey to family, March 17, 1874, TCB, MSS S-2345 B322, BL.

46. Haworth made a transcription of the speeches. See Haworth to Delano, December 15, 1873, RG 75, M234, Roll 378, NA.

47. Ibid.

48. On the deaths, see Battey, *The Life and Adventures of a Quaker*, 245; Haworth to Hoag, February 9, 1874, RG 75, M234, Roll 379, NA; Haworth to Hoag, February 16, 1874, RG 75, M234, Roll 379, NA; Haworth to Hoag, March 28, 1874, RG 75, M234, Roll 379, NA. For the calendar entries, see Mooney, *Calendar History*, 337–338; Greene, *One Hundred Summers*, 103; Quitone Kiowa Calendar, MS 20020–27, NAA, SI; Ware Calendar, MS 7268, NAA, SI; Kiowa Calendar on Canvas, MS 2002–28, NAA, SI. On Cúifágàui's response, see Beede to Hoag, March 30, 1874, RG 75, M234, Roll 379, NA.

49. On the council, see Beede to Hoag, March 30, 1874, RG 75, M234, Roll 379, NA; Surveyor to Haworth, April 1, 1874, RG 75, M234, Roll 379, NA; Battey, *The Life and Adventures of a Quaker*, 264–270.

50. Anderson, *The Conquest of Texas*, 352–353.

51. Haworth to Hoag, April 13, 1874, RG 75, M234, Roll 379, NA; Rhoads to Hoag, April 13, 1874, RG 75, M234, Roll 379, NA.

52. On the Quakers' request, see Haworth to Hoag, April 13, 1874, RG 75, M234, Roll 379, NA; Rhoades to Hoag, April 13, 1874, RG 75, M234, Roll 379, NA; Beede to Smith, May 6, 1874, RG 75, M234, Roll 379, NA. On Battey's concern, see Battey to family, March 25, 1874, TCBC, Box 1, Folder 16, WHC, UO.

53. On news of a dance, see Haworth to Hoag, May 6, 1874, RG 75, M234, Roll 379, NA. This is an odd statement as "medicine dance" usually referred to Sun Dance ceremonials, of which the Comanches had no long tradition. When they engaged in Sun Dancing, they did

so in gatherings organized by Kiowas. On Isatai as a new man of power, see *ARCIA 1874*, 220; Meadows, *Through Indian Sign Language*, 168–168; Kavanagh, *Comanche Political History*, 445–446; Hämäläinen, *The Comanche Empire*, 337; Hagan, *United States-Comanche Relations*, 105; Anderson, *The Conquest of Texas*, 358; Haley, *The Buffalo War*, 52–53. I take the language of rectification from Jonathan Z. Smith; see "A Pearl of Great Price and a Cargo of Yams," 8–9. See also Wenzel, *Bulletproof*, 10. On Isatai's dance, see *The Buffalo War*, 54. On the Quakers' concern about the dance and possible attack, see Haworth to Hoag, May 9, 1874, RG 75, M234, Roll 379, NA. Battey was also nervous about Comanches convincing Kiowas to join them in war. See *The Life and Adventures of a Quaker*, 284. The Quaker agent at the Cheyenne and Arapaho reservation also begged officials to supply rations in order to stave off a war. See Haley, *The Buffalo War*, 43.

54. Battey, *The Life and Adventures of a Quaker*, 302–304.

55. *ARCIA 1874*, 220.

56. On Cûifâgàui's actions, see Haworth to Hoag, May 9, 1874, RG 75, M234, Roll 379, NA; Haworth to Hoag, June 6, 1874, RG 75, M234, Roll 379, NA; Mooney, *Calendar History*, 338. On the Quakers' responses, see Haworth to Hoag, June 22, 1874, RG 75, M234, Roll 379, NA; Battey to family, June 22, 1874, TCBLF, YCWA, BL; Haworth to Hoag, June 27, 1874, RG 75, M234, Roll 379, NA.

57. On the Sun Dance, see Mooney, *Calendar History*, 338; Greene, *One Hundred Summers*, 103–104; Haley, *The Buffalo War*, 65–78. Battey noted Kiowa absences from Sun Dances were so unusual that he did not believe reports about the young men leaving. See Battey to family, June 30, 1874, TCBLF, YCWA, BL. On the battle, see Mooney, *Calendar History*, 202–204; Hagan, *United States-Comanche Relations*, 109; Haley, *The Buffalo War*, 97. According to Haley, Agent Richards at Anadarko also called for military aid. Battey heard that the Comanches "threw away" the new medicine man after Isatai's effort to make fighters invulnerable to bullets proved unsuccessful. See Battey to family, July 8, 1874, TCBLF, YCWA, BL. On failed ritual, or in this case a powerful leader's failure, see Hüsken, "Ritual Dynamics and Ritual Failure," 337–339.

58. Haley, *The Buffalo War*, 79–93. Haley claims that three-quarters of KCA Indians went to the reservation headquarters; see *The Buffalo War*, 80–83.

59. Battey claimed to know many who planned to come in after the Sun Dance, unless the "medicine" called for war. See Battey to family, July 5, 1874, TCBLF, YCWA, BL.

60. Meadows, *Kiowa Military Societies*, 141.

61. Ibid, 140.

62. On the fighters and their power, see *ARCIA 1874*, 220; Battey to family, June 30, 1874, TCBLF, YCWA, BL; Haley, *The Buffalo War*, 79–93.

63. AECFIA, "Minute Book," 156–163, vol. 4, AA9, PYMICR, HC. The use of the term "religion" to identify Kiowa ritual life and relations to supernatural powers is unusual for this period. Protestants involved in Indian affairs typically withheld this term, as it granted a certain amount of legitimacy, and instead employed the terms "heathen," "pagan," or "superstition." See Wenger, *We Have a Religion*, 19.

64. On Quakers' efforts and perspectives, see Haworth to Hoag, July 11, 1874, RG 75, M234, Roll 379, NA; Haley, *The Buffalo War*, 112. On military responses, see Haley, *The Buffalo War*, 109–110.

65. On fear of the census, see Haworth to Hoag, July 28, 1874, RG 75, M856, Roll 47, NA; Haworth to Smith, August 3, 1874, RG 75, M234, Roll 379; Haworth to Smith, 8 August 1874, RG 75, M234, Roll 379; Davidson to Division of Texas, August 15, 1874, RG 75, M234, Roll 379,

NA. Dees notes other census efforts that Native people feared and participated in unwillingly; see "The Scientific Study of Native American Religions," 73–82. On new conditions established by military officers, see Sanderson to Haworth, August 9, 1874, RG 75, M234, Roll 379, NA; Sanderson to Haworth, August 10, 1874, RG 75, M234, Roll 379, NA.

66. Beede to Rhoads, AECFIA, "Minute Book," 172–173, vol. 4, AA9, PYMICR, HC.

67. Nicholson to Smith, AECFIA, "Minute Book," 144–148, 169, vol. 4, AA9, PYMICR, HC.

68. Rhoads to Beede, AECFIA, "Minute Book," 172, vol. 4, AA9, PYMICR, HC. The committee's minute taker reported that Enoch Hoag, the Quaker superintendent over the region containing the KCA Reservation, approved of the use of force.

69. On Miles's actions, see Miles to Smith, AECFIA, "Minute Book," 123, vol. 4, AA9, PYMICR, HC; "Dictionary of Quaker Biography," HC; Hagan, *United States-Comanche Relations*, 109. On Quakers' responses to him, see AECFIA, "Minute Book," 132, vol. 4, AA9, PYMICR, HC; Keller, *American Protestantism*, 143–146.

70. On the battle at the Wichita headquarters, see *ARCIA 1874*, 221; Abel Big Bow, interview by Julia A. Jordan, June 17, 1967, interview T-16, OFLC, M452, Box 5, Folder 2, WHC, UO; Haley, *The Buffalo War*, 115; Mooney, *Calendar History*, 204–205. On the period after the battle, see Jordan, "Reclaiming the Past," 93. On Palo Duro, see Nye, *Bad Medicine and Good*, 188, 198; Jordan, "Reclaiming the Past," 94.

71. On the battle, see Haley, *The Buffalo War*, 169–182; Jordan, "Reclaiming the Past," 94–95. On the aftermath, see Anderson, *The Conquest of Texas*, 358; Jordan, "Reclaiming the Past," 96–98.

72. As noted earlier, see Hüsken, "Ritual Dynamics and Ritual Failure," 337–339, on failed rituals and ritual leaders.

73. Jordan, "Reclaiming the Past," 95–96; Nye, *Bad Medicine and Good*, 200–201.

74. Frost, "Indian Hostilities," *Friends' Intelligencer*, October 3, 1874.

75. On the anti-Indian newspaper coverage, see "The Indians," *NYT*, October 20, 1874; Marshall, *Miles Expedition of 1874–1875*, 4–5, 18.

76. Haley, *The Buffalo War*, 213–214.

77. "The Owl or Death Medicine," FWP, Box 62, Folder 4, OHS.

78. Ibid.

79. For another version of Cáumâmáje's interaction with Thènéàungópjè and his subsequent death, see Nye, *Bad Medicine and Good*, 222–225.

80. For a discussion of Quaker struggles over the peace testimony during the Revolutionary and Civil War years and earlier in the Peace Policy, see Graber, " 'If a War It May Be Called,' " 37–43.

81. Blight, *Race and Reunion*; Blum, *Reforging the White Republic*, 6–7.

82. Paddison, *American Heathens*, 3–4, 7–8; Chang, *Citizens of a Christian Nation*, 23, 28–30, 164.

CHAPTER 5

1. Zotom (Zotum), "A History of Indian Prison Life By Zotom (Biter) Kiowa," pages 4B, 5A, 7B, 8A, and 10A, ASSNAA, 1996.017.0195A, DRC, NCWHM. On Zótâm's Fort Marion drawings, see Szabo, *Imprisoned Art, Complex Patronage*, 3, 21–27, 69–117.

2. Szabo, *Art from Fort Marion*, 24.

3. See Wade and Rand, "The Subtle Art of Resistance," for one possible reading of this drawing.

4. Americans' concerns about potential assimilation were hardly limited to debates about Native Americans. Similar conversations emerged around the surge in European immigration and

ongoing immigration from China, as well as with newly emancipated African Americans in the South. See Brands, *The Triumph of Capitalism*, 136–144, 285.

5. Paddison, *American Heathens*, 5.

6. AECFIA, "Minute Book," 168–169, 190, vol. 4, AA9, PYMICR, HC.

7. *ARCIA 1875*, 275; Haworth to Hoag, December 14, 1875, RG75, M234, roll 380, NA; Haworth to Stickney, April 26, 1876, RG75, M234, Roll 381, NA; Galpin, *Report upon the Condition and Management*, 3–4.

8. William Nicholson to AECFIA in AECFIA, "Minute Book," 168, vol. 4. On the connection of American policy to exterminate the buffalo and contain Native peoples, see Hubbard, "Buffalo Genocide in Nineteenth-Century North America," 292–305.

9. On troops, see Burkhart to Haworth, February 22, 1878, RG75, M234, Roll 383, NA. On total bans on buffalo hunting, see Haworth to Hoag, May 31, 1875, RG75, M234, Roll 380, NA; AECFIA, "Minute Book," 195, vol. 4; Haworth to Hayt, October 15, 1877, RG75, M234, Roll 382, NA.

10. Greene, *One Hundred Summers*, 107.

11. On insufficient rations, see Haworth to Hoag, May 31, 1875, RG75, M234, Roll 380, NA; AECFIA, "Minute Book," 195, vol. 4; *ARCIA 1879*, 65. On malnutrition, see Haworth to Hayt, October 15, 1877, RG75, M234, Roll 382, NA. On government refusal to supplement, see Hayt to Haworth, undated, included in Haworth to Hayt, October 15, 1877, RG 75, M234, Roll 382, NA.

12. Mooney, *Calendar History*, 339, 341.

13. *ARCIA 1875*, 275.

14. AECFIA, "Minute Book," no page number, entry for April 4, 1877, vol. 4.

15. Laracy, "Sacred Heart Mission and Abbey," 234; Fossey and Morris, "St. Katharine Drexel and St. Patrick's Mission," 63. Benedictines began their involvement in Indian missions when Martin Marty, a Benedictine in the Dakota Territory, responded to the BCIM's call for missionaries in the late 1870s. Marty recruited Benedictines from Europe to serve as missionaries to Native people. See Rippinger, *The Benedictine Order in the United States*, 130–134. Marty later became president of the BCIM and lobbied Congress on Indian affairs.

16. Richards to Bureau of Indian Affairs, August 30, 1877, RG75, M234, Roll 382, NA.

17. Prucha, *American Indian Policy in Crisis*, 57.

18. Haworth to Nicholson, September 29, 1877, RG75, M234, Roll 382, NA; Nicholson to Hayt, October 6, 1877, RG75, M234, Roll 382, NA; Reeve, *Religion of a Different Color*, Chapter 2.

19. *ARCIA 1875*, 273.

20. *ARCIA 1877*, 88.

21. *ARCIA 1877*, 87. This focus on moving Kiowas from one stage of cultural development to another reflected a broadly shared view about human progress articulated famously by Henry Morgan in his influential 1877 work, *Ancient Society*.

22. *ARCIA 1877*, 88.

23. Champney, "The Indians at San Marco," *The Independent*, June 13, 1878.

24. Stowe, "The Indians at St. Augustine," *Christian Union*, April 18, 1877.

25. Childs, "A Picture Letter Reveals a Cheyenne Family's Love," 60.

26. "KCA Chiefs to the Great Father," June 23, 1876, RG75, M234, Roll 381, NA.

27. Á càą̀ (Going Into The Timber) was sick with what Colonel Pratt identified as a lung hemorrhage, most likely caused from tuberculosis. Pratt requested permission from the military to

send Ácàà home with the hope he might survive his illness. He sent Māyítèndè (Woman's Heart) with him. See Pratt to name illegible, April 7, 1877, RG75, M234, Roll 382, NA.

28. "Talks of the Kiowa, Comanche, and Apache Chiefs at a Council," April 30, 1877, RG75, M234, Roll 382, NA.

29. Haworth to Nicholson, May 4, 1877, RG75, M234, Roll 382, NA.

30. On surveillance by troops, see Quitone Kiowa Calendar, MS 2002–27, NAA, SI. See also "Kiowa Calendar on Canvas," MS 2002–28, NAA, SI; Ware Calendar, MS 7268, NAA, SI; Mooney, *Calendar History*, 339, 342; Greene, *One Hundred Summers*, 214. On the keeper's death and replacement, see Greene, *Silver Horn*, 107; Stokely, "Black Bear's Calendar," 353. On measles during the Sun Dance, see Mooney, *Calendar History*, 341; Greene, *Silver Horn*, 107.

31. Galpin, *Report upon the Condition and Management*, 5.

32. *ARCIA* 1876, 51.

33. Galpin, *Report upon the Condition and Management*, 6.

34. "President Grant's Indian Policy," *Methodist Quarterly Review* (July 1877).

35. Bellesiles, *1877*, 67–68. Southern editorialists were some of the loudest critics after the Little Bighorn. They used the incident to attack President Grant, whom they despised for his Reconstruction policies. See Reilly, *Frontier Newspapers*, 40–41.

36. McGloin, "Our Indian Problem," *Overland Monthly and Out West Magazine* (November 1875).

37. Whipple, "The Indian Policy," *New York Observer and Chronicle* (August 3, 1876).

38. Torquaster, "Our Indian Policy," *The Independent* (October 4, 1877).

39. Bellesiles, *1877*, 36–47.

40. AECFIA, "Minute Book," 213, vol. 4.

41. "Address from AECFIA to Rutherford B. Hayes, President of the United States," AECFIA, "Minute Book," no page number, vol. 4.

42. *Circular of the Catholic Commissioner*, 13.

43. *Manual: Catholic Indian Missionary Associations*, 1.

44. On Mrs. Sherman's work, see Sherman, *Appeal of Mrs. W. T. Sherman to the Catholic Ladies of the United States*, 1–3. On the pope's encouragement, see *Annals of the Catholic Indian Missions of America* 1, no. 1 (January 1877): 6–8.

45. On Catholic public schooling controversies in this period, see McGreevy, *Catholicism and American Freedom*, 112–116. McKevitt also notes the move toward schooling in Jesuit missions. See *Brokers of Culture*, 123.

46. Pratt, *Battlefield and Classroom*, 107–108, 116.

47. Gloege, *Guaranteed Pure*, 25, 41–44.

48. "St. Augustine in April," *Lippincott's Magazine of Popular Literature and Science* (November 1875).

49. M. E. W., "Christian Work in Florida," *New York Evangelist*, January 27, 1876.

50. Stowe, "The Indians at St. Augustine" *Christian Union*, April 18, 1877.

51. Mauro, *The Art of Americanization*, 54, 66–67, 72. Mauro argues that George Catlin actually initiated the "before and after" genre of Native representation; see 71–72.

52. Pratt, *Battlefield and Classroom*, 118.

53. Pratt, *Battlefield and Classroom*, 113–115.

54. Pratt, *Battlefield and Classroom*, 115, 118, 147.

55. On the request, see Cowen to Grant, August 5, 1875, RG75, M234, Roll 380, NA; Haworth to Edward P. Smith, August 6, 1875, RG75, M234, Roll 380, NA. On the women's response, see Haworth to Smith, August 5, 1875, RG75, M234, Roll 380, NA; Haworth to Smith, August 6, 1875, RG75, M234, Roll 380, NA.

56. Stowe, "The Indians at St. Augustine."

57. Pratt to Adjutant General of U.S. Army, October 5, 1875, RG75, M234, Roll 380, NA.

58. For more on Kiowa ledger art and how I use it, see the Introduction.

59. I take many of my cues for interpreting Fort Marion ledger drawings from museum anthropologist, Candace S. Greene. She offers one of the most succinct and helpful introductions to the art itself and the possibilities for its continued interpretation. See Greene, "Being Indian at Fort Marion," 289–316.

60. Karen Daniels Petersen wrote the first extensive study of drawings and artists from Fort Marion. She considered six major Kiowa artists: White Horse (Chẹthà̀idè), Koba, Etahdleuh (Éttàlyỉdònmàui), Ohettoint (Oheltoint), Zotom (Zótâm), and Wohaw (Gùhâudè). She listed four minor artists: Tounkeuh, Tsadeltah, Tsaitkopeta (Sétqópjè), and Zonekeuh. See *Plains Indian Art from Fort Marion*.

61. On the emergence of landscape depictions, see Jantzer-White, "Narrative and Landscape in the Drawings of Etahdleuh Doanmoe;" Graber, "Religion in Kiowa Ledgers," 42–60. On Éttàlyỉdònmàui's images of land and people, see "Drawing of a Panoramic View of a Buffalo Hunt," Manuscript 290844, NAA, SI.

62. On American flags in Plains Indian drawing, see Schmittou and Logan, "Fluidity of Meaning," 559–604.

63. Etahdleuh, "Ledger," RCHS.

64. Wohaw, Ledger Book 1, MHM Art Collections, MHM.

65. Wohaw, Ledger Book 2, MHM Art Collections, MHM.

66. Wohaw, "Ledger Book, Containing Fourteen Original Color Drawings," WA MSS S-2893, GWFC, YCWA, BL.

67. Wohaw, Ledger Book 2.

68. Wohaw, "Ledger Book, Containing Fourteen Original Color Drawings."

69. "Red-skin Fancies and Sketches, Zo-tom (Biter) Kiowa Prisoner, in Old San Marco at St. Augustine, Fla., June 13, 1876," RHPP, YCWA, BL. On thunderbirds and their association with power, see Kracht, "Kiowa Religion: An Ethnohistorical Analysis," 86.

70. Mooney, *Calendar History*, 322, 328.

71. "Exercise Book Containing Drawings by Anonymous Kiowa Artist" MS 98–54, NAA, SI. Zótâm's name is in the book, but there is disagreement about whether he is the artist of a portion or all of the drawings.

72. See also a multi-artist ledger collected by Pratt. "Sketchbook by Indian Prisoners at St. Augustine, Florida, WA MSS S-1174, RHPP, YCWA, BL.

73. On ritual as enactment of perfect material conditions and community ideals, see Smith, "The Bare Facts of Ritual," 112–127.

74. Zotom, "Ledger Book," 4100.G.1, Braun Research Library, Autry Museum of the American West.

75. Zotom (Zutom), "A History of Indian Prison Life by Zotom (Biter) Kiowa," 1996.017.0194B, ASSNAA, DRC, NCWHM.

76. Haworth to Hayt, February 27, 1878, RG75, M234, Roll 383, NA.

77. Ibid.

78. Ibid. On the connection between humans and animals among Plains Indian nations, see DeMallie and Lavenda, "Wakan," 156; Hubbard, "Buffalo Genocide in Nineteenth-Century North America," 292–305.

79. Ibid.

80. Kretch III, *The Ecological Indian*; Isenberg, *The Destruction of the Bison.*

81. White, "The Winning of the West," 319–343 and West, "Bison R Us," 213–229.

82. Hubbard, "Buffalo Genocide in Nineteenth-Century North America," 294. Hubbard takes issue with work by Krech and Isenberg cited earlier; see 298–299.

83. On Protestants' typical language for Indian ritual life, see Wenger, *We Have a Religion,* 19, 40–41.

84. Gordon, *The Mormon Question,* 119–135.

85. Blum, *Reforging the White Republic,* 3, 7, 13–15.

86. On anti-Chinese and anti-Indian sentiment and political activity, see Paddison, *American Heathens,* 8–9, 151–152; Brands, *The Triumph of Capitalism,* 56–61; Bellesiles, *1877,* 103–105. On this wider white supremacy, see Paddison, *American Heathens,* 9.

87. P. B. Hunt to Hayt, May 7, 1878, RG75, M234, Roll 383, NA.

88. *ARCIA 1878,* 58–59.

89. Ibid., 60–62.

90. *ARCIA 1879,* 62–63. The move combined the agency serving Kiowas and Comanches with that of the Wichitas.

91. *ARCIA 1878,* 60.

92. Hoxie, *A Final Promise,* xi–xv.

93. "The Indian School at Fort Marion," *Harper's Weekly* (May 11, 1878).

94. Champney, "The Indians at San Marco."

95. Miles, "Will the Indian Stay Civilized?" July 1878, clipping from a Hampton Institute newspaper, Box 30, Folder 820, RHPP, YCWA, BL.

96. Lindsey, *Indians at Hampton Institute.*

97. Pratt, "An Indian Raid at Hampton Institute," *Southern Workman* (May 7, 1878) in Box 30, Folder 820, RHPP, YCWA, BL.

98. "Hampton Commencement," May 29, 1879, *New York Evangelist.*

99. Burnham, *Spirit of Missions.*

100. Burnham, "Florida Indians," *The Churchman* (June 29, 1878): 719–720.

101. Burnham, "First Fruits of the Kiowas, Comanches, and Cheyennes," *The Churchman* (2 November 1878): 527–528.

102. Adams, *Education for Extinction,* 48–51, 101–103, 168.

103. Ibid., 149–156.

104. Mauro, *The Art of Americanization,* 77. Mauro also explains Torlino's ambiguous experience at Carlisle; see 79–80.

105. On the federal report, see Department of the Interior, Bureau of Education, *The Indian School at Carlisle Barracks,* 3–4. On Quaker praise, see "Indian Education," *Friends' Intelligencer,* October 23, 1880; "The Carlisle School for Indian Children, *The Friend,* November 26, 1881.

106. AECFIA, "Minute Book," no page number, entry for May 14, 1879, vol. 4.

107. P. B. Hunt to Hayt, May 2, 1878, RG75, M234, Roll 383, NA.

108. On hunger, see George W. Hunt to Hayt, May 28, 1878, RG75, M234, Roll 383, NA; *ARCIA 1879*, 65. On child mortality, see *ARCIA 1880*, 72; Greene, *One Hundred Summers*, 111.

109. On 1878, see Silver Horn, "Pictorial Calendar," MSS 2531, Vol. 7, NAA, SI. On 1879, see *ARCIA 1879*, 64–66; Silver Horn, "Pictorial Calendar." Mooney posited that the people could not find a buffalo and did not hold a dance in 1880. See Mooney, *Calendar History*, 346.

110. Setkopti, "Diary," MS 2531, Volume 2, NAA, SI.

111. Contained in J. B. Wicks to Commissioner of Indian Affairs, September 15, 1879, RG75, M234, Roll 125, NA.

112. Zótâm to Pratt, August 6, 1878, Box 9, Folder 339, RHPP, YCWA, BL.

113. Zótâm to Pratt, November 22, 1878, Box 9, Folder 339, RHPP, YCWA, BL.

114. Zótâm wrote his letter in English, so it's unclear how he might have used Kiowa words or concepts to name Jesus and God. Eventually, Kiowas used the term *Dwk'i* to refer to God. According to Kracht, this word denotes a personified creator, a concept that Kiowas did not have before contact with Christian missionaries. See "Kiowa Religion in Historical Perspective," 20. On a similar trajectory of a high god articulated as the "Great Spirit" after contact with Europeans in the eastern half of North America, see Cave, *Prophets of the Great Spirit*, 3.

115. On the bishop's service, see "Ordination of Two Indians, *The Churchman* (June 18, 1881): 680; *Journal of 13th Annual Convention of the Protestant Episcopal Church in the Diocese of Central New York*, 41. On Burnham and Pratt, see Burnham to Pratt, July 28, 1879, Box 2, Folder 18, MBP, YCWA, BL.

116. Wicks, "Work in Indian Territory," *Spirit of Missions* (1882): 61.

117. Wicks to Burnham, June 20, 1881, Box 2, Folder 16, MBP, YCWA, BL.

118. Wicks to Burnham, June 27, 1881, Box 2, Folder 16, MBP, YCWA, BL.

119. On calendar entries, see Ware Calendar Quitone Kiowa Calendar. On the agent's observations, see *ARCIA 1881*, 78.

120. Oakerhater to Burnham, September 2, 1881, MBC, OSU.

121. Wicks to Burnham, September 5, 1881, Box 2, Folder 17, MBP, YCWA, BL.

122. See Wicks's constant updates on Zótâm's obedience and service on September 15 and 27, as well as October 10 and 13. Box 2, Folder 17, MBP, YCWA, BL.

123. Wicks to Burnham, October 21, 1881, Box 2, Folder 17, MBP, YCWA, BL; Wicks to Burnham, September 27, 1881, Box 2, Folder 17, MBP, YCWA, BL; Wicks to Burnham, October 28, 1881, Box 2, Folder 17, MBP, YCWA, BL.

124. Calls for severalty were also often paired with an insistence that Indians be granted the same legal rights as other Americans. This claim became increasingly popular around the decision in the 1879 Standing Bear case, but was also connected to reformers' desire to break down tribal affiliations and connections. On reception of the Standing Bear case, see Reilly, *Frontier Newspapers*, 97–110. Among those organizations composed of "friends of the Indian" making calls for severalty already in the late 1870s, see Stimson, *Address on the Indian Question*, 1.

125. AECFIA, "Minute Book," no page number, entry for April 8, 1881, vol. 4.

126. Wicks to Burnham, October 10, 1881, Box 2, Folder 17, MBP, YCWA, BL; Wicks to Burnham, December 1, 1881, Box 2, Folder 17, MBP, YCWA, BL.

127. On Páutépjè's movement, see Mooney, *Calendar History*, 350; Kracht, "Kiowa Religion: An Ethnohistorical Analysis," 739; Kracht, "Kiowa Religion in Historical Perspective," 23. On calendar entries, see Silver Horn, "Ledger Book," 64–9/64, NAMA. As Irwin emphasizes, Native

movements like Páutépjè's aimed at saving Indian communities through innovation, as well as the preservation of "traditional values." See *Coming Down from Above*, 4–8.

128. LaBarre dates the introduction of peyote around 1870. See *The Peyote Cult*, 90. Wiedman and Greene echo this claim. See "Early Kiowa Peyote Ritual and Symbolism," 34. Éttàlyìdònmàui drew a picture of six peyote buttons in a ledger he shared with Koba after they arrived at the Carlisle school in 1879. Koba drew many images in the ledger before returning home to die in September 1880. See Sullivan, *Heritage Auctions American Indian Art Auction Catalog #6029*, 88–94. Kiowas probably had some knowledge of peyote long before they began to integrate it into their own ritual practice. See the story of Crow Neck's peyote shield created around the middle of the nineteenth century. See McCoy, "A Shield To Help You through Life," 78–79.

129. Hail, *Gifts of Pride and Love*, 17–33; Rand, "Primary Sources," 151–53.

130. "R. H. Pratt's List of the Twenty-Seven Kiowa Prisoners at Fort Marion, Florida, 1875 to 1878 and Commented upon by Parker Paul McKenzie," entry on Bad Eye, Box 12, Folder 8, PMP, OHS.

CHAPTER 6

1. Corwin, "The A-Nanthy Odle-Paugh Kiowa Calendar (1975)," 155–156. Bear's Hat was a translation of the Kiowa name Sétbòhon.

2. *ARCIA 1883*, 70.

3. Prucha, *The Great Father*, 211.

4. On children as "privileged media" through which parents and others (in this case, Americans) ascribe religious meaning, see Orsi, *Between Heaven and Earth*, 77.

5. This activity involved significant interaction with federal officials and mirrored a surge in white Protestant efforts to expand government's role in bolstering morality, especially through temperance and anti-vice campaigns. See Foster, *Moral Reconstruction*, 1–3, 73–81.

6. Painter, *Standing at Armageddon*, 8, 164–166; Wood, *Lynching and Spectacle*.

7. Paddison, *American Heathens*, 139–140.

8. Gordon, *The Mormon Question*, 149–154.

9. On the code and its implementation, see Prucha, *Americanizing the American Indian*, 295–305; Prucha, *American Indian Policy in Crisis*, 218–219; Wenger, *We Have a Religion*, 36; Warren, *God's Red Son*, 162–163. On the Kiowa agent, see Guy Quetone, interview by Julia A. Jordan, September 12, 1967, interview T-101, OFLC, M452, Box 5, Folder 2, WHC, OU.

10. Prucha, *The Great Father*, 231.

11. Gordon finds that congressional debate sometimes included explicit comparisons between Mormons and Native Americans, namely the need to break down church relations for the former and tribal relations for the latter. See Gordon, *The Mormon Question*, 204.

12. Hagan, *The Indian Rights Association*.

13. Milner II, "Albert K. Smiley: Friend to Friends of the Indian," 143–176.

14. Adams, *Education for Extinction*, 11–12.

15. Genetin-Pilawa, *Crooked Paths to Allotment*, 112–113, 125.

16. Butler, *Across God's Frontiers*, Chapter 6.

17. Brouillett, *Memoranda Relative to the Rights of Christian Churches on Indian Reservations*, 9.

18. On Catholic officials' efforts to defend Catholic practice among Pueblos, see Wenger, *We Have a Religion*, 20, 48–50.

19. Painter, *Standing at Armageddon*, 10.

20. Meyer, "The Fear of Cultural Decline," 397.

21. Brands, *American Colossus*, 562.

22. *ARCIA 1882*, 64.

23. At least two Kiowa young people traveled from the reservation to enroll in Carlisle in 1879. See Laura Doanmore Student File, RG 75, Series 1327, box 50, folder 2508, NA; Lucius Aitsan Student File, RG 75, Series 1327, Box 15, Folder 729, NA.

24. On 1883, see Mooney, *Calendar History*, 351; Greene, *One Hundred Summers*, 115. On 1884 and 1886, see Mooney, *Calendar History*, 352, 354. On 1887, see Goravits to White, July 3, 1888, Roll 47, "Celebrations and Dances," KAF, OHS; Mooney, *Calendar History*, 355.

25. On ritual peyote ingestion in this period, see *ARCIA 1888*, 98–99; Kracht, "Kiowa Religion in Historical Perspective," 20. On Kiowa oral history about peyote, see James Silverhorn, interview by Julia A. Jordan, June 9, 1967, interview T-19, OFLC, M452, Box 5, Folder 2, WHC, OU; James Silverhorn, interview by Julia A. Jordan, October 3, 1967, interview T-145, OFLC, M452, Box 5, Folder 2, WHC, OU. On Americans' response, see Methvin, *Reminiscences of Life among the Indians*, 176–178.

26. On Catholics, see Cassal, "Missionary Tour in the Chickasaw Nation," 409. On the MECS, see Smith, *Capture These Indians for the Lord*, Chapter 3. On the Baptists, see Smith, "Reminiscences of a Missionary," 12–13; Hicks, "The Kiowa Indians, Baptist Missionary Work, Early Beginnings," unpublished manuscript, Folder 1, GWHC, OHS; Burdette, *Thirty-Two Years' Work among the Indians*, 3–4.

27. *Transporter Supplement* 3:15 (March 25, 1882). The bishop of Arkansas visited in the fall of 1882 and failed to mention Zótâm in his report about missions in the region. See *Journal of the Proceedings of the Eleventh Annual Council*, 15–16.

28. Setkopti, "Diary," January 30, 1879, KDT, Manuscript 2531, Vol. 2, NAA, SI.

29. Setkopti, "Diary," January 3, 1879; March 22, 1879; April 6, 1879; September 23, 1879; October 25, 1879; February 15, 1882.

30. Kracht, "Kiowa Religion: An Ethnohistorical Analysis," 764–770.

31. Mooney, "The Mescal Plant and Ceremony," *Therapeutic Gazette* 12:1 (January 15, 1896): 9. Smith claims that Sétqópjè abandoned Christianity upon his return to the reservation. See *Capture These Indians for the Lord*, 93.

32. Hagan, *Taking Indian Lands*, 5. See also Banner, *How the Indians Lost Their Land*, 258–262.

33. Chang, *The Color of the Land*, 3.

34. Prucha, *The Great Father*, 225; Genetin-Pilawa, *Crooked Paths to Allotment*, 112. Although Ryan writes about an earlier period, reformers involved in Indian affairs in this period also strived for an "ideal personhood" characterized by self-reliant labor. See *The Grammar of Good Intentions*, 78.

35. Banner, *How the Indians Lost Their Land*, 257, 268–269.

36. Prucha, *The Great Father*, 223–224.

37. Cahill, *Federal Fathers and Mothers*, 30–33.

38. Prucha, *The Great Father*, 200.

39. Wicks, *Domestic Missions, Protestant Episcopal Church*, 1–2.

40. Genetin-Pilawa, *Crooked Paths to Allotment*.

41. Adams, *Education for Extinction*, 53.

42. DeMallie, *The Treaty of Medicine Lodge, 1867*, 40.

43. Genetin-Pilawa, *Crooked Paths to Allotment*, 128.

44. Ostler, *Plains Sioux and U.S. Colonialism*, 221.

45. Pommerscheim, *Broken Landscapes*, 129.

46. Battey, "Indian Ideas of Property," *The Day Star* 11:3, Box 1, Folder 4, TBC, OU.

47. *ARCIA 1887*, 83; *ARCIA 1888*, 99; *ARCIA 1889*, 192.

48. *ARCIA 1892*, 385.

49. On the Sioux allotment process, see Prucha, *American Indian Policy in Crisis*, 181. On the process in Oklahoma, see Hagan, *Taking Indian Lands*, 10–17, 82.

50. Smith, *Capture These Indians for the Lord*, 76–78.

51. Kracht, "Kiowa Religion: An Ethnohistorical Analysis," 741.

52. Dowd, *A Spirited Resistance*, xxii; Irwin, *Coming Down from Above*, 188, 293.

53. Kracht, "Kiowa Religion: An Ethnohistorical Analysis," 741–742.

54. On school, see Meadows, *Through Indian Sign Language*, 182. On Methvin, see J. J. Methvin, interview by Lillian Gassoway, December 31, 1937, interview 9536, IPP, WPA, OU. On troops, see Nye, *Carbine and Lance*, 268–270. On the Sun Dance, see Mooney, *Calendar History*, 356; Thomas, "Important History of the Kiowas: Religion and Ceremonies," unpublished manuscript, page 6, Box 62, Folder 6, FWP, OHS. On peyote, see "Order from Special Agent in Charge," June 6, 1888, "Liquor Traffic, Gambling, Peyote/Mescal Use," Roll 50, KAF, OHS; *ARCIA 1888*, 98–99.

55. On Givens's schooling, see Hagan, "Joshua Given: Kiowa Indian and Carlisle Alumnus," 17. On his education and consideration for ordination, see Carlisle Presbytery, "Minutes, 1883–1889," PHS.

56. John Jasper Methvin, "Autobiography," Chapter 17, MS 3195, HRBML.

57. Mooney, *Calendar History*, 355–359; Greene, *One Hundred Summers*, 121–127, 218.

58. Methvin, "Autobiography," 107; Smith, *Capture These Indians for the Lord*, 87.

59. Methvin, "Autobiography," 110. Methvin's number of Indian church members went from fifteen in 1889 to thirty by the fall of 1890. See *Minutes of the Annual Conference*, 125–127.

60. This is the same Páutáuljè (Lean Bison Bull) that the Methodists claimed to have made "Poor Buffalo's request" for missionaries.

61. On the Kiowa delegation, see Mooney, *The Ghost-Dance Religion and Wounded Knee*, 907; Murray, "Messenger to Wovoka: Apiatan," Box 62, Folder 6, FWP, OHS. For the specific guidelines scholars have offered, see Ostler, *The Plains Sioux and U.S. Colonialism*, 1–5; Warren, *God's Red Son*, 8, 170. Scholarship on the Ghost Dance includes Andersson, *The Lakota Dance of 1890*; DeMallie, "The Lakota Ghost Dance"; Kracht, "The Kiowa Ghost Dance"; Overholt, "The Ghost Dance of 1890"; Moses, "'The Father Tells Me So'"; Clow, "Lakota Ghost Dance after 1890"; Smoak, *Ghost Dances and Identity*; Martin, "Before and Beyond the Sioux Ghost Dance"; Warren, *God's Red Son*.

62. Focusing on the innovations brought to the Ghost Dance movement by each Indian nation can help us see the particular needs the practice addressed, as well as avoid some of the pitfalls of relying on documentary sources provided only by white Americans. I thank Michelene Pessantubbee for her helpful counsel on this question. Thanks, also, to Bill Meadows for his advice on Kiowa terms for the dance.

63. On the practice, see Murray, "Messenger to Wovoka"; Kracht, "The Kiowa Ghost Dance, 1894–1916," 460. On calendar entries, see Quitone Kiowa Calendar.

64. Scott, "Some Memories of a Soldier," Box 59, Folder 26, FWP, OHS.

65. Reilly, *The Frontier Newspapers and the Coverage of the Plains Indian Wars*, 111–128; Coward, *The Newspaper Indian*, 159–195.

66. Bureau of Indian Affairs Acting Commissioner to KCA Agent, November 22, 1890, Roll 47, "Celebrations and Dances," KAF, OHS.

67. Deers to Adams, December 29, 1890, Roll 47, "Celebrations and Dances," KAF, OHS.

68. Fort Sill Commander to Adams, late 1890 (exact date illegible), Roll 50, "Churches," KAF, OHS.

69. Untitled article, *Fayetteville Observer* (January 1, 1891).

70. Scott, *Some Memoires of a Soldier*, Part 2.

71. Kracht, "Kiowa Religion in Historical Perspective," 20; Warren, *God's Red Son*, 264.

72. Richardson, *Wounded Knee*, 1–18.

73. On Wovoka, see Warren, *God's Red Son*, 297–298. On Ấ fĭt̖u and other Kiowas' responses, see Apiatan to Adams, January 26, 1891, Roll 50, "Churches," KAF, OHS; Kracht, "The Kiowa Ghost Dance," 459; Warren, *God's Red Son*, 307–308.

74. For schooling statistics, see Adams, *Education for Extinction*, 27. On Kiowa schooling on reservation and off, see *ARCIA 1880*, 71, 75; *ARCIA 1884*, 81.

75. "An Indian Entertainment," *Christian Union* (February 10, 1887). Givens began giving speeches at Pratt events as early as 1881. See "Indian Pupils from Carlisle," *Friends' Intelligencer*, May 7, 1881. Givens also spoke at denominational and mission society gatherings. See "Women's Committee of Home Missions," *New York Evangelist* (June 7, 1888); "A Million for Missions: The American Missionary Association at Providence," *Christian Union* (November 1, 1888); Untitled article, *Christian Secretary* (December 25, 1889): 1.

76. "Indians at School: Glimpses of the Establishment at Carlisle, PA," *Wichita Daily Eagle* (July 2, 1887).

77. *ARCIA 1891*, 485. This is, of course, the Daniel Dorchester who went on to write several books on American church history.

78. Adams, *Education for Extinction*, 19, 143, 146.

79. Adams, *Education for Extinction*, 23, 30.

80. On parents' close proximity to and oversight of children in school, see *ARCIA 1888*, 97; *ARCIA 1889*, 189; *ARCIA 1890*, 188; McBeth, "Indian Boarding Schools and Ethnic Identity," 124; Greene, *One Hundred Summers*, 133–134. One boarding school student recalls that visiting parents brought Kiowa food for their children. See LaBarre, "Autobiography of a Kiowa Indian," 47. On students during V̨au̧igài's movement, see J. J. Methvin, interview by Lillian Gassoway, December 31, 1937, interview #9536, IPP, WPA, OU; *ARCIA 1887*, 81. On students during the Ghost Dance, see *ARCIA 1891*, 351. On the recalled student, see Belo Cozad Student File, RG 75, Series 1327, Box 15, Folder 733, NA. Belo's father was Fįqí, a leader among the Feather Dancers.

81. Fait, "An Autobiography," 190–191.

82. Methvin, "Measles Epidemic," 135, Box 59, Folder 16, FWP, OHS; Mooney, *Calendar History*, 223.

83. Methvin, "Measles Epidemic"; John Jasper Methvin, "Autobiography," 69.

84. Methvin, "Measles Epidemic"; Mooney, *Calendar History*, 223.

85. John Jasper Methvin, "Autobiography," 71–72.

86. Acting Commissioner to Agent, May 13, 1892, Roll 50, "Ghost Dance," KAF, OHS.

87. *ARCIA 1892*, 386.

88. Wilkins and Lomawaima claim that Congress's allotment legislation was an unprecedented example of exercising its plenary power in an unlimited or absolute fashion. See *Uneven Ground*, 98–108.

89. JC, September 26, 1892, KAF, OHS.

90. JC, September 26, 1892, KAF, OHS.

91. JC, September 28, 1892, KAF, OHS.

92. JC, October 3, 1892, KAF, OHS.

93. JC, October 6, 1892, KAF, OHS, 88–89.

94. JC, October 11, 1892, KAF, OHS, 101.

95. Klassen, "Spiritual Jurisdictions."

96. JC, October 14, 1892, 106.

97. JC, October 15, 1892, 125; JC, October 17, 1892, 129–131. Pommerscheim chronicles the commissioners' efforts to secure the agreement's ratification in Washington, D.C. See *Broken Landscapes*, 132–134.

98. Smith, *Capture These Indians for the Lord*, 95.

99. On Methvin's involvement, see Methvin to Day, October 20, 1892, Roll 50, "Churches," KAF, OHS; John Jasper Methvin, "Autobiography," 123, 142–143.

100. For councils in 1897 and 1899, see Greene, *One Hundred Summers*, 140–143; Silver Horn Pictorial Calendar, MS 2531, Vol. 7, NAA, SI. On delegations, see Stokely, "Black Bear's Calendar," 357.

101. On early Baptist activity with Lone Wolf and other Kiowas, see Hicks, Diary, June 1, 1892, Folder 1, GWHC, OHS; Burdette, *Young Women among Blanket Indians*, 4, 12; Smith, "Reminiscences of a Missionary among South-West Wild Indians," 12–13; Burdette, *Thirty-Two Years' Work among Indians*, 4–5.

102. Haffner, "Annals of Sacred Heart Abbey," 33–35, ASGA; Murphy, *Tenacious Monks*, 226–231.

103. Fossey and Morris, "St. Katharine Drexel and St. Patrick's Mission to the Indians of the Southern Plains," 66.

104. Hitta, "Historical Sketch of the Anadarko Boarding School," 38, contained in Mrs. H. C. Rooney, interview by Lillian Gassoway, November 29, 1933, interview 9318, IPP, WPA, WHC, UO.

105. Untitled article, *Indian Advocate* (1888): 2; "Saint Benedict and the Christian Civilization in the Old World," *Indian Advocate* 1, no. 1 (January 1889).

106. "Saint Benedict and the Christian Civilization in the Old World," *Indian Advocate* 1:1 (January 1889).

107. Moses, *The Indian Man*, 61.

108. Wiedman and Greene, "Early Kiowa Peyote Ritual and Symbolism"; Greene, *Silver Horn*, 64–65.

109. On the agent's concern, see *ARCIA 1891*, 351; *ARCIA 1892*, 376. On Mooney's visit, see Warren, *God's Red Son*, 321. On Cheyenne and Arapaho dancing, see Warren, *God's Red Son*, 309–311. On Fíqi's participation in the Feather Dance, see Kracht, "Kiowa Religion: An Ethnohistorical Analysis," 799–800; Warren, *God's Red Son*, 348.

110. Warren says some Ghost Dancers understood Wovoka's promised "messiah" to be Jesus, while others conceived of the messianic figure at the movement's center differently. See *God's Red Son*, 208, 262–263.

III. Greene, *Silver Horn*, 110–111. Kracht notes that the end of warfare and raiding also affected Sun Dance practice. Men had fewer reasons to make vows. Further, the end of warfare meant the decline of the buffalo doctors' activity, which had been focused on healing fighters. See "Kiowa Religion: An Ethnohistorical Analysis," 728–732.

112. Gordon, *The Mormon Question*, 220.

113. Blum, *Reforging the White Republic*.

114. Paddison, *American Heathens*.

CHAPTER 7

1. Blum, *Reforging the White Republic*, 217–218; Painter, *Standing at Armageddon*, xxx; Ngai, "Race, Nation, and Citizenship," 324. Fluhman notes how expositions and fairs in the 1890s hosted both representations of the country's diversity along with restrictions on how cultures and traditions could be represented. See *A Peculiar People*, 129–133.

2. Jacobson, *Barbarian Virtues*, 61; Painter, *Standing at Armageddon*, 164–166; Brands, *American Colossus*, 465.

3. Jacobson, *Barbarian Virtues*, 4–7, 96–97.

4. Painter, *Standing at Armageddon*, 142–154; Brands, *American Colossus*, 566, 573; Blum, *Reforging the White Republic*, 212–213, 220–222, 243; Tyrrell, *Reforming the World*, 2–7; McCullough, *The Cross of War*, 3–6.

5. Hoxie, *A Final Promise*, xi–xiv.

6. Citizenship would not be granted immediately, however, to those who accepted allotments. There was a twenty-five-year waiting period. See Banner, *How the Indians Lost Their Land*, 277–278.

7. *Proceedings of the Eleventh Annual Meeting of the Lake Mohonk Conference of Friends of the Indian*, 87.

8. On the connection between assimilation through education and land dispossession, see Jacobs, *White Mother to a Dark Race*, xxx.

9. *Proceedings of the Tenth Annual Meeting of the Lake Mohonk Conference of Friends of the Indian*, 51–53. For more on Morgan's approach to schooling while the head of the Indian office, see Ellis, *To Change Them Forever*, 10–16.

10. Protestants' concern about Catholic reservation schools was connected to their worries about parochial school expansion across the nation. By 1895, Catholics ran 4,000 schools and enrolled more 750,000 children. See McGreevy, *Catholicism and American Freedom*, 114. Many of these schools relied on federal contributions, which had grown from $54,000 in 1883 to $394,533 in 1889. See McKevitt, *Brokers of Culture*, 155.

11. *The Bureau of Catholic Indian Missions, 1874 to 1895*, 18. The Apostolic Prefect of Indian Territory, like many Protestant "friends of the Indian," preferred boarding to day schools. See Meerschart to Drexel, February 25, 1892, H10B, Box 37, Folder 17, ASBS.

12. *Proceedings of the Eleventh Annual Meeting of the Lake Mohonk Conference of Friends of the Indian*, 73–75.

13. *Proceedings of the Twelfth Annual Meeting of the Lake Mohonk Conference of Friends of the Indian*, 138. Protestant "friends of the Indian" with strong ties to the federal Indian office published several works against Catholic Indian schools. See Morgan, *Roman Catholics and Indian Education*, and Dorchester, *Romanism versus the Public School System*. Wenger also discusses Morgan and Dorchester's efforts; see *We Have a Religion*, 50.

14. Gibbons to unnamed bishop, December 5, 1898, Bureau of Indian Missions folder, AAOC.

15. *The Bureau of Catholic Indian Missions, 1874 to 1895*, 8, 18, 30–31. On bias and persecution, also see Stephan, *Crusade against the Catholic Schools*, 1–4; Stephan, *Report of the Bureau of Catholic Indian Missions for the Year Ending October 1, 1898*, 1–9; Stephan, *Brief of Objections to Certain Proposed Enactments*, 1–4.

16. *The Bureau of Catholic Indian Missions, 1874 to 1895*, 18. On Drexel's career funding missions and schools for both Native Americans and African Americans, see Bresie, "Mother Katharine Drexel's Benevolent Empire," 1–24.

17. *Petition of James Cardinal Gibbons*, 1, 5. McKevitt also observed a shift from a catechetical focus in earlier decades to an educational focus later, making Catholic missions likelier to lead to assimilation and Americanization. See *Brokers of Culture*, 149.

18. *Proceedings of the Tenth Annual Meeting of the Lake Mohonk Conference of Friends of the Indian*, 62–63. King represented the National League for the Protection of American Institutions, an organization founded in 1889 that promoted separation of church and state as Catholic institutions garnered more public resources.

19. LaBarre gathered details about the spread of Kiowa peyote rites, especially stories of people seeking healing. See "Autobiography of a Kiowa Indian," 11–15, 24–32, 160–179.

20. On these missions, see Burdette, *Thirty-Two Years' Work among Indians*; Burdette, *A Trip through Indian Country*; and Lassiter, Ellis, and Kotay, *The Jesus Road*.

21. On the Baptist missions, see Hicks, "The Kiowa Indians," Folder 1, GWHC, OHS. On Crawford's career, see Whiteley, *The Life of Isabel Crawford*. On the Baptist women missionaries among the Kiowa, see Williams Reese, *Women of Oklahoma*, Chapter 5.

22. In 1892, Methvin served two circuits on the reservation and counted about 16 whites and 65 Indians in his churches. See *Minutes of the Annual Conference*, 158–162. By 1901, at least four men served the circuits on the former KCA Reservation and the membership and attendance had grown substantially. See *Minutes of the Annual Conference*, 80–83. One of the house churches Methvin initiated was led by Cáukì (Ten) and his wife. This community eventually became the Cedar Creek Methodist Mission. The community kept what has been called the Gaukein (or Gaukey) calendar. See "Gaukey Kiowa Calendar," ASSNAA, Box 1, Folder 19, DRC, NCWHM. On the Methodist missions, see Smith, *Capture These Indians for the Lord*.

23. Hume, "Church History: Part 1," MS1028, PHS; McAfee, *Missions among the North American Indians*, 49.

24. "Annals of Sacred Heart Abbey," 33, ASGA; De Hasque, *St. Patrick's Indian Mission of Anadarko*, 5–17.

25. Comanche and Kiowa efforts to teach Ricklin sign language are commemorated in murals painted by Kiowa artists in the early twentieth century. See "Kiowa Indian Memorial Paintings," Box 59, Folder 11, FWP, OHS.

26. Enrollments were high by the mid-1890s. St. Patrick's mission records also show the baptism, confirmations, and first communions of students from Kiowa families, including surnames such as Goonaii, Tighkobo, Moore, Paddlety (spelled Podlltay), Tannedooah (spelled Tenedaw), Ohetoint (spelled Ointoint), Apiatan (spelled Ahpeahtone), Frizzlehead, and Twohatchet. See "Ledger for St. Patrick's Mission School," ASGA. See also "History of St. Patrick's Mission," 13-A, Box 2, Folder 9, ASSF.

27. "Minutes of the Session of the Presbyterian Church at Anadarko, Indian Territory," page 1, Box 1, APCR, PHS.

28. "Church Register of the Presbyterian Church at Anadarko, Indian Territory," page 136, 138, Box 1, APCR, PHS.

29. Sister Aemiliana to Drexel, October 25, 1892, H10B1, Folder 5, ASBS. Mooney observed Ricklin and the sisters' attention to medical concerns during his visit in September 1893. See Mooney, "Home Life among the Kiowas," *Friends' Intelligencer*, January 6, 1894.

30. Ricklin to Drexel, December 29, 1892, H10B, Folder 20, ASBS.

31. Burdette, *Young Women among Blanket Indians*, 59.

32. Crawford, *From Tent to Chapel at Saddle Mountain*, 53. According to Whiteley, more than 500 Indians attended the meeting. See *The Life of Isabel Crawford*, 73.

33. Methvin, *Andele*, 119–120, 132.

34. Hicks, "The Kiowa Indians." We know that Paddlety continued his relationship with the Baptists for many years. Lauretta Ballew mentioned him in a 1907 letter updating the federal Indian office on the work of the Red Stone Baptist mission. According to Ballew, Paddlety wanted to see "Ghost-medicine-men," or leaders of the Ghost Dance movement. See Reeside to name illegible, May 9, 1907, Roll 50, "Ghost Dance," KAF, OHS.

35. Burdette, *Young Women among Blanket Indians*, Chapter 7; Burdette, *Thirty-Two Years' Work among Indians*, 6.

36. Ellis, "Introduction," in Crawford, *Kiowa*, xiii.

37. Crawford, *Kiowa*, 13–14, 19–20. According to church records, Zótâm was baptized again in November 1895. See "Rainy Mountain Baptist Church Report," PMP, Box 12, Folder 11, OHS. Several Episcopal sources list that his bishop deposed him as early as 1888. See *Journal of the Second Annual Council*, 54; *Journal of the Proceedings of the Eighteenth Annual Council*, 36–37. Other sources listed him as retired. See *Annual Report of the Board of Missions*, 38. One account, however, states that Zotom renounced his ministry in writing. See *Journal of the Proceedings of the Annual Convention*, 108. Unfortunately, I was unable to verify this letter.

38. Methvin, *Andele*, 116–121.

39. Julia Given card file, RG 75, Series 1327, Box 50, Folder 2509, NA. Julia's brother was Joshua Givens, the boarding school student, licensed Presbyterian preacher, and translator.

40. Crawford, *Kiowa*, 36.

41. Lucius Aitsan card file, RG 75, Series 1327, Box 15, Folder 729, NA. Kracht offers some additional explanations for Kiowa affiliation with Christian missions, including that the power of the Christian God and Jesus was more readily available to a wider range of people, avoiding some of the restrictions associated with gaining power through vision or inheritance. See "Kiowa Religion: An Ethnohistorical Analysis," 700.

42. On preferences for on-reservation schools, see the petition for a Presbyterian school, July 1895, Roll 50, "Churches," KAF, OHS; *ARCIA 1895*, 250–252; *ARCIA 1896*, 254, 256; *ARCIA 1897*, 233; Utley, "Introduction," in Pratt, *Battlefield and Classroom*, xiii; Ellis, *To Change Them Forever*, 39–40. On examples of resistance to American officials' directives about school location, breaks, and enrollment age, see Cassel to Father Stephan, ca. 1889, H10B13, Folder 20, ASBS; *ARCIA, 1895*, 252, 254; *ARCIA, 1896*, 257; *ARCIA, 1897*, 236; Adams, *Education for Extinction*, 63. On Kiowa camps near schools, see Greene, *One Hundred Summers*, 133–134.

43. On concerns about secular schools, see Aemiliana to Drexel, September 25, 1891, H10B1, Folder 5, ASBS. On Catholic missionaries' fear about Protestant sabotage, see Ricklin to Drexel, January 26, 1892, H10B 47, Folder 20, ASBS; Ricklin to Drexel, October 27, 1893, H10B 47, Folder 20, ASBS; Aemiliana to Drexel, November 30, 1893, H10B1, Folder 5, ASBS; Aemiliana to

Drexel, January 8, 1897, H10B1, Folder 5, ASBS. Their fears were not unfounded. Methvin, especially, tried to dissuade Indians from attending St. Patrick's. See Smith, *Capture These Indians for the Lord*, 113–114.

44. KCA children persisted in using Native languages. Federal officials wrote to the agent demanding that teachers monitor children's use of English outside of classroom hours. See Morgan to Day, April 15, 1892, Box 13, Folder 4, PMP, OHS.

45. Whiteley, *The Life of Isabel Crawford*, 65.

46. "Hard Work Crowned with Success – Indian Boarding School – Dedicated – Father Isidore's Letter," *Indian Advocate* (January 1, 1893): 2.

47. Hill, "Indian Progress," *New York Evangelist* (March 19, 1896): 33.

48. Burdette, *Young Women among Blanket Indians*, 16.

49. Seeman, "Reading Indians' Deathbed Scenes," 17–47.

50. Meadows and Harragarra, "The Kiowa Drawings of Gotebo," 229–244. Missionaries Reeside and Clouse attested to Gotebo's baptism. See Burdette, *Young Women among Blanket Indians*, 21; Clouse, "Rainy Mountain," undated pamphlet, Box 12, Folder 11, PMP, OHS.

51. One scholar says efforts such as the minister's "constitute a literary reduction, abduction, and captivity" in that they "estrange the Native convert . . . from the spiritual and political roots of his or her own world." See Palmer, "The Devil in the Details," 268.

52. Meadows, *Kiowa Military Societies*, 267.

53. On Qódèbǫ̀hòn's church-related activities, see Burdette, *Young Women among Blanket Indians*, 46; "First Centennial of the Rainy Mountain Kiowa Baptist Church," January 20, 1993, Box 12, Folder 11, PMP, OHS.

54. Crawford, *Kiowa*, 61–62, 139.

55. Seeman, "Reading Indians' Deathbed Scenes," 17–47.

56. Burdette, *Young Women among Blanket Indians*, 60.

57. Crawford, *Kiowa*, 81–82.

58. Crawford, *From Tent to Chapel*, 36–37. See also Jenny Horse, interview with Julia A. Jordan, September 18, 1868, interview T-329, OFLC, M452, Box 5, Folder 2.

59. Crawford, *Kiowa*, 57–61. Whiteley recounts another story with a similar outcome; see *The Life of Isabel Crawford*, 62.

60. Gaukey calendar, PPHM; "Calendar Consultation," PPHM. Other Kiowa calendars, as well as American sources, note the 1892 measles outbreak. See Mooney, *Calendar History*, 223.

61. Greene, *One Hundred Summers*, 140–141.

62. Many Americans mistakenly referred to peyote as mescal, another natural substance that some indigenous people in the Texas-Mexico borderlands ingested.

63. Their efforts were aided by one of the Comanches' leading peyote practitioners, Quanah Parker, who held a seat on the reservation's Court of Indian Offenses.

64. Meadows, *Through Indian Sign Language*, 213–216. For another account of a typical Kiowa peyote meeting, see LaBarre, *The Peyote Cult*, 43–53. See also Niezen's argument that ritual peyote practices on the southern plains must be understood within their colonial context, including threats to Native lands. See Niezen, *Spirit Wars*, Chapter 5.

65. Silverhorn, Military Target Record Book, MS 4252, NAA, SI; Silver Horn Pictorial Calendar. See also Greene, *Silver Horn*, 42.

66. LaBarre, "Autobiography of a Kiowa Indian," 24, 160; Alice Apekaum Zanella, interview by David Jones, October 7, 1967, interview T-177-2, Box 5, Folder 2, M452, OFLC, WHC, UO;

Cecil Horse, interview by Julia Jordan, June 13, 1967, interview T-27, Box 5, Folder 2, M452, OFLC, WHC, UO; Annie Bigman, interview by David Jones, June 14, 1967, interview M-1, Box 5, Folder 2, M452, OFLC, WHC, UO.

67. On Methvin, see *History of Anadarko Presbyterian Church*, 32; Methvin, "Reminiscences of Life among the Indians," 178; John Jasper Methvin, "Autobiography," 94, MS 3195, HRBML; Methvin, *In the Limelight*, 68–70. On the agent's meeting, see Crawford, *From Tent to Chapel*, 7. On denominational papers and outlets, see untitled article, *New York Evangelist* (October 14, 1897): 31; Burdette, *Young Women among Blanket Indians*, 47–48; Proper, *The Gospel among the Blanket Indians*, 10–14; Crawford, *Kiowa*, 120–121, 160; Crawford, *From Tent to Chapel*, 30. I have found one source that documents the story of Kiowa Christians confronting both peyote practitioners and Feather Dancers. See Aitsan to Walker, October 31, 1898, AASNAA, Box 5, Folder 12, DRC NCWHM.

68. On the resurgent Ghost Dance/Feather Dance, see Mooney, *The Ghost Dance Religion and Wounded Knee*, 914; Kracht, "The Kiowa Ghost Dance," 459–461. Kiowa calendars also record Feather Dance activities in 1894 and after. See Quitone Kiowa Calendar, MS 2002-27, NAA, SI; entries for 1895 and 1898 in Silver Horn Pictorial Calendar. Black Bear's entry for summers of calendar pages A29, A31, A37, Stokely, "Black Bear's Calendar," 356–358. On Feather Dancing as a form of political opposition, see Warren, *God's Red Son*, 360–361. On Feather Dance practices, see James Silverhorn, interview by Julia A. Jordan, June 6, 1969, interview T-18, Box 5, Folder 2, M452, OFLC, WHC, UO; Guy Quetone, interview by Julia A. Jordan, March 30, 1971, interview T-638, page 13, Box 5, Folder 2, M452, OFLC, WHC, UO. On American concern, see sender illegible to Lieutenant Maury Nichols, August 23, 1894, Roll 47B, "Celebrations," KAF, OHS.

69. Quitone Kiowa Calendar; Gawkey calendar; Carrithers, untitled article, *Reformed Presbyterian and Covenanter* 30, no. 1 (January 1892): 14. Unfortunately, I cannot confirm if these references are to dances held in Kiowa camps or those held by other Indian nations, such as the Cheyenne and Arapaho, who also danced in this period and hosted some Kiowa participants.

70. Reeside to Baldwin, November 19, 1895, Roll 47B, "Celebrations," KAF, OHS.

71. Illegible to Lieutenant Maury Nichols, August 23, 1894, Roll 47 B, "Celebrations," KAF, OHS; Ballew to Baldwin, July 22, 1895, Roll 47B, "Celebrations," KAF, OHS; Clouse to Baldwin, June 26, 1897, Roll 50, "Churches," KAF, OHS.

72. Baldwin to Commanding Officer, September 26, 1895, Roll 47B, "Celebrations," KAF, OHS.

73. Crawford, *Kiowa*, 27–28; Whiteley, *The Life of Isabel Crawford*, 70. Other Baptist sources offered dramatic and negative descriptions of the Feather Dancers, including a comparison of their chants with "the howling of a pack of hungry coyotes." See Burdette, *Thirty-Two Years' Work among Indians*, 21.

74. Big Tree to Baldwin, April 19, 1896, Roll 47B, "Celebrations," KAF, OHS. Á dàuiétjè (Big Tree), along with Chálkôgái (Black Goose), Cûifãgàui (Lone Wolf), and Cómàjè (Friendship Tree) followed up this letter a month later, expressing their disappointment that the agent had not acted. See Big Tree to Baldwin, May 29, 1896, Roll 47B, "Celebrations," KAF, OHS.

75. Crawford, *Kiowa*, 102.

76. LaBarre, "Autobiography of a Kiowa Indian," 159–160.

77. Crawford, *Kiowa*, 91.

78. Kracht, "Kiowa Religion in Historical Perspective," 643–644, 704.

79. Jacobs, *White Mother to a Dark Race*, 10–11.

80. Tyrrell, *Reforming the World*, 2–7.

81. On international lessons, see LIM Minute Book, entries for December 28, 1889; February 7, 1891; May 16, 1891; March 12, 1892; February 4, 1893; February 15, 1896; February 1899; December 16, 1899; and March 25, 1900; Ladies Industrial Mission (LIM), Box 2, APCR, PHS. On lessons on domestic populations, see LIM Minute Book, entries for February 7, 1891; February 18, 1893; February 16, 1895; April 13, 1895; February 15, 1896; April 1896; April 1898; November 12, 1898; April 13, 1901; February 18, 1902; and August 22, 1902.

82. On LIM discussions of Mormons, see LIM Minute Book, entries for May 16, 1896; October 12, 1901; and November 23, 1901. On concerns about Catholics, see LIM Minute Book, entries for November 12, 1898; January 21, 1899; 17 November 17, 1900; and November 28, 1902. On the Spanish-American War, see LIM Minute Book, entries for September 1898 and January 20, 1900. On China, see LIM Minute Book, entry for February 24, 1900; February 27, 1903.

83. The committee was officially called the Cherokee Commission.

84. Hoxie, *A Final Promise*, 154–155.

85. Hagan, "Kiowas, Comanches, and Cattlemen, 1867–1906," 333–355.

86. Crawford, *Kiowa: A Woman Missionary in Indian Territory*, 117.

87. Mooney, "Home Life among the Kiowas," *Friends' Intelligencer* (4 January 1894): 14.

88. On the petitions, see US Congress, Senate, *Kiowa, Comanche, and Apache Memorial*, March 1, 1894, 53rd Congress, 2nd session, 1894. S. Misc. Doc. 102, 1–2; US Congress, Senate, *Memorial from the Kiowa, Comanche, and Apache Indian Tribes*, January 15, 1900, 56th Congress, 1st session, 1900. S. Doc. 76; Hoover, *A Developing Resistance*, 40–41. On school enrollments, see Ellis, *To Change Them Forever*, 98. Pommersheim notes that many Indian nations sent anti-allotment petitions to Congress and registered other forms of dissent to the process. See *Broken Landscapes*, 128.

89. Meadows, *Through Indian Sign Language*, 68.

90. On Zépcàuiétjè (Big Bow), see "Big Bow," undated pamphlet, Box 11, Folder 3, PMP, OHS; Rairden, *Our Work among the Kiowa Indians*, 18. On Delos Lonewolf, see Williams Reese, *Women of Oklahoma*, 140.

91. US Congress, Senate, *Kiowa, Comanche, and Apache Memorial*, 9–11.

92. Similarly, there is some evidence that Feather Dancers supported their children's attendance at government or mission schools. In 1905, Ádàuiétjè (Big Tree) informed the KCA agent that he was attending a Feather Dance and would tell everyone there to send their children to school. See Ellis, *To Change Them Forever*, 97. Historians have found that other Indian nations, namely the Pawnee, included Ghost Dancers who also fought allotment and land runs. See Warren, *God's Red Son*, 369–370.

93. US Congress, Senate, *Kiowa, Comanche, and Apache Memorial*, 8–11. The petitioners also include other known peyote practitioners, including Áisèáuidè (Many Camp Smokes), Thę́néàungópjè (Kicking Bird the Younger), Hą́ugú (Silver Horn), Ádàuiétjè (Big Tree), Black Bear, and Zǫ́tâm (Driftwood).

94. Several Kiowas with mission affiliations signed the 1893 petition against the Jerome Agreement, including Ándálé̜, Cáukị̧ (Ten), Lucius Aitsan (Etsanti), and Ôlpàu (Bison Bird). See US Congress, Senate, *Kiowa, Comanche, and Apache Memorial*, 9–11.

95. Crawford, *Kiowa*, 64–65.

96. On the strategic purchase of land by Native communities under threat, see Kantrowitz, " 'Not Quite Constitutionalized,' " 75–105.

97. Crawford, *From Tent to Chapel*, 53; Crawford, *Kiowa*, 102–103, 153–154.

98. One of the most important episodes of factionalism occurred around the decision to pursue a legal battle against allotment even after the Jerome Agreement was ratified.

99. "Home Mission Exercise: The Indians," RG 305, Box 29, Folder 13, WEC/WBHM, PHS. This pamphlet was authored by Mrs. Thomas Jefferson Morgan, one of the most prominent Protestant "friends of the Indian" and an employee of the federal Indian Office. For other articles in denominational and evangelical periodicals, see Hill, "Indian Progress," *New York Evangelist* (March 19, 1896): 33.

100. *Proceedings of the Tenth Annual Meeting*, 121; *Proceedings of the Eleventh Annual Meeting*, 143; *Proceedings of the Twelfth Annual Meeting*, 27; *Proceedings of the Thirteenth Annual Meeting*, 105–106; *Proceedings of the Fifteenth Annual Meeting*, 115.

101. Abing, "Directors of the Bureau of Catholic Indian Missions," 2. Reverend Joseph A. Stephan, 1884–1901, Marquette University, July 9, 2017, http://www.marquette.edu/library/archives/Mss/BCIM/BCIM-SC1-directors2.pdf.

102. McKevitt, *Brokers of Culture*, 137.

103. Pommersheim, *Broken Landscapes*, 135. On Congress sending a negotiator, see Hoover, "A Developing Resistance," 55.

104. *ARCIA 1901*, 321–322. He reported similar things the next year.

105. *ARCIA 1901*, 326. It was hardly unusual for students like Pedrick to return from off-reservation boarding school and find employment on the agency or in the schools. See Ahern, "An Experiment Aborted," 263.

106. Crawford, *Kiowa*, 129, 133–134.

107. *The Oklahoma Opportunity*, 3–5, 13–15. The total available land was actually two million acres. This promotion of Indian lands available for farming is especially ironic given the 1890s economic crash and its disastrous effect on farmers nationwide. See Painter, *Standing at Armageddon*, xvii, 116–117, 125.

108. *ARCIA, 1895*, 254; *ARCIA 1899*, 289; *ARCIA 1900*, 334.

109. Blue Clark, *Lone Wolf v. Hitchcock*, 57. Cûifǎgàui (Lone Wolf the Younger) also appeared at mission conferences during the allotment struggle. See Newman, "Northern Baptist Anniversaries: Second Week," *The Independent* (June 2, 1898): 18.

110. "Opening of the Indian Lands," *The Independent* (June 6, 1901).

111. Pommerscheim, *Broken Landscapes*, 135.

112. "Silver Horn Pictorial Calendar;" Stokely, "Black Bear's Calendar," 359.

113. On Puerto Rico, see LIM Minute Book, entries for June 18, 1901, and June 23, 1902. On Mormons, see LIM Minute Book, entries for October 12, 1901, and November 23, 1901. On immigrants, see LIM Minute Book, entries for August 22, 1902, and November 28, 1902.

114. On the end of the "Indian problem" and need to turn toward new populations in imperial settings, see *Proceedings of the Twenty-first Annual Meeting of the Lake Mohonk Conference*, 26–31, 40–43, 81–85, 112, 116.

115. Pommerscheim, *Broken Landscapes*, 136–138. Wilkins and Lomawaima write that the court's argument that Congress had always exercised absolute plenary power over Indian nations was a "fiction." See *Uneven Ground*, 110–116.

116. "Providential Hinges," *Baptist Home Mission Monthly* 26, no. 9 (September 1904): 318.

117. Bowerman, "The Religious Significance of the Louisiana Purchase," *Baptist Home Mission Monthly* 26, no. 9 (September 1904): 322–323.

118. "The American Indian: An Object Lesson," *Baptist Home Mission Monthly* 26, no. 9 (September 1904): 336. This celebration of the frontier continued in other Baptist materials. See Masters, *Southern Baptists and the Frontier*, 1909.

119. "For the Junior Meeting: Kiowa Indian Mission," *Baptist Home Mission Monthly* 26, no. 9 (September 1904): 348.

120. Crawford, *Kiowa*, 213, 222–223.

121. Colonel Pratt saw the letter while Cozad was a student at Carlisle. Pratt later sent the letter back to the reservation so that Cozad could translate it. Cozad discussed the letter with ethnologist James Mooney, who then sent information about the letter and a line-by-line "translation" to Pratt. See Pratt to Mallery, May 6, 1891, ASSNAA, Box 82, Folder 19, DRC NCWHM; Mooney to Pratt, undated, ASSNAA, Box 82, Folder 19, DRC NCWHM; Mooney to Pratt, May 11, 1891, ASSNAA, Box 82, Folder 19, DRC NCWHM; Mooney to Pratt, May 13, 1891, ASSNAA, Box 82, Folder 19, DRC NCWHM. For Cozad's period at Carlisle, see Belo Cozad student file, RG 75, Series 1327, Box 15, Folder 733, NA. On the importance of using Indian sources created by and for boarding school students, see Szabo, "Drawing Life's Changes," 41–51.

BIBLIOGRAPHY

⌒

ARCHIVES

Archives of the Archdiocese of Oklahoma City, Oklahoma City, Oklahoma
Archives of the Episcopal Church, Austin, Texas
Archives of the Sisters of the Blessed Sacrament, Bensalem, Pennsylvania
Archives of the Sisters of Saint Francis of Philadelphia, Aston, Pennsylvania
Archives and Special Collections, Dulaney-Brown Library, Oklahoma City University, Oklahoma City, Oklahoma
Archives of St. Gregory's Abbey, Shawnee, Oklahoma
Beinecke Rare Book and Manuscript Library, Yale University, New Haven, Connecticut
Dickinson Research Center, National Cowboy and Western Heritage Museum, Oklahoma City, Oklahoma
Gilcrease Museum, Tulsa, Oklahoma
Hargrett Rare Book and Manuscript Library, The University of Georgia Libraries, Athens, Georgia
Haverford College, Quaker and Special Collections, Haverford, Pennsylvania
Huntington Library, San Marino, California
Missouri History Museum, St. Louis, Missouri
Museum of the Great Plains, Special Collections, Lawton, Oklahoma
National Anthropological Archives, Smithsonian Institution, Suitland, Maryland
National Archives and Records Administration, Washington, DC
Oklahoma Historical Society Research Center, Oklahoma City, Oklahoma
Panhandle-Plains Historical Museum, Canyon, Texas

Presbyterian Historical Society, Philadelphia, Pennsylvania
Research Center, State Historical Society of Iowa, Iowa City, Iowa
Rice County Historical Society, Faribault, Minnesota
Smithsonian Institution, Washington DC
Special Collections and University Archives, Oklahoma State University, Stillwater, Oklahoma
University of Oklahoma, Western History Collections, Norman, Oklahoma

NEWSPAPERS AND PERIODICALS

Baptist Home Mission Monthly
Boston Masonic Mirror
Catholic Telegraph
Cheyenne Transporter & Transporter Supplement
Christian Advocate and Journal
Christian Secretary
Christian Spectator
Christian Union
Christian Watchmen
The Churchman
Columbian Star
Daily Arkansas Gazette
Daily Central City Register
Daily National Intelligencer
Daily National Journal
The Day Star
Evening Bulletin (Philadelphia)
Fayetteville Observer
Georgia Weekly Telegraph & Journal and Messenger
The Friend
Friends' Intelligencer
Friends' Review
Harper's Weekly
The Indian Advocate
The Independent
Lippincott's Magazine of Popular Literature and Science
Methodist Quarterly Review
Missionary Herald
New York Evangelist
New York Observer and Chronicle
New York Times
North American Magazine
North American Review
Observer and Telegraph
Overland Monthly and Out West Magazine
Reformed Presbyterian and Covenanter

Religious Intelligencer
San Francisco Daily Evening Bulletin
Saturday Pennsylvania Gazette
Southern Workman
Spirit of Missions
Therapeutic Gazette
United States' Telegraph
Universalist Quarterly
Vermont Chronicle
Western Reserve Chronicle
Wichita Daily Eagle

PRIMARY SOURCES: SERIALS AND GOVERNMENT DOCUMENTS

Annals of the Catholic Indian Missions of America. Washington, DC: Bureau of Catholic Indian Missions, 1877–1879.

Annual Report of the Board of Indian Commissioners. Washington, DC: Government Printing Office, 1869–1904.

Annual Report of the Commissioner of Indian Affairs. Washington, DC: Government Printing Office, 1826–1904.

Department of the Interior, Bureau of Education. *The Indian School at Carlisle Barracks*. Washington, DC: Government Printing Office, 1880.

Galpin, S. A. *Report upon the Condition and Management of Certain Indian Agencies in the Indian Territories Now under the Supervision of the Orthodox Friends*. Washington, DC: Government Printing Office, 1877.

Proceedings of the Annual Meeting of the Lake Mohonk Conference of Friends of the Indian. s.l.: The Lake Mohonk Conference, 1883–1904.

US Congress, House of Representatives, Committee on Indian Affairs. *Regulating the Indian Department: Report (to Accompany H. 488, 489, 490)*. 23rd Congress, 1st session, 1834. H. Rep. 474.

US Congress, Senate. *Kiowa, Comanche, and Apache Memorial*. 53rd Congress, 2nd session, 1894. S. Misc. Doc. 102.

US Congress, Senate. *Memorial from the Kiowa, Comanche, and Apache Indian Tribes*. 56th Congress, 1st session, 1900. S. Doc. 76.

PRIMARY SOURCES: BOOKS, PAMPHLETS, AND ARTICLES

Address to the Public of the Lake Mohonk Conference: Held at Lake Mohonk, N.Y., October 1883, in Behalf of the Civilization and Legal Protection of the Indians of the United States. Philadelphia: Executive Committee of the Indian Rights Association, 1883.

Annual Address to the Public of the Lake Mohonk Conference in Behalf of the Civilization and Legal Protection of the Indians of the United States. Philadelphia: Executive Committee of the Indian Rights Association, 1884.

Annual Report of the Board of Missions for the Fiscal Year. Domestic and Foreign Missionary Society of the Protestant Episcopal Church in the U.S.A., 1889.

Battey, Thomas C. *The Life and Adventures of a Quaker among the Indians*. Norman: University of Oklahoma Press, 1968.

Beecher, Lyman. *Plea for the West*. Cincinnati: Truman & Smith, 1835.

Benton, Angelo Ames. *The Church Cyclopaedia: A Dictionary of Church Doctrine, History, Organization, and Ritual*. New York: James Pott, 1883.

Brouillet, J. B. A. *Memoranda Relative to the Rights of Christian Churches on Indian Reservations*. Washington, DC: Bureau of Catholic Indian Missions, 1880.

Burdette, Mary G. *A Trip through the Indian Country*. Chicago: Woman's American Baptist Home Mission Society, ca. 1902.

Burdette, Mary G. *Thirty-Two Years' Work among Indians, 1877–1909*. Chicago: Woman's American Baptist Home Mission Society, 1909.

Burdette, Mary G. *Young Women among Blanket Indians: The Trio at Rainy Mountain*. Chicago: R. R. Donnelley & Sons, 1895.

Bureau of Catholic Indian Missions, 1874 to 1895. Washington, DC: Church News Publishing, 1895.

Burnham, Mary D. *Spirit of Missions, Woman's Work the Dakota League of Boston*. s.l.: s.n., 1870.

Butler, Josiah. "Pioneer School Teaching at the Comanche-Kiowa Agency School, 1870–1873." *Chronicles of Oklahoma* 6, no. 4 (December 1928): 483–528.

Cassal, Reverend Hilary. "Missionary Tour in the Chickasaw Nation and Western Indian Territory." *Chronicles of Oklahoma* 34 (Winter 1956–1957): 397–416.

Catlin, George. *An Account of an Annual Religious Ceremony Practiced by the Mandan Tribe of North American Indians*. London: s.n., 1865.

Catlin, George. *George Catlin and His Indian Gallery*. Washington, DC: Smithsonian American Art Museum, 2002.

Catlin, George. *Illustrations of the Manners, Customs and Condition of the North American Indians in a Series of Letters and Notes Written during Eight Years of Travel and Adventure among the Wildest and Most Remarkable Tribes Now Existing*. 7th ed. London: H. G. Bohn, 1848.

Catlin, George. *Letters and Notes on the Manners, Customs, and Conditions of the North American Indians Written during Eight Years' Travel (1832–1839) amongst the Wildest Tribes of Indians in North America*. New York: Dover Publications, 1973.

Circular of the Catholic Commissioner of Indian Missions to the Catholics of the United States. Baltimore, MD: John Murphy, 1874.

Crawford, Isabel Alice Hartley. *From Tent to Chapel at Saddle Mountain*. Chicago: Women's American Baptist Home Mission Society, 1903.

Crawford, Isabel Alice Hartley. *Kiowa: A Woman Missionary in Indian Territory*. Lincoln: University of Nebraska Press, 1998.

De Hasque, Urban. *St. Patrick's Indian Mission of Anadarko, Oklahoma, 1891–1915*. Oklahoma City: St. Joseph's Orphanage, 1915.

De Smet, Pierre-Jean. *Western Missions and Missionaries: A Series of Letters*. New York: J. B. Kirker, 1863.

Dorchester, Daniel. *Romanism versus the Public School System*. New York: Phillips & Hunt, 1888.

Evarts, Jeremiah. *Cherokee Removal: The "William Penn" Essays and Other Writings*. Knoxville: University of Tennessee Press, 1981.

Fait, Anna R. "An Autobiography." *Chronicles of Oklahoma* 32, no. 2 (1954–1955): 185–194.

Journal of the Proceedings of the Annual Convention of the Protestant Episcopal Church in the State of New York. s.l.: The Diocese, 1894.

Journal of the Proceedings of the Eighteenth Annual Council of the Diocese of Arkansas. Little Rock, AR: Press Printing, 1890.

Journal of the Proceedings of the Eleventh Annual Council of the Protestant Episcopal Church in the Diocese of Arkansas. Little Rock, AR: Kellogg Printing, 1883.

Journal of the Second Annual Council of the Protestant Episcopal Church in Colorado. Longmont, CO: Printed for the Council, 1888.

Journal of the Thirteenth Annual Convention of the Protestant Episcopal Church in the Diocese of Central New York. Utica, NY: Curtiss & Childs, 1881.

LaBarre, Weston. *The Autobiography of a Kiowa Indian*. Madison, WI: Microcard Foundation, 1957.

Long, Stephen H. *Account of an Expedition from Pittsburgh to the Rocky Mountains Performed in the Years 1819–20*. Philadelphia: H. C. Carey and L. Lea, 1822.

Loomis, A. W. *Scenes in the Indian Country*. Philadelphia: Presbyterian Board of Publication, 1859.

Manual: Catholic Indian Missionary Associations. Washington DC: Bureau of Catholic Indian Missions, 1875.

Marshall, J. T. *Miles Expedition of 1874–1875: An Eyewitness Account of the Red River War*. Austin, TX: Encino Press, 1971.

Masters, Victor I. *Southern Baptists and Frontier Missions*. Atlanta, GA: Home Mission Board, Southern Baptist Convention, 1909.

McAfee, George F. *Missions among the North American Indians under the Care of the Missions of the Presbyterian Church in the United States of America*. New York: Woman's Board of Home Missions, 1903.

McCoy, Isaac. *History of Baptist Indian Missions: Embracing Remarks on the Former and Present Condition of the Aboriginal Tribes, Their Settlement within the Indian Territory and the Future Prospects*. Washington, DC: William M. Morrison, 1840.

Memorial of the Society of Friends in Regard to the Indians. Baltimore, MD: Rose, 1868.

Methvin, J. J. *Andele: Or, The Mexican-Kiowa Captive. A Story of Real Life among the Indians*. Albuquerque: University of New Mexico Press, 1996.

Methvin, J. J. *In the Limelight: Or, History of Anadarko (Caddo County) and Vicinity from the Earliest Days*. Anadarko, OK: Plummer, 1929.

Methvin, J. J. "Reminiscences of Life among the Indians." *Chronicles of Oklahoma* 5, no. 2 (June 1927): 166–179.

Minutes of the Annual Conference of the Methodist Episcopal Church, South for the Year 1887. Nashville, TN: Publishing House of the Methodist Episcopal Church, South, 1888.

Mooney, James. *Calendar History of the Kiowa Indians*. Washington, DC: Smithsonian Institution Press, 1979.

Mooney, James. *The Ghost-Dance Religion and Wounded Knee*. New York: Dover Publications, 1973.

Morgan, Thomas Jefferson. *Roman Catholics and Indian Education: An Address*. Boston: American Citizen, 1893.

Morse, Jedediah. *Report to the Secretary of War of the United States on Indian Affairs, Comprising a Narrative of a Tour Performed in the Summer of 1820, Under a Commission from the President of the United States, For the Purpose of Ascertaining, For the Use of the Government, the Actual State of the Indian Tribes in our Country*. New Haven, CT: S. Converse, 1822.

Petition of the Catholic Church for the Agency of the Chippewas of Lake Superior. Washington, DC: H. Polkinghorn, 1873.

Petition of James Cardinal Gibbons. s.l.: s.n., 1898.

Pratt, Richard Henry. *Battlefield and Classroom: Four Decades with the American Indian, 1867–1904*. Norman: University of Oklahoma Press, 2003.

Proper, Rev. D. D. *The Gospel among the Blanket Indians*. New York: American Baptist Home Missionary Society, n.d.

Rairden, A. B. *Our Work among the Kiowa Indians, Revised*. New York: American Baptist Home Missionary Society, 1896.

Scott, Hugh Lenox. "Notes on the Kado, or Sun Dance of the Kiowa." *American Anthropologist* 13, no. 3 (July 1, 1911): 345–379.

Scott, Hugh Lenox. *Some Memoires of a Soldier*. New York: Century, ca. 1928.

Sherman, Ellen Ewing. *Appeal of Mrs. W. T. Sherman to the Catholic Ladies of the United States*. St. Louis: n.d., 1875.

Steele, James W. *The Oklahoma Opportunity: Opening of the Kiowa, Comanche and Apache Reservations*. Chicago: J. C. Winship, 1900.

Stephan, James Cardinal. "Brief of Objections to Certain Proposed Enactments, Covering Appropriations for Indian Education," s.l.: s.n., 1895.

Stephan, James Cardinal. *Crusade against the Catholic Schools*. s.l.: s.n., 1895.

Stephan, James Cardinal. "Report of the Bureau of Catholic Indian Missions for the Year Ending October 1, 1898." s.l.: s.n., 1898.

Stimson, H. A. *Address on the Indian Question, Delivered by Rev. H. A. Stimson, of Minneapolis, Minn. Before the American Missionary Association*. s.l.: s.n., 1879.

Tatum, Lawrie. "Lawrie Tatum's Letters." *Prairie Lore* 4, no. 1 (July 1967): 50–61.

Tatum, Lawrie. *Our Red Brothers and the Peace Policy of President Ulysses S. Grant*. Lincoln: University of Nebraska Press, 1970.

Wicks, J. B. *Domestic Missions, Protestant Episcopal Church in the United States of America the Church's Work among the Indians: Letters from the Rev. J. B. White and Others*. New York: s.n., ca. 1880.

SECONDARY SOURCES

Adams, David Wallace. *Education for Extinction: American Indians and the Boarding School Experience, 1875–1928*. Lawrence: University Press of Kansas, 1995.

Addis, Cameron. "The Whitman Massacre: Religion and Manifest Destiny on the Columbia Plateau, 1809–1858." *Journal of the Early Republic* 25, no. 2 (July 1, 2005): 221–258.

Adelman, Jeremy, and Stephen Aron. "From Borderlands to Borders: Empires, Nation-States, and the Peoples in between in North American History." *The American Historical Review* 104, no. 3 (June 1, 1999): 814–841.

Agnew, Brad. "Leavenworth and Dodge." In *Frontier Adventurers: American Exploration in Oklahoma*, edited by Joseph Allen Stout, 91–100. Oklahoma City: Oklahoma Historical Society, 1976.

Ahern, Wilbert H. "An Experiment Aborted: Returned Indian Students in the Indian School Service, 1881–1908." *Ethnohistory* 44, no. 2 (April 1997): 263–304.

Altman, Michael. *Heathen, Hindoo, Hindu: American Representations of India, 1721–1893*. New York: Oxford University Press, 2017.

Anbinder, Tyler. "Ulysses S. Grant, Nativist." *Civil War History* 43, no. 2 (January 4, 2012): 119–141.

Anderson, Gary Clayton. *The Conquest of Texas: Ethnic Cleansing in the Promised Land, 1820–1875*. Norman: University of Oklahoma Press, 2005.

Anderson, Gary Clayton. *The Indian Southwest, 1580–1830: Ethnogenesis and Reinvention*. Norman: University of Oklahoma Press, 1999.

Andersson, Rani-Henrik. *The Lakota Ghost Dance of 1890*. Lincoln: University of Nebraska Press, 2008.

Andrew, John A. *From Revivals to Removal: Jeremiah Evarts, the Cherokee Nation, and the Search for the Soul of America*. Athens: University of Georgia Press, 1992.

Archambault, JoAllyn. "Sun Dance." In *Handbook of North American Indians: Plains*, vol. 13, edited by Raymond DeMallie, 983–995. Washington, DC: Government Printing Office, 2001.

Arenson, Adam, and Andrew R. Graybill, eds. *Civil War Wests: Testing the Limits of the United States*. Berkeley: University of California Press, 2015.

Asad, Talal. *Genealogies of Religion: Discipline and Reasons of Power in Christianity and Islam*. Baltimore, MD: Johns Hopkins University Press, 1993.

Baird, W. David. "Cyrus Byington and the Presbyterian Choctaw Mission." In *Churchmen and the Western Indians, 1820–1920*, edited by Clyde A. Milner and Floyd A. O'Neil, 5–40. Norman: University of Oklahoma, 1985.

Baird, W. David, and Danney Goble. *Oklahoma: A History*. Norman: University of Oklahoma Press, 2011.

Banner, Stuart. *How the Indians Lost Their Land: Law and Power on the Frontier*. Cambridge, MA: Harvard University Press, 2007.

Basso, Keith H. *Wisdom Sits in Places: Landscape and Language among the Western Apache*. Albuquerque: University of New Mexico Press, 1996.

Belich, James. *Replenishing the Earth: The Settler Revolution and the Rise of the Anglo-World, 1783–1939*. New York: Oxford University Press, 2009.

Belknap, Lucille S. *Beginnings: Oklahoma, Norman, the Little Church, the History of St. John's Episcopal Church, 1892–1980*. Norman, OK: Transcript Press, 1980.

Bellesiles, Michael A. *1877: America's Year of Living Violently*. New York: New Press, 2010.

Berlo, Janet. *Plains Indian Drawings, 1865–1935: Pages from a Visual History*. New York: Harry N. Abrams, 1996.

Berlo, Janet. "Wo-Haw's Notebooks: 19th Century Kiowa Indian Drawings in the Collections of the Missouri Historical Society." *Gateway Heritage: Quarterly Journal of the Missouri Historical Society* 3, no. 2 (Fall 1982): 2–13.

Blackhawk, Ned. *Violence over the Land: Indians and Empires in the Early American West*. Cambridge, MA: Harvard University Press, 2006.

Blight, David W. *Race and Reunion: The Civil War in American Memory*. Cambridge, MA: Belknap Press, 2002.

Blum, Edward J. *Reforging the White Republic: Race, Religion, and American Nationalism, 1865–1898*. Baton Rouge: Louisiana State University Press, 2007.

Boone, Elizabeth Hill, and Walter Mignolo. *Writing without Words: Alternative Literacies in Mesoamerica and the Andes*. Durham, NC: Duke University Press, 1994.

Botkin, Samuel L. "Indian Missions of the Episcopal Church in Oklahoma." *Chronicles of Oklahoma* 34 (1956): 40–47.

Bowes, John P. "American Indian Removal Beyond the Removal Act." *Native American and Indigenous Studies* 1, no. 1 (Spring 2014): 65–87.

Brander Rasmussen, Birgit. *Queequeg's Coffin: Indigenous Literacies and Early American Literature*. Durham, NC: Duke University Press, 2012.

Brands, H. D. *American Colossus: The Triumph of Capitalism, 1865–1900*. New York: Doubleday, 2010.

Brantlinger, Patrick. *Dark Vanishings: Discourse on the Extinction of Primitive Races, 1800–1930*. Ithaca, NY: Cornell University Press, 2003.

Bresie, Amanda. "Mother Katharine Drexel's Benevolent Empire: The Bureau of Catholic Indian Missions and Education of Native Americans, 1885–1935." *U.S. Catholic Historian* 32, no. 3 (Summer 2014): 1–24.

Brooks, James. *Captives and Cousins: Slavery, Kinship, and Community in the Southwest Borderlands*. Chapel Hill: University of North Carolina Press, 2002.

Buckley, Cornelius M. "Overland with Optimism: The Jesuit Missionary Party of 1841." *Oregon Historical Quarterly* 97, no. 1 (1996): 8–25.

Bunson, Margaret. *Faith in the Wilderness: The Story of the Catholic Indian Missions*. Huntington, IN: Our Sunday Visitor, 2000.

Butler, Anne M. *Across God's Frontiers: Catholic Sisters in the American West, 1850–1920*. Chapel Hill: University of North Carolina Press, 2012.

Butler, Jon. *Awash in a Sea of Faith: Christianizing the American People*. Cambridge, MA: Harvard University Press, 1990.

Butler, Jon, Grant Wacker, and Randall Herbert Balmer. *Religion in American Life: A Short History*. New York: Oxford University Press, 2003.

Byler, Charles A. *Civil-Military Relations on the Frontier and Beyond, 1865–1917*. Greenwood Publishing Group, 2006.

Cahill, Cathleen D. *Federal Fathers and Mothers: A Social History of the United States Indian Service, 1869–1933*. Chapel Hill: University of North Carolina Press, 2011.

Callahan, Richard, Jr., ed. *New Territories, New Perspectives: The Religious Impact of the Louisiana Purchase*. Columbia: University of Missouri Press, 2008.

Calloway, Colin G. *One Vast Winter Count: The Native American West before Lewis and Clark*. Lincoln: University of Nebraska Press, 2003.

Calloway, Colin G. *Our Hearts Fell to the Ground: Plains Indian Views of How the West Was Lost*. New York: Bedford, St. Martin's, 1996.

Carriker, Robert. "Admiring Advocate of the Great Plains: Father Pierre-Jean de Smet, S. J., on the Middle Missouri." *Great Plains Quarterly* 14, no. 4 (1994): 243–256.

Cave, Alfred. *Prophets of the Great Spirit: Native American Revitalization Movements in Eastern North America*. Lincoln: University of Nebraska Press, 2014.

Chang, David A. *The Color of the Land: Race, Nation, and the Politics of Landownership in Oklahoma, 1832–1929*. Chapel Hill: University of North Carolina Press, 2010.

Chang, Derek. *Citizens of a Christian Nation: Evangelical Missions and the Problem of Race in the Nineteenth Century*. Philadelphia: University of Pennsylvania Press, 2010.

Chidester, David. *Empire of Religion: Imperialism and Comparative Religion*. Chicago: University of Chicago Press, 2014.

Chidester, David. *Savage Systems: Colonialism and Comparative Religion in Southern Africa*. Charlottesville: University Press of Virginia, 1996.

Childs, Ann Waybright. "A Picture Letter Reveals a Cheyenne Family's Love for Relatives Being Held Prisoner in Florida." *Wild West* 12, no. 6 (April 2000): 60–61.

Christensen, Scott R. *Sagwitch: Shoshone Chieftain, Mormon Elder, 1822–1887*. Logan: Utah State University Press, 1999.

Clark, Blue. *Lone Wolf v. Hitchcock: Treaty Rights and Indian Law at the End of the Nineteenth Century*. Lincoln: University of Nebraska Press, 1999.

Clatterbuck, Mark. *Demons, Saints, and Patriots: Catholic Visions of Native America Through the Indian Sentinel, 1902–1962*. Milwaukee: Marquette University Press, 2009.

Clow, Richard. "Lakota Ghost Dance after 1890." *South Dakota History* 20 (Winter 1990): 323–333.

Comer, Douglas C. *Ritual Ground: Bent's Old Fort, World Formation, and the Annexation of the Southwest*. Berkeley: University of California Press, 1996.

Conroy-Krutz, Emily. *Christian Imperialism: Converting the World in the Early American Republic*. Ithaca, NY: Cornell University Press, 2015.

Corrigan, John. *Emptiness: Feeling Christian in America*. Chicago: University of Chicago Press, 2015.

Corwin, Hugh. "The A-nan-thy Odle-Paugh Kiowa Calendar." *Prairie Lore* (October 1967): 66–83.

Corwin, Hugh. "The Ananthy Odle-paugh Kiowa Calendar." *Prairie Lore* (April 1968): 226–228.

Corwin, Hugh. "The A-Nanthy Odle-Paugh Kiowa Calendar." *Prairie Lore* (January 1971): 130–153.

Corwin, Hugh. "The A-Nanthy Odle-Paugh Kiowa Calendar." *Prairie Lore* (October 1971): 107–125.

Corwin, Hugh. "The A-Nanthy Odle-Paugh Kiowa Calendar." *Prairie Lore* (January 1975): 154–163.

Corwin, Hugh. *The Kiowa Indians: Their History and Life Stories*. Lawton, OK: H. D. Corwin, 1958.

Coward, John M. *The Newspaper Indian: Native American Identity in the Press, 1820–90*. Chicago: University of Illinois Press, 1999.

Cutler, Lee. "Lawrie Tatum and the Kiowa Agency: 1869–1873." *Arizona and the West* 13, no. 3 (Autumn 1971): 221–244.

Dees, Sarah E. "The Scientific Study of Native American Religions, 1879–1903." PhD dissertation, Indiana University, 2015.

DeLay, Brian. *War of a Thousand Deserts: Indian Raids and the U.S.-Mexican War*. New Haven, CT: Yale University Press, 2008.

Deloria, Philip Joseph. *Indians in Unexpected Places*. Lawrence: University Press of Kansas, 2004.

DeMallie, Raymond J. "Early Kiowa and Comanche Treaties: The Treaties of 1835 and 1837." *American Indian Journal* 9 (1986): 16–21.

DeMallie, Raymond J. *The Kiowa Treaty of 1853*. Treaty Rights Workshop. Washington, DC: Institute for the Development of Indian Law, 1977.

DeMallie, Raymond J. "The Lakota Ghost Dance: An Ethnohistorical Account." *Pacific Historical Review* 51, no. 4 (November 1982): 385–405.

DeMallie, Raymond J. "Teton." In *Handbook of North American Indians*, edited by William C. Sturtevant, Vol. XIII, Plains, part 2, 794–820. Washington, DC: Smithsonian Institution, 2001.

DeMallie, Raymond J. "Touching the Pen: Plains Indian Treaty Councils in Ethnohistorical Perspective." In *Ethnicity on the Great Plains*, edited by Frederick C. Luebke, 38–51. Lincoln: University of Nebraska Press, 1980.

DeMallie, Raymond J. *The Treaty of Medicine Lodge, 1867: Between the United States and the Kiowa, Comanche and Apache Indians*. Washington, DC: Institute for the Development of Indian Law, 1976.

DeMallie, Raymond J. *The Treaty on the Little Arkansas River, 1865*. Washington, DC: Institute for the Development of Indian Law, 1977.

DeMallie, Raymond J. *The Unratified Treaty between the Kiowas, Comanches and Apaches and the United States*. Washington, DC: Institute for the Development of Indian Law, 1977.

DeMallie, Raymond J., and Robert H. Lavenda. "Wakan: Plains Siouan Concepts of Power." In *The Anthropology of Power: Ethnographic Studies from Asia, Oceania, and the New World*, edited by Raymond D. Fogelson and Richard N. Adams, 153–165. New York: Academic Press, 1977.

Dennis, Matthew. *Seneca Possessed: Indians, Witchcraft, and Power in the Early American Republic*. Philadelphia: University of Pennsylvania Press, 2010.

Dichtl, John R. *Frontiers of Faith: Bringing Catholicism to the West in the Early Republic*. Lexington: University Press of Kentucky, 2008.

Dippie, Brian W. *The Vanishing American: White Attitudes and U.S. Indian Policy*. Middletown, CT: Wesleyan University Press, 1982.

Dowd, Gregory Evans. *A Spirited Resistance: The North American Indian Struggle for Unity, 1745–1815*. Baltimore, MD: Johns Hopkins University Press, 1992.

Downs, Gregory P., and Kate Masur. Introduction to *The World the Civil War Made*, edited by Gregory P. Downs and Kate Masur. Chapel Hill: University of North Carolina Press, 2015.

Drescher, Seymour. *Abolition: A History of Slavery and Antislavery*. New York: Cambridge University Press, 2009.

DuVal, Kathleen. "Debating Identity, Sovereignty, and Civilization: The Arkansas Valley after the Louisiana Purchase." *Journal of the Early Republic* 26, no. 1 (2006): 25–58.

Eastman, Carolyn. "The Indian Censures the White Man: 'Indian Eloquence' and American Reading Audiences in the Early Republic." *William and Mary Quarterly* 65, no. 3 (2008): 535–564.

Eisler, Benita. *The Red Man's Bones: George Catlin, Artist and Showman*. New York: W.W. Norton, 2013.

Ellis, Clyde. Introduction to *Kiowa: A Woman Missionary in Indian Territory*, by Isabel Crawford. Lincoln: University of Nebraska Press, 1998.

Ellis, Clyde. *To Change Them Forever: Indian Education at the Rainy Mountain Boarding School, 1893–1920*. Norman: University of Oklahoma Press, 1996.

Ewers, John C. *Murals in the Round: Painted Tipis of the Kiowa and Kiowa-Apache Indians: An Exhibition of Tipi Models Made for James Mooney of the Smithsonian Institution during His Field Studies of Indian History and Art in Southwestern Oklahoma, 1891–1904*. Washington, DC: Smithsonian Institution Press, 1978.

Fenn, Elizabeth A. *Encounters at the Heart of the World: A History of the Mandan People*. New York: Hill and Wang, 2015.

Fessenden, Tracy. *Culture and Redemption: Religion, the Secular, and American Literature*. Princeton, NJ: Princeton University Press, 2007.

Fisher, Linford D. *The Indian Great Awakening: Religion and the Shaping of Native Cultures in Early America*. New York: Oxford University Press, 2012.

Fluhman, Spencer. *"A Peculiar People:" Anti-Mormonism and the Making of Religion in Nineteenth-Century America*. Chapel Hill: University of North Carolina Press, 2014.

Foner, Eric. *Reconstruction: America's Unfinished Revolution, 1863–1877*. New York: Harper Collins, 2002.

Fossey, Richard, and Stephanie Morris. "St. Katharine Drexel and St. Patrick's Mission to the Indians of the Southern Plains: A Study in Saintly Administration." *Catholic Southwest* 18 (2007): 61–84.

Foster, Gaines M. *Moral Reconstruction: Christian Lobbyists and the Federal Legislation of Morality, 1865–1920*. Chapel Hill: University of North Carolina Press, 2002.

Fowler, Loretta. "The Great Plains from the Arrival of the Horse to 1885." In *The Cambridge History of the Native Peoples of the Americas*, Vol. 1: *North America,* Part 2, edited by Bruce G. Trigger and Wilcomb E. Washburn, 1–56. New York: Cambridge University Press, 1996.

Fowles, Severin M. *An Archaeology of Doings: Secularism and the Study of Pueblo Religion*. Santa Fe: School for Advanced Research Press, 2013.

Franklin, Brian Russell. "America's Missions: The Home Mission Movement and the Story of the Early Republic." PhD Dissertation, Southern Methodist University, 2012.

Gage, Justin Randolph. "Intertribal Communication, Literacy, and the Spread of the Ghost Dance." PhD dissertation, University of Arkansas, 2015.

Genetin-Pilawa, C. Joseph. *Crooked Paths to Allotment: The Fight over Federal Indian Policy after the Civil War*. Chapel Hill: University of North Carolina Press, 2012.

Genetin-Pilawa, C. Joseph. "Ely Parker and the Contentious Peace Policy." *Western Historical Quarterly* 41, no. 2 (Summer 2010): 196–217.

Gibson, Arrell Morgan. "Native Americans and the Civil War." *American Indian Quarterly* 9, no. 4 (January 1985): 385–410.

Gin Lum, Kathryn. *Damned Nation: Hell in America from Revolution to Reconstruction*. New York: Oxford University Press, 2014.

Gloege, Timothy. *Guaranteed Pure: The Moody Bible Institute, Business, and the Making of Modern Evangelicalism*. Chapel Hill: University of North Carolina Press, 2015.

Goldschmidt, Henry, and Elizabeth A. McAlister, eds. *Race, Nation, and Religion in the Americas*. New York: Oxford University Press, 2004.

Gordon, Sarah Barringer. *The Mormon Question: Polygamy and Constitutional Conflict in Nineteenth-Century America*. Chapel Hill: University of North Carolina Press, 2002.

Graber, Jennifer. "From Drone War to Indian War." In *Faith in the New Millennium: The Future of Religion and American Politics*, edited by Matthew Avery Sutton and Darren Dochuk, 91–109. New York: Oxford University Press, 2016.

Graber, Jennifer. "'If a War It May Be Called': The Peace Policy with American Indians." *Religion and American Culture: A Journal of Interpretation* 24, no. 1 (Winter 2014): 36–69.

Graber, Jennifer. "The Imperial Angle: Martin Marty Narrates U.S. Religious History," unpublished paper.

Graber, Jennifer. "Religion in Kiowa Ledgers Expanding the Canon of American Religious Literature." *American Literary History* 26, no. 1 (Spring 2014): 42–60.

Green, Steven K. *The Bible, the School, and the Constitution: The Clash That Shaped Modern Church-State Doctrine*. New York: Oxford University Press, 2012.

Green, Steven K. *The Second Disestablishment: Church and State in Nineteenth-Century America*. New York: Oxford University Press, 2010.

Greenberg, Bruce. "The Mi'kmaq Hieroglyphic Prayer Book: Writing and Christianity in Maritime Canada, 1675–1921." In *The Language Encounter in the Americas, 1492–1800*, edited by Edward G. Gray and Norman Fiering, 189–211. New York: Berghahn Books, 2000.

Greene, Candace S. "Being Indian at Fort Marion: Revisiting Three Drawings." *American Indian Quarterly* 37, no. 4 (Fall 2013): 289–316.

Greene, Candace S. "Buffalo and Longhorn: A Medicine Complex Revealed." *American Indian Art Magazine* 38, no. 4 (Autumn 2013): 42–53.

Greene, Candace S. "Exploring the Three 'Little Bluffs' of the Kiowa." *Plains Anthropologist* 41, no. 157 (August 1, 1996): 221–242.

Greene, Candace S. "From Bison Robes to Ledgers: Changing Contexts in Plains Drawings." *European Review of Native American Studies* 18, no. 1 (2004): 21–29.

Greene, Candace S. *One Hundred Summers: A Kiowa Calendar Record*. Lincoln: University of Nebraska Press, 2009.

Greene, Candace S. *Silver Horn: Master Illustrator of the Kiowas*. Norman: University of Oklahoma Press, 2001.

Greene, Candace S., and Russell Thornton. *The Year the Stars Fell: Lakota Winter Counts at the Smithsonian*. Washington, DC: Smithsonian National Museum of Natural History, 2007.

Grimsley, Mark. "'Rebels' and 'Redskins': U.S. Military Conduct toward White Southerners and Native Americans in Comparative Perspective." In *Civilians in the Path of War*, edited by Mark Grimsley and Clifford J. Rogers, 137–162. Lincoln: University of Nebraska Press, 2002.

Guyatt, Nicholas. *Bind Us Apart: How Enlightened Americans Invented Racial Segregation*. New York: Basic Books, 2016.

Hagan, William T. *The Indian Rights Association: The Herbert Welsh Years, 1882–1904*. Tucson: University of Arizona Press, 1985.

Hagan, William T. "Joshua Given: Kiowa Indian and Carlisle Alumnus." Published lecture, Mary Baldwin College, 1977.

Hagan, William T. "Kiowas, Comanches, and Cattlemen, 1867–1906: A Case Study of the Failure of U.S. Reservation Policy." *Pacific Historical Review* 40, no. 3 (August 1971): 333–355.

Hagan, William T. *Taking Indian Lands: The Cherokee (Jerome) Commission, 1889–1893*. Norman: University of Oklahoma Press, 2003.

Hagan, William T. *United States-Comanche Relations: The Reservation Years*. New Haven, CT: Yale University Press, 1976.

Haley, James L. *The Buffalo War: The History of the Red River Indian Uprising of 1874*. Norman: University of Oklahoma Press, 1985.

Hall, Catherine. *Civilising Subjects: Metropole and Colony in the English Imagination 1830–1867*. Chicago: The University of Chicago Press, 2002.

Hall, Margaret. *History of Anadarko Presbyterian Church*, 1889–1989. s.l.: Gene Hall, 1989.

Hämäläinen, Pekka. *The Comanche Empire*. New Haven, CT: Yale University Press, 2009.

Hatch, Nathan O. *The Democratization of American Christianity*. New Haven, CT: Yale University Press, 1989.

Hausdoerffer, John. *Catlin's Lament: Indians, Manifest Destiny, and the Ethics of Nature*. Lawrence: University Press of Kansas, 2009.

Hardorff, Richard. *Washita Memories: Eyewitness Views of Custer's Attack on Black Kettle's Village*. Norman: University of Oklahoma Press, 2006.

Haselby, Sam. *The Origins of American Religious Nationalism*. New York: Oxford University Press, 2015.

Hershberger, Mary. "Mobilizing Women, Anticipating Abolition: The Struggle against Indian Removal in the 1830s." *Journal of American History* 86, no. 1 (June 1999): 15–40.

Higham, John. *Strangers in the Land: Patterns of American Nativism, 1860–1925*. New Brunswick, NJ: Rutgers University Press, 2002.

Hittman, Michael. "The 1870 Ghost Dance at the Walker River Reservation: A Reconstruction." *Ethnohistory* 20, no. 3 (1973): 247.

Hoig, Stan. *Tribal Wars of the Southern Plains*. Norman: University of Oklahoma Press, 1993.

Holler, Clyde. *Black Elk's Religion: The Sun Dance and Lakota Catholicism*. Syracuse, NY: Syracuse University Press, 1995.

Hoover, David Sanders. "A Developing Resistance: Fighting Allotment on the Kiowa, Comanche, and Apache Reservation." Master's thesis, Southeastern Oklahoma State University, 2001.

Horsman, Reginald. "The Indian Policy of an 'Empire of Liberty.'" In *Native Americans and the Early Republic*, edited by Frederick E. Hoxie, 37–61. Charlottesville: University of Virginia Press, 1999.

Horsman, Reginald. *Race and Manifest Destiny: The Origins of American Racial Anglo-Saxonism*. Cambridge, MA: Harvard University Press, 1981.

Hoxie, Frederick E. *A Final Promise: The Campaign to Assimilate the Indians, 1880–1920*. Lincoln: University of Nebraska Press, 1984.

Hubbard, Tasha. "Buffalo Genocide in Nineteenth-Century North America." In *Colonial Genocide in Indigenous North America*, edited by Andrew Woolford, Jeff Benvenuto, and Alexander Laban Hinton, 292–305. Durham, NC: Duke University Press, 2014.

Hüsken, Ute. "Ritual Dynamics and Ritual Failure." In *When Rituals Go Wrong: Mistakes, Failures, and the Dynamics of Ritual*, edited by Ute Hüsken, 337–366. Boston, MA: Brill, 2007.

Hutchison, William R. *Errand to the World: American Protestant Thought and Foreign Missions*. Chicago: University of Chicago Press, 1987.

Hyde, Anne Farrar. *Empires, Nations, and Families: A History of the North American West, 1800–1860*. Lincoln: University of Nebraska Press, 2011.

Illick, Joseph E. "'Some of Our Best Indians Are Friends': Quaker Attitudes and Actions Regarding the Western Indians during the Grant Administration." *Western Historical Quarterly* 2, no. 3 (July 1971): 283–294.

Irwin, Lee. *Coming Down from Above: Prophecy, Resistance, and Renewal in Native American Religions*. Norman: University of Oklahoma Press, 2008.

Isenberg, Andrew C. *The Destruction of the Bison: An Environmental History, 1750–1920*. New York: Cambridge University Press, 2001.

Jacobs, Margaret D. *White Mother to a Dark Race: Settler Colonialism, Maternalism, and the Removal of Indigenous Children in the American West and Australia, 1880–1940*. Lincoln: University of Nebraska Press, 2009.

Jacobson, Matthew Frye. *Barbarian Virtues: The United States Encounters Foreign Peoples at Home and Abroad, 1876–1917*. New York: Hill and Wang, 2000.

Jacobson, Matthew Frye. *Whiteness of a Different Color: European Immigrants and the Alchemy of Race*. Cambridge, MA: Harvard University Press, 1998.

Jacoby, Karl. "Indigenous Empires and Native Nations: Beyond History and Ethnohistory in Pekka Hämäläinen's *The Comanche Empire*." *History and Theory* 52 (February 2013): 60–66.

Jacoby, Karl. *Shadows at Dawn: A Borderlands Massacre and the Violence of History*. New York: Penguin Press, 2008.

Jantzer-White, Marilee. "Narrative and Landscape in the Drawings of Etahdleuh Doanmoe." In *Plains Indian Drawing, 1865–1935: Pages from a Visual History*, edited by Janet Catherine Berlo, 50–55. New York: American Federation of Arts and the Drawing Center, 1996.

Jaye, Barbara H. and William P. Mitchell. *Picturing Faith: A Facsimile Edition of the Pictographic Quechua Catechism in the Huntington Free Library*. New York: Huntington Free Library, 1999.

John, Elizabeth A. H. "An Earlier Chapter in Kiowa History." *New Mexico Historical Review* 60, no. 4 (October 1985): 379–397.

John, G. E. "Cultural Nationalism, Westward Expansion and the Production of Imperial Landscape: George Catlin's Native American West." *ECUMENE* 8, no. 2 (April 2001): 175–203.

Johnson, Sylvester A. *African American Religions, 1500–2000: Colonialism, Democracy, and Freedom*. New York: Cambridge University Press, 2015.

Johnson, Sylvester. "Religion and American Empire in Mississippi." In *Gods of the Mississippi*, edited by Michael Pasquier, 36–55. Bloomington: Indiana University Press, 2013.

Jordan, Michael Paul. "Reclaiming the Past: Descendants' Organizations, Historical Consciousness, and Intellectual Property in Kiowa Society." PhD dissertation, University of Oklahoma, 2011.

Kantrowitz, Stephen. "'Not Quite Constitutionalized': The Meanings of 'Civilization' and the Limits of Native American Citizenship." In *The World the Civil War Made*, edited by Gregory P. Downs and Kate Masur, 75–105. Chapel Hill: University of North Carolina Press, 2015.

Kaplan, Amy. "Manifest Domesticity." *American Literature* 70, no. 3 (September 1, 1998): 581–606.

Kastor, Peter J. "'What Are the Advantages of the Acquisition?': Inventing Expansion in the Early American Republic." *American Quarterly* 60, no. 4 (2008): 1003–1035.

Keller, Robert H. *American Protestantism and United States Indian Policy, 1869–82*. Lincoln: University of Nebraska Press, 1983.

Kelman, Ari. *A Misplaced Massacre: Struggling over the Memory of Sand Creek*. Cambridge, MA: Harvard University Press, 2013.

Kerber, Linda K. "The Abolitionist Perception of the Indian." *The Journal of American History* 62, no. 2 (September 1, 1975): 271–295.

Keyser, James D. *Art of the Warriors: Rock Art of the American Plains*. Salt Lake City: University of Utah Press, 2004.

Killoren, John J. *"Come, Blackrobe": De Smet and the Indian Tragedy*. Norman: University of Oklahoma Press, 1994.

King, Richard. *Orientalism and Religion: Postcolonial Theory, India and "the Mystic East."* New York: Routledge, 1999.

Klassen, Pamela E. "Spiritual Jurisdictions: Treaty People and the Queen of Canada." In *Ekklesia: Three Inquiries in Church, State, and the People*, edited by Paul C. Johnson, Pamela E. Klassen, and Winnifred Fallers Sullivan. Chicago: University of Chicago Press, 2018.

Kling, David W. "The New Divinity and the Origins of the American Board of Commissioners for Foreign Missions." *Church History* 72, no. 4 (December 1, 2003): 791–819.

Kracht, Benjamin R. "The Kiowa Ghost Dance, 1894–1916: An Unheralded Revitalization Movement." *Ethnohistory* 39, no. 4 (October 1, 1992): 452–477.

Kracht, Benjamin R. "Kiowa Religion: An Ethnohistorical Analysis of Ritual Symbolism, 1832–1987." PhD dissertation, Southern Methodist University, 1989.

Kracht, Benjamin R. "Kiowa Religion in Historical Perspective." *American Indian Quarterly* 21, no. 1 (January 1, 1997): 15–33.

Kramer, Paul A. "Power and Connection: Imperial Histories of the United States in the World." *The American Historical Review* 116, no. 5 (December 2011): 1348–1391.

Kretch, Shepard, III. *The Ecological Indian: Myth and History.* New York: W. W. Norton, 2000.

LaBarre, Weston. *The Peyote Cult: New Enlarged Edition.* Brooklyn, NY: Shoe String Press, 1964.

Laracy, Brother John. "Sacred Heart Mission and Abbey." *Chronicles of Oklahoma* 5, no. 2 (June 1927): 234–250.

Lassiter, Luke E., Clyde Ellis, and Ralph Kotay. *The Jesus Road: Kiowas, Christianity, and Indian Hymns.* Lincoln: University of Nebraska Press, 2002.

La Vere, David. *Contrary Neighbors: Southern Plains and Removed Indians in Indian Territory.* Norman: University of Oklahoma Press, 2000.

Levine, Richard R. "Indian Fighters and Indian Reformers: Grant's Indian Peace Policy and the Conservative Consensus." *Civil War History* 31, no. 4 (1985): 329–352.

Levy, Jerrold E. "Kiowa." In *Handbook of North American Indians*, Vol. 13: *Plains*, edited by Raymond J. DeMallie, 907–925. Washington, DC: Smithsonian Institution, 2001.

Liebersohn, Harry. "Introduction: The Civilizing Mission." *Journal of World History* 27, no. 3 (September 2016): 383–387.

Lincoln, Bruce. *Religion, Empire and Torture: The Case of Achamenian Persia, with a Postscript on Abu Ghraib.* Chicago: University of Chicago Press, 2007.

Lindsey, Donald F. *Indians at Hampton Institute, 1877–1923.* Urbana: University of Illinois Press, 1995.

Lofton, Kathryn. "Religious History as Religious Studies." *Religion* 42, no. 3 (2012): 383–394.

Long, Charles H. "Religion, Discourse and Hermeneutics: New Approaches in the Study of Religion." In *The Next Steps in Studying Religion: A Graduate's Guide*, edited by Mathieu E. Courville, 183–197. New York: Continuum International Publishing Group, 2007.

Lookingbill, Brad D. *War Dance at Fort Marion: Plains Indian War Prisoners.* Norman: University of Oklahoma Press, 2006.

Maroukis, Thomas Constantine. "The Peyote Controversy and the Demise of the Society of American Indians." *American Indian Quarterly* 37, no. 3 (Summer 2013): 159–180.

Maroukis, Thomas Constantine. *The Peyote Road: Religious Freedom and the Native American Church.* Norman: University of Oklahoma Press, 2010.

Masuzawa, Tomoko. *The Invention of World Religions, Or, How European Universalism Was Preserved in the Language of Pluralism.* Chicago: University of Chicago Press, 2005.

Marr, Timothy. *The Cultural Roots of American Islamicism.* Cambridge; New York: Cambridge University Press, 2006.

Marriott, Alice. *Kiowa Years: A Study in Culture Impact.* New York: Macmillan, 1968.

Marriott, Alice. *The Ten Grandmothers.* Norman: University of Oklahoma Press, 1945.

Martin, Joel W. "Before and beyond the Sioux Ghost Dance: Native American Prophetic Movements and the Study of Religion." *Journal of the American Academy of Religion* 59, no. 4 (Winter 1991): 677–701.

Martin, Joel W. "Introduction." In *Native Americans, Christianity, and the Reshaping of the American Religious Landscape*, edited by Joel W. Martin and Mark A. Nicholas, 1–20. Chapel Hill: University of North Carolina Press, 2010.

Martin, Joel W. *Sacred Revolt: The Muskogees' Struggle for a New World*. Boston, MA: Beacon Press, 1993.

Martin, Michael. "Bi'äñki's Ghost Dance Map: Thanatoptic Cartography and the Native American Spirit World." *Imago Mundi* 65, no. 1 (January 2013): 106–114.

Mauro, Hayes Peter. *The Art of Americanization at the Carlisle Indian School*. Albuquerque: University of New Mexico Press, 2011.

McBeth, Sally J. "Indian Boarding Schools and Ethnic Identity: An Example from the Southern Plains Tribes of Oklahoma." *Plains Anthropologist* 28, no. 100 (May 1, 1983): 119–128.

McCoy, Ronald. "'A Shield to Help You through Life': Kiowa Shield Designs and Origin Stories Collected by James Mooney, 1891–1906." *American Indian Art Magazine* 28, no. 3 (Summer 2003): 70–81.

McCoy, Ronald. "'I Have a Mysterious Way': Kiowa Shield Designs and Origin Stories Collected by James Mooney, 1891–1906." *American Indian Art Magazine* 29, no. 1 (Winter 2003): 64–75.

McCullough, Matthew. *The Cross of War: Christian Nationalism and U.S. Expansion in the Spanish-American War*. Madison: University of Wisconsin Press, 2014.

McGreevy, John T. *American Jesuits and the World: How an Embattled Religious Order Made Modern Catholicism Global*. Princeton, NJ: Princeton University Press, 2016.

McGreevy, John T. *Catholicism and American Freedom: A History*. New York: W. W. Norton, 2003.

McKevitt, Gerald. *Brokers of Culture: Italian Jesuits in the American West, 1848–1919*. Stanford, CA: Stanford University Press, 2010.

McLoughlin, William G. *Champions of the Cherokees: Evan and John B. Jones*. Princeton, NJ: Princeton University Press, 1990.

McLoughlin, William G., and Walter H. Conser. *The Cherokees and Christianity, 1794–1870: Essays on Acculturation and Cultural Persistence*. Athens: University of Georgia Press, 1994.

McNally, Michael David. *Ojibwe Singers: Hymns, Grief, and a Native Culture in Motion*. New York: Oxford University Press, 2000.

Meadows, William C. "Black Goose's Map of the Kiowa-Comanche-Apache Reservation in Oklahoma Territory." *Great Plains Quarterly* 26 (Fall 2006): 265–282.

Meadows, William C. *Kiowa, Apache, and Comanche Military Societies: Enduring Veterans, 1800 to the Present*. Austin: University of Texas Press, 1999.

Meadows, William C. *Kiowa Military Societies: Ethnohistory and Ritual*. Norman: University of Oklahoma Press, 2010.

Meadows, William C. *Through Indian Sign Language: The Fort Sill Ledgers of Hugh Lenox Scott and Iseeo, 1889–1897*. Norman: University of Oklahoma Press, 2015.

Meadows, William C., and Kenny Harragarra. "The Kiowa Drawings of Gotebo (1847–1927): A Self-Portrait of Cultural and Religious Transition." *Plains Anthropologist* 52, no. 202 (May 2007): 229–244.

Meyer, Paul R. "The Fear of Cultural Decline: Josiah Strong's Thought about Reform and Expansion." *Church History* 42, no. 3 (September 1973): 396–405.

Mielke, Laura L. *Moving Encounters, Sympathy and the Indian Question in Antebellum Literature*. Amherst: University of Massachusetts Press, 2008.

Milner, Clyde A., II. "Albert K. Smiley: Friend to Friends of the Indian." In *Churchmen and the Western Indians, 1820–1920*, edited by Clyde A. Milner II and Floyd A. O'Neil, 143–176. Norman: University of Oklahoma Press, 1985.

Mintz, Steven. *Moralists and Modernizers: America's Pre-Civil War Reformers*. Baltimore, MD: Johns Hopkins University Press, 1995.

Modern, John Lardas. *Secularism in Antebellum America: With Reference to Ghosts, Protestant Subcultures, Machines, and Their Metaphors; Featuring Discussions of Mass Media, Moby-Dick, Spirituality, Phrenology, Anthropology, Sing Sing State Penitentiary, and Sex with the New Motive Power*. Chicago: University of Chicago Press, 2011.

Moses, L. G. "'The Father Tells Me So!' Wovoka: The Ghost Dance Prophet." *American Indian Quarterly* 9, no. 3 (July 1, 1985): 335–351.

Moses, L. G. *The Indian Man: A Biography of James Mooney*. Urbana: University of Illinois Press, 1984.

Murphy, Joseph F. *Tenacious Monks: The Oklahoma Benedictines, 1875–1975: Indian Missionaries, Catholic Founders, Educators, Agriculturalists*. Shawnee, OK: Benedictine Color Press, 1974.

Ngai, Mae M. "Race, Nation, and Citizenship in Late Nineteenth-Century America, 1878–1900," In *The Columbia Documentary History of Race and Ethnicity in America*, edited by Ronald H. Bayor, 309–338. New York: Columbia University Press, 2004.

Niezen, Ronald. *Spirit Wars: Native North American Religions in the Age of Nation Building*. Berkeley: University of California Press, 2000.

Nye, Wilbur Sturtevant. *Bad Medicine and Good: Tales of the Kiowas*. Norman: University of Oklahoma Press, 1962.

Nye, Wilbur Sturtevant. *Carbine and Lance: The Story of Old Fort Sill*. Norman: University of Oklahoma Press, 1969.

O'Daniel, V. F. *The Right Rev. Edward Dominic Fenwick, O.P.: Founder of the Dominicans in the United States, Pioneer Missionary in Kentucky, Apostle of Ohio, First Bishop of Cincinnati*. Washington, DC: Dominicana, 1920.

Oman, Kerry R. "The Beginning of the End: The Indian Peace Commission of 1867–1868," *Great Plains Quarterly* 22 (Winter 2002): 35–51.

Orsi, Robert A. *History and Presence*. Cambridge, MA: Belknap Press, 2016.

Ostler, Jeffrey. *The Plains Sioux and U.S. Colonialism from Lewis and Clark to Wounded Knee*. New York: Cambridge University Press, 2004.

Overholt, Thomas W. "The Ghost Dance of 1890 and the Nature of the Prophetic Process." *Ethnohistory* 21, no. 1 (January 1, 1974): 37–63.

Paddison, Joshua. *American Heathens: Religion, Race, and Reconstruction in California*. Berkeley: University of California Press, 2012.

Paddison, Joshua. "Anti-Catholicism and Race in Post-Civil War San Francisco." *Pacific Historical Review* 78, no. 4 (2009): 505–544.

Painter, Nell Irwin. *Standing at Armageddon: A Grassroots History of the Progressive Era*. New York: W. W. Norton, 2008.

Palmer, Vera B. "'The Devil in the Details': Controverting an American Indian Conversion Narrative." In *Theorizing Native Studies*, edited by Audra Simpson and Andrea Smith, 266–295. Durham, NC: Duke University Press, 2014.

Parsons, Elsie Worthington Clews. *Kiowa Tales*. New York: G. E. Stechert, 1929.

Pasquier, Michael. *Fathers on the Frontier: French Missionaries and the Roman Catholic Priesthood in the United States, 1789–1870.* Oxford: Oxford University Press, 2010.

Pasquier, Michael. Introduction to *Gods of the Mississippi,* by Michael Pasquier, 1–16. Bloomington: Indiana University Press, 2013.

Perdue, Theda, and Michael D. Green, *The Cherokee Nation and the Trail of Tears.* New York: Penguin, 2008.

Pesantubbee, Michelene E. *Choctaw Women in a Chaotic World: The Clash of Cultures in the Colonial Southeast.* Albuquerque: University of New Mexico Press, 2005.

Petersen, Karen Daniels. *Plains Indian Art from Fort Marion.* Norman: University of Oklahoma Press, 1971.

Pinheiro, John C. *Missionaries of Republicanism: A Religious History of the Mexican-American War.* New York: Oxford University Press, 2014.

Point, Nicolas, S.J. *Wilderness Kingdom—Indian Life in the Rocky Mountains: 1840–1847, The Journals and Paintings of Nicolas Point, S.J.* Chicago: Loyola University Press, 1967.

Pointer, Richard W. *Encounters of the Spirit: Native Americans and European Colonial Religion.* Bloomington: Indiana University Press, 2007.

Pommersheim, Frank. *Broken Landscape: Indians, Indian Tribes, and the Constitution.* New York: Oxford University Press, 2009.

Powers, Ramon, and James N. Leiker. "Cholera among the Plains Indians: Perceptions, Causes, Consequences." *Western Historical Quarterly* 29, no. 3 (October 1, 1998): 317–340.

Pratt, Mary Louise. *Imperial Eyes: Travel Writing and Transculturation.* New York: Routledge, 2007.

Prentiss, Craig R., ed. *Religion and the Creation of Race and Ethnicity: An Introduction.* New York: New York University, 2003.

Prucha, Francis Paul. *American Indian Policy in Crisis: Christian Reformers and the Indian, 1865–1900.* Norman: University of Oklahoma Press, 1975.

Prucha, Francis Paul. *Americanizing the American Indians.* Cambridge, MA: Harvard University Press, 1973.

Prucha, Francis Paul. *Documents of United States Indian Policy.* Lincoln: University of Nebraska Press, 2000.

Prucha, Francis Paul. *The Great Father: The United States Government and the American Indians.* Lincoln: University of Nebraska Press, 1984.

Rahill, Peter James. *The Catholic Indian Missions and Grant's Peace Policy, 1870–1884.* Washington, DC: Catholic University of America Press, 1953.

Rand, Jacki Thompson. *Kiowa Humanity and the Invasion of the State.* Lincoln: University of Nebraska Press, 2008.

Rand, Jacki Thompson. "Primary Sources: Indian Goods and the History of American Colonialism and the 19th-Century Reservation." In *Clearing a Path: Theorizing the Past in Native American Studies,* edited by Nancy Shoemaker, 137–160. New York: Routledge, 2002.

Reeve, W. Paul. *Religion of a Different Color: Race and the Mormon Struggle for Whiteness.* New York: Oxford University Press, 2015.

Reilly, Hugh J. *The Frontier Newspapers and the Coverage of the Plains Indian Wars.* Santa Barbara, CA: Praeger, 2010.

Richardson, Heather Cox. "North and West of Reconstruction: Studies in Political Economy." In *Reconstructions: New Perspectives on the Postbellum United States,* edited by Thomas J. Brown, 66–90. New York: Oxford University Press, 2006.

Richardson, Heather Cox. *Wounded Knee: Party Politics and the Road to an American Massacre.* New York: Basic Books, 2010.

Richter, Daniel K. "'Believing That Many of the Red People Suffer Much for the Want of Food': Hunting, Agriculture, and a Quaker Construction of Indianness in the Early Republic." *Journal of the Early Republic* 19, no. 4 (December 1, 1999): 601–628.

Rippinger, Joel. *The Benedictine Order in the United States: An Interpretative History.* Collegeville, MN: Liturgical Press, 1990.

Rochford, Thomas M. "Father Nicolas Point: Missionary and Artist." *Oregon Historical Quarterly* 97, no. 1 (1996): 46–69.

Rockwell, Stephen J. *Indian Affairs and the Administrative State in the Nineteenth Century.* New York: Cambridge University Press, 2010.

Ryan, Susan M. *The Grammar of Good Intentions: Race and the Antebellum Culture of Benevolence.* Ithaca, NY: Cornell University Press, 2004.

Schmittou, Douglas A., and Michael H. Logan. "Fluidity of Meaning: Flag Imagery in Plains Indian Art." *American Indian Quarterly* 26, no. 4 (October 1, 2002): 559–604.

Seeman, Erik R. "Reading Indians' Deathbed Scenes: Ethnohistorical and Representational Approaches." *The Journal of American History* 88, no. 1 (2001): 17–47.

Sheehan, Bernard W. *Seeds of Extinction: Jeffersonian Philanthropy and the American Indian.* New York: W. W. Norton, 1974.

Shoemaker, Nancy. "How Indians Got to Be Red." *The American Historical Review* 102, no. 3 (June 1, 1997): 625–644.

Silverman, David J. *Red Brethren: The Brothertown and Stockbridge Indians and the Problem of Race in Early America.* Ithaca, NY: Cornell University Press, 2010.

Slotkin, Richard. *The Fatal Environment: The Myth of the Frontier in the Age of Industrialization, 1800–1890.* New York: Atheneum, 1985.

Slotkin, Richard. *Regeneration through Violence: The Mythology of the American Frontier, 1600–1860.* Middletown, CT: Wesleyan University Press, 1973.

Smallwood, James. "Major Stephen Harriman Long's Account from 1820." In *Frontier Adventurers: American Exploration in Oklahoma*, edited by Joseph Allen Stout, 55–60. Oklahoma City: Oklahoma Historical Society, 1976.

Smith, Jonathan Z. "The Bare Facts of Ritual." *History of Religions* 20, no. 1–2 (1980): 112–127.

Smith, Jonathan Z. "A Pearl of Great Price and a Cargo of Yams: A Study in Situational Incongruity." *History of Religions* 16, no. 1 (August 1976): 1–19.

Smith, Tash. *Capture These Indians for the Lord: Indians, Methodists, and Oklahomans, 1844–1939.* Tucson: University of Arizona Press, 2014.

Smits, David D. "The Frontier Army and the Destruction of the Buffalo: 1865–1883." *Western Historical Quarterly* 25, no. 3 (October 1, 1994): 313–338.

Smoak, Gregory Ellis. *Ghost Dances and Identity: Prophetic Religion and American Indian Ethnogenesis in the Nineteenth Century.* Berkeley: University of California Press, 2008.

Stokely, Michelle D. "Black Bear's Calendar: Picturing Southern Plains History." *Great Plains Quarterly* 34, no. 4 (2014): 317–339.

Sullivan, Delia. *Heritage Auctions American Indian Art Auction Catalog #6029.* Dallas, TX: Heritage Capital, 2009.

Szabo, Joyce M. *Art from Fort Marion: The Silberman Collection.* Norman: University of Oklahoma Press, 2009.

Szabo, Joyce M. "Drawing Life's Changes: Late Nineteenth-Century Plains Drawings from the Hampton Institute and Carlisle Indian School." *European Review of Native American Studies* 18, no. 1 (2004): 41–51.

Szabo, Joyce M. *Howling Wolf and the History of Ledger Art*. Albuquerque: University of New Mexico Press, 1994.

Szabo, Joyce M. *Imprisoned Art, Complex Patronage: Plains Drawings by Howling Wolf and Zotom at the Autry National Center*. Santa Fe, NM: School for Advanced Research Press, 2011.

Szabo, Joyce M. "Shields and Lodges, Warriors and Chiefs: Kiowa Drawings as Historical Records." *Ethnohistory* 41, no. 1 (Winter 1993): 1–24.

Thiel, Mark G. "Catholic Ladders and Native American Evangelization." *U.S. Catholic Historian* 27, no. 1 (2009): 49–70.

Tiro, Karim M. "'We Wish to Do You Good': The Quaker Mission to the Oneida Nation, 1790–1840." *Journal of the Early Republic* 26, no. 3 (October 1, 2006): 353–376.

Tone-Pah-Hote, Jenny Elizabeth. "Envisioning Nationhood: Kiowa Expressive Culture, 1875–1939." PhD dissertation, University of Minnesota, 2009.

Trafzer, Clifford E., and Margery Ann Beach. "Smohalla, the Washani, and Religion as a Factor in Northwestern Indian History." *American Indian Quarterly* 9, no. 3 (1985): 309–324.

Tyrrell, Ian. *Reforming the World: The Creation of America's Moral Empire*. Princeton, NJ: Princeton University Press, 2013.

Tyson, Carl. "Captain Randolph Barnes Marcy, 1849–1852." In *Frontier Adventurers: American Exploration in Oklahoma*, edited by Joseph Allen Stout, 124–131. Oklahoma City: Oklahoma Historical Society, 1976.

Utley, Robert Marshall. *The Indian Frontier of the American West, 1846–1890*. Albuquerque: University of New Mexico Press, 1984.

Utley, Robert Marshall. Introduction to *Battlefield and Classroom: Four Decades with the American Indian, 1867–1904* by Richard Henry Pratt. Norman: University of Oklahoma Press, 1964.

Vecsey, Christopher. "The Good News in Print and Image: Catholic Evangeliteracy in Native America." *U.S. Catholic Historian* 27, no. 1 (Winter 2009): 1–19.

Viola, Herman J. *Diplomats in Buckskins: A History of Indian Delegations in Washington City*. Washington, DC: Smithsonian Institution Press, 1981.

Voget, Fred W. *The Shoshoni-Crow Sun Dance*. Norman: University of Oklahoma Press, 1984.

Wade, Edwin L., and Jacki Thompson Rand. "The Subtle Art of Resistance: Encounter and Accommodation in the Art of Fort Marion." In *Plains Indian Drawings, 1865–1935: Pages from a Visual History*, edited by Janet Catherin Berlo, 45–49. New York: Harry Abrams, 1996.

Wallace, Anthony F. C. *The Death and Rebirth of the Seneca*. New York: Random House: 1969.

Warde, Mary Jane. "Alternative Perspectives on the Battle of Wolf Creek of 1838." *Indigenous Nations Studies Journal* 2, no. 2 (Fall 2001): 3–14.

Warren, Louis S. *God's Red Son: The Ghost Dance Religion and the Making of Modern America*. New York: Basic Books, 2017.

Warren, Stephen. *The Worlds the Shawnees Made: Migration and Violence in Early America*. Chapel Hill: The University of North Carolina Press, 2014.

Watson, Blake A. *Buying America from the Indians: Johnson v. McIntosh and the History of Native Land Rights*. Norman: University of Oklahoma Press, 2012.

Watson, Kelly L. *Insatiable Appetites: Imperial Encounters with Cannibals in the North Atlantic World*. New York: New York University Press, 2015.

Wenger, Tisa Joy. *We Have a Religion: The 1920s Pueblo Indian Dance Controversy and American Religious Freedom.* Chapel Hill: University of North Carolina Press, 2009.

Wenzel, Jennifer. *Bulletproof: Afterlives of Anticolonial Prophecy in South Africa and Beyond.* Chicago: University of Chicago Press, 2009.

West, Elliott. "Bison R Us: The Buffalo as Cultural Icon." In *The Essential West: Collected Essays,* 213–229. Norman: University of Oklahoma Press, 2012.

West, Elliott. "Reconstructing Race." *The Western Historical Quarterly* 34, no. 1 (April 1, 2003): 6–26.

White, Kris A., and Janice St. Laurent. "Mysterious Journey: The Catholic Ladder of 1840." *Oregon Historical Quarterly* 97, no. 1 (Spring 1996): 70–88.

White, Richard. "The Winning of the West: The Expansion of the Western Sioux in the Eighteenth and Nineteenth Centuries." *Journal of American History* 65, no. 2 (1978): 319–343.

Whiteley, Marilyn Fardig. *The Life of Isabel Crawford: More Than I Asked For.* Eugene, OR: Pickwick Publishers, 2015.

Wiedman, Dennis, and Candace Greene. "Early Kiowa Peyote Ritual and Symbolism: The 1891 Drawing Books of Silverhorn (Haungooah)." *American Indian Art Magazine* 13, no. 4 (1988): 32–41.

Wilkins, David E., and K. Tsianina Lomawaima. *Uneven Ground: American Indian Sovereignty and Federal Law.* Norman: University of Oklahoma Press, 2002.

Williams Reese, Linda. *Women of Oklahoma, 1890–1920.* Norman: University of Oklahoma Press, 1997.

Winter, Joseph C. *Tobacco Use by Native North Americans: Sacred Smoke and Silent Killer.* Norman: University of Oklahoma Press, 2001.

Wood, Amy Louise. *Lynching and Spectacle: Witnessing Racial Violence in America, 1890–1940.* Chapel Hill: University of North Carolina Press, 2011.

Wood, Gordon S. *Empire of Liberty: A History of the Early Republic, 1789–1815.* New York: Oxford University Press, 2009.

Zappia, Natale A. *Traders and Raiders: The Indigenous World of the Colorado Basin, 1540–1859.* Chapel Hill: University of North Carolina Press, 2014.

INDEX

⌒ ───

Page numbers followed by *f* and *pl* refer to figures and plates.